Latinos in an Aging

This book fosters a deeper understanding of the growing Latino elderly population and its implications on society. It examines post-WWII demographic and social changes and summarizes research from sociology, psychology, economics, and public health to shed light on the economic, physical, and mental well-being of older Latinos. The political and cultural implications including possible policy changes are also considered. Written in an engaging style, each chapter opens with a vignette that puts a human face on the issues. Boxed exhibits highlight social programs and policies, and physical and mental health challenges that impact Latino elders. Web alerts direct readers to sites that feature more detailed information related to the chapter's issues. Each chapter also features an introduction, examples, tables, figures, a summary, and discussion questions. The self-contained chapters can be read in any order.

Latinos in an Aging World: Social, Psychological, and Economic Perspectives explores:

- real world problems individuals face in dealing with poverty, immigration, and health and retirement decisions;
- the latest data on Latinos as compared to research on African- and Asian-Americans where appropriate;
- the unique historical, demographic, social, familial, and economic situations of various Latino subgroups including those from Mexico, Puerto Rico, and Cuba;
- how ethnicity affects one's position of wealth and power and sense of citizenship;
- the consequence of life-long disadvantages and stigmatization on economic, physical, and mental well-being;
- the impact of one's neighborhood and the proximity to those from similar cultures on quality of life.

Intended for courses on Latinos and aging, diversity, race and ethnicity, minorities and aging, adult development and aging, the psychology or sociology or politics of aging, geriatric social work, public health and aging, global aging, social or family policy, and health and society taught in the behavioral and social sciences, ethnic, or Latin American/Chicano Studies, this book also appeals to researchers and practitioners who work with Hispanic families.

Ronald J. Angel is a Professor of Sociology at the University of Texas at Austin.

Jacqueline L. Angel is a Professor of Sociology and Public Policy at the University of Texas at Austin.

TEXTBOOKS IN AGING SERIES

Currently, more than 500 million people are aged 65 and older, accounting for about 8% of the world's population. To enhance students' understanding of the issues associated with aging, an increasing number of academic programs include a life span perspective or opt to incorporate consideration of aging processes among the topics they include in the curriculum. The Routledge/Taylor and Francis *Textbooks in Aging Series* is designed to address the growing need for new educational materials in the field of gerontology. Featuring both full-length and supplemental texts, the series offers cutting-edge interdisciplinary material in gerontology and adult development and aging, with authored or edited volumes by renowned gerontologists who address contemporary topics in a highly readable format. The series features texts covering classic topics in adult development and aging approached in fresh ways as well as volumes presenting hot topics from emerging research findings. These texts are relevant to courses in human development and family studies, psychology, gerontology, human services, sociology, social work, and health-related fields. Undergraduate or graduate instructors can use these texts by selecting a series volume as a companion to the standard text in an introductory course, by combining several of the series volumes to use as instructional materials in a course, or by assigning one series volume as the primary text for an undergraduate or graduate course or seminar. If you are interested in submitting a proposal for the series please contact debra.riegert@taylorandfrancis.com.

The books in this series include:
Latinos in an Aging World
Social, Psychological, and Economic Perspectives
Ronald J. Angel and Jacqueline L. Angel (2015)

Latinos in an Aging World

SOCIAL, PSYCHOLOGICAL, AND ECONOMIC PERSPECTIVES

Ronald J. Angel and
Jacqueline L. Angel

NEW YORK AND LONDON

First published 2015
by Routledge
711 Third Avenue, New York, NY 10017

and by Routledge
27 Church Road, Hove, East Sussex BN3 2FA

Routledge is an imprint of the Taylor & Francis Group, an informa business

Library of Congress Cataloging in Publication Data
A catalog record for this book has been requested

ISBN: 978-1-84872-536-2 (hbk)
ISBN: 978-1-84872-537-9 (pbk)
ISBN: 978-1-315-81458-2 (ebk)

Typeset in StoneSerif
by Wearset Ltd, Boldon, Tyne and Wear

Printed and bound in the United States of America by Publishers Graphics, LLC on sustainably sourced paper.

CONTENTS

ABOUT THE AUTHORS

Ronald J. Angel received his PhD in Sociology from the University of Wisconsin Madison in 1981. He is the author of five books, more than 70 referred journal articles, and numerous chapters and reports. Throughout his career Ronald Angel been engaged in cutting-edge research based on multi-method techniques to address questions related to racial and ethnic disparities in wealth, income, health, and retirement security. His current research interests focus on social welfare and retirement systems, as well as access to and use of medical care by Hispanics and other minority populations. He is currently involved in the development of a research agenda focused on health, retirement, and social welfare systems in Latin America and Europe.

Since 1993 he has served as Principal Investigator of the Austin site of the Hispanic Established Populations for the Epidemiologic Study of the Elderly (Hispanic EPESE), a study that has resulted in numerous publications that further the field of minority aging and welfare: www.icpsr.umich. edu/icpsrweb/NACDA/studies/02851. He also served as Principal Investigator of the San Antonio site of a major and highly innovative multi-method study of the lives of poor families: www.jhu.edu/~welfare. This *Three City Study* focused on the lives of poor families, most of which were Latino or African American, in Boston, Chicago, and San Antonio after the introduction of welfare reform.

In a recent qualitative study of the displaced victims of Hurricane Katrina funded by NSF, Ronald Angel investigated the nature of the response by civil society organizations to the disaster and the role of federal and state agencies in fostering or impeding their participation in assisting hurricane victims to recover. In general Angel's work relates directly to issues of social organization, stratification, health risks, and social welfare.

Ronald Angel served as Editor of the *Journal of Health and Social Behavior*, a major outlet for work in medical sociology and health policy from 1994 to 1997, and he has served on the editorial boards of numerous other journals.

He has also served in numerous consultative positions to foundations and the federal government.

Jacqueline L. Angel (PhD, Rutgers, 1989) is currently a Professor of Public Affairs and Sociology and a Faculty Affiliate at the Population Research Center and LBJ School's Center for Health and Social Policy at the University of Texas at Austin. Prior to joining the U.T. Faculty, she did her post-doctoral training at Rutgers in mental health services research and the Pennsylvania State University Program in Demography of Aging. Her research addresses the relationships linking family structures, inequality, and health across the life course, including a special focus on minority aging, the Hispanic population, and older Mexican Americans.

Dr. Angel is the Principal Investigator on a National Institute of Minority Health and Health Disparities (MD) R01 study examining the risk of long-term care in older Mexican-American families and, since its inception, a Co-Investigator on the Hispanic Established Populations for the Epidemiologic Study of the Elderly (H-EPESE). In addition, she is Co-organizer of the NIA-funded (R-13) grant for the Conference Series on Aging in the Americas: Mexico and the United States.

She is the author/coauthor/editor of numerous publications, including 60 journal articles, 20 book chapters, and 7 books. Some of her recent publications include: *Aging, Health and Longevity in the Mexican-Origin Population*, co-edited with Fernando Torres-Gil and Kyriakos Markides; *Handbook of the Sociology of Aging* with Rick Settersten; and *Hispanic Families at Risk: The New Economy, Work, and the Welfare State*, co-authored with Ronald Angel.

Jacqueline Angel has served as an advisor to numerous non-governmental organizations and other agencies that provide basic services to the elderly. She is currently Chair-elect of the Behavioral and Social Sciences Section of the Gerontological Society of America (GSA). In Austin, she is a member of the President's Council at Family Eldercare and a 2013 recipient of the Jackie Lelong Visionary Leader Award. Dr. Angel is a Fellow of the Behavioral and Social Sciences section of the GSA and a Senior Fellow at the Sealy Center on Aging, UTMB School of Medicine. In 2010, she received the GSA Senior Service Scholar Award, in 2012 she was awarded the Jacob's Institute of Women's Health Charles E. Gibbs Leadership Prize for the best manuscript in 2011, and in 2013 the Outstanding Publication Book Award (with Richard Settersten) from the American Sociological Association's Section on Aging in the Life Course.

FOREWORD

*Rosemary Blieszner & Karen A. Roberto,
Series Editors*

Aging is one of the most important phenomena of the 21st century. Today, more than 500 million people are aged 65 and older, accounting for about 8% of the world's population. By 2030, that total is projected to increase to one billion older adults, or 13% of the world's total population. In the United States alone, between 2011 and 2030, about 10,000 baby boomers will turn 65 each day (Cohn & Taylor, 2010). By 2030, the first members of the baby boom generation, born in 1946, will be 84 years of age, and the youngest members, born in 1964, will be 65 (Federal Interagency Forum on Aging-Related Statistics, 2010). Thus, with the aging of the population in the United States and across the globe, more people than ever before will be living into their seventh, eighth, and ninth decades of life and beyond.

To enhance students' understanding of the promises and challenges associated with individual and societal aging, an increasing number of academic programs are including a lifespan or life course perspective along with their disciplinary focus, or opting to incorporate consideration of aging processes and outcomes among the topics they include in the curriculum. Thus, the new Routledge/ Taylor & Francis *Textbooks in Aging Series*, an interdisciplinary set of both full-length and supplemental volumes on aging, is timely and exciting. The series offers cutting-edge material in gerontology and adult development and aging, with the volumes authored or edited by renowned gerontologists who lend their expertise to a variety of contemporary topics in a highly readable format that will appeal to both beginning and more advanced students.

Our vision for the series includes texts covering classic topics in adult development and aging approached in fresh ways as well as volumes presenting hot topics from recently emerging research findings. These texts will be relevant to courses and programs in human development and family studies, psychology, gerontology, health-related fields and professions, human services, social work, those in other behavioral and social sciences areas, and courses in humanities and arts and other fields for which a background in adult development and aging would be relevant to the instructional goals.

Both undergraduate and graduate course instructors could use these topical volumes in several ways. They might assign one or two as companions to a standard, comprehensive textbook in introductory courses. Another approach would be to select several volumes to use in courses that would integrate specific, complementary topics. Still another possibility would be to select a volume to use as the text for a course or seminar. In addition, these more specialized volumes may be of interest to researchers interested in obtaining an overview of the literature in the areas covered by the series topics.

The *Textbooks in Aging Series* begins with *Latinos in an Aging World* by Dr. Ronald J. Angel, Professor of Sociology, and Dr. Jacqueline L. Angel, Professor of Public Affairs and Sociology and a Faculty Affiliate at the Population Research Center and the LBJ School's Center for Health and Social Policy, both at the University of Texas at Austin. Dr. Ronald Angel's research encompasses the areas of medical sociology, social welfare, poverty, minority groups, demography, and epidemiology. Dr. Jacqueline Angel focuses on elucidating the links among family structures, inequality, and health across the life course, including emphasis on older Hispanics and the impact of social policies on the health and well-being of aging immigrants.

Members of Hispanic groups who immigrated to the United States often face economic and social barriers to assimilation that can have an impact on their aging processes and outcomes. *Latinos in an Aging World* provides a thorough analysis of myriad intersecting influences on growing older among Hispanic members of the U.S. population. The authors consider the effects of culture, attitudes, age, gender, fertility, employment status and productivity, religion, caregiving, politics and policies, intergenerational solidarity, and more. They are particularly concerned with examining the consequences of ongoing socioeconomic disadvantages and stigmatization for health and well-being in the last part of life. They integrate work from multiple disciplines to showcase the growing cultural and social diversity of the U.S. population and the implications of such diversity for society at large and for older members of minority groups in particular. This book is suitable for courses in gerontology, adult development and aging, family studies, human development across the lifespan, demography, and aging policies.

As the older population grows larger, it will also grow more racially and ethnically diverse. By 2050, members of minority groups will constitute the majority of the U.S. population, with the largest proportion of them expected to be Hispanics. Thus, we consider it quite fitting that the first volume of the *Textbooks in Aging Series* focuses on this crucial change in U.S. history.

PREFACE

In the United States today over half of all births are to minority mothers and immigration continues to add to the number of Hispanics and Asians. These changes have profound social, economic, and political implications for the nation as a whole, as well as for the physical and mental health of these groups. The United States has always been and continues to be ethnically diverse and multicultural. Spanish and a host of Asian languages are common and the Census Bureau and other federal, state, and local agencies are forced to collect data and provide information in several languages. This fact is not welcomed by all. In both Europe and the United States perceived threats to racial, ethnic and cultural homogeneity give rise to political parties and groups opposed to immigration and multiculturalism. On a daily basis one hears vehement calls for a stop to immigration and harsh treatment for the undocumented population that has already arrived.

All nations of the developed world, and even many of the countries of the developing world, face new cultural, religious, and political realities as the result of immigration and population aging. Since immigrants and minority groups tend to be young and have high fertility these ethnic and cultural changes interact with age differences to create potentially significant conflicts among age and cultural groups. While the younger age ranges become increasingly ethnic, the older age ranges remain heavily old-stock.

Changes in the age structure, as well as the social and cultural composition of populations have profound implications for the welfare state. The Civil Rights Act of 1964 and Voting Rights Act of 1965 and much other legislation of Lyndon Johnson's Great Society and War on Poverty resulted from a national sense of injustice and the demands of the less fortunate who had been systematically excluded from the American Dream. They were also made possible by the fact that the post-war economy was growing rapidly and generosity in terms of welfare state extension could be easily accommodated. Today that generosity, and the solidarity among different age, ethnic, and racial groups that it fosters, is in jeopardy. Most developed nations are experiencing protracted periods of slow economic growth and the need for fiscal retrenchment. Spain recently revoked the right to free health care it had previously offered to undocumented residents. An increasingly negative political rhetoric and gridlock in government reflect deep resentment of the expense of the welfare state, especially the portion that supports foreigners and minorities.

The objective of this book is to foster a deeper understanding of the growing cultural and social diversity of the population of the United States and its implications for society at large, and for minority group elderly individuals in particular. Social Security and other programs for the elderly are based on an ideal of solidarity among generations in which younger people support and care for their elders in the expectation that they will receive similar care from younger generations. Such solidarity ideally creates a sense of common purpose that promotes a sense of citizenship. Large social and cultural differences threaten to undermine the possibility of generational and group solidarity.

In this book we examine the post-World War II demographic and social changes that have created our current situation, and summarize over 30 years of our own research and that of others on Hispanics and other minorities, with a particular focus on the consequence of life-long disadvantages and stigmatization for economic well-being and physical and mental health in old age. According to Census Bureau estimates, by 2050 minority Americans will make up the majority of the population. A large fraction of those will be Hispanic and the largest fraction will be those of Mexican origin. Although the population over 65 will remain predominantly White and non-Hispanic, the fraction of Hispanics and other minority group members in the older age ranges is growing.

The following chapters summarize research from sociology, psychology, economics, ethnography, public health, and other disciplines that sheds light on the economic well-being as well as the physical and mental health of older Hispanics. Each substantive chapter begins with a short story based on our previous research and experiences that is focused on the problems that individuals face and that are discussed in the chapter. Each chapter provides the most up-to-date data and information on the Hispanic population and compares it to the Black and where possible the Asian population. The book of necessity deals with social policy, as well as political and economic processes, since they are central to determining individuals' lives and circumstances. It will, therefore, be of use to individuals interested in racial and ethnic relations, social stratification, gender, and group political processes, especially those students majoring in the behavioral and social sciences. We also summarize research on racial and ethnic disparities in individual physical and mental health outcomes, as well as with the negative psychological consequences associated with stigma and marginalization. This perspective will be particularly insightful for both undergraduates and graduate students in allied health and the professions, such as social work, nursing, and pharmacy, who will also find this book of interest given the increasing diversity of the client populations they serve. A focus on economics, politics, and other objective structures is necessary to avoid blaming the victims or attributing to individual or purely psychological factors complex outcomes that have a major social structural component.

TEACHING ENHANCEMENTS

Some unique pedagogical features of the book include the following:

- Introductory vignettes as part of Chapters 2 through 9 that present individuals and families dealing with the dilemmas discussed in the chapter. These individuals and families are fictional but are based on real cases that we have encountered in previous research or in our own lives and put a human face on what might otherwise appear as impersonal policy and numbers.
- Exhibits present useful information that is somewhat tangential to the flow of the chapter. These exhibits provide more detailed information that the reader can use as desired.
- Tables and figures that summarize the most current and reliable information available on the situations of Hispanics and others over the life course. These form the basis of our discussion of the consequences of the aging of the population at large and the Hispanic population in particular.
- Discussion questions at the end of each chapter to stimulate critical thinking and promote peer interaction. These probes can also be used in essay exams or surprise quizzes to verify whether students are retaining the key ideas covered in the readings and in lectures.

- Web icons that direct students to more detailed information concerning the themes covered in the discussion.

We would like to thank our colleagues who informed our thinking about these topics, especially in our home departments the Lyndon Baines Johnson School of Public Affairs and the Department of Sociology at the University of Texas at Austin. We are also indebted to the following reviewers for their useful suggestions. They are: Stan Ingman, University of North Texas, Bronwynne Evans, Arizona State University, and two anonymous reviewers.

Introduction
A Brave New World: Ethnic Diversity and Population Aging

The United States is a nation of immigrants. Even the ancestors of Native Americans immigrated from some other continent. Over the centuries immigrants have come from many nations at different historical periods and under different political and economic circumstances. Yet for most of our nation's history immigrants arrived from Europe. Today, though, they arrive primarily from Latin America and Asia. New immigrants are rarely openly embraced by previous arrivals. Even newly arrived Europeans were stereotyped and rejected by old-stock natives. Eventually, though the immigrants assimilated into the new culture, learned its language and values, and attained middle-class status. Although many new immigrants continue to move into the middle class within a generation or two, many others, and even some who have been citizens for several generations, remain trapped in an underclass. Certain Hispanic families who became American citizens when the Southwest was seized from Mexico have not yet moved into the middle class. These families often live in isolated rural and urban communities and neighborhoods that are plagued by crime, violence, and drug abuse. Although we reject simplistic culture of poverty explanations of impaired group mobility, life in communities in which the role models one sees are criminals or drug dealers, and in which the payoff to legitimate hard work pales in comparison, can only harm a young person's self-concept and his or her possibilities for educational, occupational, and social attainment.

The data we present in this book clearly shows that the time and circumstances of a group's arrival and the complex assimilation and incorporation experiences that it undergoes greatly influence its members' economic and social well-being, as well as their physical and mental health. Both in Europe and the United States, the assimilation of new arrivals, especially when they are from very different cultures, creates significant challenges for social policy and the institutions that are charged with their support. Although the United States is a nation of immigrants, most Americans were born in the United States and are second-, third-, or later-generation natives. This is certainly true of European migrants, many of whom have long ago lost any connection to their nations of origin. As Richard Alba, an expert on immigration, points out, specific European identities and ethnicities have been replaced by a more general "European-origin" identity for those groups that arrived during the heyday of immigration from that continent. The same is not true for Americans of Latin American extraction. Even long-term residents who have been citizens for centuries often retain a distinct identity, one that they may affirm, but also one that is often forced upon them by the larger society.

In previous years, high birth rates among all groups resulted in a young population in which the number of working-age individuals relative to those of retirement age remained high, meaning that several workers were available to contribute to the support of each retiree. Since Social Security is a pay-as-you-go system, meaning that the benefits that individuals receive come directly from current workers, the ratio of workers to retirees is important, as is the ethnic composition of each age range. As birth rates have dropped and as the population has aged the number of workers relative to retirees has dropped dramatically. In 1960 there were approximately 5.1 workers for each retiree; by 2010 this number dropped to 2.9, and by 2050 it will decline further to 2.0. Given the higher birth rate among Hispanics than among non-Hispanic Whites, in the future the fraction of the working-age population consisting of Hispanics and other minority group members will increase dramatically. If, because of restricted opportunities and low educational levels, the productivity of many of these workers is impaired, the nation's capacity to care for the elderly, provide for defense, educate the young, repair decaying infrastructure, and more will be seriously limited. In addition, the ability of those future workers to save for their own retirements, to educate their children, support their aging parents, and improve their economic and social situations will be compromised.

All nations of the developed world, and even many of the countries of the developing world, face new racial, ethnic, cultural, and religious realities as the result of aging and rapid changes in population composition. Low fertility in European nations means that immigration is a vitally important source of new workers. Yet this new reality is unwelcome for many and poses serious challenges to governments. In Spain, a country with a reputation for producing large families, fertility today is far below replacement, as for much of the rest of Europe. In the absence of immigration from Africa and Eastern Europe, the population would shrink. In the countries of Latin America the doubling of the proportion of the population over 65 that took over 100 years in European nations is occurring in less than 30 years, and in some cases fewer. These nations will not have the time that European nations had to adapt Social Security, health, long-term care, and other institutions to the new reality of aging populations, and they must do so from a far lower resource base. In the United States fertility levels remain at replacement level because of the relatively high fertility of Hispanics, although even their fertility has been dropping.

Changes in the social and culture composition of populations have profound implications for the welfare state. The Civil Rights Act of 1964 and Voting Rights Act of 1965 and much other legislation of the Great Society and War on Poverty resulted from a national sense of injustice and the demands of the less fortunate who had been systematically excluded from the American Dream. They were also made possible by the fact that the post-war economy was growing rapidly and generosity in terms of welfare state expansion could be easily accommodated. Today that prosperity and the generosity that it fostered are in jeopardy. Most developed nations are facing serious fiscal constraints brought about by massive state deficits and limited revenues. These seriously threaten the situation of immigrants, and especially the undocumented, in nations that have tolerated their presence or even encouraged their arrival because their labor was needed. Spain recently revoked the right to free health care it had previously offered to undocumented residents. An increasingly negative political rhetoric and gridlock in government reflect deep resentment of the expense of the welfare state, especially that portion that supports foreigners and minorities.

THE OBJECTIVE OF THIS BOOK

The objective of the book is to foster a deeper understanding of the growing cultural and social diversity of the population of the United States and the implications of this diversity for society at large, and for minority group elderly individuals in particular. Although we deal with other racial and ethnic groups our focus is primarily on Hispanics, the largest minority group in the nation. In addition to a close examination of the demographic and economic situation of the various nation-of-origin subgroups, including the Mexican-origin, Puerto Rican, and other Hispanic populations, we examine the unique histories of each of these groups in the United States and review what is known of the structural and cultural assimilation processes and their consequences for the elderly and their families.

A major focus is on the social and structural sources of solidarity and alienation and the consequences of divisive ethnic conflict on the moral fabric of our nation. American politics has always included an ethnic element as different groups have vied for wealth and power. Ethnicity and ethnic interests continue to affect public life. Although a growing fraction of the population is Hispanic, especially in certain states, relatively few Hispanics occupy positions of power or influence in government, the corporate world, or in education. Ethnicity also affects individuals' sense of solidarity and citizenship. Traditional Social Security systems in which current retirees are supported by current workers are based on a principle of solidarity among generations. This solidarity arises from the fact that collectively younger people support their elders in the expectation that they will be supported by younger generations in turn. Such solidarity ideally creates a sense of common purpose and group membership and promotes a sense of belonging and citizenship. Large social and cultural differences, though, in addition to a growing old-age dependency burden, threaten to undermine generational and group solidarity. As the fiscal and instrumental burdens of the support of a rapidly growing elderly population grows, new arrangements for the support of the elderly must be found. As part of that effort we examine the potential role of non-governmental organizations (NGOs), including faith-based organizations (FBOs), and other civil society entities in complementing formal governmental efforts at elder support.

As part of our task we examine the post-World War II demographic and social changes that have created our current situation, and summarize over 30 years of our own research and that of others on the economic and social welfare of Hispanics and other minorities, with a particular focus on the consequence of life-long disadvantages and stigmatization for economic well-being and physical and mental health in old age. According to Census Bureau estimates, by 2050 the minority Americans will make up the majority of the population. A large fraction of those will be Hispanic and the largest fraction will be those of Mexican origin. Although the population over the age of 65 will remain predominantly White and non-Hispanic, the fraction of Hispanics and other minority group members in the older age ranges is growing.

In the following chapters we summarize research in sociology, psychology, economics, ethnography, public health, and other disciplines that sheds light on the economic well-being as well as the physical and mental health of older Hispanics. We also deal with the political implications of the profound cultural and political changes that could accompany rapid aging and very different racial and ethnic compositions among age groups. We deal with social policy, as well as political and economic issues, since laws and their implementation are central to determining the opportunities available to individuals. Among other outcomes, we focus on individual physical and mental health and the negative psychological consequences associated with stigma and marginalization. A focus on economics, politics, and other objective structures is necessary to avoid blaming the victims or attributing to individual or to purely psychological factors complex outcomes that have a major social structural component.

In the following chapters we employ the labels "Latino" and "Hispanic" interchangeably. When possible we present data for specific nation-of-origin groups. We are not always able to differentiate among nation-of-origin groups since official statistics frequently do not differentiate among Hispanic subgroups and provide information only for the combined category. It is important to emphasize that because individuals of Mexican origin make up over 60% of the Hispanic population, statistics that refer to Hispanics as a group are heavily influenced by the Mexican-origin component. We must also note that we use the label "Mexican-origin" rather than "Mexican-American" to refer to this subgroup since it consists of both citizens and non-citizens.

CHAPTER DESCRIPTIONS

The book consists of 10 chapters, each of which is self-contained and deals with a different aspect of the core theme of the individual and social consequences of a growing Latino population in conjunction with the aging of the population as a whole. Each chapter ends with a summary of the major points covered in the chapter and includes a set of questions that provide the opportunities for discussion of major issues that relate to the topic of each chapter. The substantive chapters begin with vignettes, or stories of individuals and families, that put a human face on the issues dealt with in that chapter. Although the characters involved are fictitious, their situations reflect the experiences of people we have encountered in our research and in our lives. Their experiences reflect real world problems that individuals face in dealing with poverty, few assets, immigration problems, declining health, and aging parents. What follows is a description of each chapter.

In Chapter 1 we define the problem and discuss the meaning of the label "Hispanic." We review the immigration and incorporation histories of the major Hispanic subgroups. We also discuss theories of assimilation and multiculturalism, as well as relevant theories related to social capital and social networks as they relate to race, ethnicity, and gender. These theories provide a conceptual framework, or frameworks, for understanding the complex associations we describe in later chapters. Throughout the book we draw upon intersectionality theory, which draws our attention to the fact that although single characteristics such as race, ethnicity, gender, or sexual orientation are each associated with certain social vulnerabilities, the combination of ascribed and achieved social characteristics place certain individuals, families, and groups at greater risk of poverty, poor health, and restricted mobility opportunities. In this chapter we also review the history of specific Hispanic subgroups in the United States.

In Chapter 2 we present a demographic, economic, and social profile of the Hispanic population and document important differences among specific Hispanic subgroups based on their immigration histories and legal status. The fact that Puerto Ricans are citizens by birth and that Cubans receive special status as refugees makes the situations of these two groups different than that of Mexican immigrants, who are neither citizens by birth nor refugees. In this chapter we review the ways in which Hispanics are classified and identified by the Census Bureau and other governmental agencies. Many Hispanics consider themselves to be a unique racial category, complicating the Census Bureau's classification task. In addition, many members of the Hispanic population have parents from different Hispanic or racial groups. Intermarriage among Hispanics and non-Hispanics is common and further complicates the characterization and classification of individuals.

In Chapter 3 and the following chapters, we approach the situation of Hispanics from an intersectional perspective and examine the economic and social situations of men and women, including their educational experiences and attainment, their marital histories and family situations, and their labor force participation. Education, family, and work make up core identities that objectively determine one's life chances, including one's income and wealth, but they also affect one's social standing and sense of self-worth. Membership in a stigmatized or devalued group, or the burden of a socially devalued identity, can have seriously negative psychological effects. It can also have the opposite effect and lead one to reject the stigma and reaffirm one's own identity as a member of the stigmatized group as a rejection of the majority view. Contemporary examples include demands for the legalization of gay marriage, protection of the rights of transgendered individuals, and the embrace of tribal identities by Native Americans.

In Chapter 4 we examine the situation of older immigrants and their families, and identify the social resources available to them in the communities to which they migrate. We show that while older immigrant parents are highly dependent on their younger family members, they also often draw on social resources available in ethnic communities. In many cases they replicate much of the cultural and social support system of the old country in the new area. The term "chain migration" is a label that is employed to characterize migration of individuals from the same community in the sending nation to a particular area in the receiving country. Such chain migration eases the stress of moving to a new environment.

In Chapter 5 we review the literature on the major health risks that older minority Americans, including Hispanics, face as a result of the disadvantages they experience throughout life. As we shall see, a longer life does not necessarily mean a better or healthier life. In this chapter we present new data that shows that despite their relatively long average lifespans, Hispanics spend a large fraction of the years past 65 in poor health and plagued by functional limitations.

In Chapter 6 we examine the family situations and living arrangements of older Hispanics in the larger context of the options in care and living arrangements for older people generally. A major focus is on the changing nature of families' eldercare roles and an examination of the social, economic, and cultural forces that affect both the desire and capacity of adult children to contribute to their parent's care. We begin with the perhaps unsurprising observation that most older individuals prefer to stay in their own homes for as long as possible, even when their health deteriorates, and even after their spouse is gone. When an older person can no longer live alone, someone must make the decision as to where they will live. Traditionally they would move in with children, but given the need for women to work and other changes in the family, other options including formal institutional care must be considered, even if that is a choice of last resort.

Chapter 7 turns to Hispanic communities and presents findings from research that documents the impact of neighborhood quality on older residents' lives. In this chapter we review research related to the relationship between neighborhood affluence, perceived safety, and ethnic homogeneity on physical and mental health outcomes. In Chapter 8 we review research focused on the burden of caring for someone with complex and extensive needs and summarize research that shows that the ongoing strain of caring for a dependent family member can lead to caregiver burnout and seriously undermine the caregiver's own physical and mental health.

Chapter 9 builds on previous chapters and further investigates the serious gaps in income and especially in wealth between minority Americans and non-Hispanic White Americans. In this chapter we discuss the issue of financial literacy and examine what individuals with few resources need to know about financial management. Given their low levels of income and wealth we develop the concept of "survival strategies" that involve understanding the social welfare system and ways in which to access services to which one is entitled. It is clear that financial literacy has a very different meaning for lower-class individuals than it has for middle-class individuals. In this chapter we review the efforts of NGOs in furthering the financial literacy and survival skills of individuals with low incomes and few accumulated assets.

In Chapter 10 we summarize and synthesize the major points of the earlier chapters and review the social, political, and economic implications of the growing Hispanic population for America's future. In this chapter we discuss major legislative initiatives, including those related to immigration reform on the political system. We discuss the implications of the radical change in the population distribution of Hispanics for local politics and municipal governance. We end with a discussion of the role of NGOs and other civil society organizations in advocacy and service provision to older populations, including Hispanics. It is clear that even in developed nations governmental agencies will not be able to address all of the needs of rapidly aging populations. In the future new experiments in public/private approaches to addressing the needs of aging Hispanics and others will be necessary.

CHAPTER 1

A Majority Minority Nation

THE STRANGERS AMONG US

Over the centuries the Roma, descendants of an ancient nomadic tribe with origins in Northern India, settled in many European countries and migrated even as far as the United States (McGarry, 2010). They are one of the ethnic groups that are referred to as "gypsies," with all of the negative connotations that the term conveys. What one immediately notices about the Roma almost everywhere they settle is that they are generally not welcome and do not fit easily into the host society. The Roma live at the physical and social margins of the cities to which they have migrated; there they face discrimination and rejection as unwelcome outsiders (Nolan, 2011). The Roma are not the only outsiders who face rejection. In 2010 during a speech before the conservative Christian Democratic Union (CDU) in Potsdam, German Chancellor Angela Merkel announced that Germany's attempt to create a multicultural society had been an utter failure (Siebold, 2010). Expressing similar sentiments, President Nicolas Sarkozy of France appealed to conservative sentiments during his failed 2012 re-election campaign by proclaiming that France had too many immigrants (Samuel, 2012). Recently, Prime Minister David Cameron of the United Kingdom pledged to restrict the use of social services by immigrants (Castle & Cowell, 2013). As an austerity measure Spain, which had been providing medical care to all residents, has informed illegal immigrants that they will no longer receive care at public expense (Govan, 2012).

These statements and actions reflect a new austerity and the difficulty that Europe faces as new waves of immigrants from its old colonies and from Islamic nations outside Europe change the cultural and ethnic face of the Continent. This situation underscores the dilemma that arises when economic reality clashes with traditional cultural identities and values. The fear that immigrants represent a potential social service burden is not confined to Europe. Reflecting public opinion, on March 25, 2013 Hong Kong's Supreme Court ruled unanimously that a Philippine woman who had worked as a domestic in the city for 27 years was not entitled to legal residency, a status that would have allowed her to stay permanently and given her access to publicly funded medical care and other social services (Bradsher, 2013).

In Europe, immigration is a demographic and economic necessity even as the fear of threats to traditional cultural values among Europeans grows. During the 1960s labor shortages in Germany gave rise to a guest worker program that recruited Turks, among others, as temporary laborers. Ideally, these guest workers were to remain as long as they were needed and then return home. Of course they stayed and brought their families to join them and are now an integral part of German society, even though they are far from fully integrated. Their culture and religion make them difficult to assimilate; they are often portrayed as criminals and thugs and are overrepresented in correctional facilities (Albrecht, 1997; Kulish, 2008). Turkish communities remain segregated and are often the victims of serious violence (Thränhardt, 1995; White, 1997).

Something similar happened in the United States when in 1942 the growing need for manual labor brought on by World War II resulted in what came to be known as the "Bracero" program. As part of this program Mexican nationals were allowed to enter the country temporarily to work in various industries and in agriculture (Cohen, 2011; Snodgrass, 2011). The Braceros, a name based on the Spanish word "brazo," meaning "arm," were expected to return to Mexico after their contracts expired, and many in fact did. After the formal end of the program in 1964, though, the need for agricultural labor did not end, and many Mexicans continued to enter the United States both legally and illegally. Those who are in the country illegally find themselves in a unique limbo; they are not eligible for public programs and they have far less legal recourse for the protection of their rights than citizens (Motomura, 2010). As in Germany, the labor needs of the U.S. economy began a process that cannot be easily reversed.

These are only a few of many examples of the mingling of peoples with different cultures, languages, religions, and values. Native Americans, as a colonized people, share many of the characteristics of the Roma. Although they are citizens, in many ways they remain separate and less than fully incorporated into mainstream society. The Mexicans who became U.S. citizens after the Mexican–American War, when the United States annexed the northern part of Mexico, are another example. They have been citizens for generations, but in many areas of the Southwest they remain separate and incompletely assimilated. Globalization, the increasing ability of individuals to migrate, and the labor demands of host countries make encounters among different racial, ethnic, and religious groups inevitable. When an immigrant group remains small it might go unnoticed. When the presence of a large number of new arrivals begins to alter the cultural and social landscape of a country, though, their presence can quickly become a problem for longer-term residents. What is clear is that large-scale immigration, as well as colonization, results in societies that are far from socially or culturally homogeneous and often produces marginalized and stigmatized groups that do not share in the economic or social life of the nation.

In this book we examine the situation of Hispanics in the United States and investigate the full range of factors that affect the social welfare and physical and mental health of the Hispanic population at large, as well as that of various subgroups. We also investigate the potential impact of a growing and relatively young Hispanic population on the larger society and its institutions. In subsequent chapters we examine a specific aspect of the situation of Hispanics in the United States and examine their demographic and social profile in order to determine the extent to which they are becoming similar to other Americans and the extent to which a significant subgroup remains apart and outside the economic and political mainstream.

Like the term "Asian," the label "Hispanic" includes individuals with many different national origins; it includes individuals and families that have been citizens for generations, as well as new arrivals, and it includes individuals with very different assimilation and incorporation experiences into U.S. society. As we illustrate, Hispanics as a group are changing the cultural face of the nation, not always in ways that are welcomed by the mainstream. That change, though, is inevitable and irreversible. In the future Hispanics will make up a large fraction of the labor force; at the same time they will make up a growing fraction of the elderly population. What is clear is that the Hispanic population cannot be ignored and that understanding their unique contribution to U.S. culture, as well as their unique needs and vulnerabilities, is imperative for understanding the possibilities for our collective future.

Before beginning our detailed examination of this population, in this chapter we review theories of assimilation and multiculturalism that are often the objects of heated debate and disagreement, but that provide useful means for thinking about the ways that different cultures interact when they come into contact, and of the consequences of the mingling of peoples from different worlds. We review social theories that deal with practical problems and normative principles related to citizenship, human rights, and cultural diversity. We begin with the assumption that one's cultural and ethnic identity are central to one's sense of self and that marginalization and stigmatization based on cultural markers undermine individuals' and groups' health and well-being. An appreciation by others of the value of one's cultural identity is central to one's psychological health. Health, both physical and mental, is influenced by social factors. As we show, a sophisticated understanding of issues related to immigration, social policy, politics, and economics is central to addressing the factors that affect individuals' physical and psychological health.

MELTING POT OR CULTURAL MOSAIC

Although some social theorists and others continue to cling to the melting pot ideal of immigrant incorporation, in which immigration creates a new common cultural identity, continuing social and cultural diversity remains a core reality of most modern societies. Modern nation states, especially those that have experienced colonization, often include groups with different languages, cultural backgrounds, religions, regional or tribal affiliations, and more that intersect systems of social and economic stratification to privilege certain groups and disadvantage others. A nation may have a common official language, but often daily life involves many different languages or dialects. The continuing migration of peoples ensures that cultural and linguistic homogeneity will remain rare. Even the Scandinavian countries are today dealing with issues of cultural diversity as Muslim immigration threatens traditional cultural identities.

Perhaps the hope for a cultural melting pot was naive. Today many social theorists reject the ideal of complete assimilation and advocate multiculturalism, both as a reflection of the reality of complex societies and as a normative ideal that recognizes the value of cultural differences (Kymlicka, 1995, 2007; Kymlicka & Norman, 2000b). Multiculturalism, which we discuss in greater detail later in the chapter, emphasizes the positive aspects of the retention of important aspects of one's culture of origin, including its language and religion. One's culture is an important part of one's identity and the recognition of its value by others is important in one's psychological well-being. From a multicultural perspective the recognition of the value of other cultures enriches societies and allows citizens to understand the world from other cultures' perspectives and to live together without conflict. Whether multiculturalism is compatible with basic human nature or whether it is an unrealistic ideal remains to be seen. What is readily observable in most nations, though, are serious conflicts among different cultural groups that are accompanied by serious differences in social, economic, and political power.

For Europe, large-scale immigration is a relatively recent phenomenon. Even as the nations of the old Continent sent their tired and poor to the new world in search of freedom and economic opportunity, they themselves remained largely unaffected by immigration. Unlike the United States, which early on embraced its identity as a nation of immigrants, until recently the nations of Europe have not thought of themselves in that way, even as significant numbers of immigrants from other parts of Europe and their old colonies arrived. Today the reality of large-scale immigration by individuals from the Muslim nations to the south and east has radically altered the traditional demographic and social fabric of Europe (Caldwell, 2009). Like other affluent countries, the nations of Western Europe rely on cheap labor from the developing world, and they are increasingly dependent on the higher fertility of immigrants to sustain their populations in the face of declining native birth rates. In today's globalized economy, in which financial capital flows freely from nation to nation, labor too is far more fluid. Despite the growing resentment of the newcomers, without immigration the populations of European nations would shrink and low-paid service-sector jobs would go unfilled (Castles, 2004).

Migration, of course, is not a new phenomenon. From our origins on the African continent humans have migrated to every corner of the planet. Yet migration today raises a new set of issues and considerations in both Europe and the United States that are different than those characteristic of migration flows from Europe to the Americas during the 19th and early 20th centuries. The origins of the new migration and the social and political contexts in which immigrants arrive are different than in earlier times. In Europe major social strains result from the fact that many of the new immigrants are from Muslim nations and bring with them customs and practices that are not only foreign but objectionable to many native Europeans. France's banning of the burka in public places is an example of a clash of incompatible values. For the French the burka represents a denial of a woman's basic freedom as an individual and a denial of the fundamental principles of the French Republic.

The official French policy of "laïcité" (laicism or secularism), a term that refers to the practice and philosophy of the strict separation of church and state, conflicts with the cultural beliefs of individuals who wish to abide by conservative religious principles even in public. The controversy is not confined to France. In 2009 over half of voters in Switzerland voted for a constitutional ban on the construction of new minarets. Politicians including Geert Wilders in the Netherlands, Jean-Marie le Pen in France, and Lars Hedegaard in Denmark have capitalized upon growing anti-Islamic sentiments among voters eager to hear their message. Whatever the ultimate outcome of the clash of cultures, though, it is clear that the old Europe is gone forever and that the face of a new Europe is being drawn by immigrants. Exhibit 1.1 lists a few of the anti-immigrant political parties that have attracted a growing number of voters in Europe in recent years.

Today migration to the United States is primarily from Asia and Latin America. Although the incorporation of these new immigrants into American culture presents different problems than those of Muslims in Europe, the new arrivals are not welcomed with open arms. Immigrants from Latin America, primarily from Mexico, provide cheap labor to sectors of the economy that probably could not function without them. These new immigrants have higher fertility than natives and hold more traditional values concerning family, gender, and marriage. Since they are not Muslim, though, they do not give rise to the same level of fear of cultural conflict as is the case in Europe. Yet the fact that Hispanics have a high rate of Spanish-language retention and

Exhibit 1.1 Selected Anti-Immigration Parties in Europe

The nations of Europe have all seen the rise of parties opposed to immigration. Most are conservative and many are far-right populist parties. Most oppose the European Union (EU) and seek greater national and local autonomy. Some are new parties and others are older parties that have taken stronger anti-EU and immigration stances. The economic crisis of 2008 affected all countries, but resulted in greater unemployment and more stringent austerity in some, which fueled anti-European and anti-immigrant sentiments. Information on these and many other parties from both the left and right is available on the Web. Search anti-immigrant parties 🌐 https://sites.google.com/site/breivikmanifesto/2083/book-3/108.

Austria: The *Freedom Party* opposes immigration as a threat to Austrian cultural identity. It especially opposes Muslim immigration and what it fears is the "Islamization" of Austria.

Belgium: Vlams Belang is a far-right Flemish party that advocates the independence of Flanders and strict limitations on immigration with strict rules that immigrants assimilate and adopt Flemish culture.

France: Le Front National led by Marine Le Pen is a far-right party strongly opposed to the EU and to immigration. The party has become the third most popular party in France.

Germany: PRO-NRW (Pro-North Rhine-Westphalia) is a newly formed party that opposes immigration, and especially Muslim immigration. It has won several seats in district and municipal councils.

Greece: Golden Dawn is a new far-right party led by Nikolaos G. Michaloliakos. The party strongly opposes the austerity measures imposed on Greece after the 2008 economic crisis and it is vehemently anti-immigrant. Its members have been implicated in attacks on immigrants and gay people.

Holland: The *Party for Freedom*, founded by Geert Wilders, opposes the immigration of Muslims and the supposed "Islamization" of the Netherlands.

Italy: Lega Nord is a conservative regional party in Northern Italy with a specific federalist agenda. It opposes immigration from Muslim countries, although it supports immigration from non-Muslim countries, in order to protect the Christian heritage of the nation.

Norway: Some observers have described the *Progress Party* as conservative, although they do not necessarily accept the label. The party is, however, in favor of far more restrictive asylum and immigration policies.

Sweden: The *Swedish Democrats* is a far-right populist party that is increasing in popularity among the Swedish population and is strongly opposed to immigration as a threat to national identity.

Switzerland: The *Swiss People's Party* is a conservative, right-wing party that is opposed to immigration in the fear that immigrants will become a drain on the Swiss welfare state. Such a position is increasingly popular in Scandinavian countries also.

remain incompletely assimilated into mainstream culture causes some observers, such as Samuel Huntington, a noted political scientist, to characterize large-scale immigration from Mexico as a cultural threat to the United States (Huntington, 2004). Noted historian Arthur M. Schlesinger Jr. warns against the divisiveness of a focus on subgroup identities rather than on a more inclusive American identity (Schlesinger, 1998). Such concerns can only be made worse by the fact that a large number of Hispanic residents are undocumented (Passel & Cohn, 2011). Despite objections to high rates of immigration and especially the presence of large numbers of undocumented residents, though, as in Europe, immigrants and their children are changing the ethnic face of the nation.

WHO ARE HISPANICS AND WHERE DO THEY COME FROM?

Immigration to the United States has occurred in multiple waves since the Pilgrims arrived at Plymouth Rock in 1620. Native Americans had arrived many centuries earlier, but our story begins with the founding of the modern nation. Along with subsequent waves of immigrants, theories of immigrant incorporation and explanations of their assimilation and acculturation experiences have changed (Sezgin, 2012). Early waves of immigrants arrived from different parts of Europe and theories of immigrant incorporation reflected what was termed "Anglo conformity," a process in which the newcomers learned English and adopted the culture and social profile of the original settlers. Other theories were based on the image of a "melting pot," in which individuals from different nations mingled, and much like a metal alloy created a new and uniquely American culture and national identity (Gordon, 1964; Handlin, 1959). Such theories focused on processes of assimilation and acculturation and reflected the belief that within a few generations newcomers would lose their culture and language of origin and become largely indistinguishable from one another. For immigrants from Europe such a characterization was largely accurate. Richard Alba, a noted immigration scholar, notes that immigrants from European nations have indeed become indistinguishable and today comprise what we might label "European Americans," a group that has made up the White and politically powerful majority through most of our history (Alba, 1990).

The incorporation experiences of the large number of non-Europeans who have arrived more recently have been very different and have given rise to a new set of theories that attempt to offer explanations for the fact that not all members of certain groups meld into the middle class within a few generations. Nor do they reject their native cultures and become fully acculturated. Segmented assimilation theory focuses primarily on the Hispanic population and is based on the observation that even after several generations certain individuals and families remain trapped in what is essentially an underclass (Portes, 1995; Portes & Zhou, 1993; Stepick & Stepick, 2010; Telles & Ortiz, 2008). The result is stratification within specific immigrant groups as a segment of the group becomes educated and economically successful, while another segment does not.

Several explanations for this differential success have been offered, including racism and the adoption of a set of behavioral patterns learned from other stigmatized groups (Portes & Zhou, 1993; Waters, 1999). Critics of segmented assimilation theory claim that it overstates the difficulties of today's immigrants relative to those who arrived earlier (Foner & Alba, 2006; Waldinger & Perlmann, 1997). Several writers have examined the applicability of segmented assimilation theory and variations of it to European nations (Silberman, Alba, & Fournier, 2007; Vermeulen, 2010). For the most part they find similarities, as well as differences that result from specific national origin differences in religion, language, and race that define the boundaries between groups, as well as the nature of the labor markets they enter.

In later chapters we examine the relative socioeconomic success of different Hispanic groups and delve into the reasons for the low levels of education, labor force disadvantage, and limited social mobility that characterize large segments of the population. First, though, it is necessary to be more specific about the population with which we are dealing. The label "Hispanic," like the term "Asian," reflects a largely artificial administrative category that includes groups with many different origins, cultures, and immigration histories. Individual Hispanics are members of specific national origin groups including Mexicans, Cubans, Puerto Ricans, Dominicans, Nicaraguans, and many more. Many marry non-Hispanics and have children with mixed ethnic origins. What they have in common is Spanish, although as a major world language it is very different depending upon the nation in which it is spoken, and many Hispanics in the United States no longer speak or understand Spanish.

The various Hispanic subgroups arrived at different historical moments and under very different circumstances, and in order to understand their situation it is necessary to know something of those circumstances. Figure 1.1 presents a breakdown of the population of the United States by race and ethnicity. Over 60% of the population is non-Hispanic and White. Hispanics make up over 16% and African Americans approximately 13% of the total. Asians make up 5% and other races less than 4%. Figure 1.2 shows that among the more than 50 million Hispanics identified by the 2010 Census, 63% are of Mexican origin, 9% are Puerto Rican, 4% Cuban, and 24% of Central or South American origin. These figures do not include the relatively small populations of Spaniards and individuals from other Spanish-speaking nations. Given their small sizes, in what follows we combine individuals from Central and South America into a single category.

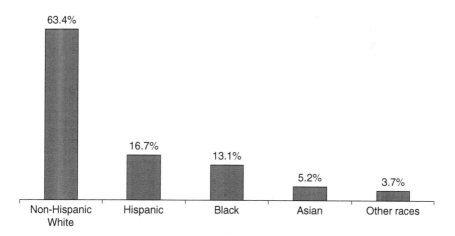

FIGURE 1.1   *U.S. Population by Race and Hispanic Ethnicity: 2011.*
Source: U.S. Census Bureau (2013).
Note: Other races include Asian and Pacific Islanders and people reporting two or more races.

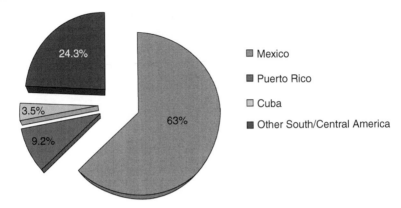

FIGURE 1.2 *U.S. Hispanic Population by Nativity: 2010.*
Source: Ennis, Ríos-Vargas, and Albert (2011).

Historically the various Hispanic subgroups have been concentrated in different parts of the country. In 1848, as part of the treaty ending the Mexican–American War, the United States annexed a huge part of northern Mexico (Castillo, 1990). Prior to that time individuals in what are today the states of Arizona, California, Colorado, and New Mexico were Mexicans. Texas had been admitted to the Union in 1845 and after the war its southern border was set at the Rio Grande. Mexican citizens in these regions were given the option of becoming U.S. citizens or returning to what was left of Mexico (Mora, 2011). That colonized population included the original Mexican Americans. In later years other Mexicans came to the United States to work in agriculture, mining, construction, and other activities, including manufacturing during the war years (Henderson, 2011). Immigration continues today, resulting in a Mexican-origin population that ranges from families that have been here for several generations to new arrivals, a large number of whom are undocumented (Cohen, 2011; Massey, Rugh, & Pren, 2010; Passel & Cohn, 2011).

Puerto Ricans have traditionally been concentrated in the Northeastern United States, as well as on the island of Puerto Rico. They differ from Mexicans in that they are citizens of the United States from birth since Puerto Rico is a territory of the United States, which acquired the island in 1848 after the Spanish–American War. In 1917 Puerto Ricans were granted U.S. citizenship with full citizenship rights, including the right to travel freely to the mainland (Cabranes, 1978). Although they are citizens, Puerto Ricans both on the island of Puerto Rico and on the mainland have low levels of education, high rates of unemployment, and high rates of poverty (Collazo, Ryan, & Bauman, 2010).

Cubans are very different than either Mexicans or Puerto Ricans in their immigration and incorporation experiences (Portes & Bach, 1985; Portes & Rumbaut, 2006; Suro, 1998). Cuban migration to the United States began during the Spanish colonial period in the 18th century when parts of the Southern United States, including Florida, Louisiana, and Texas, had important Spanish ties. Over the years a steady stream of Cubans migrated to Florida to work in the tobacco and other industries and they also settled in other parts of the country. The largest and most dramatic migrations, though, occurred during the 20th century. After the revolution in 1959 hundreds of thousands of Cubans immigrated to the United States. During the 1980s over 100,000 additional Cubans arrived as part of the Mariel boat lift in which, along with those seeking to escape communism, Fidel Castro expelled many prisoners and mentally ill individuals. The first wave of Cuban immigrants were treated as political refugees and granted immediate citizenship. Although subsequent waves of immigrants were not granted immediate citizenship their route to citizenship was much easier than was the case for other immigrants. As a group Cubans have been highly successful, due largely to the high levels of human capital that those escaping Castro's communist regime brought with them.

MULTICULTURAL AMERICA

As we have noted, both in the United States and in Europe many long-term residents fear that the maintenance or resurgence of identities based on race, ethnicity, or culture represent serious threats to solidarity and a sense of national unity (Caldwell, 2009; Schlesinger, 1998). Yet many individuals reject the notion that they should completely abandon their old cultural identities and acculturate into the larger culture. Today individuals proudly affirm identities based on gender and sexual preference, as well as race, religion, and ethnicity. Rather than willfully abandoning their cultures and language individuals embrace their cultural uniqueness. For certain marginalized groups, including Native Americans, a unique identity is forced upon them by the larger society. For others, such as those Mexican Americans who proudly adopt the label "Chicano," the reaffirmation of one's cultural identity and language represents a political act. For a stigmatized group the affirmation of one's unique identity represents a political act that involves the rejection of the negative stereotype the larger society imposes upon it.

The second half of the 20th century saw the emergence of new social movements based on more specific identities. This has been part of a process in which identity politics has replaced a politics based on social class solidarity (Giddens, 1994, 1998). Another way of stating this change is that a demand for recognition of one's cultural, social, and personal identity has superseded or even replaced demands for the redistribution of resources and power from the rich to the poor, which was the objective of the Old Left and traditional socialist movements. This change has been accompanied by the emergence of a renewed focus on civil society (Batliwala & Brown, 2006; Keck & Sikkink, 1998). For some observers the massive explosion in the number of international and more local non-governmental organizations (NGOs) that occurred after World War II is a reflection of a new civil society vitality in which more specific issues and identities, rather than class solidarity, become the focus of individual and group action (Boli & Thomas, 1999). Those who continue to believe in a more general labor or social democratic agenda often see this fragmentation of interests as a threat to the defense of more general social rights (Roman, 2004).

The Civil Rights Movement, the women's movement, the environmental movement, and demands by Latinos, Native Americans, gays and lesbians, and others have given rise to the normative ethical principle that individuals need not be expected to completely adopt the cultural and social practices of the majority, and that their personal racial, ethnic, sexual, and religious identities be respected. These new social movements are based on the belief that one can be both a citizen of a nation state and a member of a specific cultural, linguistic, sexual, or other group. Rather than seeing diversity as a threat to solidarity, from this multicultural perspective diversity can be seen as a strength. The recognition of the legitimacy of an individual's or group's identity is, at the very least, a basic human right since such identities form core aspects of one's self-concept (Taylor, 1994).

This new multicultural perspective reflects the reality of different cultures and groups living together. Whether they can do so in harmony depends upon their mutual recognition and acceptance. Given the fact that Hispanics, Asians, Native Americans, and other groups represent major segments of our society, it is useful to examine the sources and

content of multicultural theories and ask how they can contribute to the development of a new, more inclusionary
perspective. Strains and conflicts among groups are an inevitable part of human life, but attempts to at least raise the
possibility of mutual acceptance and coexistence are worth-
while. The alternative is a rejection of the other and a
failure to understand or appreciate the value of different
cultures.

We return to the theme of migration and the inevitable
mingling of peoples and cultures that it entails. In today's
globalized economy, labor, as well as capital, are increasingly international commodities (Balibar, 2004; Schierup,
Hansen, & Castles, 2006). As we have noted, though, this
new reality runs into opposition fueled by traditional preju-
dices concerning local solidarity and cultural identity, as
well as an often irrational fear of the outsider. Calls for
secure borders in the United States, Europe, and elsewhere
and the rise of anti-immigrant sentiments that form the
core platforms of political parties of the far right are part of
a discourse in which the problem of immigration is framed
by a populist rhetoric that focuses on real or perceived
threats to national security and identity.

In response to these growing fears, even centrist parties
are forced to adopt aspects of this rhetoric and take a
stronger stance toward immigration, and especially illegal
immigration. Yet demographic reality and the economic
needs of developed nations result in a tacit acceptance of
immigration. Despite calls for stronger sanctions against
illegal immigrants and those who employ them, few countries do all that might be possible to seal borders and discourage undocumented immigration. The demand for
cheap labor in the advanced welfare states creates a fundamental conflict between restrictive immigration policies
and the needs of competitive labor markets (Castles, 2004).

The growing racial and cultural heterogeneity that has
come to characterize the large cities of the industrialized
world results directly from this new international migration
and the increasing ability of people to move from one
nation to another, invited or not. The European Union, like
Australia, Canada, and the United States, which have been
defined by immigration, today confronts a new multiethnic
reality that accompanies a highly dynamic global economy.
This new reality makes the myth of assimilation clear. Yet
an inclusive and fully participatory multiculturalism
remains elusive and we are left to ask whether a truly multi-
ethnic nation in which all groups, irrespective of their

cultural origin, religion, sexual orientation, or other characteristics, are treated as equal is possible. The reality is that
new immigrants find that rather than enjoying the rights of
citizens, or denizens who can look forward to the possibility
of eventually becoming citizens, the reality is permanent
residential and social marginalization. The fact that the new
immigrants are racially, ethnically, and culturally different
than the receiving populations gives this segregation a distinctly racist aspect (Schierup et al., 2006).

IS MULTICULTURALISM TRULY POSSIBLE?

During the last two decades certain social theorists and
critics have begun to address the difficult ethical issues
related to cultural and social group membership, identity,
and social rights (Benhabib, 2002; Fraser & Honneth, 2003;
Kymlicka, 1995, 2007; Kymlicka & Norman, 2000b; Taylor,
1994). These observers of contemporary societies go beyond
the documentation of demographic and economic differences among groups to an examination of the normative
dimensions of citizenship rights and the new multicultural
political and social reality. These discussions focus on the
rights and obligations of individuals from different racial
and cultural groups, many of whom are immigrants. This
debate raises fundamental questions concerning the changing nature of the nation state system, as well as the nature
and function of civil society in defining rights and determining access to political and social power and influence.

Although the language of the debate is a bit specialized,
the core issues relate directly to the objective of this book,
which is to understand the conditions under which individuals from very different backgrounds can live together in
mutual respect and understanding. Another way of posing
the question relates to the extent to which one can retain
important aspects of one's unique identity, including one's
cultural identity, and still enjoy the rights and privileges of
full citizenship. Clearly, a fairly high degree of acculturation
is necessary for anyone to become a citizen of a new nation.
One must, at the very least, learn the language, but competent citizenship also requires a mastery of customs
deemed to be appropriate in the new context. The real question for our purposes has to do with the degree of cultural
maintenance that is possible and whether individuals can
ever arrive at a true understanding and acceptance of

others. Bilingual classrooms that include English speakers who wish to learn Spanish or other languages suggest that the acceptance of a broader view of a national culture is possible. On the other hand, the group conflicts and xenophobia that we discussed earlier must inevitably temper any excessive optimism.

The debate over multiculturalism, which we summarize briefly, is informed by a complex post-colonial politics and the recognition of important differences between colonized indigenous populations (indigenous minority groups), refugees, and asylum seekers who have been forced to leave their homelands because of political unrest or natural disaster, and voluntary migrants who move in search of economic opportunities or political or religious freedom (Kymlicka, 1995; Kymlicka & Norman, 2000a; Valadez, 2001). It would be useful to briefly review the differences between these groups since they relate directly to the situation of different minority populations. While there may be a general acceptance of the principle that the social and economic marginalization of colonized groups, such as Native Americans who were involuntarily incorporated into a nation, justifies special treatment, often including the right to their own territory and the right to at least some degree of legal self-determination and special recognition of their cultural heritage, the situation of refugees, and certainly that of voluntary immigrants, is different.

Cubans occupy a unique political status among Hispanics since they are refugees from a government the United States classifies as hostile. Since the 1980s, though, refugees and asylum seekers have come from many other nations, including the former Soviet Union, Vietnam, Laos, Cambodia, the former Yugoslavia, Iraq, and Somalia (Singer & Wilson, 2007). Most immigrants, however, are not refugees but rather have economic motivations for moving. Individuals who voluntarily leave their homelands and migrate to a new country are expected to assimilate rapidly and more completely, and they have few legitimate claims to special privileges. These economic migrants include Mexicans who are not forced out of their home country but come in search of work and a better life. Voluntary immigrants are expected to follow legal procedures for entry, learn the host country's official language, and observe its mores and practices, at least in public. When they do not conform to these expectations, and especially when they retain certain cultural practices that members of the host society find objectionable, they are stigmatized and rejected. Yet in reality, voluntary migrants are often not allowed to fully incorporate into the host society, and remain trapped in the legal and social limbo of guest or temporary worker status, or that of illegal resident or undocumented alien. A large number of Mexican immigrants often fall into this category.

The presence of large numbers of new immigrants, especially the undocumented, results in ongoing calls for large-scale deportations, both in Europe and the United States, but for the most part economic realities determine official governmental actions. Once individuals and families have arrived and established themselves, and even had children who have little contact with the country of origin, mass deportations are largely impossible. The more realistic response, in fact, is amnesty and policies that attempt at least to regularize and control the immigrants' situation (DeParle, 2008; Orrenius & Zavodny, 2003). Current discussions concerning policies that provide a route to citizenship for undocumented Mexican residents in the United States reflect the acceptance even among conservatives of the reality of immigrants' presence and their contribution to the economy. They are also motivated by the situations of specific groups. The "DREAM Act," which we discuss further in later chapters, would provide individuals who were brought to the United States illegally as infants by their parents a route to citizenship, or at least relief from the fear of deportation. This law, which has yet to be passed, represents a response to the tragic situation of individuals who are illegal through no fault of their own (Olivas, 2009).

REDISTRIBUTION AND RECOGNITION

The rise of social and political movements based on race, ethnicity, gender, and sexual orientation reflect a shift toward a concern for what has been termed "recognition." This term refers to the demand that one's individual identity, including one's cultural identity, be recognized as legitimate and valuable by the larger society (Fraser & Honneth, 2003). Rather than replacing the old politics of redistribution, which focuses on reducing income and wealth inequality, this new politics of recognition adds a new dimension. Both recognition and redistribution are central to social inclusion. While demands for recognition are based on the basic human need that one's personal and cultural identity be respected, such respect must also be accompanied by equity in access to material and political resources. The most serious danger that immigrants and indigenous populations face is exclusion from the means of economic and political power. The supportive and defensive civil society organizations that marginalized groups establish, including churches and professional associations, do not necessarily create ties to the larger culture or serve as avenues to economic or political power. The basic problem arises from the fact that marginalized individuals and groups lack the ability to make their voices heard, a problem we shall address below.

As we mentioned earlier, multiculturalism is not universally accepted and it is not only cultural conservatives who are suspicious. Even for progressives who find certain cultural beliefs and practices of other cultural groups objectionable, multiculturalism has less appeal. Susan Okin, a noted feminist, observes that most if not all traditional cultures are patriarchal and therefore in direct conflict with Western feminist values (Okin, 1988). Acceptance of the attitudes and behaviors associated with patriarchal social arrangements is incompatible with any political position that demands complete gender equality. Again the French rejection of the burka as a symbol of female oppression serves as a clear example. For Western feminists complete gender equality in access to education and economic and political power represents a core value. These feminist objections reveal a clear dilemma for defenders of multiculturalism who may wish to affirm both the autonomy of the individual and the rights of specific cultural groups to engage in practices that deny such complete autonomy to women and others.

MULTICULTURALISM, RECOGNITION, AND PSYCHOLOGICAL HEALTH

Fundamentalism, which we might define as the strict, if not inflexible, adherence to a set of beliefs, principles, or rules is clearly incompatible with multiculturalism and it can solidify differences among groups. Unfortunately, fundamentalist positions are common in the world and undermine the evolution of more inclusive societies. As we noted earlier, a major problem in modern nation states arises from the fact that cultural and social group differences are associated with differences in income, wealth, and political power. Fundamentalist or politically motivated perspectives often view these differences as evidence of the inferiority of disadvantaged groups. As we document in later chapters, Hispanics as a group have far less wealth, less education, and lower incomes than the majority of non-Hispanic Whites (Hispanic Institute for Americans for Secure Retirement, 2009). These differences in material wealth create serious problems for recognition and for the ability of Hispanics to move up the economic and social ladders. Understanding the sources of these disadvantages represents a major challenge that we confront in later chapters. Here, though, we frame the problem in terms of ethical and normative principles related to the definition of a just and truly democratic society.

Jürgen Habermas, one of the 20th century's foremost philosophers and social critics, focuses on the requirements for effective and equitable interaction among individuals and groups (Habermas, 1971, 1984, 1987). Habermas's objective is in effect to identify the moral characteristics of a just and equitable society. Ultimately, such a society is one in which everyone is treated equitably and in which, by definition, no one remains powerless, a far cry from most contemporary societies. Habermas employs the term "communicative competence" to characterize a situation in which all participants in a deliberative process in which the outcome can be of great importance are equally capable of effectively presenting their opinions and being heard. In the present context we can think of such an exchange as one involving political and economic decisions. In an ideal situation all participants can effectively express and defend their points of view, as well as their individual and group interests. An important prerequisite for such a situation, of course, is that all participants accept the rights of others to express their opinions and remain open to the possibility of being convinced by a strong argument. Unfortunately, in the real world of competition for scarce resources this is often not the case.

Advocates of a similar approach to human interaction labeled "deliberative" or "discursive" democracy also focus on the requirement for effective exchanges in which the outcomes can be of major significance (Dryzek, 2010; Fishkin, 2009). Such theories set out the requirements for effective democratic participation. Among these are that all participants in the exchange be sincere and willing to consider all evidence provided. It also requires that, as for Habermas, all participants be equal in terms of factors that allow their opinions to be heard and that allow them to influence the outcome of the deliberations. Large differences in education or economic power that grant those with greater resources greater weight in determining whatever course of action will ultimately undermine the possibility of democracy and justice.

Such normative theoretical discussions might strike some readers as hopelessly abstract or idealistic and unrelated to the struggles of oppressed groups. Yet the debate reminds us that we are dealing with basically moral issues, as well as the political and economic sources of group inequality. One serious potential criticism of such idealized normative theories is that the requirements for communicative competence and democratic participation *presuppose* the outcome of that process. In order for the discourse to even begin the conditions for equity and justice must be fairly well in place, which itself presupposes certain institutional arrangements that insure a high level of equality in material, cultural, and social resources. A society in which open communication occurs at every level of the political structure requires an enlightened State and powerful citizenry with clear oversight potential. It also requires that all individuals and groups have equal access to economic, social, and political resources and enjoy complete recognition as competent and deserving citizens. Such a society remains an ideal rather than a reality.

It is not easy, or perhaps even possible, to identify situations in which groups that are in power willingly, and in recognition of what is morally correct, allow excluded groups to share power. In order to gain recognition, or more basic political, social, and economic equality, groups that are socially stigmatized must struggle. We would do well to arrive at a much weaker form of consensus than that proposed by Habermas based on negotiation that does not require that one abandon one's most basic beliefs, but in which the participants do not immediately reject others' world views. Fundamentalism, as well as overtly racist and exclusionary beliefs that deny the basic humanity and autonomy of others, make civilized discourse impossible.

Theoretical and normative discussions of this sort are useful in clarifying the basic requirements for a just and equitable society. They help to identify a set of desired or ideal social arrangements and draw attention to how current arrangements fall short. Not everyone, of course, finds such theoretical discussions interesting or useful. We mention multicultural and communicative theories here because they strike us as dealing with central moral issues, especially with reference to cultural and social group differences. George Herbert Mead was among the first of a number of social psychologists to point out that our self-concepts are created and maintained in reciprocal interactions with others (Mead, 1934). Charles Horton Cooley's concept of the "looking glass self" also emphasized the fact that our concept of who we are, our basic sense of self, reflects what others communicate about how they see us (Cooley, 1902).

The impressions that we receive from others concerning their evaluations of us clearly reflect visible aspects of race and ethnicity, as well as social class markers such as language, dress, and other characteristics. It is for this reason that multiculturalists identify recognition as being of major importance in the creation of a positive self-image (Taylor, 1994). A stigmatized identity and the perceived experience of discrimination can undermine one's self-concept as well as one's mental and physical health (Williams & Mohammed, 2009). Clearly poverty and social rejection can undermine health directly by making access to care unaffordable, but it can also cause psychological harm through a lack of recognition of the value of one's cultural and personal identity. This fact makes it imperative to understand the social and institutional sources of inequality and powerlessness since they are central not only to the maintenance of social inequalities, but also to the physical and mental well-being of those who are excluded.

A NEW INSTITUTIONAL ORDER

These theoretical considerations raise the question as to the conditions under which greater social equity could be achieved and major differences in economic and political power between groups eliminated or at least reduced. Answering that question requires an understanding of the institutional context within which individuals and groups interact and which creates and maintains differentials in individuals' and groups' ability to control important aspects of their lives. Such an understanding might make it possible to alter those institutional arrangements in order to reduce inequalities and conflict between cultural and social groups. In the discussions of communicative competence that might inform research and inform remedial action to address issues of group exclusion, what is lacking is a greater focus on the institutional environments in which interactions between groups take place and in which exclusion occurs. Given human beings' propensity to interact with their own kind, venues for interaction with other groups who differ in culture and social class can be limited. Large differences in power and the separation of one group from another are clearly incompatible with open communication. Interactions between the lord of the manor and his serfs were by definition formal and unequal; they violated the basic requirements of deliberative democracy. The same holds for any institutional arrangement that creates and perpetuates large power differentials among groups, including unequal educational systems, discriminatory justice systems, and exclusionary political processes.

The literature on social networks provides two theoretical concepts that might be useful in understanding the nature of interactions among groups. Several years ago sociologist Mark Granovetter developed a theoretical perspective in which he distinguished between what he termed "strong" and "weak" ties (Granovetter, 1973). Ties refer to relationships with other people that can vary in terms of intimacy, support, and information. Strong ties are those that characterize close relationships, such as those with family members and close friends. These are the emotionally and materially supportive relationships on which one can rely in times of crisis or that the poor rely on for daily survival (Edin & Lein, 1997; Stack, 1974). When one needs money for food or some other immediate need, one usually calls upon a close family member or friend.

Weak ties, on the other hand, consist of less intimate relationships that can be more instrumental. These include relationships with teachers, employers, co-workers, colleagues, and other more formal and less intimate contacts. Weak ties characterize professional relationships that one can call upon for professional purposes. They allow one to communicate and interact with a larger network and they are more information rich than strong ties. As a consequence, they can further economic, political, or professional ends. One's cousin might know of a job at the local hardware store, but a member of one's professional association can provide information on jobs, business possibilities, and other opportunities in different parts of the country or even internationally. Poor families and communities tend to rely heavily on strong ties for basic survival, but they have few weak ties to individuals in positions of power who might help improve their lot (Edin & Lein, 1997; Stack, 1974).

Political scientist Robert Putnam has described similar aspects of networks that are salient for our purposes. Putnam notes that institutions and organizations can be characterized in terms of two important qualities of the relationships they foster. Like Granovetter's strong and weak ties, this distinction focuses on the exclusivity and inclusivity of relationships (Putnam, 2000). Bonding social ties, as the name implies, bond individuals to one another. They are inward looking, which means that they tend to be exclusive, that is, they define an in-group that can be homogeneous in terms of some characteristic. Bonding ties, in this regard, are similar to Granovetter's strong ties. Examples include ethnic fraternal organizations and exclusive country clubs. Bridging relationships, on the other hand, are outward looking and include people from different social groups. They are inclusive of others and are similar to Granovetter's weak ties. Examples include the Civil Rights Movement, the women's rights movement, the environmental movement, ecumenical religious organizations, and international scientific associations. The essence of these organizations is that they can foster communication and understanding among individuals from very different social backgrounds.

Organizations can have aspects of each; they can bond and bridge. Again to use Putnam's examples, the Black church brings together people of the same race but of different social classes; the Knights of Columbus bonds along religious and gender lines while bridging different ethnic communities; Internet chat rooms can bring individuals with similar ideologies and educations together across all sorts of other social distinctions. When organizations bond together on cultural, religious, or ethnic bases and make no attempt to bridge by reaching out to other cultural, religious, or ethnic groups, the possibility of the ideal of a multicultural society is weakened. On the other hand, true attempts to bridge promise a greater sense of community, while allowing individuals to retain aspects of their core cultural and social identities.

In order to further the recognition and mutual understanding, interaction and open-mindedness are necessary. From our perspective the most useful approach to understanding the situation of Hispanics and other vulnerable groups is to combine the objectives of communicative competence and deliberative democracy with traditional interest group politics to create a politics of inclusion. Communicative competence is an ideal that we should strive for, but the need, by those who are excluded, to struggle to be allowed into the conversation is an ongoing reality, but in more effective ways than in the past. Those struggles occur within specific institutional contexts and understanding how institutions create and maintain inequalities, as well as how they might be redesigned to help eliminate them, leads us to institutional theory (Campbell, 2004; Campbell & Pedersen, 2001). In the following chapters we examine institutions of all sorts, including the family, education, religion, work, social welfare, and more, and the role they have in determining the welfare of Hispanics.

ACTIVE CITIZENSHIP

We have touched on several themes in this short discussion of multiculturalism. We end by raising the question of political participation since politics is the arena in which power is exercised. The term "active citizenship" has been used in many areas of political action to refer to the ability of individuals and groups to act effectively to engage the state and other major actors to further their interests and group objectives. Individuals band together in organizations that are often affiliated with larger social movements to protect the environment, further human rights, oppose oppressive political regimes, and more. Political and economic power remain unequally distributed in the world, with serious implications for the future of humanity. Many individuals in the world today are far from enjoying the ability to be active citizens in the countries in which they reside. Our task involves understanding the historical and social forces that perpetuate the lack of basic dignity that active citizenship would provide to those who currently do not have it.

As we noted earlier, the new waves of immigrants are different in many ways than the older waves. Although Hispanics have traditionally engaged in machine politics, it was of a different type than the sort of machine politics that characterized the older urban immigrant experience of other groups and it had different results, including passivity and a sense of political incapacity (DeSipio, 2006). Hispanics certainly engage in local political efforts and form self-help groups focused on issues of local importance, but these local efforts do not necessarily translate into effective political movements at the national level. The size of the Hispanic population makes them a potentially powerful voting bloc, but Hispanics are hardly homogeneous in terms of their political affiliations. While Hispanics may tend to be conservative in terms of social issues, they are hardly of one opinion, even on issues such as immigration reform.

In addition to normative considerations of the ideal communicative context, we must develop a more sophisticated understanding of how institutions operate to perpetuate systems of social stratification. Within the framework of globalization and the international flow of labor, institutional theory provides the opportunity to examine the political and institutional contexts within which migration occurs and the cultural and social change it brings about. Identities, those of both immigrants and the long-term residents of the communities in which immigrants arrive, are formed and maintained by political, religious, cultural, and legal institutions. Group and individual identities do not emerge from a vacuum, nor do they directly reflect prescribed beliefs, norms, practices, or symbolic systems of larger collectivities independent of their more local institutional contexts.

Culture inheres in institutions, as does one's sense of self. Institutions provide opportunities for change, at the same time that they constrain individual consciousness and freedom of action. But what are institutions? From a general perspective, institutions consist of the taken-for-granted rules of the game or the norms and belief systems that constrain individual actions in all areas of life. From this perspective one speaks of the institution of marriage, the institution of the family, the institution of religion, and education, justice, and more as the embodiment of established principles and practices. From another perspective, institutions refer to specific corporate bodies or organizations. One can identify specific institutions, such as the Presbyterian Church, Harvard University, the Senate, and the Supreme Court. All of these entities are institutions in both senses of the term; they are identifiable entities that embody specific moral and ethical principles.

Recent work in institutional theory focuses on the role of ideas, in addition to readily observable interests, in determining institutional evolution (Campbell, 2004). Social institutions and their key actors help define and redefine social reality by providing cognitive frames, or ways of interpreting social reality, in terms of which social actions are understood and responded to by individuals. The objective of many civil society organizations, including NGOs and others, is to influence the ways in which social problems are viewed by the public. This effort involves "framing" the problem in new ways that change people's perceptions in order to change the image of the immigrant from that of dangerous foreigner to that of a potentially productive addition to society. These efforts to further a multicultural agenda are in direct opposition to the frames promoted by the far right that portray immigration as a dangerous threat. What is clear is that discussions of multiculturalism, incorporation, and cultural assimilation are dominated by interested and engaged individuals who work though institutions that embody and institutionalize various political perspectives. Understanding the role of such institutions in the process of migration and the success or failure of migrant incorporation is essential to understanding how structure and agency interact to determine the direction and outcome of cultural change, as well as the degree of stigmatization or acceptance that immigrants experience. In the chapters of this book we examine various aspects of the Hispanic experience in the United States and relate it to the various institutions that determine their levels of education, their labor force experiences, their opportunities for social mobility, their income and wealth, their retirement experiences, their political participation, and more.

SUMMARY AND CONCLUSIONS

The United States is becoming more Hispanic. Hispanics from different nations have over the years migrated to the United States and given a distinct feel to specific parts of the country. Cubans, Puerto Ricans, Dominicans, Mexicans, and others have followed earlier immigrants to give rise to Latin communities in New York, Chicago, Los Angeles, Dallas, and other cities. Some cities, like San Antonio, Texas, are identified with their Mexican heritage. In this chapter we have reviewed theories of immigrant incorporation and followed the shift from "Anglo conformity" and "melting pot" theories, which held that immigrants would over time adopt the language, culture, and behavior of previous immigrants and form a new hybrid identity, to "multiculturalist" theories that hold that one's unique cultural identity is central to one's basic identity and psychological well-being. Rather than rejecting one's identity one should expect that it be recognized and respected by others. Debate over the possibility of a truly multicultural society continues and, as we noted, much political rhetoric in the

United States and Europe rejects the notion that different cultures and belief systems can coexist.

Yet immigration is a reality that defines our globalized modern world. People living in poverty in the developing world inevitably move to richer nations in search of a better life. Electronic media and the availability of means of transportation mean that millions will attempt to move from Africa to Europe and from Latin America to the United States. Many international migrants are refugees fleeing political upheaval and war. Despite calls for sealing borders and deporting undocumented residents, the need for cheap labor keeps the door to immigration open. In the United States immigration from Mexico and Latin America has a long history. Among Hispanics, the Mexican-origin population makes up the largest segment, over 60%. This fact reflects both the proximity of the two nations and the fact that American industry and agriculture have always depended on cheap labor.

Both in the United States and Europe attempts to introduce temporary guest worker programs have come up against the reality that once migrants from developing nations arrive they bring their families and remain. In Germany the Turkish community includes many families whose older members arrived as guest workers. In the United States the Bracero Program begun during World War II brought many Mexican workers into the country to fill jobs in industry and agriculture. These workers took advantage of the new opportunities and began a process that insured a porous border and the continuing flow of Mexicans into the United States, where they have become an important part of the labor force.

Hispanics as a whole, and particularly the Mexican-origin and Puerto Rican populations, remain socioeconomically disadvantaged and politically and socially marginalized. These individuals have extremely low levels of income and assets, the consequences of which we will discuss further in later chapters. As we will discuss further, Hispanics are underrepresented in the professions and are overrepresented in low-wage occupations. Few Hispanics hold high-level elected office. In this chapter we introduced "segmented assimilation" theory that is based on the observation that while certain immigrants rapidly move into the middle class, others remain in the lower classes even after many generations. The impaired mobility and low levels of education among Hispanics has serious short- and long-term negative implications for the nation as a whole. Given their high fertility Hispanics will make up a larger fraction of the labor force in years to come. As we note throughout the following chapters, if their productivity is impaired by low levels of education and poor health the productivity of the labor force as a whole will be impaired. This chapter has offered a number of theoretical perspectives that can provide a vocabulary for understanding the complexity of the Hispanic experience in more than a simple descriptive or mechanical way. In the next chapter we begin with description and compare the social and economic situation of Hispanics to that of Asians and non-Hispanics.

DISCUSSION QUESTIONS

1. In earlier centuries immigrants to the United States were primarily from Europe. Summarize some of the major commonalities and differences among immigrants from different European nations and list some ways in which they differed from immigrants today. Discuss whether the cultural and social differences characteristic of contemporary immigrants are likely to make their incorporation experiences more difficult and less complete than those of earlier European immigrants.

2. Multiculturalists maintain that since one's cultural identity is central to one's overall sense of personal worth it is imperative that an individual's culture or subculture be respected by others. Advocates for various groups believe that this holds even for aspects of identity such as sexual orientation. To what extent is the view that "culture" is a central and important part of an individual's or a group's identity useful? To what extent is it true? Have immigrants from Europe lost their "cultural" identity? To what extent are social class and such identifying factors as skin color and religious practices more important in determining life chances than culture?

3. Discuss the moral implications of "guest worker" programs. Is it ethical to bring workers from poor countries to serve as temporary workers with few of the rights that citizens enjoy? If developed nations need cheap labor, should immigration policy make provision for a more stable status that includes clearer and stronger protections for individual immigrants' rights? Should guest workers be allowed to vote in local and national elections? Should they have the opportunity to become citizens?

4. Should groups like Native Americans and Alaska Natives be entitled to special privileges because of the fact that they were colonized? Could one make similar arguments for African Americans whose ancestors were brought as slaves? Could this argument be extended to Mexican-origin individuals whose ancestors were Mexican citizens prior to the annexation of the north of Mexico by the United States in 1848?

5. Discuss the moral issues involved in calls for mass deportations. Should all undocumented residents be treated equally? Are there extenuating circumstances that might justify allowing certain undocumented immigrants a route to permanent residence or even citizenship? Should individuals who were brought into this country by their parents when they were children and incapable of deciding for themselves, but who have grown up here, be exempt from deportation?

6. Choose one or two countries in Europe, South America, or Asia and identify any active anti-immigration political parties or parties with strong anti-immigration positions. Summarize their arguments and the reasons for their anti-immigration positions. From what you can find, does it appear that they are winning a greater number of voters to their positions?

LITERATURE CITED

Alba, R. D. (1990). *Ethnic identity: The transformation of White America.* New Haven, CT: Yale University Press.

Albrecht, H.-J. (1997). Ethnic minorities, crime, and criminal justice in Germany. *Crime and Justice, 21,* 31–99.

Balibar, E. (2004). *We, the people of Europe? Reflections on transnational citizenship.* Princeton, NJ: Princeton University Press.

Batliwala, S., & Brown, L. D. (Eds.). (2006). *Transnational civil society: An introduction.* Bloomfield, CT: Kumarian Press, Inc.

Benhabib, S. (2002). *The claims of culture: Equality and diversity in the global era.* Princeton, NJ: Princeton University Press.

Boli, J., & Thomas, G. M. (Eds.). (1999). *Constructing world culture: International nongovernmental organizations since 1875.* Palo Alto, CA: Stanford University Press.

Bradsher, K. (2013, March 25). Hong Kong court denies residency to domestics. *New York Times,* pp. A4–A6. Retrieved May 1, 2014, from www.nytimes.com/2013/03/26/world/asia/hong-kong-court-denies-foreign-domestic-helpers-right-to-permanent-residency.html?pagewanted=all.

Cabranes, J. A. (1978). Citizenship and the American Empire: Notes on the legislative history of the United States citizenship of Puerto Ricans. *University of Pennsylvania Law Review, 127*(2), 391–492.

Caldwell, C. (2009). *Reflections on the revolution in Europe: Immigration, Islam, and the West.* New York, NY: Doubleday.

Campbell, J. L. (2004). *Institutional change and globalization.* Princeton, NJ: Princeton University Press.

Campbell, J. L., & Pedersen, O. K. (Eds.). (2001). *The rise of neoliberalism and institutional analysis.* Princeton, NJ: Princeton University Press.

Castillo, R. G. del. (1990). *The Treaty of Guadalupe Hidalgo: A legacy of conflict.* Norman, OK: University of Oklahoma Press.

Castle, S., & Cowell, A. (2013, March 25). Britain pledges to curtail benefits for immigrants. *New York Times,* p. A5. Retrieved May 1, 2014, from www.nytimes.com/2013/03/26/world/europe/cameron-pledges-tighter-rules-for-immigrants-in-britain.html.

Castles, S. (2004). Why migration policies fail. *Ethnic and Racial Studies, 27*(2), 205–27.

Cohen, D. (2011). *Braceros: Migrant citizens and transnational subjects in the postwar United States and Mexico.* Chapel Hill, NC: University of North Carolina Press.

Collazo, S. G., Ryan, C. L., & Bauman, K. J. (2010). *Profile of the Puerto Rican population in United States and Puerto Rico: 2008.* Paper presented at the Annual Meeting of the Population Association of America, Dallas, TX.

Cooley, C. H. (1902). *Human nature and the social order.* New York, NY: Charles Scribner's Sons.

DeParle, J. (2008, June 10). Spain, like U.S., grapples with immigration. *New York Times.* Retrieved March 11, 2013, from www.nytimes.com/2008/06/10/world/europe/10iht-10migrate.13592054.html?_r=0.

DeSipio, L. (2006). Latino civic and political participation. In M. Tienda, F. Mitchell, & National Research Council Panel on Hispanics in the United States, Committee on Population (Eds.), *Hispanics and the future of America* (pp. 447–79). Washington, DC: National Academies Press.

Dryzek, J. S. (2010). *Foundations and frontiers of deliberative governance.* New York, NY: Oxford University Press.

Edin, K., & Lein, L. (1997). *Making ends meet: How single mothers survive welfare and low-wage work.* New York, NY: Russell Sage Foundation.

Ennis, S. R., Ríos-Vargas, M., & Albert, N. G. (2011). *The Hispanic population: 2010.* Washington, DC: U.S. Census Bureau.

Fishkin, J. S. (2009). *When the people speak: Deliberative democracy and public consultation.* New York, NY: Oxford University Press.

Foner, N., & Alba, R. (2006). *The second generation from the last great wave of immigration: Setting the record straight.* Washington, DC: Migration Information Source. Retrieved March 10, 2013 from www.migrationinformation.org/Feature/display.cfm?id=439.

Fraser, N., & Honneth, A. (2003). *Redistribution or recognition? A political-philosophical exchange.* New York, NY: Verso.

Giddens, A. (1994). *Beyond left and right: The future of radical politics.* Stanford, CA: Stanford University Press.

Giddens, A. (1998). *The third way: The renewal of social democracy.* Malden, MA: Polity Press.

Gordon, M. M. (1964). *Assimilation in American life: The role of race, religion, and national origins.* New York and London: Oxford University Press.

Govan, F. (2012, May 10). Spanish illegal immigrants no longer given free health care. *The Telegraph*. Retrieved May 27, 2013 from www.telegraph.co.uk/news/worldnews/europe/spain/9258093/Spanish-illegal-immigrants-no-longer-given-free-health-care.html.

Granovetter, M. S. (1973). The strength of weak ties. *American Journal of Sociology, 78*(6), 1360–80.

Habermas, J. (1971). *Knowledge and human interests*. Boston, MA: Beacon Press.

Habermas, J. (1984). *The theory of communicative action, volume 1: Reason and the rationalization of society*. Boston, MA: Beacon Press.

Habermas, J. (1987). *The theory of communicative action, volume 2: Lifeworld and system – A critique of functionalist reason*. Boston, MA: Beacon Press.

Handlin, O. (Ed.). (1959). *Immigration as a factor in American history*. Englewood Cliffs, NJ: Prentice-Hall.

Henderson, T. J. (2011). Mexican immigration to the United States. In W. H. Beezley (Ed.), *A companion to Mexican history and culture* (pp. 604–15). Hoboken, NJ: Wiley-Blackwell.

Hispanic Institute for Americans for Secure Retirement. (2009). *Hispanics and retirement: Challenges and opportunities*. Washington, DC: Americans For Security Retirement and The Hispanic Institute. Retrieved March 14, 2013 from www.thehispanicinstitute.net/node/1890.

Huntington, S. P. (2004). The Hispanic challenge. *Foreign Policy, 141*, 30–45.

Keck, M. E., & Sikkink, K. (1998). *Activists beyond borders: Advocacy networks in international politics*. Ithaca, NY: Cornell University Press.

Kulish, N. (2008, January 14). Attack jolts Germany into fray on immigrant crime. *New York Times*. Retrieved March 11, 2013 from www.nytimes.com/2008/01/14/world/europe/14germany.html.

Kymlicka, W. (1995). *Multicultural citizenship: A liberal theory of minority rights*. New York: Oxford University Press.

Kymlicka, W. (2007). *Multicultural odysseys: Navigating the new international politics of diversity*. Oxford: Oxford University Press.

Kymlicka, W., & Norman, W. (2000a). Citizenship in culturally diverse societies: Issues, contexts, concepts. In *Citizenship in diverse societies* (pp. 1–41). Oxford and New York: Oxford University Press.

Kymlicka, W., & Norman, W. (Eds.). (2000b). *Citizenship in diverse societies*. Oxford and New York: Oxford University Press.

Massey, D. S., Rugh, J. S., & Pren, K. A. (2010). The geography of undocumented Mexican migration. *Mexican Studies, 26*(1), 129–52.

McGarry, A. (2010). *Who speaks for Roma? Political representation of a transnational minority community*. New York, NY: Continuum International Publishing Group.

Mead, G. H. (1934). *Mind, self, and society*. Chicago, IL: University of Chicago Press.

Mora, A. (2011). *Border dilemmas: Racial and national uncertainties in New Mexico, 1848–1912*. Durham, NC: Duke University Press.

Motomura, H. (2010). The rights of others: Legal claims and immigration outside the law. *Duke Law Journal, 59*, 1723–86.

Nolan, A. (2011). "Aggravated violations", Roma housing rights and forced expulsions in Italy: Recent developments under the European Social Charter Collective Complaints System. *Human Rights Law Review, 11*(2), 343–61.

Okin, S. M. (1988). Feminism and multiculturalism: Some tensions. *Ethics, 108*(4), 661–84.

Olivas, M. A. (2009). The political economy of the Dream Act and the legislative process: A case study of comprehensive immigration reform. *Wayne Law Review, 55*(1), 1757–810.

Orrenius, P. M., & Zavodny, M. (2003). Do amnesty programs reduce undocumented immigration? Evidence from IRCA. *Demography, 40*(3), 437–50.

Passel, J., & Cohn, D. (2011). *Unauthorized immigrant population: National and state trends, 2010.* Washington, DC: Pew Research Hispanic Center. Retrieved March 10, 2013 from www.pewhispanic.org/2011/02/01/unauthorized-immigrant-population-brnational-and-state-trends-2010.

Portes, A. (1995). Children of immigrants: Segmented assimilation and its determinants. In A. Portes (Ed.), *The economic sociology of immigration: Essays on networks, ethnicity, and entrepreneurship* (pp. 248–79). New York, NY: Russell Sage Foundation.

Portes, A., & Bach, R. L. (1985). *Latin journey: Cuban and Mexican immigrants in the United States.* Berkeley and Los Angeles, CA: University of California Press.

Portes, A., & Rumbaut, R. G. (2006). *Immigrant America: A portrait.* Berkeley and Los Angeles, CA: University of California Press.

Portes, A., & Zhou, M. (1993). The new second generation: Segmented assimilation and its variants. *Annals of the American Academy of Political and Social Science, 530*, 74–96.

Putnam, R. (2000). *Bowling alone: The collapse and revival of American community.* New York, NY: Simon & Schuster.

Roman, J. (2004). The trade union solution or the NGO problem? The fight for global labor rights. *Development in Practice, 14*(1–2), 100–9.

Samuel, H. (2012, March 6). Nicolas Sarkozy appeals to far-right saying "too many immigrants" in France. *Telegraph.* Retrieved March 11, 2013 from www.telegraph.co.uk/news/worldnews/nicolas-sarkozy/9127441/Nicolas-Sarkozy-appeals-to-far-Right-saying-too-many-immigrants-in-France.html.

Schierup, C.-U., Hansen, P., & Castles, S. (2006). *Migration, citizenship, and the European welfare state: A European dilemma.* Oxford: Oxford University Press.

Schlesinger, A. M. (1998). *The disuniting of America: Reflections on a multicultural society* (Rev. and enlarged ed.). New York, NY: W.W. Norton & Company, Inc.

Sezgin, U. (2012). Assimilation versus absorption. In P. J. Hayes (Ed.), *The making of modern immigration: An encyclopedia of people and ideas* (pp. 29–61). Santa Barbara, CA: ABC-CLIO, LLC.

Siebold, S. (2010, October 17). Merkel says German multiculturalism has failed. *Reuters.* Retrieved January 12, 2013, from http://uk.reuters.com/article/2010/10/16/uk-germany-merkel-immigration-idUKTRE69F19T20101016.

Silberman, R., Alba, R., & Fournier, I. (2007). Segmented assimilation in France? Discrimination in the labour market against the second generation. *Ethnic and Racial Studies, 30*(1), 1–27.

Singer, A., & Wilson, J. H. (2007). *Refugee resettlement in metropolitan America.* Washington, DC: Migration Information Source. Retrieved March 14, 2013, from www.migrationpolicy.org/article/refugee-resettlement-metropolitan-america/.

Snodgrass, M. (2011). Patronage and progress: The Bracero Program from the perspective of Mexico. In L. Fink (Ed.), *Workers across the Americas: The transnational turn in labor history* (pp. 245–66). New York, NY: Oxford University Press.

Stack, C. B. (1974). *All our kin: Strategies for survival in a Black community.* New York, NY: Basic Books.

Stepick, A., & Stepick, C. D. (2010). The complexities and confusions of segmented assimilation. *Ethnic and Racial Studies, 33*(7), 1149–67.

Suro, R. (1998). *Strangers among us: Latino lives in a changing America.* New York, NY: Vintage Books.

Taylor, C. (1994). The politics of recognition. In A. Gutman (Ed.), *Multiculturalism: Examining the politics of recognition* (pp. 25–73). Princeton, NJ: Princeton University Press.

Telles, E. E., & Ortiz, V. (2008). *Generations of exclusion: Mexican Americans, assimilation, and race.* New York, NY: Russell Sage Foundation.

Thränhardt, D. (1995). Germany: An undeclared immigration country. *Journal of Ethnic and Migration Studies, 21*(1), 19–35.

Valadez, J. M. (2001). *Deliberative democracy, political legitimacy, and self-determination in multicultural societies.* Boulder, CO: Westview Press.

Vermeulen, H. (2010). Segmented assimilation and cross-national comparative research on integration of immigrants and their children. *Ethnic and Racial Studies, 33*(7), 1214–30.

Waldinger, R., & Perlmann, J. (1997). Second generation decline? Immigrant children past and present: A reconsideration. *International Migration Review, 31*(4), 893–922.

Waters, M. (1999). *Black identities: West Indian immigrant dreams and American realities.* Cambridge, MA: Harvard University Press.

White, J. B. (1997). Turks in the new Germany. *American Anthropologist, 99*(4), 754–69.

Williams, D. R., & Mohammed, S. A. (2009). Discrimination and racial disparities in health: Evidence and needed research. *Journal of Behavioral Medicine, 32*, 20–47.

CHAPTER 2

Demographic, Educational, and Occupational Profile

IS HISPANIC A RACE?

Roberto Mondragon, a second-generation Mexican American from San Antonio, Texas, was born in the United States. His parents had lived most of their lives in Monterrey, Mexico, but had immigrated to the United States before Roberto was born. Roberto had two younger brothers and an older sister. The parents worked overtime and made great sacrifices to make sure their children received the best education possible. Roberto graduated near the top of his class at Alamo High School in San Antonio. With the help of his high school counselor he applied for and won a prestigious scholarship to Fordham University in the Bronx, where he majored in biology. He intended to apply to medical school after he earned his Bachelor's degree. During his junior year Roberto met Anna Hernandez, a sociology major who was also a junior, in a medical sociology course. The two dated a few times during their junior year, but the relationship blossomed in their senior year and they decided to get married soon after graduation.

The next year Roberto entered medical school at Columbia and Anna entered the graduate sociology program at New York University. Within a year Anna was pregnant and after a normal pregnancy gave birth to a healthy boy whom they named Antonio. The year was 1999. A year later the family received a census form as part of the 2000 Census. The questions were easy to answer until they got to the questions about race and ethnicity. The difficulty arose from the fact that Roberto, Anna, and Antonio were mixtures of different Hispanic subgroups. Roberto's parents were both born in Mexico. Anna's mother, Nancy Lyons, was a non-Hispanic White nurse who was born in Winchester, Massachusetts. Her father, Fernando Hernandez, was a neurosurgeon who had been born in San Juan, Puerto Rico and raised and educated on the island before moving to New York.

When they arrived at the race and ethnicity questions Roberto listed himself as Mexican. He also listed Antonio as Mexican but Anna objected, saying that he was Puerto Rican. In the end they decided upon a mixed ethnicity category, which was a write-in option. In answering the race question, Roberto, like a certain fraction of Hispanics, did not want to check White or Black for himself or Antonio since he felt that their race was Hispanic. Since Anna's mother was non-Hispanic White she listed herself as White, but Roberto insisted that he was Hispanic. The couple could not agree on Antonio's race since Anna wanted to list him as White. In the end they also listed him as Hispanic.

WHAT'S IN A NAME?

This hypothetical example illustrates the difficulty that individuals from various backgrounds can have in fitting themselves into administrative categories intended to determine race and ethnicity. It might lead us to question the utility of racial and ethnic classifications for any purpose. Hispanic ethnicity may provide information on origin, but of what real use is that information? Racial classifications have changed since the 19th century and those listed on the census form reflect political and social decisions rather than meaningful scientific distinctions. This administrative and social focus on race and Hispanic ethnicity, and our disinterest in specific European ethnicities, reflects political forces and contemporary realities. Blacks and Hispanics are disadvantaged groups with long histories of marginalization in terms of economic and political power. Racial and ethnic classifications reveal little of biological origins, genetic makeup, or any other characteristic that is common to all members of the category; rather they tell us more about the social realities that affect the lives of certain groups at certain historical moments. Yet the classification is important for theoretical and practical purposes.

In this chapter we examine the major cultural, social, and economic characteristics of Hispanics and compare them to non-Hispanic Whites, Blacks, and Asians. Where possible we differentiate among Hispanics on the basis of nation of origin. Often, however, information is only available for Hispanics as a group. Given the fact that individuals of Mexican origin make up over 60% of the Hispanic population, aggregate Hispanic statistics based on representative samples of Hispanics are heavily influenced by the Mexican-origin component. Asians, of course, also comprise multiple nationalities with very different immigration experiences. Given the large number of specific Asian groups and the relative shortage of data that provides detailed breakdowns, we treat Asians as a single category, conceding that such an approach masks significant intragroup differences.

In the previous chapter we documented important differences among specific Hispanic subgroups based on their immigration histories and legal status in the United States. In order to examine their characteristics we must accurately categorize individuals belonging to different groups. Unfortunately, although the conceptual categories might be clear, in practice such classification can be difficult and even contentious, as our opening vignette illustrates (Nasser, 2013). How, for example, would one classify someone who is half-Cuban and half-non-Hispanic, or someone whose father is Puerto Rican and whose mother is Mexican American, or someone who is one-quarter African American, one-quarter Nicaraguan, and one-half non-Hispanic White? Clearly many combinations are possible and some classification rule is necessary for the purpose of presenting statistics and characterizing populations.

In this book we employ the official United States Census operationalization of Hispanic ethnicity, which is based on one's self-identification (Humes, Jones, & Ramirez, 2011). In the Census Bureau's scheme the identification of someone as Hispanic is based on two questions, one that refers to race and the other to specific Hispanic origin group (Humes et al., 2011). The race question asks the respondent to choose one of five racial categories: (1) White; (2) Black or African American; (3) American Indian or Alaska Native; (4) Asian; (5) Native Hawaiian or Other Pacific Islander. For those who do not wish to choose one of these categories a sixth classification is possible: (6) Some Other Race. Someone of Hispanic origin could identify Hispanic as his or her race. In a separate question the respondent is asked if he or she is Hispanic or Latino. The response options include (1) not Hispanic or Latino; (2) Cuban; (3) Mexican; (4) Puerto Rican; (5) South or Central American; or (6) other Spanish culture or origin regardless of race (Humes et al., 2011). The last category provided the opportunity for the respondent to enter a nationality that is not listed or to choose multiple categories.

The race and Hispanic categories are combined when data are reported and Hispanics can be of any race. Research by the Census Bureau finds many Latinos do not identify with the current race categories and consider their race to be Hispanic (Compton, Bentley, Ennis, & Rastogi, 2013). In the 2010 Census, 53% of Hispanics identified themselves as White; 2.5% as Black or African American; 1.4% as American Indian or Alaska Native; 0.4% as Asian; 0.1% as Native Hawaiian or Other Pacific Islander; and 36.7% as Some Other Race (Compton et al., 2013). The remaining 6% chose more than one race category. The fact that nearly 40% of Hispanic respondents identified themselves as of some other race indicates that for this population the standard racial categories do not reflect their subjective reality. This situation might lead us to reconsider the concept of race altogether and to combine the race and ethnicity questions into one self-identification.

As a group Hispanics are the largest minority group in the nation, making up nearly 17% of the population. As we mentioned earlier, Hispanics of Mexican origin make up the largest segment of the total Hispanic population. Given the sheer size of the Mexican-origin population, their cultural and economic impact is disproportionate. The various Hispanic nationalities have historically been regionally concentrated, although there has always been some degree of dispersion. Today individuals of Mexican origin, who had been concentrated in the Southwest and in cities like Los Angeles and Chicago, have moved to many parts of the South and other parts of the country (Terrazas, 2010). Despite this growing dispersion, though, the various Hispanic subgroups still tend to cluster in specific regions and metropolitan areas. This concentration reflects the colonization and immigration history of each group and the periods during which it occurred.

The top panel of Table 2.1 lists the 10 cities with the largest number of Hispanics. The lower panel lists the 10 cities or areas with the highest concentrations of Hispanics. Many Americans are aware of the very Mexican feel of tourist centers like San Antonio, a city in which over 60% of the population is of Mexican origin (U.S. Census Bureau, 2013). Almost everyone is aware of the high concentrations of Mexicans in Los Angeles (LA), although most middle-class Americans have never visited East LA, which is nearly 100% Mexican. Other cities have high concentrations of Hispanics. New York leads the list with nearly two million Hispanics. As a global city, New York is the destination of

Hispanics from all over Latin America. Given its historical tie to the island of Puerto Rico, a large fraction of New Yorkers are Puerto Rican, but the presence of Dominicans, Salvadoreans, Hondurans, and others means that one can hear many Spanish accents in the small shops and businesses of Manhattan and other boroughs.

Chicago has a large Mexican-origin population as well as a large Puerto Rican population. Neighborhoods like "Little Village" in South Lawndale have a distinctly Latin flavor. The presence of a large number of Hispanics means that they are inevitably an important part of the local economy. As we will discuss at length in subsequent

TABLE 2.1 *Ten Places With the Highest Number and Percentage of Hispanics or Latinos: 2010*

HISPANIC OR LATINO POPULATION		
PLACE	RANK	NUMBER
New York, NY	1	2,336,076
Los Angeles, CA	2	1,838,822
Houston, TX	3	919,668
San Antonio, TX	4	838,952
Chicago, IL	5	778,862
Phoenix, AZ	6	589,877
El Paso, TX	7	523,721
Dallas, TX	8	507,309
San Diego, CA	9	376,020
San Jose, CA	10	313,636
PLACE	RANK	PERCENT
East Los Angeles, CA	1	97.1
Laredo, TX	2	95.6
Hialeah, FL	3	94.7
Brownsville, TX	4	93.2
McAllen, TX	5	84.6
El Paso, TX	6	80.7
Santa Ana, CA	7	78.2
Salinas, CA	8	75.0
Oxnard, CA	9	73.5
Downey, CA	10	70.7

Source: Ennis, Ríos-Vargas, & Albert (2011).

chapters, Hispanics tend to hold jobs in the service, construction, and agricultural sectors in which they often lack health insurance and retirement plans. In a very real sense, then, many of the major cities of the country are maintained by Hispanic labor.

The second panel of Table 2.1 reveals major concentrations of Hispanics in certain places. Of the nine locations listed in which Hispanics make up over 70% of the population, nine are in California and Texas, reflecting the fact that those states were at one time part of Mexico and continue to have locations with high concentrations of Mexican-origin individuals. The high concentration of Hispanics in Hialeah, Florida, in which nearly 95% of the population is Hispanic, reflects the importance of Cubans to the culture and economy of South Florida. Many other cities and localities in the country have high concentrations of Hispanics who live in specific barrios. These concentrations have been referred to as "ethnic enclaves" and, as in the "Little Havanas" of South Florida, residents can interact with others in their idiomatic Spanish and go about their business as if they were back on the island. Research that we review in Chapter 7 reveals that such ethnic enclaves can have a protective influence on the physical and mental health of residents. Interaction with co-ethnics and the reproduction of the culture of home neutralizes many of the stresses associated with immigration and life in a foreign country.

THE IMPLICATIONS OF DIFFERENT AGE STRUCTURES

Although opposition to immigration and proposals for allowing illegal immigrants to become citizens is widespread, Hispanics make an important contribution to the nation in the form of people and labor. Their higher fertility is part of the reason that the population of the United States as a whole remains above the replacement level. This higher fertility, though, means that they are younger as a group than non-Hispanic White Americans. This fact has important social and cultural implications since it means that Hispanics will become an even larger segment of the population in the future.

Just as age is an important characteristic of individuals, the age structure of a population has important social, economic, and political consequences (Angel & Settersten, 2014). When individuals are young they need education but not much medical care. When they grow up, they need employment and the ability to save to buy a home, educate children, and prepare for old age. The elderly need little education and more medical care, and their earning capacities rapidly decline. For the most part their asset accumulation is over and they must live on whatever they have managed to save. A population with a large proportion of children needs schools and day care; one with a large fraction of old people needs institutions focused on the needs of the elderly, including long-term care facilities, elder housing, senior transportation, nutrition programs, and more. A population with a large proportion of working-age adults relative to those who are young or old results in what some have termed a "demographic dividend," since in such a situation many workers are available to support those who are too young or old to work (Cotlear, 2011).

Given the importance of age structures in defining the needs of individuals and society at large, and the fact that subgroups differ greatly in their age structure, the topic deserves a bit more discussion since it relates directly to the impact of the Hispanic population on various social institutions. In the process of development nations experience a process known as the "demographic transition" (Cotlear, 2011). Initially, when social conditions result in high mortality, as was the case in European nations prior to the Industrial Revolution, birth rates are high as well. The combination of high birth rates and high mortality results in stable but relatively small populations. Beginning in the 18th century in Europe, mortality began to drop as living conditions improved (Caldwell, Caldwell, Caldwell, McDonald, & Schindlmayr, 2006). Because of a lack of effective contraception and traditional practices, though, birth rates remained high, resulting in rapidly growing populations (Caldwell et al., 2006). Eventually, as individuals could expect their children to survive, and as they gained access to effective contraception, birth rates dropped and population sizes again stabilized, albeit at a much larger size.

At this point in the demographic transition a new phenomenon occurs: populations age rapidly and the number of older individuals relative to working-age individuals increases (National Research Council, 2012). Today lifespans are increasing in all developed and developing nations. In nations that, only a generation or two ago, had high fertility today have fertility rates that are well below replacement level. In Spain, a conservative Catholic country with traditionally high fertility, the fertility rate had dropped to

1.48 children per woman by 2012 (Central Intelligence Agency, 2012). In order for a population to remain stable in size each woman must replace herself and one male, which means that women must on average have at least 2.1 children. The fraction compensates the inevitable loss associated with infant mortality. At rates below replacement populations inevitably shrink, and as they move into the later stages of the demographic transition they become old and lose their "demographic dividend," a term that refers to the potential economic benefit of a large number of prime-age adults relative to the dependent young and old. Instead of a large number of workers for each retiree, they enter a phase in which there are relatively few workers for each retiree. As Figure 2.1 shows, among women aged 15 to 44 in the United States, birth rates vary greatly by race and Hispanic ethnicity (Hamilton, Martin, & Ventura, 2012). Other data not presented here show that Hispanic women immigrants who have spent less than 6 years in the United States have the highest fertility (Frank & Heuveline, 2005).

When Social Security was introduced in 1935 each retiree was supported by approximately 40 workers. In 1960 there were approximately five workers for each retiree; by 2010 the number had dropped to fewer than three; and by 2040 it will drop to two, and decrease even further after that (Old-Age Survivors and Disability Insurance Board of Trustees, 2012). One can easily see that given the higher birth rate among Hispanics, in the future the proportion of working-age Hispanics in the labor force will inevitably grow.

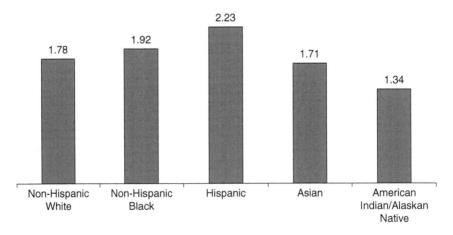

FIGURE 2.1 *Children Ever Born by Race and Hispanic Origin: 2011.*
Source: National Center for Health Statistics (2012).

The rapid aging of populations has other important social implications. When a nation's fertility rate is below the replacement level, the only way in which overall population size and a reasonable worker-to-retiree ratio can be maintained is through immigration. As we mentioned in the previous chapter, today European nations are forced to confront the reality of immigration and the fact that their economies depend upon it (Castles, 2004; DeParle, 2008). What this means, though, is that different age groups will have different ethnic and cultural profiles (Caldwell, 2009). Immigration to Europe is primarily from the Muslim nations of the South and East (Pew Forum on Religion and Public Life, 2010). In the United States immigrants come primarily from Latin America and Asia. Given immigrants' higher fertility this means that in the very near future in the United States the working-age population will be culturally and socially different than the retired population (Torres-Gil & Treas, 2009). One of the two workers that will be responsible for each retiree will be a member of a minority group, and very probably Hispanic. At the same time the retired population will be predominantly non-Hispanic and White. Clearly, the political and social implications are profound. If the productivity of those minority workers is impaired by low levels of education and poor health they will not be able to bear the burden, nor might they welcome it if they feel that they have been unjustly treated.

To further illustrate the point, in Figure 2.2 we present age pyramids for Hispanics, Asians, and non-Hispanic Blacks and Whites. Age pyramids are a convenient way of describing the age and sex composition of a population. The label "pyramid" refers to the fact that in young populations the younger age ranges are much larger than the older age ranges and thus the figure takes on the shape of a pyramid. This age profile was typical of all societies prior to the demographic transition and is typical of developing nations today. In the developed world age pyramids no longer take that shape and in very old societies like Japan they are basically rectangular or even inverted. In Figure 2.2 the Hispanic age profile resembles more of a pyramid than do those of Asians or non-Hispanic Whites. The Asian pyramid reflects a large adult population relative to children and youth. Non-Hispanic Blacks are somewhat intermediate.

The point is vitally important to ethnic relations in the future. A very compelling illustration of the potential consequences of group differences in age structure and fertility has been offered by Stephen Murdock, who served as the

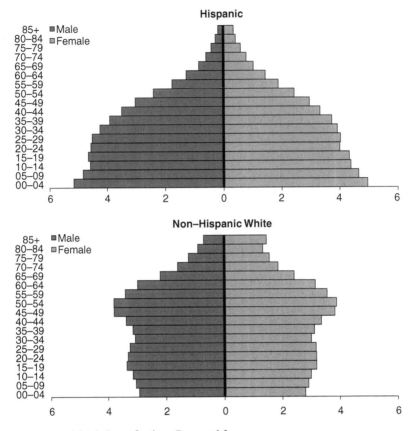

FIGURE 2.2 *2010 Population Pyramids.*

Source: U.S. Census Bureau (2011) 2010 Census Summary File 2; www.census.gov/prod/cen2010/doc/sf2.pdf.

Director of the U.S. Census Bureau and the Office of the State Demographer, Texas, and who is keenly aware of the consequences of group differences in age structure. Figure 2.3 shows that in 2000 the proportion of Anglo and Hispanic children between the ages of five and nine was the same. Each represented approximately 40% of that age group. As one moves up the age range, though, the proportion of Anglos increases, such that among those aged 65 and older over 70% were Anglo, while fewer than 20% were Hispanic. The figure clearly demonstrates the Social Security problem we face. In a pay-as-you go system in which payments to retirees come directly from the contributions of those who are working, in the future a predominantly non-Hispanic White population, will depend on a largely minority workforce for support.

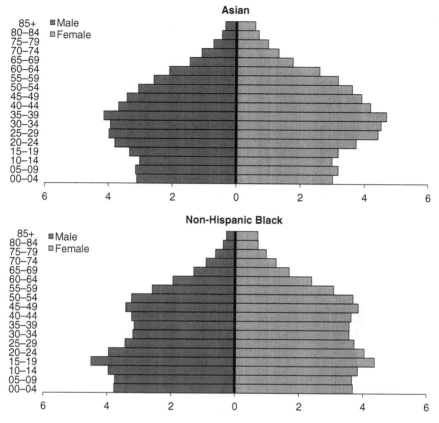

FIGURE 2.2 *Continued*

MARRIAGE AND DIVORCE

Age profiles clearly reflect other social and cultural factors. Hispanics' young age profile reflects higher fertility, cultural norms, and other factors. In order to better understand this population let us examine other important characteristics. Figure 2.4 shows that among female individuals aged 18 and older, Mexicans are less likely to be married than non-Hispanic Whites and more likely to be married than Blacks. Once married, though, Hispanic women are less likely than others to divorce. Figure 2.5 shows that Hispanics' divorce rates are far lower than those of non-Hispanic Whites or Blacks. These figures clearly show the decline in marriage among Blacks that reflects a large number of disruptive social forces, including racism, as well as high rates of out-of-wedlock childbirth and father absence (Moynihan,

Smeeding, & Rainwater, 2006; Wilson, 1996). These negative social forces have clearly not affected Hispanic marriage rates to the same degree, but one imagines that given their socioeconomic and educational profile, they may become more similar to Blacks in the future. These data, then, show that Hispanics have higher fertility but are less likely to be married than non-Hispanics. Of course, the Hispanic population is younger and since these data refer to women as young as 15, the lower marriage rate may reflect a higher proportion of very young individuals. Nonetheless,

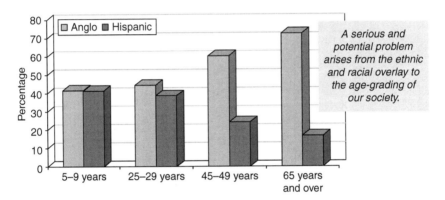

FIGURE 2.3 *Percentage of Texas Population by Age Group and Ethnicity: 2000.*
Source: Murdock (2004, slide 30).

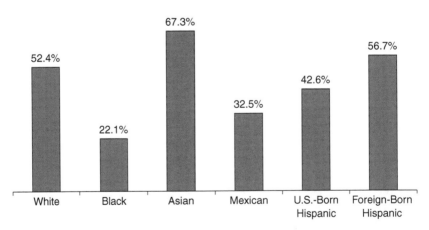

FIGURE 2.4 *First Marriage Rates of Never-married Women Aged 18 and Older by Race, Ethnicity, and Hispanic Nativity Status: 2010.*
Source: U.S. Census Bureau, American Community Survey, 2010.
1. Data from the 2007–11 American Community Survey; women 15 and older.

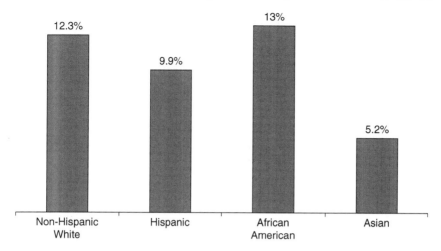

FIGURE 2.5 *Divorce Rate for Ever-married Women Ages 18 and Older by Race and Hispanic Origin: 2012.*
U.S. Census Bureau (2012).

this pattern challenges previous assumptions regarding marriage and fertility among Hispanics and should make us question all cultural and group stereotypes.

EDUCATION

In caste societies or those with clear social class distinctions one's opportunities for occupational attainment and social advancement are heavily influenced by the circumstances of one's birth. In more meritocratic systems, on the other hand, one's own efforts have a significant effect on one's success. In the United States a major mechanism for self-advancement is education. Individuals with a college education earn more than individuals with only a high school education, and they enjoy greater job security and are more likely to have health insurance and a retirement plan (Angel & Angel, 2009). Yet the opportunities for educational achievement are influenced to a large extent by racial and ethnic group membership. Hispanics, on average, have the lowest levels of education of any minority group (Tienda & Mitchell, 2006). Since, as we have noted, those of Mexican origin make up the majority of the Hispanic category, these low levels of education reflect the Mexican experience, although Puerto Ricans also have low levels of education.

Low average levels of education, though, mask other differences that are revealed when we examine different types of education. The most serious situation in terms of limited opportunities for occupational and social advancement occurs when an individual fails to complete high school. Although some high school dropouts do well, the majority face a lifetime of restricted opportunities and earn on average about $270,000 less over their lifetimes than high school graduates (Orfield, Losen, Wald, & Swanson, 2004). Figure 2.6 presents high school graduation rates for non-Hispanic Whites, Blacks, and Hispanics aged 25 years and older. It shows that Hispanics as a group are less likely to have a high school diploma or equivalent than non-Hispanic Whites or Blacks.

Among Hispanics, those of Mexican origin are the least likely to graduate; over 40% drop out before receiving a diploma. For most high school dropouts their education is finished; only 3.8% of Hispanic dropouts receive a General Equivalency Diploma (GED) (Ryan & Siebens, 2012).

High rates of high school dropout of course mean that a large fraction of Hispanics, and especially those of Mexican origin, are not even in the running for higher levels of education. Data on college attendance and graduation rates reflect this educational handicap. Among Hispanics, 13% have some college as opposed to 22% of Whites, 25% of Blacks, and 17% of Asians. For a disproportionate number of Hispanics post-secondary education consists of

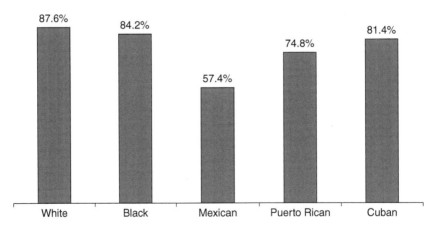

FIGURE 2.6 *High School Graduate by Race and Hispanic Origin 25 Years and Older: 2010.*
Source: U.S. Statistical Abstract (2012, table 229).

community college (Kurlaender, 2006). In general, though, only about a quarter of community college enrollees transfer to 4-year colleges (Pew Research Hispanic Center, 2005). Although community college can provide one with useful vocational skills, it is not a route to professional or managerial positions.

Figure 2.7 presents college graduation rates for Cubans, Puerto Ricans, and Mexicans, as well as non-Hispanic Whites and Blacks. Although Cubans' college graduation rate is lower than that of non-Hispanic Whites, it is far higher than that of Blacks or the other two Hispanic groups.

Hispanics of Mexican origin have an extremely low college graduation rate; only about 10% are college graduates. Combined with the high rate of high school dropout, this reality means that the group as a whole is poorly prepared to move into influential positions in education, business, or government.

The disproportionately small percentage of Hispanics with Bachelor's degrees necessarily means that a smaller proportion of these groups will be eligible for graduate or professional training. Figure 2.8 presents data on the proportion of each group with postgraduate education. It clearly shows that, given their lower completion rates at lower levels of education, Hispanics are less likely than other groups to earn advanced or professional degrees. They are less likely than Blacks to earn a Master's degree (2.7%) and are similar to Blacks in their rates of doctoral and

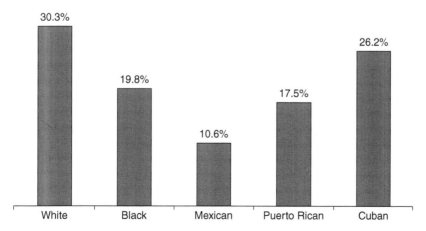

FIGURE 2.7 *College Graduate or More by Race and Hispanic Origin: 2010.*

Source: U.S. Statistical Abstract (2012, table 229).

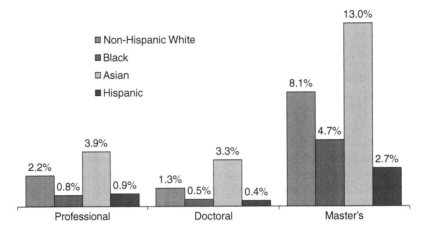

FIGURE 2.8 *Graduate School and Professional School Achievement: 2009.*
Source: Ryan and Siebens (2012).

professional education. For both groups, less than 1% possesses the levels of education that are required for many of the most powerful and prestigious positions. This educational deficit represents a serious barrier to social, economic, and political power for both groups (Pew Research Hispanic Center, 2005). As a consequence, the number of Hispanic and Black CEOs, Congresspersons, Senators, or influential professors, doctors, and lawyers remains limited.

EMPLOYMENT

Education, of course, serves as preparation for employment and a career. A career implies not only a good salary, but also access to health insurance, a retirement plan, and some degree of job security. Such careers require high levels of education, so Hispanics and Blacks enter the arena with a serious handicap. Table 2.2 presents important employment characteristics for non-Hispanic White, non-Hispanic Black, and Mexican-origin Hispanics. The table shows high labor force participation rates among Mexican males. Nearly 62% are employed compared to just over 40% of Blacks. Over 80% of all three groups is employed full-time.

However, Mexicans are less likely than either non-Hispanic Whites or Blacks to be employed in the public sector where they would be more likely to have access to employer-sponsored health plans and retirement plans.

TABLE 2.2 *Employment Characteristics of Employed Population by Race and Mexican Origin*

CHARACTERISTIC	NON-HISPANIC WHITE	NON-HISPANIC BLACK	MEXICAN ORIGIN
Total Employment (in thousands)	114,690	15,051	12,698
Men (%)	54.0	46.2	61.8
Employment Hours			
Full-time	80.1	82.0	80.6
Employment Sector (%)			
Private	78.5	76.9	84.1
Public	14.2	19.3	9.9
Self-employed	7.3	3.8	6.0
Union Membership[a,b]	11.6	13.5	9.7

Sources: Bureau of Labor Statistics, Current Population Survey (2011).

Notes
a. Union membership based on the number of employed workers, not total employment.
b. Union membership available for all Hispanics, and not Mexican origin only.

Table 2.2 also reflects the relatively low levels of union membership among U.S. workers, but it also shows that membership is particularly low among Mexicans, again perhaps reflecting their lower representation in unionized public-sector jobs and concentration in agriculture, construction, and small enterprises.

Figure 2.9 provides evidence of Hispanics' occupational ghettoization. Given the group's low levels of education, they are seriously underrepresented in the professions. In the private sector, Mexicans are more likely to work in small firms that do not offer health insurance or retirement plans (Angel, Angel, & Montez, 2009). Such jobs often do not offer group health insurance plans to their workers and are unlikely to pay enough to allow workers to purchase private health insurance for themselves and their families or to save for retirement.

These occupational disadvantages inevitably translate into earnings and wealth disadvantages. Figure 2.10 presents the median weekly income of Hispanic, African-American, Asian, and non-Hispanic White males. It shows that Hispanic males' average weekly earnings are only 71% of non-Hispanic White males' weekly earnings and 90% of African-American males' weekly earnings. Hispanic males earn only 61% of what Asian males earn.

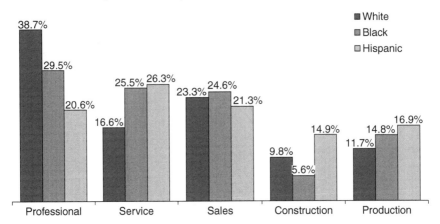

FIGURE 2.9 *Occupation Sectors by Race and Hispanic Ethnicity: 2012.*
Source: Current Population Survey (2012).

Table 2.3 provides information on household income for non-Hispanic White, Black, Asian, and Hispanic households of all ages for 2009 and 2010 after the economic collapse of 2008. It shows that while all groups lost some ground from 2009 to 2010, Hispanics suffered a smaller loss than others, although their household incomes remain low compared to Asians and non-Hispanic Whites. Hispanics' household income, though, remains above that of Blacks.

Table 2.4 provides information on the financial situation of households in which the head is over 65. The

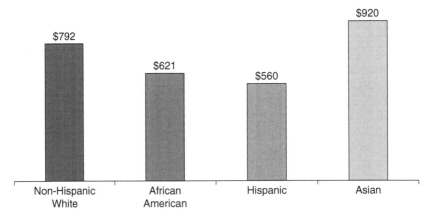

FIGURE 2.10 *Hispanic Male Workers Earn Less per Week than Non-Hispanic Whites and Blacks (in Dollars): 2007.*
Source: Bureau of Labor Statistics (2008).

TABLE 2.3 *Household Income by Race and Hispanic Ethnicity*

RACE AND HISPANIC ORIGIN OF HOUSEHOLD	2009	2010	PERCENTAGE CHANGE IN REAL MEDIAN INCOME
Non-Hispanic White	$55,360	$54,620	−1.3
Black	$33,122	$32,068	−3.2
Asian	$66,550	$64,308	−3.4
Hispanic Origin	$38,667	$37,759	−2.3

Source: DeNavas, Proctor, & Semega (2011).

previous table showed that income differences are large, but this table shows that wealth differences among groups are huge. By the time the head of household reaches 65 the household's earning capacity is probably declining and its total net worth is in all probability as high as it will ever be. For most individuals security in old age depends on the liquidation of assets and savings to supplement Social Security. Social Security is a major source of financial security in old age, but it was never meant to be one's sole source of retirement income. For a large fraction (20%) of the older population, though, including a large fraction (40%) of Hispanics, Social Security is their only source of income (Social Security Administration, 2010). Individuals in this situation have almost no discretionary income. In the absence of Social Security benefits, over half of women would fall below or close to the poverty line (Angel & Mudrazijia, 2011).

TABLE 2.4 *Housing Equity and Non-Housing Assets (in US$) for Elderly Households (65 and older) by Race, Hispanic Ethnicity, and Household Headship Status, 2010*

	NON-HISPANIC WHITE	NON-HISPANIC BLACK	MEXICAN ORIGIN	OTHER HISPANIC
Couple or Single Male:				
Housing Equity	182,740	97,609	93,614	102,887
Non-Housing Assets	458,375	103,934	90,852	106,576
Single Female:				
Housing Equity	116,408	64,113	59,740	40,223
Non-Housing Assets	216,238	33,908	28,911	19,459

Source: Health and Retirement Study (2010).

Given the clear handicap that female-headed house-holds face in terms of wealth accumulation, a topic that we discuss at greater length in Chapter 3, in Table 2.4 we present housing equity and non-housing assets separately by the gender of the head of household. Among couple-headed households or those with a single male head, both housing and non-housing assets are far higher for non-Hispanic Whites than for non-Hispanic Blacks, Mexicans, and Other Hispanics. Mexicans fall far below non-Hispanic Whites in both forms of assets, and they fall below Other Hispanics. The second panel of Table 2.4 clearly shows the serious lack of wealth among Black, Mexican, and Other Hispanic female-headed households. Even non-Hispanic White female-headed households are handicapped com-pared to couple-headed or male-headed households. Mexican and Other Hispanic female-headed households have less than $30,000 in non-housing assets. Clearly, these households have very little by way of a personal safety net and are at very high risk of becoming dependent on chil-dren or public programs for such basic necessities as medical care, housing, and nutrition.

SUMMARY AND CONCLUSIONS

This chapter set the stage for the subsequent chapters by documenting the serious educational, occupational, and income disadvantages that affect the Hispanic community. These clearly affect the well-being of individuals and fam-ilies, but they also limit the economic and political clout of the community as a whole. As we noted, Hispanics are less likely than non-Hispanic Whites to enter the corridors of power. The chapter also illustrated important differences among the various Hispanic groups. Hispanics of Mexican origin are clearly the most seriously handicapped in terms of education, a handicap that translates directly into lower occupational attainment, lower income, and limited wealth. Puerto Ricans, despite the fact that they are U.S. citizens by birth, also fare poorly as a group. Cubans, on the other hand, do much better and on many indictors approximate non-Hispanic Whites.

Although Asians and Blacks share minority group status with Hispanics, they differ significantly on the major social indicators that we have examined. Blacks are similar to or worse than Hispanics on certain indicators. Asians, on the other hand, fare much better in terms of education and income. They, in fact, are not disadvantaged as the term is usually employed. With these basic facts in mind, in the next chapter we examine the role of gender in the Hispanic experience. Although we can identify clear occupational and income disadvantages associated with both gender and ethnicity, their joint impact can place Hispanic women at a particular disadvantage. Hispanic families are increasingly affected by the disruptive social forces that have placed serious strains on Black families. Smaller families, marital disruption, and migration in addition to the unemployment, disorganization, and crime that plague many urban neighborhoods may result in an increasing level of family disruption in the years to come. These changes have serious implications for everyone, but especially for women's roles as wives, mothers, and workers. In Chapter 3 we examine changing cultural norms, and Hispanic women's changing social situation.

The label "Hispanic" masks large differences in culture, regional concentration, education and wealth, immigration history, and more among subgroups whose roots lie in the Caribbean, Mexico, or the rest of Latin America. The timing and circumstances of the incorporation of different subgroups has had a profound impact on their social and political circumstances. Old-stock Mexican Americans who became citizens as the result of the annexation of the north of Mexico into what is now the Southwest have been citizens for generations, even as many remain isolated in economically deprived areas. Puerto Ricans also became citizens when the United States seized the island after the Spanish–American War. Cubans are refugees who received special status and an easier path to citizenship than regular immigrants from other nations. Among Hispanics, Cubans have been highly successful economically and politically and have turned Miami into a Little Havana.

Today Hispanics are fanning out across the country, a phenomenon we discuss in greater detail in later chapters. States like North Carolina, which was home to almost no Mexican-origin individuals just 20 years ago, now have large and growing Mexican-origin populations. These new immigrants support the economic base of the communities into which they move, and they give those places a new and more international flavor.

Hispanics also contribute to population stability. Their relatively high fertility means that a disproportionate number of births are to Hispanic mothers. This fact has profound implications for the ethnic composition of different age ranges, a topic we return to frequently throughout the book. Hispanics are also culturally distinct from the majority population in many ways. In Europe the arrival of individuals from Muslim countries has resulted in a backlash based on the fear that traditional cultural values are under assault. Many new immigrants wish to retain aspects of their traditional cultures, and they reject the notion that they should assimilate completely. Immigrants from Latin America are clearly different in that even though they speak Spanish, they fairly quickly learn English and are for the most part members of familiar religious denominations.

In this chapter we showed that Hispanics are more likely than non-Hispanics to marry and less likely to divorce, patterns consistent with "familism," a cultural orientation that many have attributed to Hispanics that includes a high value placed on marriage and family. Both in this chapter and in later chapters, though, we note trends in family disruption that accompany low levels of education and blocked mobility chances for both men and women that are straining the traditional family. Increasingly, Hispanics may come to adopt the family profile of African Americans that includes high levels of single motherhood.

For Hispanics a major barrier to individual social mobility and to group political and economic power results from seriously low levels of education. Hispanics are less likely than other groups to complete secondary education, which means that they are not able to go on to college or university. Among Hispanics, higher levels of education often means community or 2-year colleges. Without basic college education they do not move on to graduate or professional schools and are underrepresented in the professions.

DISCUSSION QUESTIONS

1. Are race and ethnicity biologically or genetically based categorizations? What characteristics of individuals or groups do categorizations of the sort employed by the Census Bureau reflect? Are such categorizations in reality socially constructed? Might it make sense to abandon the use of such categories in official documents?

2. Summarize the "demographic transition" and discuss its implications for population aging. We used the term "demographic dividend" to describe a situation in which the size of the working-age population is large

relative to the dependent population, that consists of children too young to work and the elderly who are no longer in the workforce. Given the aging of the population of the United States, discuss the implications for Social Security and discuss the possible range of options for dealing with the consequences of rapid population aging. What might be some of the political hurdles to any reform of Social Security?

3. Although Hispanics have higher marriage rates and lower divorce rates than non-Hispanics, the disruptive social forces associated with low levels of education, high rates of poverty, and blocked social mobility chances are leading to higher rates of family disruption and single motherhood among these groups. Discuss the social sources of strain on the family and propose public policy and program reforms that might help address the problem of family disruption, not only for Hispanics, but in general. Debate the proposition that the government and social policy are not responsible for preserving the institution of marriage.

4. The Hispanic population has on average very low levels of education, which translates into lower-status jobs with lower pay and few benefits. As a consequence, Hispanics are more likely than non-Hispanic Whites to lack health insurance or retirement plans. Do low levels of education among Hispanics represent a public problem that government should address? How might low levels of education among Hispanics affect the economy at large?

5. Professor Samuel P. Huntington, chairman of the Harvard Academy for International and Area Studies, published an article in *Foreign Policy* magazine in which he claimed that Mexican immigrants refuse to assimilate and that because of their large numbers the cultural identity of the United States is threatened. According to Huntington we are in danger of becoming two nations with two languages and cultures and he feels this change is dangerous. Discuss the proposition that Mexican immigration, because of its magnitude and the fact that a large number of immigrants are undocumented and poorly educated, poses a danger to our collective cultural identity. Discuss whether this proposition misrepresents the nature of Mexican immigration. Are Mexican immigrants in reality significantly different than earlier immigrant groups in terms of their ability and desire to assimilate and acculturate?

LITERATURE CITED

Angel, J. L., & Mudrazijia, S. (2011). Raising the retirement age: Is it fair for low-income workers and minorities? *Public Policy and Aging Report, 21*(2), 14–21.

Angel, J. L., & Settersten, R. A. (2014). The new realities of aging: Social and economic contexts. In L. Waite (Ed.), *Perspectives on the future of the sociology of aging* (pp. 11–31). Washington, DC: The National Academies Press.

Angel, R. J., & Angel, J. L. (2009). *Hispanic families at risk: The new economy, work, and the welfare state.* New York, NY: Springer Sciences.

Angel, R. J., Angel, J. L., & Montez, J. K. (2009). The work/health insurance nexus: A weak link for Mexican-origin men. *Social Science Quarterly, 90*(5), 1112–33.

Caldwell, C. (2009). *Reflections on the revolution in Europe: Immigration, Islam, and the West.* New York, NY: Doubleday.

Caldwell, J. C., Caldwell, B. K., Caldwell, P., McDonald, P. F., & Schindlmayr, T. (2006). *Demographic transition theory.* Dordrecht, the Netherlands: Springer Science.

Castles, S. (2004). Why migration policies fail. *Ethnic and Racial Studies, 27*(2), 205–27.

Central Intelligence Agency. (2012). Total fertility rate (children born/woman). In *The world factbook.* Washington, DC: Central Intelligence Agency.

Compton, E., Bentley, M., Ennis, S., & Rastogi, S. (2013). Final report of the Alternative Questionnaire Experiment focus group research. In *Focus group report executive summary* (appendix D). Washington, DC: U.S. Census Bureau.

Cotlear, D. (Ed.). (2011). *Population aging: Is Latin America ready?* Washington, DC: The World Bank.

DeNavas, C., Proctor, D. D., & Semega, J. L. (2011). Income, poverty, and health insurance coverage in the United States: 2010. In *Current Population Reports* (pp. 60–239, table 1). Retrieved from www.census.gov/prod/2011pubs/p60-239.pdf.

DeParle, J. (2008, June 10). Spain, like U.S., grapples with immigration. *New York Times.* Retrieved March 11, 2013 from: www.nytimes.com/2008/06/10/world/europe/10iht-10migrate.13592054.html?_r=0.

Ennis, S. R., Ríos-Vargas, M., & Albert, N. G. (2011). *The Hispanic population: 2010.* Washington, DC: U.S. Census Bureau.

Frank, R., & Heuveline, P. (2005). A crossover in Mexican and Mexican-American fertility rates: Evidence and explanations for an emerging paradox. *Demographic Research, 12*(4), 77–104.

Hamilton, B. E., Martin, J. A., & Ventura, S. J. (2012). Births: Preliminary data for 2011. *National Vital Statistics Reports, 61*(5), 1–20.

Humes, K. R., Jones, N. A., & Ramirez, R. R. (2011). Overview of race and Hispanic origin: 2010. In *2010 Census Briefs.* Washington, DC: U.S. Census Bureau.

Kurlaender, M. (2006). Choosing community college: Factors affecting Latino college choice. New Directions for Community Colleges, *133*, 7–16.

Moynihan, D. P., Smeeding, T. M., & Rainwater, L. (Eds.). (2006). *The future of the family.* New York, NY: Russell Sage Foundation.

Murdock, S. H. (2004). Population change in Texas: Implications for human and socioeconomic resources in the 21st century. slide #30. San Antonio, TX: University of Texas, San Antonio.

Nasser, H. El. (2013, January 4). Census rethinks Hispanic on questionnaire. *USA Today*. Retrieved May 1, 2014, from www.usatoday.com/story/news/nation/2013/01/03/hispanics-may-be-added-to-census-race-category/1808087.

National Research Council. (2012). *Aging and the macroeconomy: Long-term implications of an older population*. Washington, DC: National Academies Press.

Old-Age Survivors and Disability Insurance Board of Trustees. (2012). *2012 OASDI Trustees Report*. Baltimore, MD: Social Security Administration.

Orfield, G., Losen, D., Wald, J., & Swanson, C. B. (2004). *Losing our future: How minority youth are being left behind by the graduation rate crisis*. Cambridge, MA: The Civil Rights Project at Harvard University.

Pew Forum on Religion and Public Life. (2010). *Muslim networks and movements in Western Europe*. Retrieved April 2, 2010, from www.pewforum.org/Muslim/Muslim-Networks-and-Movements-in-Western-Europe.aspx.

Pew Research Hispanic Center. (2005). Hispanics in schools and colleges. In *Hispanic trends: Hispanics – A people in motion*. Washington, DC: Pew Research Center.

Ryan, C. L., & Siebens, J. (2012). *Educational attainment for the population 25 years and over by age, sex, race and Hispanic origin: 2009*. Washington, DC: U.S. Census Bureau.

Social Security Administration. (2010). *Income of the population 55 or older, 2008*. Baltimore, MD: Social Security Administration.

Terrazas, A. (2010). Mexican immigrants in the United States. In *National vital statistics reports*. Washington, DC: Migration Policy Institute.

Tienda, M., & Mitchell, F. (Eds.). (2006). *Multiple origins, uncertain destinies: Hispanics and the American future*. Washington, DC: The National Academy Press.

Torres-Gil, F., & Treas, J. (2009). Immigration and aging: The nexus of complexity and promise. *Generations: Journal of the American Society on Aging, 32*(4), 6–10.

U.S. Census Bureau, American FactFinder. (2013). *2007–2011 American community survey*. Retrieved March 27, 2013, from http://factfinder2.census.gov/faces/tableservices/jsf/pages/productview.xhtml?pid=ACS_11_5YR_DP05.

Wilson, W. J. (1996). *When work disappears: The world of the urban poor*. New York, NY: Knopf.

CHAPTER 3

At the Intersection of Gender, Ethnicity, and Nativity

A LONG DAY FOR LITTLE REWARD

It is 8:30 in the evening and Sandra has finally put Sara, her 2-year-old daughter, to bed and joined Roberto, her 10-year-old son who is named after his maternal grandfather, at the dinner table, where the boy has begun doing his homework. Sandra got home at 6:30 after a long day at work as a waitress at a local Tex-Mex diner and after picking Sara up from her grandmother's apartment where the child usually stays while Sandra works. Sara had supper at her grandmother's. When Sandra got home she prepared supper for Roberto and herself. Although tonight Roberto has begun his homework, he rarely completes his assignments and is often not even at home at this hour. He is not doing well at school and Sandra is frequently called in to deal with disciplinary problems. She realizes that as he gets older she has less and less control over the boy's behavior.

Roberto's father is a Mexican national who was in the country without documentation when Sandra became pregnant. The couple was married, but the father was deported after a third drunk driving arrest. Sandra knows that he moved in with his mother in a small village in the state of Guerrero, but she has not heard from him for over a year and he provides nothing for Roberto's support. Sara's father is a U.S. citizen of mixed race, Mexican and Black. He and Sandra were never married and Sara was born out of wedlock. Although he is a citizen, Sara's father has several felony convictions and little education. He is essentially unemployable and works sporadically as a day laborer in the landscape business. He occasionally sends Sandra a little money, diapers or other goods, but the contributions are small and too infrequent to make much of a difference.

Sandra's parents were both Mexican immigrants and she was born and still lives in San Antonio, Texas. She has had several jobs as a waitress, but none have paid well and the customers rarely give large tips. Given Texas's restricted welfare system, Sandra and the two children receive only $223 in cash assistance per month (Temporary Assistance to Needy Families). The family qualifies for $526 in Food Stamps (Supplemental Nutrition Assistance Program), and after a 2-year wait received a Section 8 housing voucher that allowed them to move to a better neighborhood and a nicer apartment, although Sandra is still worried about gangs and violence. She had seen several drug deals take place in the courtyard.

Sandra is finally able to begin an assignment for a course that she is taking at the local community college as part of a licensed practical nurse program. She attends classes three times a week in the evening when her mother can care for Sara. Sandra dropped out of high school at 15 but earned her GED in her 20s. She is now 35. In the hope of improving her employment prospects she has tried to finish the community college program for 5 years, but problems with the children and her work schedule have made it difficult for her to make much progress. She has had to drop out in the middle of the semester several times. Sandra has no savings, no retirement plan, no life insurance, nor any health insurance for herself. She was able to get Medicaid for Sara because of her low income. Roberto never sees a doctor.

During the day Sara stays with Sandra's mother or with an aunt who lives close by and does not work. Sometimes these arrangements fall through and Sandra misses work. If she misses too many times she is usually fired, but she has little control over the circumstances. Roberto occasionally acts up at school and has been sent home. When that happens he is on his own until she returns home in the evening. The family has no car so getting to work, going to doctor's appointments, or anything else means taking the bus. By 9:30 Roberto has given up on his homework and has moved to the other room to watch TV. He returns to badger Sandra for a new pair of Nikes, which some of the other kids wear, while she is trying to study. Although she can hardly afford such name brands, Sandra feels bad that she cannot provide her children the material things that they might like. By 10 p.m., Sandra can hardly stay awake and goes into her bedroom, where Sara is sleeping, to read for a while. Within half an hour she is asleep. Roberto is still watching TV and will go to bed when he chooses. Tomorrow will be pretty much the same.

THE RACIAL AND ETHNIC FEMINIZATION OF POVERTY

Sandra is a composite of several women we studied as part of an ethnographic study of the lives of low-income families in Boston, Chicago, and San Antonio after the welfare reforms of the 1990s (Angel, Lein, & Henrici, 2006). The sample for the study consisted of low-income families in poor neighborhoods. We spent a great deal of time with these families in order to learn how they managed. Since the study focused on the survival strategies of poor families, it was predominantly Black and Latino, with a large fraction of single mothers. We did not start out to collect a sample of Blacks and Latinos; however, the reality of class in America means that if one focuses on poverty one inevitably draws samples that are largely minority. Low-income Blacks and Latinos live in poor neighborhoods that consist largely of other Black or Latino families. In these neighborhoods housing values and educational levels are low; rates of single motherhood are high; and crime and social disorganization are major problems. One does, of course, find non-Hispanic White women in poor neighborhoods, but they are rarer and our impression during the study was that they had particularly serious problems.

The women we interviewed had much in common with Sandra. Most did not have enough income to cover all of their expenses and at the end of the month things got tight. Other sources of income, including an occasional child support payment, or assistance from some other relative helped, but there was clearly no way that individuals in our sample could save money. If they had been able to save they would not have qualified for public assistance programs that require that one be nearly destitute. Retirement planners advise individuals to save a substantial fraction of their incomes beginning as early as possible. Without such savings one faces serious deprivation in old age. Yet only about 40% of all workers have any sort of retirement plan, and the rate is even lower for Hispanics and females (Copeland, 2012). Surveys indicate that as many as half of Americans are worried that they do not have enough saved to last through their retirement years (Brandon, 2012; Morin & Fry, 2012). Many, in fact, borrow from their retirement plans to deal with emergencies and everyday expenses (Treasury Inspector General for Tax Administration, 2010). Imagining that someone in Sandra's situation could save to buy a home, send her children to college, and prepare for retirement is simply unrealistic. Our and other studies of female-headed minority families show that in order to survive they must pool resources with others in similar situations (Edin & Lein, 1997; Henrici, 2006; Stack, 1974).

One wonders, of course, why these particular families are living in situations in which they are at risk of poverty and welfare dependency and from which they find it nearly impossible to escape. One might wonder whether it is something about them as individuals, or something about their social situations and life circumstances that undermines even the most noble attempts to get ahead. Conservative social critics like Charles Murray take a cultural view and blame aspects of the welfare state that foster dependency and result in what he and others have identified as an underclass characterized by high rates of single motherhood, unemployment, and criminality (Murray, 1994, 1999, 2006). According to Murray, this phenomenon is even occurring in Britain, although at a different pace than in the United States (Murray, 1990).

Other observers look past the individual and identify a set of interacting structural factors that account for the persistence of poverty and powerlessness among certain groups (Andersen & Collins, 2004; Best, Edelman, Krieger, Hamilton, & Eliason, 2011; Collins, 1998, 2000; Crenshaw, 1990–1). Based on findings from a longitudinal field study of 162 young unmarried mothers living in Philadelphia's blighted urban neighborhoods, Edin and Kefalas conclude that for these women marriage is for the most part an unrealistic expectation. While the young women they studied might wish to find a supportive husband, given the lack of marriageable males their chances are extremely low. As a result, having children out of wedlock is the only realistic option that has taken on a positive value that represents an opportunity for a young woman to prove her worth. For structural reasons, then, in these communities single motherhood has become normative (Edin & Kefalas, 2005).

The situations of these young women illustrate the interaction of forces that structure the lives of individuals with few social or material resources who are trapped in disorganized neighborhoods with few opportunities. Intersectionality theory offers a useful perspective for understanding these individuals' enhanced vulnerability. The root "intersection" emphasizes the interaction of multiple social identities and sources of social disadvantage. From this perspective, no single socially ascribed characteristic or individual trait can explain the degree of social exclusion that characterizes certain neighborhoods, nor the vulnerability of certain individuals to violence, criminal prosecution, discrimination, or other negative outcomes. Although characteristics such as race, ethnicity, and gender are independently associated with risk factors for negative outcomes, such as domestic violence or poverty, in combination they have synergistic effects that greatly increase the risk of such outcomes (Andersen & Collins, 2004; Collins, 1998, 2000; McCall, 2005). As we saw in the last chapter, although female-headed households have far fewer assets and income than couple- or male-headed households, Black and Latino female-headed households have even fewer. Although single motherhood represents an independent risk factor for poverty, in combination with minority group status, low educational levels, and few occupational or marriage opportunities its negative impact is greatly enhanced.

Whether one uses the label or not, the core concept of intersectionality theory is extremely important since it draws attention to the complexity of the forces that place individuals and families at elevated risk of the negative outcomes associated with poverty and social disorganization, including family disruption, neighborhood disorder, domestic violence, and impaired social mobility. Focusing solely on one characteristic, such as race or ethnicity, ignores this complexity and can result in simplistic explanations of the difficulties that certain individuals and families face.

The example of immigrant health helps illustrate the point. As we discuss in greater detail in Chapter 5, a large body of research finds that recent Latino immigrants, perhaps because the healthiest individuals are able to migrate, enjoy relatively good health in comparison to natives. This health advantage, though, shrinks and eventually disappears the longer immigrants remain in the United States (Angel, Buckley, & Sakamoto, 2001; Cho, Frisbie, Hummer, & Rogers, 2004; Hummer, Benjamins, & Rogers, 2004; Landale & Oropesa, 2007; Padilla, Boardman, Hummer, & Espitia, 2002). One set of explanations focuses on acculturation and the supposed negative effects of immigrants' adoption of the deleterious health habits of the native population, such as smoking, drinking to excess, and overeating (Finch & Vega, 2003). Such explanations, though, ignore the complexity of the immigrant experience and the ways in which the intersection of multiple factors can affect the health of different groups in different ways (Viruell-Fuentes, Miranda, & Abdulrahim, 2012; Zambrana & Carter-Pokras, 2010). Our discussion of segmented assimilation in Chapter 1 pointed out the complexity of the process of social mobility and the multiple possibilities associated with different structural factors. Cultural explanations alone are insufficient to explain the different degrees of incorporation and of health levels among members of any subgroup or population.

In this chapter, and in the following chapters, we approach the situation of Hispanics from an intersectional perspective and examine the economic and social consequences of low levels of educational attainment, changing marital and family patterns, and patterns of labor force participation. Education, family, and work provide an individual with core social identities that objectively determine one's life chances, including one's income and wealth, but they also affect his or her social standing, physical and mental health, and sense of self-worth. Membership in a stigmatized or devalued group or the burden of a socially devalued identity can have seriously negative psychological consequences.

CHANGING FAMILY LIFE

Many of the social and demographic changes that have greatly altered marriage and family patterns in recent years, including lowered fertility, higher rates of marital disruption, and out-of-wedlock childbearing have serious implications for women, and especially women with little education and few job skills. These new trends result in the feminization as well as the racialization and greater ethnic concentration of poverty. Figure 3.1 shows that out-of-wedlock births are

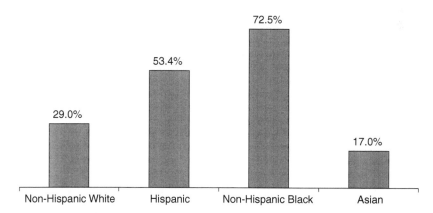

FIGURE 3.1 *Percentage of Births to Unmarried Women by Race and Hispanic Origin: 2010.*
Source: Martin et al. (2012).

much more common among Blacks and Hispanics than among non-Hispanic Whites or Asians. In 2010 nearly three-quarters of births in the Black population and over half of births in the Hispanic population were to single mothers (Martin et al., 2012).

Among Hispanics, out-of-wedlock births increase among second and later generation females, a pattern that some scholars have described as negative assimilation to emphasize the fact that the tie between marriage and fertility weakens with time in the United States (Pew Research Center, 2013). Some observers, like Charles Murray, mentioned above, see this negative assimilation as one of many interrelated causes of the serious social pathology that plagues certain neighborhoods. In 1965, sociologist Daniel Patrick Moynihan, who was at the time Assistant Secretary of Labor, produced a report entitled "The Negro Family: The Case for National Action" in which he identified a "ghetto culture," characterized by a lack of responsible males and high rates of single motherhood among other factors, as causes of the social pathology that characterizes many low-income Black neighborhoods (Moynihan, 1965). The increase in single motherhood among second and later generation Hispanics may indicate that forces similar to those that have undermined the Black family are increasingly affecting the Hispanic family.

Both Moynihan's and Murray's positions have been criticized for essentially blaming the victims and placing insufficient attention on the structural causes of the marginal situation in which ghettoized groups live (Murray, 1990; Ryan, 1971). From a different perspective, sociologist William Julius Wilson, while recognizing the existence of an urban underclass characterized by serious social pathologies, including the decline of the family, attributes its existence to structural factors, primarily the disappearance of employment opportunities in the neighborhoods in which Black families have been trapped by racism and a history of social exclusion (Wilson, 1978, 1987). Whatever the causes, though, there is little disagreement that rates of single motherhood in low-income and minority communities are increasing. The indisputable fact of the matter is that female-headed families are at very high risk of poverty, and are often trapped in neighborhoods in which children are exposed to serious social pathologies (Angel & Angel, 1993).

Although Hispanics have traditionally been characterized as highly familistic, or family oriented, we have presented evidence that this characterization may be overstated.

Hispanic families are being affected by the same disruptive social forces that affect other groups. Migration, changing marriage and fertility patterns, and increasing labor force involvement by women are changing Hispanic family life profoundly. Such changes have important implications for older minority group members. Hispanics continue to avoid nursing homes and remain in the community, either by choice or necessity (Espino et al., 2002; Herrera, Angel, Diaz, & Angel, 2012). There they are cared for primarily by daughters and daughters-in-law (Angel, Rote, & Markides, 2013). As social norms and marriage patterns change, though, younger women find that they must work at the same time that they are responsible for their own children. In the future, the capacity of daughters or daughters-in-law to act as primary caregivers to older parents and in-laws may diminish (Herrera, Benson, Angel, Markides, & Torres-Gil, 2013). The result will inevitably be that, despite a preference to avoid nursing homes, older Hispanics with few assets will have to turn to Medicaid to pay for institutional or community care, or they will be forced to spend much of their time alone in situations in which they are highly vulnerable to self-neglect and injury (Parra-Cardona, Ruben, Meyer, Schiamberg, & Post, 2007).

In light of the changes that affect women's ability to care for older relatives it would be useful to examine aspects of the socioeconomic and social situations of Hispanic women and inquire as to how those might affect women's potential caregiving role. For a growing number of Hispanic women, as is the case for other groups, the male-breadwinner model of family life, in which a wife stayed home to care for children, grandparents, and the household while her husband worked outside the home to support the family, no longer holds. These changes mean that the past is no guide for the future.

A DISTINCTIVE FORM OF POVERTY

During the 20th century women's labor force participation increased dramatically (Toossi, 2002), although patterns of entry into and exit from the labor force continued to be affected by changing marriage and family responsibilities (Goldin, 1989). What is indisputable, though, is that the large-scale entry of women into the labor force has accompanied changing work and family roles. At the same time that their commitment to work increased women's political and economic power grew. Until early in the 20th century women in what are today developed nations had restricted civil and political rights (Doepke, Tertilt, & Voena, 2012). They were not allowed to vote or to exercise complete control over property. Today women can vote, enter the professions, and own property without having to seek their husband's approval. As Figure 3.2 shows, since 1970 the proportion of women in the labor force has increased by over 15%. Yet, for many of these women work provides low pay and no health insurance or retirement plan. For women like Sandra, with whose story we began this chapter, many of whom work in the low-wage service sector, work is definitely not a route to social or economic mobility. For a head of family earning even twice or three times the federal minimum wage ($7.25 per hour in 2013), saving is virtually impossible. For a single women who works uncertain hours for low wages in the service sector, providing for herself and her family is often a hand-to-mouth prospect.

Although many, if not most, Latino immigrants and longer-term residents eventually make it into the middle class, as we discussed in the earlier chapter when we reviewed segmented assimilation theory, a substantial fraction of immigrants do not make this move within one, two, or even later generations. A substantial fraction of long-term residents and individuals from families who have been citizens for generations remain in the lower classes (Portes, Fernández-Kelly, & Haller, 2005; Portes & Hao, 2002; Portes & Zhou, 1993; Rumbaut, 1997; Tienda & Mitchell, 2006). As journalist Roberto Soro, among others, notes, Hispanic poverty is distinctive (Suro, 1998). Soro is referring to the fact that for

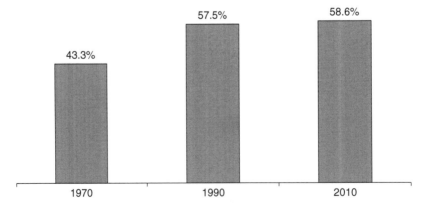

FIGURE 3.2 *Trends in Women's Employment Status: 1970–2010.*
Source: U.S. Bureau of Labor Statistics (2011).

certain members of these groups work is not the route to prosperity.

Given the fact that the minimum wage is very low, even a couple in which both spouses work full-time all year can fall below the poverty line if they have children. In 2013 a couple-headed household with three children in which both adults work full-time 5 days a week for 50 weeks a year at the federal minimum wage of $7.25 an hour would have earned around $29,000 before taxes. In that year the poverty threshold was $27,500 for a family of five (Office of the Assistant Secretary for Planning and Evaluation, 2013). Clearly, a family has to make substantially more than minimum wage to even begin to approximate a middle-class lifestyle. Employed male heads of household whose wives do not work are often unable to make enough to move much above poverty. In 2010, among men aged 35 to 44 in the labor force for at least 27 weeks, Hispanics were far more likely to be in poverty (16.8%) compared to Whites (7.2%), Blacks (9%), or Asians (3.2%) (U.S. Bureau of Labor Statistics, 2012b). Given their lower earning power, women in similar situations face even greater difficulties in escaping poverty.

EMPLOYMENT AND EARNINGS

Figure 3.3 presents labor force participation rates for non-Hispanic White, Black, Asian, and Hispanic men and women. Among men, Hispanics have the highest labor

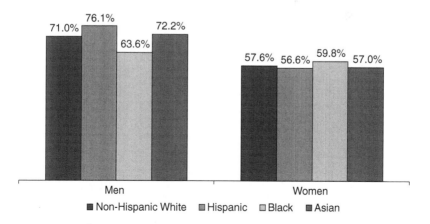

FIGURE 3.3 *Labor Force Participation Rates by Sex, Race, and Hispanic Ethnicity: 2012.*

Source: U.S. Bureau of Labor Statistics (2013c) Table 3.3, www.bls.gov/emp/ep_table_303.htm.

force participation rate, substantially higher than that of Black men. Among women, on the other hand, Blacks have the highest rate and Hispanics the lowest. Women from Mexico are the least likely to be employed (46% compared to 52% for Caribbeans, 61% for South Americans, and 63% for Central Americans) (Gonzales, 2008). In addition to somewhat lower labor force participation rates, in 2011 Hispanic women had lower median weekly earnings ($518) than Asian ($751), non-Hispanic White ($703), and African-American ($595) women (U.S. Bureau of Labor Statistics, 2013b). Among foreign-born Hispanic women, median weekly earnings were substantially lower than those of the U.S.-born ($400 versus $540) (Gonzales, 2008).

As we have noted, today most immigrants to the United States are Hispanic, a large fraction of whom are undocumented (Alsalam, 2010). Nearly 60% of undocumented immigrants are from Mexico (Passel & Cohn, 2009). As we discussed in earlier chapters, these individuals are drawn to the United States by employment opportunities that result from the need for cheap labor. Their attractiveness to U.S. employers is due to the fact that they take jobs that citizens will not perform for the wages offered (Camarota & Jensenius, 2009). Such jobs largely involve manual labor. Recent Hispanic immigrants, and especially unauthorized immigrants without technical skills, enter the labor force at the bottom where they earn very little and from which they find it difficult to escape. For Americans, reasonably priced produce, landscaping, affordable housing, and bargain-priced dry cleaning depends on undocumented Mexican labor. Their importance to our economy is made clear by the fact that one in four farmworkers is undocumented (Passel & Cohn, 2009).

Clearly their legal status makes it difficult for undocumented immigrants to enjoy any social mobility. Since they have limited legal recourse, they are easily exploited by unscrupulous employers. One might imagine that during recessions, such as the protracted global recession that began in 2008 and that affected the sectors in which Mexican immigrant labor works, immigrants would make the relatively short trip home to Mexico where the cost of living is lower. They could return to find work when economic conditions improve. Indeed, such cyclical migration has been common, but recent changes in immigration policy have increased border enforcement and made it more difficult for non-citizens to move easily between the United States and Mexico. As a result, undocumented residents are less likely to return to Mexico for short periods and hence remain in the United States even during economic downturns (Massey & Pren, 2012).

Immigrants face clear barriers to immediate movement into the middle class, but even among longer-term Hispanic residents income, and as a consequence wealth, remains on average low. Figure 3.4 presents data on the median annual earnings of U.S.-born and foreign-born Hispanics aged 25 and older and compares those to the median annual incomes of other groups of the same age. Data from 2011 reveal a clear Hispanic disadvantage that is most serious for the foreign-born. Asians have the highest annual salary, followed by non-Hispanic Whites, Blacks, and Hispanics (U.S. Bureau of Labor Statistics, 2013c). In 2012, foreign-born Hispanic workers earned weekly about three-quarters as much as the native-born (U.S. Bureau of Labor Statistics, 2012a).

Employment in the low-wage service sector is a major factor accounting for lower earnings among Hispanics. Table 3.1 presents information on the proportion of Hispanics, Blacks, Asians, and non-Hispanic Whites in selected occupations. Since we do not present all sectors, the percentages do not add to 100. The table clearly shows, though, that a smaller fraction of Hispanics are in management and business than non-Hispanics. Among Hispanics the proportion of the foreign-born in management and

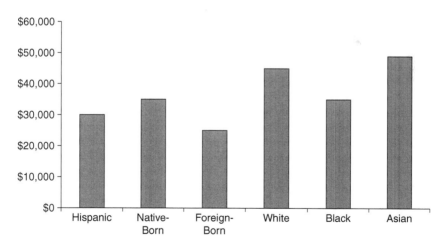

FIGURE 3.4 *Median Personal Earnings for Full-time, Year-Round Workers, by Race, Hispanic Ethnicity, and Nativity: 2011.*
Source: Pew Hispanic Center tabulations of 2000 Census (5% IPUMS) and 2011 American Community Survey (1% IPUMS).

TABLE 3.1 *Occupation by Race, Hispanic Ethnicity, and Nativity, 2011 (%)*

| | HISPANIC | | NON-HISPANIC | | |
	NATIVE-BORN	FOREIGN-BORN	WHITE	BLACK	ASIAN
Management and Business	8.9	5.3	14.9	8.6	14.7
Food Preparation and Serving	7.3	10.4	5.4	6.5	6.8
Cleaning and Maintenance	4.5	14.0	3.1	5.8	2.3
Farming, Fishing, and Forestry	0.9	4.5	0.6	0.3	0.3
Construction and Extraction	5.5	12.8	5.2	3.3	1.4
Installation, Repair, and Production	8.7	14.5	8.9	8.6	8.3

Source: Motel and Patten (2012).

business is even lower. Foreign-born Hispanics are concentrated in food service, cleaning and maintenance, construction, and installation. They are more likely than any other group to work in agriculture.

Gender interacts with ethnicity, race, and immigration status to magnify labor force disparities. Hispanic and African-American women are far more likely than non-Hispanic White or Asian women to work in the service sector, agriculture, and building and grounds cleaning and maintenance (U.S. Bureau of Labor Statistics, 2013a). Among Hispanics, immigrants are highly concentrated in occupations that not only pay little, but also rarely provide health or retirement benefits (Gonzales, 2008).

A NEW UNDERCLASS?

The severity and persistence of the poverty experienced by Hispanic individuals and households reflects lifelong processes that impede education, employment, income, and asset accumulation. Figure 3.5 presents data on youth unemployment from the 2010 U.S. Bureau of Labor Statistics to illustrate the fact that economic insecurity at later ages has its root early in the life course. These data show that unemployment rates are particularly serious for young Hispanics and Blacks. Over a third of young Blacks are unemployed, as are 22% of Hispanics. Asian youth unemployment remains high as well when compared to that of non-Hispanic Whites. The high youth unemployment rate among minorities has serious implications for their future

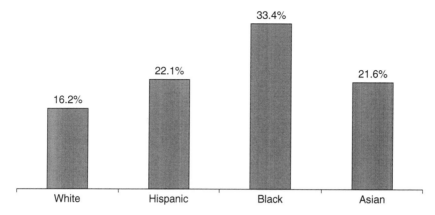

FIGURE 3.5 *Youth Unemployment Rate: 2010.*
Source: U.S. Bureau of Labor Statistics (2010, table 1).

productivity. The lack of work experience accompanies high rates of high school dropout, meaning that many young minority individuals have no tie to either the educational system or the labor force. Working reinforces work-related values, including punctuality and dependability, and socializes a young person into a positive social role. High unemployment rates among young minority men and women denies them these important opportunities, with potentially life-long consequences.

INHERITANCES AND GIFTS

The concentration of Hispanics in specific sectors of the economy has implications for income in later life. Low incomes during the working years translate directly into low savings rates and little asset accumulation. Retirement counselors advise that one should save 10 or 15%, or even a higher percentage, of one's income on a long-term basis starting early in life. Ideally, an employer matches at least a portion of that amount. In reality, though, if one is forced to spend all of one's income on basic food, shelter, transportation, and other daily necessities, the possibility of saving is clearly limited. Individuals in this situation are unable to take advantage of compound interest or the rest of the financial apparatus that assures a financially secure old age. As a result, Hispanic families have little wealth to pass on to future generations. This fact has seriously negative consequences for individuals, families, and the community at large. Data from the Federal Reserve Board's Survey of Consumer Finances reveal significant racial and ethnic variation in the percentage of households that receive an inheritance (Wolff & Gittleman, 2011). As Figure 3.6 shows, non-Hispanic White households are far more likely to receive a monetary gift or inheritance than African-American or Hispanic households. Slightly more than 5% of Hispanic households receive an inheritance of any size.

In addition to a lower likelihood of receiving a wealth transfer, the amounts of money that Hispanic families receive is far lower than that of non-Hispanic White families, a fact that clearly accounts for the lower aggregate wealth of this population. A study reported by the Urban Institute for the period 1999–2007 revealed large differences in net worth among families (McKernan, Ratcliffe, Simms, & Zhang, 2012). Among Black families, median net worth, that is, assets minus debts, amounted to $18,181. For Hispanics the amount was $33,619 and for non-Hispanic White families it was $122,927. These rather dramatic differences reflect fewer assets rather than more debt among Blacks and Hispanics. When they examined large gifts and inheritances, the Urban Institute researchers found that Black and Hispanic families were five times less likely than non-Hispanic White families to receive large gifts or inheritances, a finding consistent with the results reported by the Federal Reserve mentioned above. Over time and across generations such impaired asset accumulation means that

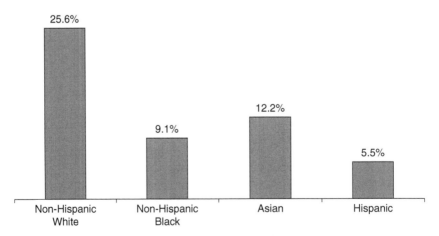

FIGURE 3.6 *Percentage of Households Receiving Gifts and Inheritances: 2007.*
Source: Survey of Consumer Finances, Wolff and Gittleman (2011).

minority groups collectively possess less wealth with which to help their members go to university and become professionals, buy homes, or start businesses. As a result opportunities for economic and social mobility remain more limited than those of individuals who are members of more affluent groups.

RETIREMENT INCOME AND FINANCIAL SECURITY

Almost by definition a good job is one that not only pays well, but also provides health insurance and a retirement plan. An employer-sponsored pension or a well-funded 401(k) plan is essential for a dignified and comfortable retirement. As we discuss more extensively in later chapters, in the absence of a retirement plan one is dependent on Social Security, which might allow one to survive, but does not leave one with much more. For older Hispanics and Blacks, Social Security is often the only or a more significant source of income than is the case for older non-Hispanic Whites (Office of Retirement and Disability Policy, 2012). Social Security accounts for almost 80% of the total retirement incomes of African-American and Hispanic elderly households (Waid & Koenig, 2012). About one-quarter of older African Americans and Hispanics rely on Social Security for *all* of their family income, compared to only 14% of older non-Hispanic Whites (Waid & Koenig, 2012). Although Social Security is the single most important source of income for minority elderly, many of these retirees receive only minimal Social Security or survivorship benefits (Social Security Administration, 2012). Median Social Security household income for minority elderly is 26% lower than for non-Hispanic Whites. In 2010, Hispanic and Black households received $13,942 and $14,356, respectively, compared to $18,833 for non-Hispanic Whites (Office of Retirement and Disability Policy, 2012). In light of the fact that Hispanic and Black households have fewer assets and less income from other sources than non-Hispanic White households, their collective economic potential is limited and old minority group members have little with which to aid future generations.

Although Social Security is far from adequate to provide an affluent retirement, it has clearly improved the economic situation of the elderly. Prior to the passage of Social Security severe poverty was common among older individuals. Over time Social Security has greatly reduced poverty among the elderly. In 1960, 25 years after the passage of the Social Security Act, the poverty rate among those aged 65 or older was still 35%, but because of increased per-capita funding by 1995 it had dropped to 10% (Engelhardt & Gruber, 2004). As important as Social Security is, though, it was never intended to serve as one's sole source of income. True financial security in old age requires additional income from other sources, including a private employer-based retirement plan. Such a private retirement plan can make the difference between a minimally adequate income and one that allows a person the freedom to enjoy his or her retirement and to help younger generations. A private retirement plan is a very real component of one's overall wealth.

Figure 3.7 shows the sources of the retirement income disadvantage among African-American and Mexican-origin individuals over 65. The data are from the 2010 Health and Retirement Study, a major study of the income and wealth of older Americans (Health and Retirement Study, 2013). The figure shows the clear advantage that non-Hispanic White individuals have over both minority groups in terms of assets. Of non-Hispanic Whites, 31% report asset income compared to only around 10% of African Americans and individuals of Mexican origin. The figure also reveals the serious lack of retirement plan income among Mexican-origin elderly. As a consequence, nearly 60% of their total

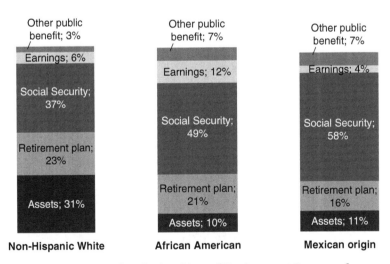

FIGURE 3.7 *Sources and Relative Size of Retirement Income for Elderly Individuals by Race and Mexican Origin: 2010.*
Source: Health and Retirement Study (2010).

income is from Social Security. Yet, in absolute terms, non-Hispanic Whites receive more money from Social Security than do minorities. The average annual benefit for non-Hispanic Whites is about $13,400, which is almost $1,700 higher than that of non-Hispanic Blacks and $3,000 higher than that of Mexican-origin individuals (Social Security Administration, 2012).

The low rate of pension plan participation by Mexican-origin households means that even with Social Security many will have little choice other than to continue working, if that is possible. Supreme Court justices, professors, or hedge-fund managers may be able to work on into their 80s, but for many low-wage workers poor health and difficult physical labor often make continuing to work impossible. If one has inadequate retirement income and can no longer work, the options are few. One can perhaps rely on financial help from children, but they have financial responsibilities for their own children and must save for their own retirements. In the absence of other sources of income one simply has to do without needed goods and services, including medical care or even adequate nutrition.

Even when they do participate in employer-sponsored 401(k) plans, Hispanics are less likely than other groups to contribute sufficiently. A recent online survey of employed individuals between the ages of 25 and 69 conducted by ING, a major international insurance company that offers Retirement plans, revealed racial and ethnic differences in planning and saving for retirement (ING Retirement Research Institute, 2012b). Nearly half of all respondents felt that they were "not very" or "not at all" prepared financially for retirement. Hispanics, though, felt the least prepared. In addition to low rates of participation, Hispanics report the lowest average balances in 401(k) plans. The ING study revealed that Hispanics' plans averaged $54,000 in value compared to $69,000 for the sample as a whole (ING retirement Research Institute, 2012a). Asian respondents reported the highest average plan balance of $81,000. The study also revealed that among Hispanics who were participating in a defined-contribution plan, 19% were contributing less than $50 per pay period compared to 13% for the sample as a whole. Such low contributions are clearly inadequate to insure that the amount saved will last one through retirement.

The study revealed other shortcomings in Hispanics' retirement planning. Fifty-seven percent of Hispanics, for example, have never calculated how much money they will need to maintain their current lifestyle, and 70% did not have a formal plan for reaching their retirement goals. Hispanics are also less likely than others to be saving in other ways, including Individual Retirement Accounts (IRAs), Roth IRAs, or Certificates of Deposit (CDs). Over half of Hispanics in the ING study, compared to slightly over 40% of the sample as a whole, reported that they did not save. The reality, therefore, is that Hispanics are far less likely than non-Hispanic Whites to participate in a retirement plan of any sort, and those that do are less likely to have a defined-benefit plan that would guarantee an income for life, or to have saved enough in defined-contribution savings plans.

THE ECONOMIC REALITY OF RETIREMENT SECURITY FOR WOMEN

These race, nativity, and Hispanic ethnicity disadvantages in retirement coverage have particularly important implications for the economic security of women in later life. For women, trade-offs between domestic labor and market work have huge implications for retirement security. Historically, women's retirement security has been tied to marriage. Many women, especially those born before the baby boom, never worked outside the home or did so only part-time. Dependence on their husband's income and health benefits continued into the retirement years. During the second half of the 20th century, though, this pattern began to change as women's labor force participation increased and as traditional marriage patterns gave way to lower fertility and higher divorce rates.

The decline of the "male breadwinner" family pattern in which the wife assumed responsibility for domestic tasks and the husband worked for wages means that today women are more likely to participate in employer-sponsored retirement plans and assume responsibility for their own retirement security or to contribute to the family's retirement security. Of course, many women continue to rely on their husband's retirement plan, but in a large fraction of households both partners have a retirement plan. Table 3.2 presents sources of retirement coverage for married women aged 25 and older by race and Hispanic ethnicity during the period from 2004 to 2006. It shows that during that period

TABLE 3.2 *Source of Retirement Coverage for Married Women Aged 25 and Older by Race/Ethnicity*

	NON-HISPANIC WHITE		AFRICAN-AMERICAN		MEXICAN-ORIGIN	
	N	%	N	%	N	%
No Coverage	37,860	31.9	4,088	37.7	8,236	63.4
Own Coverage Only	26,285	21.6	2,027	18.2	1,754	13.0
Own and Spouse Coverage	25,806	21.2	1,991	18.0	1,738	13.0
Spouse Coverage Only	31,177	25.4	2,939	26.1	1,419	10.5
Total	121,128	100.0	11,045	100.0	13,147	100.0

Source: 2004 and 2006 March Supplements to the Current Population Survey.

Note
All percentages are weighted.

over 60% of Hispanic women had no retirement coverage at all, compared to 37% of African-American women and 32% of non-Hispanic White women. This low level of retirement coverage among Hispanic women reflects the fact that they are less likely than Black or non-Hispanic White women to have their own retirement plan or to be covered by a spouse.

WORKING AFTER 65

We mentioned earlier that one response to the lack of an adequate retirement income is to continue working. Working after 65, even part-time, can increase one's financial security and allow one to engage in potentially rewarding activities. Given longer lifespans, people are increasingly delaying retirement past 65. Today the average individual aged 65 can expect to live nearly another 20 years. Eligibility for full Social Security benefits reflects this increased longevity. Individuals who were born after 1943 can receive full benefits at age 66; those born after 1960 receive full benefits at 67. Such increased longevity places serious strains on pension plans and creates the risk that one's defined-contribution retirement plan will run out well before one dies. In the Health and Retirement Study of workers aged 50 to 61 conducted by the Institute of Social Research at the University of Michigan in 2009, 65% reported that they expected to be working full-time past age

62, and about 57% said they planned to work full-time after they reached the normal retirement age (Jacobsen, Mather, Lee, & Lent, 2011). In general, men are more likely than women to continue working after reaching age 65 (Angel & Mudrazijia, 2011).

Several factors are associated with the decision to work past 65. Perhaps the most important is health. Approximately one out of every four Americans in their 60s has a health problem that limits their ability to work or to perform basic physical tasks (Kingson & Morrissey, 2012). One's ability to continue working of course depends on the nature of the work one is qualified to perform. Heavy manual labor requires better physical health than academic work. Blue-collar workers who comprise over 40% of the labor force are often forced to retire early because of health problems caused by a lifetime spent working in physically demanding and stressful jobs (General Accounting Office, 1999).

In an analysis of reasons for early retirement carried out in 2008, twice as many blue-collar workers as white-collar workers reported that poor health was a critical factor in their decision to retire early (Angel & Mudrazijia, 2011). Data in Figure 3.7 from the same survey show that racial and ethnic minorities make up a disproportionate share of blue-collar workers. They are consequently at higher risk of being forced out of the labor force than non-Hispanic Whites for health reasons. Among women (data not shown), African-American and Hispanic blue-collar workers in poor health have the lowest chance of continuing to work after age 65 compared to non-Hispanic White blue-collar workers.

Even for individuals in good health, the opportunities for employment are limited, especially for individuals with little education. Research from the Center for Retirement at Boston College shows that both women and men with low levels of education have fewer job prospects than highly educated workers (Munnell & Jivan, 2005).

SUMMARY AND CONCLUSIONS

In this chapter we introduced the theoretical concept of intersectionality to draw attention to the fact that the vulnerability that certain individuals and groups experience results from the interaction of a number of structural factors. These factors include racism, the unequal distribution of educational and occupational opportunities that are themselves associated with race and ethnicity, and residential segregation in neighborhoods and ecological areas characterized by few employment opportunities, high levels of social pathology, and serious physical decline. While the observation that many low-income neighborhoods include a large number of minority group members, or single mothers, it is important to understand the multiple sources of vulnerability of these individuals and communities. These sources operate interactively to place Blacks and Hispanics at a disadvantage, and operate through such factors as impaired educational opportunities that in turn result in fewer opportunities for well-paying employment and diminished earnings and wealth accumulation. Ultimately, this complex interaction of factors traps individuals and groups in situations from which escape becomes almost impossible.

An intersectionality perspective is useful in understanding how multiple factors, including migration, the need for adult women to work, and limited family resources, affect families' abilities to care for aging parents. Traditionally, aging and infirm parents have been cared for by daughters and daughters-in-law. Given the forces that undermine traditional family forms, the capacity of women to assume full responsibility for aging parents or in-laws may decrease. Hispanics, who have often been characterized as "familistic" may in the future come to resemble African Americans in terms of out-of-wedlock fertility. It may simply be the case that despite preferences, the changes that are undermining traditional family forms may lead to a decline in marriage and marital fertility.

In this chapter we documented the extent of poverty and its correlates among Hispanics. For Hispanics, largely because of serious educational deficits among other factors, work is not a guarantee of a middle-class existence. Again, a major source of the problem of course emerges from the fact that low levels of education result in very low wages. Individuals who earn even substantially more than the minimum wage can barely make ends meet and are unable to save. We also showed that immigrants tend to be employed in sectors of the economy in which their earnings are low and in which they have few benefits, such as health insurance and retirement plans. Again reflecting the intersection of statuses, immigrant women are the least likely to be employed and they have particularly low earnings.

Low earnings, of course, are associated with little savings and low wealth. Hispanics, like Blacks, have on average only a fraction of the assets of non-Hispanic Whites. Again, single Hispanic women are at an even more serious disadvantage. This means that Hispanics are less able to help their children acquire educations, buy homes, start businesses, and save for their own retirements. Indeed given the low level of assets owned by older Hispanics, rather than helping their children, many adult children may be forced to provide financial assistance to their parents, further undermining their own capacity to save for their own retirements or to help their own children. Low levels of asset accumulation mean that the community as a whole has little wealth, with implications for political power and influence.

DISCUSSION QUESTIONS

1. Deconstruct the concept of "intersectionality." To what characteristics of individuals and social organization does it draw our attention? In your opinion, is the concept theoretically and practically useful? That is, does it help us gain insights into social and individual characteristics that place certain groups and individuals at greater risk of negative outcomes? Give some examples of individuals or groups for whom the combination of identities or characteristics magnifies their social vulnerability. Are there combinations of characteristics that place certain groups and individuals in advantaged positions?

2. Retirement planners and other financial advisors urge individuals to save as much as possible for future expenditures, including retirement. Yet a large proportion of individuals save very little and have almost no retirement savings. Discuss some of the potential reasons for this low rate of savings. Are the reasons purely individual, such as a lack of discipline and overspending, or do structural factors related to the labor market, minimum wage laws, the lack of mandatory retirement plans, etc. play at least some role?

3. Many "culture of poverty" explanations for low achievement levels, poverty, crime, out-of-wedlock pregnancy, unemployment, and more have been proposed. From the perspective of such theories individuals are socialized into a subculture characterized by

many negative characteristics. This socialization results in a sense of diminished self-worth, feelings of hopelessness and helplessness, and the adoption of a set of values and behaviors that inhibits achievement and social mobility. Charles Murray identifies high rates of single motherhood, criminality, and separation from the labor force as characteristics of this subculture. Critics of cultural or subcultural theories of poverty believe that such theories blame the victims, and that the disorganization, crime, poverty, and other negative outcomes that certain individuals and groups suffer result from racism, blocked opportunities, and the lack of employment possibilities that are part of an unequal and inequitable social structure that impedes the possibility of social mobility. Debate the reasonableness and utility of each position.

4. Immigration reform is a politically sensitive topic about which many individuals have very strong feelings. Undocumented immigrants are denied most social services except emergency room medical care, and they have few rights or avenues to redress grievances, such as exploitation by employers. Depending on one's point of view undocumented immigrants are either criminals or disadvantaged citizens of the world who provide needed labor to richer countries. Discuss the reasons for the high levels of undocumented immigration in most developed nations and summarize some of the realistic options for dealing with the issue.

5. Latinos as a group, and Mexican-origin Latinos in particular, have very low levels of education. Mexican-origin high school students drop out at alarming rates and those who obtain high school degrees are less likely than non-Hispanic White graduates to go on to higher education. Those that do are more likely to attend 2-year colleges than 4-year institutions and are consequently less likely to go on to graduate or professional school. This educational deficit is a clear impediment to individual and group mobility. How, in your opinion, might this educational deficit be addressed? What are the political and perhaps cultural barriers that must be addressed?

LITERATURE CITED

Alsalam, N. (2010). *The role of immigrants in the U.S. labor market: An update*. Washington, DC: Congressional Budget Office.

Andersen, M. L., & Collins, P. H. (Eds.). (2004). *Race, class, & gender: An anthology*. Beverly, MA: Wadsworth.

Angel, J. L., Buckley, C. J., & Sakamoto, A. (2001). Duration or disadvantage? Exploring nativity, ethnicity, and health in midlife. *Journal of Gerontology: Social Sciences, 56*(5), S275–84.

Angel, J. L., & Mudrazijia, S. (2011). Raising the retirement age: Is it fair for low-income workers and minorities? *Public Policy and Aging Report, 21*(2), 14–21.

Angel, J. L., Rote, S., & Markides, K. (2013). *Nativity, late-life family caregiving, and the Mexican-origin population in the United States*. Paper presented at the Gerontological Society of America Annual Meeting. New Orleans, LA.

Angel, R., & Angel, J. L. (1993). *Painful inheritance: Health and the new generation of fatherless families*. Madison, WE: University of Wisconsin Press.

Angel, R. J., Lein, L., & Henrici, J. (2006). *Poor families in America's health care crisis*. New York, NY: Cambridge University Press.

Best, R. K., Edelman, L. B., Hamilton Krieger, L., & Eliason, S. R. (2011). Multiple disadvantages: An empirical test of intersectionality theory in EEO litigation. *Law & Society Review, 45*(4), 991–1025.

Brandon, E. (2012, May 8). The new ideal retirement age: 67. *US News and World Report*. Retrieved April 11, 2013, from http://money.usnews.com/money/blogs/planning-to-retire/2012/05/08/the-new-ideal-retirement-age-67.

Camarota, S. A., & Jensenius, K. (2009). *Jobs Americans won't do? A detailed look at immigrant employment by occupation*. Washington, DC: Center for Immigration Studies.

Cho, Y., Frisbie, P. W., Hummer, R. A., & Rogers, R. G. (2004). Nativity, duration of residence, and the health of Hispanic adults in the United States. *Immigration Migration Review, 38*(1), 184–211.

Collins, P. H. (1998). The tie that binds: race, gender and US violence. *Ethnic and Racial Studies, 21*(5), 917–38.

Collins, P. H. (2000). Gender, Black feminism, and Black political economy. *The Annals of the American Academy of Political and Social Science, 568*(1), 41–53.

Copeland, C. (2012). *Employment-based retirement plan participation: Geographic differences and trends, 2011*. Washington, DC: Employee Benefit Research Institute. Retrieved April 11, 2013, from www.ebri.org/pdf/briefspdf/EBRI_IB_11-2012_No378_RetParticip.pdf.

Crenshaw, K. (1990–1). Mapping the margins: Intersectionality, identity politics, and violence against women of color. *Stanford Law Review, 43*, 1241–300.

Doepke, M., Tertilt, M., & Voena, A. (2012). The economics and politics of women's rights. *Annual Review of Economics, 4*(1), 339–72.

Edin, K., & Kefalas, M. (2005). *Promises I can keep: Why poor women put motherhood before marriage*. Berkeley, CA: University of California Press.

Edin, K., & Lein, L. (1997). *Making ends meet: How single mothers survive welfare and low-wage work*. New York, NY: Russell Sage Foundation.

Engelhardt, G., & Gruber, J. (2004). *Social security and the evolution of elderly poverty* (NBER Working Paper 10466). Cambridge, MA: National Bureau of Economic Research.

Espino, D. V., DelAguila, D., Mouton, C. P., Alford, C., Parker, R. W., Miles, T. P., & Olivares, O. (2002). Characteristics of Mexican-American elders with dementia presenting to a community-based memory evaluation program. *Ethnicity and Disease, 12*, 517–21.

Finch, B. K., & Vega, W. A. (2003). Acculturation, stress, social support, and self-rated health among Latinos in California. *Journal of Immigrant Health, 5*(3), 100–17.

General Accounting Office. (1999). *Social Security reform: Implications of raising the retirement age.* Washington, DC: Government Accountability Office.

Goldin, C. (1989). Life-cycle labor-force participation of married women: Historical evidence and implications. *Journal of Labor Economics, 7*(1), 20–47.

Gonzales, F. (2008). *Hispanic women in the United States, 2007: Fact sheet.* Washington, DC: Pew Hispanic Center.

Health and Retirement Study. (2013). *2010 core data description and usage: Version 3.0.* Ann Arbor, MI: Institute for Social Research University of Michigan.

Henrici, J. (Ed.). (2006). *Doing without: Women and work after welfare reform.* Tucson, AZ: University of Arizona Press.

Herrera, A., Angel, J. L., Diaz, C., & Angel, R. J. (2012). Estimating the demand for long-term care among aging Mexican Americans: Cultural preferences versus economic realities. In J. L. Angel, F. Torres-Gil, & K. Markides (Eds.), *Aging, health, and longevity in the Mexican-origin population* (pp. 259–76). New York, NY: Springer Sciences.

Herrera, A., Benson, R., Angel, J. L., Markides, K., & Torres-Gil, F. (2013). Effectiveness and reach of caregiver services funded by the Older Americans Act to vulnerable older Hispanics and African Americans. *Home Health Care Services Quarterly.*

Hummer, R. M., Benjamins, M., & Rogers, R. (Eds.). (2004). *Race/ethnic disparities in health and mortality among the elderly: A documentation and examination of social factors.* Washington, DC: National Academies Press.

ING Retirement Research Institute. (2012a). *Hispanic fact sheet.* Windsor, CT: ING.

ING Retirement Research Institute. (2012b). *Retirement revealed study.* Windsor, CT: ING.

Jacobsen, L. A., Mather, M., Lee, M., & Lent, M. (2011). America's aging population. *Population Bulletin, 66*(1), 1–20.

Kingson, E., & Morrissey, M. (2012, May 30). Can workers offset Social Security cuts by working longer? In *Retirement.* Washington, DC: Economic Policy Institute.

Landale, N. S., & Oropesa, R. S. (2007). Hispanic families: Stability and change. *Annual Review of Sociology, 33*, 381–405.

Martin, J. A., Hamilton, B. E., Ventura, S. J., Osterman, M. J. K., Wilson, E. C., & Mathews, T. J. (2012). Table 15: Births and birth rates for unmarried women, by age and race and Hispanic origin of mother – United States, 2010. In *National Vital Statistics Reports.* Hyattsville, MD: National Center for Health Statistics.

Massey, D. S., & Pren, K. A. (2012). Origins of the new Latino underclass. *Race and Social Problems, 4*(1), 5–17.

McCall, L. (2005). The complexity of intersectionality. *Signs, 30*(3), 1771–800.

McKernan, S.-M., Ratcliffe, C., Simms, M., & Zhang, S. (2012). Do financial support and inheritance contribute to the racial wealth gap? in *Opportunity and ownership facts.* Washington, DC: The Urban Institute.

Morin, R., & Fry, R. (2012). *More Americans worry about financing retirement: Adults in their late 30s most concerned.* Washington, DC: Pew Research Center. Retrieved April 11, 2013, from www.pewsocialtrends.org/2012/10/22/more-americans-worry-about-financing-retirement.

Motel, S., & Patten, E. (2012). Statistical portrait of Hispanics in the United States, 2011. In *Pew Research Hispanic Trends Project.* Washington, DC: Pew Research Center.

Moynihan, D. P. (1965). *The Negro family: The case for national action.* Washington, DC: Office of Policy Planning and Research, U.S. Department of Labor.

Munnell, A. H., & Jivan, N. (2005). *What makes older women work?* Chestnut Hill, MA: Center for Retirement Research, Boston College.

Murray, C. (1990). *The emerging British underclass.* London: Institute of Economic Affairs.

Murray, C. (1994). *Losing ground.* New York, NY: Basic Books.

Murray, C. (1999). *The underclass revisited.* Washington, DC: AEI Press.

Murray, C. (2006). *In our hands: A plan to replace the welfare state.* Blue Ridge Summit, PA: AEI Press.

Office of the Assistant Secretary for Planning and Evaluation. (2013). Annual update of the HHS poverty guidelines. In *Federal Register.* Washington, DC: U.S. Health and Human Services Department.

Office of Retirement and Disability Policy. (2012). Table 5.B4: Percentage distribution of persons in Social Security beneficiary families, by race, Hispanic origin, and sex, 2010. In *Family Social Security income of persons 65 or older.* Baltimore, MD: Social Security Administration.

Padilla, Y. C., Boardman, J. D., Hummer, R. A., & Espitia, M. (2002). Is the Mexican American "epidemiologic paradox" advantage at birth maintained through early childhood? *Social Forces, 80*(3), 1101–23.

Parra-Cardona, J. R., Meyer, E., Schiamberg, L., & Post, L. (2007). Elder abuse and neglect in Latino families: An ecological and culturally relevant theoretical framework for clinical practice. *Journal of Family Process, 46,* 451–70.

Passel, J., & Cohn, D. (2009). *A portrait of unauthorized immigrants in the United States.* Washington, DC: Pew Hispanic Center.

Pew Research Center. (2013). Second-generation Americans: A portrait of the adult children of immigrants. In *Social and demographic trends.* Washington, DC: Pew Research Center.

Portes, A., Fernández-Kelly, P., & Haller, W. (2005). Segmented assimilation on the ground: The new second generation in early adulthood. *Ethnic and Racial Studies, 28,* 1000–40.

Portes, A., & Hao, L. (2002). The price of uniformity: Language, family, and personality adjustment in the immigrant second generation. *Ethnic and Racial Studies, 25*(6), 889–912.

Portes, A., & Zhou, M. (1993). The new second generation: Segmented assimilation and its variants. *Annals of the American Academy of Political and Social Science, 530,* 74–96.

Rumbaut, R. (1997). Assimilation and its discontents: Between rhetoric and reality. *International Migration Review, 31*(4), 923–60.

Ryan, W. (1971). *Blaming the victim.* New York, NY: Vintage Books.

Social Security Administration. (2012). Table 10.5. In *Income of the population 55 or older, 2010.* Baltimore, MD: Social Security Administration.

Stack, C. B. (1974). *All our kin: Strategies for survival in a Black community.* New York, NY: Basic Books.

Suro, R. (1998). *Strangers among us: Latino lives in a changing America.* New York, NY: Vintage Books.

Tienda, M., & Mitchell, F. (2006). *Hispanics and the future of America.* Washington, DC: National Academy Press.

Toossi, M. (2002). A century of change: The U.S. labor force, 1950–2050. *Monthly Labor Review,* May, 14–28.

Treasury Inspector General for Tax Administration. (2010). *Statistical trends in retirement plans.* Retrieved April 11, 2013, from www.treasury.gov/tigta/aud itreports/2010reports/201010097fr.pdf.

U.S. Bureau of Labor Statistics. (2012a). Table 5: Median usual weekly earnings of full-time wage and salary workers for the foreign born and native born by selected characteristics, 2011–2012 annual averages. Washington, DC: U.S. Department of Labor.

U.S. Bureau of Labor Statistics. (2012b). Report 1035: People in the labor force for 27 or more weeks: Poverty status, by age, sex, race, and Hispanic or Latino Ethnicity, 2010. Washington, DC: U.S. Department of Labor.

U.S. Bureau of Labor Statistics. (2013a). Table 12. Employed women by occupation, race, and Hispanic or Latino ethnicity, 2011 annual averages. In *Women in the labor force: A databook.* Washington, DC: U.S. Department of Labor.

U.S. Bureau of Labor Statistics. (2013b). Table 16: Median usual weekly earnings of full-time wage and salary workers in current dollars by race, Hispanic or Latino ethnicity, and sex, 1979–2011 annual averages. In *Women in the labor force: A databook.* Washington, DC: U.S. Department of Labor.

U.S. Bureau of Labor Statistics. (2013c). Table 3: Usual median weekly earnings of full-time wage and salary workers by age, race, Hispanic or Latino ethnicity, sex, third quarter 2013 averages, not seasonally adjusted. Washington, DC: U.S. Department of Labor.

Viruell-Fuentes, E. A., Miranda, P. Y., & Abdulrahim, S. (2012). More than culture: Structural racism, intersectionality theory, and immigrant health. *Social Science & Medicine,* *75*(12), 2099–106.

Waid, M., & Koenig, G. (2012). Social Security: A key retirement income source for older minorities. In *Fact Sheet.* Washington, DC: AARP Public Policy Institute.

Wilson, W. J. (1978). *The declining significance of race: Blacks and changing American institutions.* Chicago, IL: University of Chicago Press.

Wilson, W. J. (1987). *The truly disadvantaged: The inner city, the underclass, and public policy.* Chicago, IL: University of Chicago Press.

Wolff, E. N., & Gittleman, M. (2011). *Inheritances and the distribution of wealth or whatever happened to the great inheritance boom? Results from the SCF and PSID* (NBER Working Paper). Cambridge, MA: National Bureau of Economic Research.

Zambrana, R. E., & Carter-Pokras, O. (2010). Role of acculturation research in advancing science and practice in reducing health care disparities among Latinos. *American Journal of Public Health, 100*(1), 18–23.

CHAPTER 4

Transnational Families and Intergenerational Solidarity

THE TIES THAT BIND

Rosa, who is 76, winced in pain as the nurse, with the help of her daughter Gloria and son-in-law Jaime, moved her from the hospital bed to the wheelchair. Today Rosa is being discharged from East Side Presbyterian, a community hospital that had been bought by a for-profit hospital chain 10 years ago. She has been in the hospital for nearly a week after arriving at the emergency room with severe chest and abdominal pain. The cause was a severe gall bladder attack that required surgery, so Rosa was admitted to the hospital. During her stay doctors discovered that she had severely elevated blood glucose, high blood pressure, and a significant aortic stenosis, a narrowing of the heart valve leading from the heart. She underwent surgery to remove her gall bladder, but the doctors decided to monitor the stenosis rather than treat it given Rosa's age and medical condition, and the fact that she did not have serious symptoms. Because of pain, unstable blood pressure, and heart arrhythmia, Rosa's stay was far longer than usual.

After completing the discharge paperwork, Gloria and Jaime, accompanied by a member of the hospital staff, wheeled Rosa to Jaime's Audi for the drive back to the couple's home. When Rosa arrived in the country 2 years ago she was vibrant and animated and was constantly active. She is highly respected by her family and dearly loved by Gloria. Rosa had come to the United States to help with her new granddaughter Hortencia, and was a great help with the new baby and in supervising the couple's older son, Estefan, who is 10. Today, though, Rosa seems small and frail in the large wheelchair. The illness and age have clearly taken something from her, and it is clear to everyone that she is not the same person she was when she arrived.

Rosa is a Mexican citizen and lives alone in an apartment in Monterrey close to her son and his family. Her son is a structural engineer who works for a successful construction company. Rosa's husband, Luis, died 20 years ago of a heart attack. He left his wife an estate large enough for her to live on without working. Gloria, who is now in her mid-30s, was born in Monterrey. She was working as a secretary in Mexico City when she met Jaime, who is in his early 40s. After a traditional courtship they married and Gloria quickly gave birth to Estefan. After 2 years of marriage the couple immigrated to the United States and settled in East Los Angeles, where they began what is now a thriving furniture import business. Gloria and Jaime are part of the American Dream. They are purchasing a 2,500-square-foot home and Jaime is extremely proud of his new Audi. The couple also owns a pickup, which they use for furniture delivery. When Rosa arrived it was Gloria's hope that she would stay permanently.

Two weeks after Rosa's discharge from the hospital the family received a shock. In the mail they received a bill for $68,287.96. Had she been living in Mexico Rosa would have been treated at a public hospital and would have owed very little. She has no health insurance in the United States and does not qualify for Medicare. Although parents are able to immigrate fairly easily under the family reunification provisions of the immigration laws, their families must agree to assume the responsibility for all expenses that the aging person incurs, including medical expenses. Soon the reality hit. Since her release Rosa has seemed a bit crestfallen, perhaps even depressed. Rather than helping with household tasks and child care, she became dependent and Gloria had to stay home to care for her and Hortencia rather than accompanying Jaime to the furniture business where she has been responsible for the books.

After several weeks of negotiations the hospital agreed to lower the bill to $38,000. From savings and with the help of her brother, Gloria was able to pay $6,000 and put the rest on a payment plan. Given the size of the remaining bill, it may never actually be paid off. As the reality of Rosa's declining health set in and as the family faced the reality of even larger medical bills in the future, the decision was made. Two weeks later, Gloria helped her brother load Rosa's belongings into his pickup. As they drove away on their way back to Monterrey Gloria could not help but sob, knowing that she will only see her mother occasionally and probably only a few times more before her mother is dead.

TRANSNATIONAL FAMILIES

This fictional family and their situation illustrates one of the major dilemmas that families face if they wish to bring non-citizen older parents to the United States for more than a short visit. Although an older parent can help with household tasks and grandchildren, they are unlikely to be able to earn much, if they earn anything at all, and as we explain in greater detail below, immigration law requires that their families assume total financial responsibility for them for at least 5 years. Although we have no statistics, this fact must discourage some families from reuniting with older parents, and it may motivate certain parents to return home to Mexico. In this chapter we examine the situation of older immigrants and their families, and identify the social resources available to them in the communities to which they migrate. As we will see, while older immigrant parents are highly dependent on their younger family members, they also draw on other social resources available in the community. Those resources often consist of individuals and organizations from the migrant's community or region of origin in Mexico.

"Chain migration" is a label that is employed to characterize migration of individuals from the same community in the sending nation to a particular area in the receiving country. The image of links emphasizes the interdependence of individuals in the process. Early migrants brave the unknown in search of a better life. They must cross borders, often without proper documentation; they must evade detection and find transportation to the new location in the United States. When they arrive in the new location they do not know anyone and must learn the language and the laws and customs of the new place. Later migrants benefit from these experiences. They draw upon their predecessors' knowledge of the migration process and the ways in which to manage the crossing, and they benefit from the early arrivals' knowledge of the new environment. Over time a whole community can evolve with aspects of the culture of the sending community. One important study that we draw upon in this chapter followed migrants from Guanajuato, Mexico, an area from which many residents have migrated, to specific destinations in Chicago and Dallas. The study clearly showed a preference for cities and neighborhoods to which earlier migrants from the same communities in Guanajuato had migrated (Montes de Oca, Molina, & Avalos, 2008).

For the most part, migrants tend to be young and in search of work opportunities and a better life. Older parents tend to stay home since their options for employment are limited or nonexistent. The study of Guanajuato migrants showed that migrants' ties with family members, usually spouses, children, and parents whom they left back in Guanajuato, remain strong initially. With time, though, and especially after the death of parents, those ties weaken and contact with the old country diminishes, a process that occurred with generations of European immigrants in previous centuries. Today most European-origin Americans have no remaining ties to their countries of origin.

The motivations for chain migration emerge from several sources. As we mentioned, earlier migrants provide useful information to later migrants, both about the migration process itself and navigating the institutions and bureaucracies of the receiving area. It is clearly much easier for an immigrant to adapt to an environment in which he or she deals with people from back home who speak his or her language and follow familiar customs than to adapt to an environment that is completely foreign. Neighborhoods and communities with a large number of individuals from one's own group have been referred to as "ethnic enclaves." Such enclaves, as well as associations of individuals from one's home country and even one's local community of origin, can make adaptation to a foreign environment easier and less threatening. Such enclaves can also provide important employment and economic opportunities (Portes & Rumbaut, 2006). Some evidence suggests that older Mexican-origin individuals who live in a neighborhood with a high proportion of Mexican-origin inhabitants enjoy better health than those who live in neighborhoods with fewer individuals from the same ethnic group. This positive effect of higher concentrations of co-ethnics holds despite the socioeconomic disadvantages typical of predominantly Mexican-origin neighborhoods (Aranda, Ray, Al-Snih, Ottenbacher, & Markides, 2011; Eschbach, Ostir, Patel, Markides, & Goodwin, 2004; Gerst et al., 2011).

Nonetheless, even with the assistance of earlier arrivals, migration is always difficult since it uproots the migrant from his or her familiar environment and deposits him or her in a foreign world in which much is strange and unfamiliar. Adapting to a new environment may be easy for children and younger adults, but it presents major challenges to later-life migrants. Our opening vignette illustrated a unique problem for immigrant families that we explore in this chapter. Gloria and Jaime are a relatively successful and prosperous immigrant couple. The dilemma they faced when they attempted to bring an elderly parent to live with them illustrates the fact that even for a family with resources, a parent's medical crisis can result in financial disaster. A family with fewer resources, or one with undocumented members, would have even less capacity to cope. Given the inevitable decline in health and functional capacity that accompanies aging, health care assumes a major role in older individuals' lives.

When a citizen of the United States turns 65 he or she can rely on Medicare (Broder & Blazer, 2011). Medicare, though, does not extend to recent immigrants. The lack of citizenship or permanent resident status freezes an older individual out of most public programs (Angel, 2003; Nam, 2008; Nam & Jung, 2008). Citizens with few assets and little income whose health deteriorates to a point at which they require nursing home or specialized care can turn to Medicaid. Non-citizens do not qualify for Medicaid, and unless they have substantial resources, which few immigrant families do, formal long-term care is not an option. These individuals remain dependent on their family or, like Rosa, they must return to Mexico.

TYPES OF VISAS

All nations restrict immigration and often create preferred categories that allow individuals with valuable skills or material assets easier access. The right to immigrate to the United States is granted by specific statutes that differentiate among types of applicants. These give preference to the family members of citizens or legal residents and to highly skilled or talented individuals. It would be useful to briefly review the ways in which visas are granted and to outline the policy of "family reunification" to better understand its implications for older would-be immigrants and their families in the United States. Clearly, not everyone who might wish to can immigrate to the United States legally. The number of visas that are granted to foreigners is limited, except for immediate family members. The State Department issues various types of visas that allow individuals to stay in the country for different lengths of time for specific purposes. Foreigners can, of course, apply for nonimmigrant visas to come to the United States for short periods as visitors, as students, or for other purposes. We are not concerned with these limited visa types, although they are clearly one source of illegal immigration when foreigners who are allowed in for a limited time stay beyond that period. Rather, we are concerned with two large categories of visas that allow an individual to stay for longer periods, often permanently. Unlike tourist visas, these allow individuals to seek employment. The first large category includes foreign nationals who do not have relatives in the United States, and the second foreign nationals who are the relatives of U.S. citizens (U.S. Department of State, 2013b). See the 🌐 that gives the specific criteria for the subgroups within these categories http://travel.state.gov/content/visas/english/general/all-visa-categories.html.

Let us briefly describe the first category, that for immigrants who are not sponsored by relatives already in the United States, and then describe the second category, which includes relatives of U.S. citizens. The non-relative category is divided into five priority subcategories. The first subcategory, and the one with the highest priority, includes persons with extraordinary ability, outstanding professors and researchers, and multinational executives or managers. The second subcategory includes professionals holding advanced degrees and persons with a degree of expertise significantly above that ordinarily encountered in the workplace. Applicants in this subcategory must have an offer of employment in order to receive a visa. The third subcategory includes skilled workers, professionals who qualify for jobs with at least a baccalaureate, and unskilled workers. The fourth subcategory includes certain special groups and occupations, such as interpreters, foreign-born workers who experience a threat as the result of U.S. employment in Iraq or Afghanistan, and ministers and religious workers. The fifth subcategory includes individuals who intend to invest in commercial enterprises (U.S. Bureau of Consular Affairs, 2013). The number of visas issued in these employment-based and special qualification categories is limited to 140,000 annually.

The second large category of immigrants, which itself has two large subcategories, including immediate relatives and more distant relatives of U.S. citizens or permanent residents, is governed by different rules. These immigrants must be sponsored by their U.S. relative, who must agree to certain conditions we mention below. Most importantly, though, there is no annual limit to the number of visas issued to immediate relatives (U.S. Department of State, 2012). Immediate relatives include the U.S. citizen's spouse, unmarried children under the age of 21, adopted children, and parents. The details of the family reunification provisions are somewhat complicated and the basic distinctions are presented in Exhibit 4.1.

Those who are interested in more detail can visit www.uscis.gov/family/family-us-citizens/parents/bringing-parents-live-united-states-permanent-residents. Unlike employment visas for which the wait can vary depending on demand, there is no waiting period for receiving a visa for immediate relatives. The second family visa category consists of more distant relatives, such as grown children, brothers

---

Exhibit 4.1 Family-based Immigrant Visa

Immediate Relative Immigrant Visas (Unlimited): These visa types are based on a close family relationship with a United States (U.S.) citizen described as an Immediate Relative (IR). The number of immigrants in these categories is not limited each fiscal year. Immediate relative visa types include:

IR-1: Spouse of a U.S. citizen
IR-2: Unmarried Child under 21 years of age of a U.S. citizen
IR-3: Orphan adopted abroad by a U.S. citizen
IR-4: Orphan to be adopted in the U.S. by a U.S. citizen
IR-5: Parent of a U.S. citizen who is at least 21 years old

Family Preference Immigrant Visas (Limited): These visa types are for specific, more distant, family relationships with a U.S. citizen and some specified relationships with a Lawful Permanent Resident (LPR). There are fiscal year numerical limitations on family preference immigrants, shown at the end of each category. The **family preference categories** are:

Family First Preference (F1): Unmarried sons and daughters of U.S. citizens, and their minor children, if any. (23,400)

Family Second Preference (F2): Spouses, minor children, and unmarried sons and daughters (age 21 and over) of LPRs. At least 77% of all visas available for this category will go to the spouses and children; the remainder is allocated to unmarried sons and daughters. (114,200)

Family Third Preference (F3): Married sons and daughters of U.S. citizens, and their spouses and minor children. (23,400)

Family Fourth Preference (F4): Brothers and sisters of U.S. citizens, and their spouses and minor children, provided the U.S. citizens are at least 21 years of age. (65,000)

Source: U.S. Department of State,
http://travel.state.gov/visa/immigrants/types/types_1306.html

and sisters, the spouses of green card holders, the children of green card holders, and others (U.S. Department of State, 2013a). The number of visas issued annually in this category is limited and the waiting period can vary between 4 and 14 years.

Although the number of visas available to immediate relatives is unlimited, other provisions of the law can complicate attempts to reunify families. Recent changes in immigration law establish potentially onerous requirements for sponsorship of a family member (U.S. Department of State, 2013b). As we explain in detail below, in order to sponsor a family member one must agree to assume full financial responsibility for that relative for at least 5 years. The sponsor must also prove that he or she has enough income or assets to do so (U.S. Department of State, 2013a).

The core objective of requiring sponsorship is to insure that a new immigrant does not become a "public charge." Exhibit 4.2 presents the Department of Homeland Security's definition of a public charge and the official statutory rule against admitting individuals who are likely to become public charges (U.S. Citizenship and Immigration Services, 2009). The Personal Responsibility and Work Opportunity Reconciliation Act of 1996 (PRWORA), commonly referred to as welfare reform, excludes even legal immigrants from receiving Supplemental Security Income (SSI), Food Stamps, or most other publicly funded governmental services for a period of 5 years unless they fall into certain exempt categories (Broder & Blazer, 2011; Nam, 2008; Nam & Jung, 2008). SSI is particularly important for older individuals since it provides support to those who do not qualify for regular Social Security (Nicholas & Wiseman, 2009). As a result of this law, older immigrants do not have the same access to SSI as U.S. citizens, a fact that clearly influences the extent of financial burden that family sponsors must assume (Treas, 2007).

Although exact numbers are unavailable, the risk of serious medical emergencies and the practical burden of sponsorship must discourage many families who might wish to bring aging parents to live with them in the United States from doing so. While migration benefits families in that it improves the economic situation of the family as a whole, including those who stay behind in Mexico, it tears the extended family apart and often forces children to abandon their parents. The sponsorship provision, then, has important potential consequences for families that could affect their decisions as to which family members to sponsor (Espenshade, Baraka, & Huber, 1997).

Exhibit 4.2 Public Charge Rules

Q. Who is a public charge and how is the status determined?

A. For purposes of determining inadmissibility, "public charge" means an individual who is likely to become primarily dependent on the government for subsistence, as demonstrated by either the receipt of public cash assistance for income maintenance or institutionalization for long-term care at government expense. A number of factors must be considered when making a determination that a person is likely to become a public charge.

Under Section 212(a)(4) of the Immigration and Nationality Act (INA), an individual seeking admission to the United States or seeking to adjust status to that of an individual lawfully admitted for permanent residence (green card) is inadmissible if the individual, "at the time of application for admission or adjustment of status, is likely at any time to become a public charge." Public charge does not apply in naturalization proceedings. If an individual is inadmissible, admission to the United States or adjustment of status is not granted.

Q. How is it determined whether someone is likely to become a public charge for admission or adjustment purposes?

A. Inadmissibility based on the public charge ground is determined by the totality of the circumstances. This means that the adjudicating officer must weigh both the positive and negative factors when determining the likelihood that someone might become a public charge. At a minimum, a U.S. Citizenship and Immigration Services (USCIS) officer must consider the following factors when making a public charge determination:

- Age
- Health
- Family status
- Assets
- Resources
- Financial status
- Education and skills

Source: U.S. Office of Citizenship and Immigration Services (2009)

This brief review of immigration law makes it clear that the humane desire to allow families to reunite and the need to insure that immigrants do not become public charges are fundamentally contradictory (Miranda, 1998). While sponsoring children or a spouse may represent a reasonable financial risk since young people are for the most part healthy, older individuals are at far greater risk of ill health and of the inability to contribute to family finances (Treas & Torres-Gil, 2009). This reality is part of the lives of many transnational families who must redefine their relationships with family members and navigate a new bi-national or even multi-national reality (Balibar, 2004; Bryceson & Vuorela, 2002), as well as negotiate their cultural identities in a new environment (Ehrkamp & Leitner, 2001).

ECONOMIC GLOBALIZATION: THE DRIVING FORCE?

Although political strife and war force many people all over the world to flee their homes, the forces that give rise to the phenomenon of family transnationalism are primarily economic. Individuals migrate in search of economic opportunities. The labor market for highly trained professionals is international, and they migrate to certain major metropolises that serve as the hubs of global information and financial networks (Beaverstock, 2012; Castells, 2000; Sassen, 2006). Even unskilled labor, though, is an increasingly international commodity. Immigrants from outside the European Union provide essential labor to the developed nations of Europe, as do Mexican immigrants in the United States (Borjas & Katz, 2007; Caldwell, 2009; Massey, Durand, & Malone, 2003). Given the high demand for such labor, attempts to stop or even slow immigration almost inevitably fail (Castles, 2004).

For these reasons transnational families will most likely become more common in the years to come and alter relations among generations and nations. Many countries allow dual and even multiple citizenship. As we noted earlier, though, the phenomenon of transnationalism is not new, although it is probably different in nature today than it was in the past. Large-scale immigration from Europe in the 19th and early 20th centuries created families with members in North and South America as well as in Europe. In previous centuries, though, maintaining contact was more difficult. What may be different today is the regions from which the immigrants come and a greater ability to travel, communicate, and stay in touch with family members in the country of origin. This ability to communicate and the close association among immigrants in their new communities give rise to new possibilities for mutual support. Transnational grassroots networks and organizations allow migrants to engage in mutual support and maintain close ties to their communities of origin.

Although migration limits the possibility of frequent and immediate family interactions, it often strengthens other ties, including those that provide material support.

BUILDING NEW COMMUNITIES

Social institutions outside the family, including faith-based organizations and social clubs consisting of other members of the nation or even community of origin, are central to the lives of immigrants. These organizations provide essential emotional and moral support, but they also provide important material support and information that help immigrants navigate the new environment (Hirschman, 2004). Although Protestant and Evangelical groups have made inroads both in the United States and Latin America, Hispanics remain predominantly Catholic. In the United States one-third of Roman Catholics are Hispanic, and a large fraction are recent immigrants from Mexico (D'Antonio, 2011). The Catholic Church provides Mexican-origin immigrants and their families with information concerning housing and employment opportunities, and it offers counseling and other vital social services. The Catholic Church often sponsors English immersion classes to help Mexican-origin immigrants speak and write English and learn American customs.

Among the services that churches and other organizations provide is information about sources of assistance for aging parents. Most older Hispanics are citizens and they have grown old in the United States, yet as for non-Hispanics few are aware of formal governmental services that are available through governmental programs such as Area Agencies on Aging or other local, state, and nongovernmental agencies and organizations. For families with aging immigrant parents, information concerning program eligibility and access are vital. The role of the Catholic Church in dealing with immigrants includes offering refuge for illegal immigrants (Tareen, 2008). The sanctuary movement serves as a surrogate family for undocumented workers in many large cities like Chicago, Los Angeles, and Seattle. The Church facilitates remittances to families and organizations back home in Mexico.

Exhibit 4.3 illustrates the support systems for older individuals who migrated from Mexico to the United States in later life. It is excerpted from the study of migrants from Guanajuato, Mexico we mentioned earlier. In this study ethnographers interviewed and observed individuals and families that settled in Chicago and Dallas. It illustrates the

Exhibit 4.3 Transnational Support Networks

Dolores, a 45-year-old female from a small community in the municipality of Ocampo in the central Mexican state of Guanajuato, had to leave her mother behind when she migrated to Chicago. Leaving one's aging mother behind in a place that is so far away could not have been easy, but what makes the reality bearable for Dolores is the fact that her mother is part of a large network of mutually supportive neighbors. As Dolores explained to the ethnographers who related her story, "My mom lives alone in Taranda [which refers to Tarandacuao, a municipality in Guanajuato], but what gives me comfort is knowing that her neighbors live close by, and one or another of them is always looking in on her [author's translation]" (Montes de Oca Zavala, Molina, & Avalos, 2008).

The mother's network of neighbors is only one of multiple local and transnational networks that serve many purposes. At the same time that they support individuals like Dolores's mother, they link individuals from Guanajuato to family members and other individuals from their home communities to those who have moved and facilitate the exchange of resources. Guanajuato is a state with a long tradition of migration to the United States, and individuals from specific communities migrate to specific neighborhoods, such as Oak Cliff and East Dallas in Dallas, and Little Village in Chicago. In these receiving communities, organizations that consist of individuals from the same sending area provide information as well as moral and material support to new arrivals, and help define community in a city that might otherwise remain very foreign. These networks are defined by the contacts that migrants make at church, at their children's schools, and in their workplaces.

Although informal family and neighborhood contacts are important, in the receiving cities more formal organizational structures operate as well, including those based in the Church and other civic organizations. Among the most important support organizations are "Guanajuato houses." These organizations are officially sponsored and supported by the Government of the State of Guanajuato in recognition of the fact that a large fraction of the State's population has migrated to the United States.

The result of this migration is the emergence of a transnational reality in which rather than living their entire lives in a traditional agricultural village, individuals and families are spread far apart. In the old days Dolores would have assumed the daily responsibility for her mother, but in the new post-traditional world in which she lives she cannot. The new reality for a large fraction of the population of Guanajuato is that tradition must be recreated in a new place and with those who are available.

Source: Montes de Oca Zavala, Molina, and Avalos (2008)

central role of organizations sponsored by the Government of Guanajuato in helping migrants from that state recreate aspects of their communities of origin in the destination cities. Such organizations clearly facilitate material and cultural exchanges between communities in the United States and Mexico.

Although our focus has been on immigrants from Mexico, we must point out that the massive emigration of younger people has serious consequences for the communities that they abandon. Guanajuato has been a traditional sending area and much of the younger population of the region has emigrated. Clearly, communities that have lost their younger generations are not the vital and vibrant

---

Exhibit 4.4 The Old Folks Left Behind

Dolores, like a large fraction of the population of the State of Guanajuato, left home in search of new opportunities, but the departure of the young has transformed the communities they left in profound ways. Although high rates of out-migration characterize the state as a whole, certain municipalities are particularly affected. Ocampo, a municipality in the north of the state, has experienced massive out-migration and the economic profile as well as the social profile of the municipality has changed. The shortage of water is a physical correlate of the absence of basic resources and opportunities that force younger people to leave. Unlike other areas in Mexico that are characterized by the coming and going of migrants, often on a seasonal basis, from Ocampo they only leave. They have no real choice.

The loss of the young has changed the traditional world of the elderly dramatically. In traditional times Ocampo was made up of individuals of all ages. Old people looked to the young for respect and support. Like Dolores's mother, though, today they live in a very changed world, one that is made up primarily of old people, single women, and youth with serious problems who cannot leave. The sons, daughters, nieces, and nephews that were once part of large and supportive extended families have gone to the United States. Initially, family members send money back home, but these remittances are infrequent, and with time often diminish in frequency and amount, finally ending altogether, leaving those who have been left behind on their own or dependent on the Mexican social support system. In Ocampo the elderly depend on their social networks for survival since government support is limited.

Although they need the remittances and understand the reality of the need for the young to leave home, they have lost their traditional way of life and are left with only memories. Those memories, though, only serve to remind the elderly of the world they have lost.

Source: Montes de Oca Zavala (2008)

places that they were in the past. Exhibit 4.4 illustrates the hardship and tragedy of the changed world that results from the exodus of young people to the United States. For the old people who are left behind the multigenerational young society in which they grew up is gone forever.

REMITTANCES

Migration not only serves the purpose of improving the economic lot of the migrant, but it can improve the economic situation of family members who remain behind. The money that migrants "remit," or send back to their home countries, can greatly improve the situation of parents, spouses, and children (Congressional Budget Office, 2011). It can, in fact, contribute greatly to the local community and add substantially to the local economy. For Mexico and other Latin American nations the money that both legal and illegal immigrants to the United States send back home represents a significant source of foreign currency (Villagran, 2013). In 2008 two-thirds of Latino migrants to the United States sent money to family members back home in Mexico and Latin America (Benítez-Silva, Cárceles-Poveda, & Eren, 2011).

Perhaps because their motivation for coming to the United States is more purely economic, undocumented immigrants are far more likely than legal immigrants to send money home to Mexico. Approximately 75% of undocumented workers, as opposed to 55% of legal immigrants, send money home (Benítez-Silva et al., 2011). For many undocumented migrants the choice to come to the United States to work is part of a family survival strategy. In 2008, the average monthly remittances was $404 dollars per month (Benítez-Silva et al., 2011). These flows represent an important source of income for the millions of Latin American families and for national economies. In 2012 Mexico was the largest recipient of remittances, $22.4 billion, which accounted for 2.3% of the gross domestic product (GDP) (Maldonado & Hayem, 2013). Although Haiti, a far smaller country than Mexico, received $1.98 billion in 2013, that amount accounted for a quarter of that country's GDP (Maldonado & Hayem, 2013).

In 2012 nearly one-and-a-half million families in Mexico received money from relatives in the United States. (Villagran, 2013). While this represents less than 1% of Mexico's population, certain states such as Michoacán,

Oaxaca, and Guerrero are especially dependent on this support (Villagran, 2013). As one would expect, remittances declined during the 2008 economic recession when immigrants found it more difficult to find work (Kitroeff, 2013). In 2012 the average remittance a Mexican worker sent back to his or her family was about $290 per month (Villagran, 2013). Despite that decrease remittances remain important and have helped reduce poverty in Mexico over the last decade.

GROWING OLD A LONG WAY FROM HOME

For all of the reasons we have discussed, it is not surprising that the rigors of international migration and acculturation into a new society mean that it selects the young. Children migrate with their parents and have little say in the matter. Young adults migrate primarily in search of economic opportunities. Their youth means that they are more easily able to learn a new language and customs, adapt to a new environment, and find work. Older migrants are in a very different situation since they are not as adaptable or employable as younger individuals. This fact gives rise to important differences within the older Latino population. Those older individuals who came when they were children or young adults had the opportunity to become more fully assimilated and acculturated. Indeed, those who came as children are not much different than the native-born. Most older immigrants are in this group; they have lived the majority of their lives in the United States (Office of Immigration Statistics, 2009). In this chapter we have focused on the much smaller group of immigrants who came later in life and whose incorporation was less complete. This group is clearly far more vulnerable and more dependent than the native-born or those who immigrated early in life.

As we showed earlier, although the immigration laws and the difficulties inherent in international migration in mature adulthood serve as significant disincentives, the number of later-life immigrants has risen during the last quarter-century (Brown, 2009). Between 1990 and 2010 the number of immigrants of all ethnicities aged 65 and older increased from 2.7 million to about 4.6 million (U.S. Census Bureau, 2012). Today, older immigrants over 65 account for 12% of the 40 million immigrants in the United States (Batalova, 2012). The number is expected to grow to 16 million by 2050 (Brown, 2009). In California, the largest state in the nation, nearly one in three seniors is now foreign-born (Brown, 2009). The largest number of immigrants aged 65 and over come from Mexico (Terrazas, 2009). One of every seven older immigrants in the United States in 2010 was born in Mexico.

STAY IN THE UNITED STATES OR RETURN HOME?

As has been the case for all immigrant groups for whom returning to their country of origin was a possibility, certain older Mexican immigrants return to Mexico. They do so primarily because of family and economic ties that serve as motivations to return. The most commonly stated motivation for returning to Mexico is to reunite with family members (Massey, Alarcón, Durand, & González, 1987). Immigrants who left spouses back in Mexico have a particularly strong motivation to go back (Kanaiaupuni, 2000; Massey & Pren, 2012). Other ties include the ownership of property in Mexico. Owning a home in Mexico is a major pull factor. Almost half of Mexicans over 50 living in the United States own property in Mexico (Porter & Malkin, 2005).

In addition to family and home ownership, the lower cost of living in Mexico represents a clear draw (Porter & Malkin, 2005). Compared to the United States, the cost of living in Mexico is low. This fact is especially salient for someone without a pension or only a small one. Some estimates suggest that 10 million workers of Mexican origin return to Mexico because they are unable to afford to grow old in the United States (Porter & Malkin, 2005). Limited resources can be stretched much further in Mexico than in the United States. As our opening vignette illustrated, medical care costs can be ruinous in the United States, even with Medicare. In Mexico, everyone has access to basic health care, and out-of-pocket expenses are lower than in the United States. Whether that health care is of similar quality remains in question, but that the cost of care is lower is indisputable. As Exhibit 4.5 illustrates with a recently returned Hispanic immigrant, a little money goes a long way in old age in Mexico.

In Mexico some government officials fear that the nation is ill prepared to support potentially millions of returning retirees who have spent their working lives in the United States. Mexico is aging rapidly and has a limited

Exhibit 4.5 For Aging Immigrants, a Little Goes a Long Way in Mexico

"In little Mexico the money seems like a lot," said Roselino Sebastián Castañeda, 72, who returned 9 years ago to his hometown in Tierra Caliente, Guerrero, after 35 years of shuttling from California to Texas to Louisiana to Colorado to Montana. He knows he could never afford to live in the United States on the $350 a month he collects from Social Security, the half of his benefit not swallowed by child support for a daughter in Arizona. But in Mexico, he said, "if I stop drinking and stop partying, I can live on that."

Source: Porter and Malkin (2005)

social welfare system for the elderly (Porter & Malkin, 2005). A rapid increase in the number of older individuals in need of medical care could easily overwhelm the health care system. The United States, though, is equally unprepared to care for this older Mexican-origin population (Porter & Malkin, 2005). About one-fifth (18%) of older people of Mexican origin have incomes below the poverty line, a far higher rate than the 9% below the poverty line in the elderly population as a whole (Brown & Patten, 2013). If one were to include illegal immigrants, the numbers living in poverty would no doubt be even higher.

Whether older immigrants from Mexico stay until they die or return home at some point is each family's decision, but it is made within the constraints of the immigration laws. Now that she has returned to Monterrey, Rosa and her family are part of the old but growing phenomenon of transnationalism. The family has branches in two countries. Given Rosa's economic security she does not count on remittances from Gloria and Jaime, but their separation means that their relationship is different. For early immigrants to the United States from Europe, the move often meant permanent separation from those they left behind. Today Turks in Germany, Algerians in France, Bolivians in Peru, Mexicans in the United States, and migrants in many other countries return, sometimes frequently, to visit family members in their countries of origin. Transportation over long distances is much simpler and less expensive than in the past, and in many cases the distances are not far. Even today, though, refugees, such as Cubans in the United States, cannot easily return home, even though their country of origin is only 90 miles away. For undocumented Mexican residents of the United States, stricter border controls have made return visits much more difficult (Massey & Pren, 2012).

OLDER IMMIGRANTS: A PUBLIC CHARGE?

As we discussed in Chapter 2, both Europe and the United States are currently engaged in polarizing debates concerning immigration, and especially policies dealing with undocumented immigration (Caldwell, 2009; Huntington, 2004). Absorbing an increasing number of older immigrants entails potentially significant social costs. On the positive side, if the situations of the approximately 11 million undocumented workers were regularized so that they could work legally and pay taxes, public revenues would increase (Pew Research Center for the People & the Press, 2013). Some opponents to granting permanent residency or citizenship to the undocumented argue that such a policy has a potentially hidden cost. Some data suggest that legal immigrants are sponsoring their aging parents at a growing rate, notwithstanding the disincentives we have mentioned concerning the potential costs of sponsorship (Carr & Tienda, 2013).

If undocumented immigrants who currently do not have the right to sponsor their aging parents were granted permanent residency or citizenship, the number of sponsored parents could increase substantially. Greater immigration of older parents could offset the presumed payoff in terms of increased tax revenues paid by their children. After the required 5-year waiting period the parents would qualify for many public housing, nutrition, and health programs, including Medicaid. Some of those aging family members would be eligible for Medicaid-funded long-term care. The rising cost of Medicaid is a major drain on state budgets and raises serious questions concerning future funding (Bass & Vekshin, 2013). Even with the federal government picking up the vast majority of the cost of Medicaid expansion under Obamacare, the potential burden of paying even 10% of the eventual bill leads some states to reject expansion.

UNCOLLECTED BENEFITS

Although the potential for additional costs clearly accompanies any regularization of the situation of the undocumented, it is important to emphasize that, while some may work informally and do not pay federal, state, local, Social Security, or Medicaid taxes, others do and some never collect. The Congressional Budget Office reports that in fact most undocumented immigrants have paid taxes over their working lives, but under current law they are not entitled to benefits. The Internal Revenue Service estimates that about six million undocumented immigrants file individual income tax returns each year (Congressional Budget Office, 2007). About half of undocumented workers pay Social Security taxes, although they are very unlikely to collect benefits (Feinleib & Warner, 2005). Contributions from undocumented workers make up almost 10%, or $300 billion, of the Social Security trust fund (Joshi, 2013). These contributions help support retirement and disability entitlement programs, which are projected to run out of money in 2033. Undocumented workers contribute about $15 billion a year to the Social Security Trust Fund, while taking out only $1 billion in benefits. A 2006 study carried out by the Office of the Texas State Comptroller projected that by 2010 the 1.4 million undocumented immigrants would contribute $19 billion to the state's economy in 2010 and $43 billion by 2025 (Combs, 2006).

UNFULFILLED DREAMS AND LOST OPPORTUNITIES

We end by shifting our attention to a truly unique tragedy related to the desire of individuals living in impoverished situations to migrate to improve their own lot and that of their children. The phenomenon of transnational families represents a response to globalization and the need for cheap labor in developed nations. The individuals who provide that labor often arrive illegally, but since they are human, eventually they bring their families, including children. Those children, often hardly more than infants, grow up in the United States far from their origins. Yet, despite the fact that they did not come of their own free will or that they know little of their country of origin, they are not citizens of the United States and they do not share in the rights of citizens. In fact, they are illegal and subject to deportation to places that are as foreign to them as they would be to any of us born in the United States.

Exhibit 4.6 presents a composite example, drawn from several actual cases, of the situation of young people who find themselves in this situation. The exhibit illustrates the legal and social limbo in which children who are not citizens can find themselves. The tragedy of the situation of

Exhibit 4.6 A Unique Tragedy

Emily Gutierrez graduated in the top 10% of her class at Central High School in a large Southeastern city where she had earned the admiration of the faculty. She was a member of the honors society during all four of her high school years. She played first violin in the orchestra and had lettered in track and field. In her senior year Emily had been elected president of her class. By all estimates Emily should have gone on to a prestigious private university or the flagship public university in her state. But that was not to be.

Despite her hard work and numerous accomplishments, the school counselor had bad news. He knew Emily's situation. She had been brought to the United States from Mexico by her parents at age five and was not a citizen. Like millions of other Mexicans, Emily's parents had sought a better life for themselves and their children. They had labored for years in the poultry industry to buy a home and send their children to school. They did not have enough money to pay for college or university, though. Because of her undocumented status Emily did not qualify for state or federal loans. Without a loan Emily was not able to attend college, and she joined her parents at the plant at which they worked since the owner did not require proof of citizenship. Since Emily was not a citizen she did not qualify for a work permit that would have allowed her to look for a better job.

Emily had grown up as an American. She had internalized American values of hard work and fair play, but her situation seemed anything but fair. She spoke excellent English and some Spanish at home, but she was not fluent in that language. She had never even visited Mexico since her parents were afraid to go back as they feared they would not be able to return to the United States. For Emily, Mexico was as foreign and unknown as it is to most Americans.

Emily could not legally get a driver's license but occasionally drove anyway. One afternoon she was stopped for running a stop sign and when she could not prove who she was she was arrested and eventually turned over to the Immigration Service who began deportation proceedings against her and her family. With the help of a church group the Immigration Service suspended the deportation proceedings, but Emily and her family live under the constant threat that they will be sent back to Mexico. What Emily would do there she does not know. Meanwhile, Emily's promising future has faded. Without citizenship or legal recourse to a work permit or school loans, her educational aspirations have been dashed along with any hope she might find a better job. She will never become the doctor or lawyer or scientist that she might have been and the nation will have lost the productive potential of a young individual with much to contribute.

these young people creates a clear moral dilemma for the country. Their plight is clearly different than that of individuals who made the choice to cross the border on their own. In light of the hardships and blocked educational and occupational opportunities faced by young people in this situation, legislation that would exempt young people who were brought to this country as children from immediate deportation has been proposed. The DREAM Act, which stands for the Development, Relief, and Education for Alien Minors, is a bipartisan legislative proposal introduced in 2001 by Orin Hatch (R-UT) and Richard Durbin (D-IL) that would give approximately 65,000 undocumented students a pathway to legalization and citizenship.

The law would provide opportunities to a group of children brought to the United States illegally and who have grown up as Americans to earn a college degree, serve in the military, find employment, and vote. The Act involves a lengthy and rigorous process that qualified applicants must undergo (Miranda, 2010). These young people must first document that they entered the country when they were under 16 years old, prove that they have lived in the United States continuously for 5 years, have obtained a high school diploma or General Equivalency Diploma, are of good character, and have no criminal convictions. They are also required to pay a $465 fee. After the applicant gains conditional legal permanent residency status, he or she can apply for permanent green card status if they are able to prove that they have (1) gone to college or served in the U.S. military for at least 2 years, (2) passed a second criminal background check, and (3) demonstrated good moral character. If approved, applicants can establish state residency and apply for student loans and work study programs. This process entails some risks. If applicants are unable to fulfill these requirements they will lose their legal status and be subject to deportation.

The DREAM Act would clearly represent a first step toward citizenship or legal residency that would represent the recognition of a reality brought about as much by demand for labor in the United States as the decisions of parents. Yet, as one might expect, the legislation faces opposition. Some individuals feel that it is unfair to would-be immigrants who obey the law and attempt to enter the country legally. It is important to point out, though, that the situation of individuals who find themselves in this limbo has more than just individual consequences. The legal situation of young people who cannot participate in the economic and civic life of the nation affects society as a whole. Young people who are not allowed to use their talents in ways that enhance our overall productivity represent a squandered resource. If these individuals are unable to save for their retirements or to save and invest because they are barred from well-paying jobs, they are at risk of becoming public charges, an eventuality that our current immigration law is designed to avoid. The passage of the DREAM Act, or some variation of it, would represent the acceptance of a reality that is unlikely to change and that presents the nation with a very real moral dilemma. The demand for cheap labor in service, construction, and agricultural sectors insures that the problem will persist.

Because the U.S. Congress has so far failed to deal with the problem and pass the legislation, President Obama issued the Deferred Action for Childhood Arrivals memorandum directing the Department of Homeland Security to implement a rule that would defer action against undocumented minors and grant them a temporary 2-year work permit if they meet certain qualifications. To be eligible, applicants must be between ages 15 and 30 and have lived in the United States continuously for 5 years. Those who have been convicted of a felony, one serious misdemeanor, or three minor misdemeanors are ineligible to apply.

The DREAM Act and the broader regularization of the undocumented population would have other beneficial effects. Legalized, or at least decriminalized, individuals pay more in taxes than they receive in return (Lee & Miller, 1997; McNatt & Benassi, 2006; Congressional Budget Office, 2007). Estimates suggest that offering undocumented youth a pathway to citizenship would result in an additional contribution of approximately $329 billion to the national economy over the next 20 years (Guzmán & Jara, 2012).

Policies designed to deal with the reality of undocumented immigrants, who may be formally illegal but who are not criminals in a simplistic sense, are both humane and realistic. They have important implications in the context of transnational families. Most of these individuals are not looking for a handout. They accept the necessity of hard work and sacrifice, a fact to which the often perilous journeys they undertake to get here attest. They seek and should receive only the opportunity to contribute to the economy and the general welfare of the nation at the same time that they improve their own situations. Clearly, individuals should not be allowed to become public charges, nor should they be allowed to remain if they do so, other than as the result of serious illness or injury. Although we may see progress and movement on the DREAM Act and immigration reform more broadly, immigration remains a visceral and controversial topic for which simplistic solutions do not exist (Torres-Gil, Suh, & Angel, 2013). Nonetheless, as we become a majority–minority nation, dealing with the situations of undocumented individuals of all ages will become even more of a priority.

SUMMARY AND CONCLUSIONS

In this chapter we dealt with the growing phenomenon of transnational families. The United States was built by migrants who at different periods came from different parts of the world. In previous centuries the distances covered and the difficulty of communication meant that maintaining contact and providing mutual support was more difficult than it is today. Especially in the case of Mexico, but also in the case of other countries, communication and remittances of money from migrants are extremely important to families and communities in the countries of origin. The fact that a large number of families have members who are citizens of different countries has important implications for immigration policy and for public policies related to ways of dealing with a large population of undocumented residents.

As part of the discussion we reviewed immigration and welfare policy in order to illustrate the difficulties that immigrant families face when they bring an aging parent from another country to the United States. Family reunification represents a humane ideal that allows immigrants to rebuild their lives and families in this country. Under current law, though, sponsoring a family member requires that one assume nearly complete financial responsibility for that person for a period of at least 5 years. The objective of this requirement is to insure that immigrants do not become public charges. Unfortunately, family reunification and the desire to avoid attracting individuals who might become public charges conflict in the case of older parents. The sponsorship of a young person or a spouse may present few problems, and the sponsored family member can contribute to a household's economic welfare by working or freeing others to work. An aging parent may contribute domestic labor and perhaps bring some income with them, but the real problem that we illustrated arises when the older person needs medical or long-term care. Aging increases the risk of serious illness and without Medicare a sponsoring family is responsible for any medical debt that the elderly parent incurs. In addition, without access to Medicaid a family of modest means has no way of paying for long-term care.

The phenomenon of transnationalism is fueled by the phenomenon of "chain migration," a term that refers to a process in which later migrants move to destinations in which earlier migrants have settled. Such chain migration takes advantage of the knowledge about the immigration process and the new environment, as well as potential support and assistance in finding housing and work. We illustrated how chain migration creates communities that consist of individuals with ties to a common place of origin. We also illustrated how migrants form civic organizations for mutual support and how they draw upon the support of other organizations, including the Catholic Church.

As has historically been the case a certain number of migrants eventually return home. In the case of Hispanics, and especially those from Mexico, there are several reasons for returning home even after one has spent many years in the United States. Many immigrants have families back in Mexico with whom they might reunite. Others have homes and property that draw them back. A major motivation for returning is the relatively low cost of living in Mexico where a limited income can go much further than in the United States.

DISCUSSION QUESTIONS

1. The increase in transnational families creates situations in which members of a family are citizens of different countries. Many individuals are citizens of more than one country and have multiple passports. Nationality and citizenship in a specific country defines the nation-state system that has characterized the world over the last few centuries. Does the rise of massive migration and transnationalism signal the end of the nation-state system or some fundamental change in its structure and function? Speculate on the short- and long-term consequences for national identity of large-scale human migration.

2. Discuss the logic of family reunification in terms of immigration law. Does the humane intention of family reunification create potential problems for the receiving society? Should the eligible family members be restricted to spouses and children rather than including parents and more distant relatives? Discuss the logic of sponsorship that requires families to assume complete responsibility for the relatives they bring to the United States for a period of at least 5 years. Is this a logical and justifiable policy?

3. Should the United States eliminate all limits on the number of highly skilled immigrants? Should foreign students who receive advanced degrees in the United States be allowed easy access to citizenship? Should foreigners with substantial assets who agree to begin businesses or invest in the U.S. economy be given preference? Should famous artists and writers be given preference? Discuss the benefits and drawbacks to the adoption of such policies.

4. Summarize the moral bases of arguments for and against allowing undocumented residents to become citizens or at least to vote and to apply for certain government programs. Are there circumstances in which individuals who are in the country illegally should be allowed to become permanent legal residents or even citizens?

5. How should immigration policy deal with undocumented residents who were brought into the country by their parents when they were children? These individuals have grown up in the United States and often know nothing about their country of origin. Is it reasonable to deport such individuals? Should non-citizens who volunteer to fight in our armed services be allowed to become citizens on the basis of their service?

6. Current law criminalizes illegal immigration and provides legal sanctions for employers who knowingly employ undocumented workers, yet the number of undocumented workers remains large. Why is the government not more aggressive than it is in locating and deporting undocumented immigrants? Would it be possible to reduce the number of undocumented immigrants completely? What sanctions should be applied to individuals and organizations that knowingly employ undocumented workers? Should someone who employs an undocumented domestic laborer knowing their undocumented status be sanctioned?

LITERATURE CITED

Angel, J. L. (2003). Devolution and the social welfare of elderly immigrants: Who will bear the burden? *Public Administration Review, 63*, 79–89.

Aranda, M. P., Ray, L. A., Al-Snih, S., Ottenbacher, K. J., & Markides, K. S. (2011). The protective effect of the neighborhood composition on increasing frailty among older Mexican Americans: A barrio advantage? *Journal of Aging and Health, 23*(7), 1189–217.

Balibar, E. (2004). *We, the people of Europe? Reflections on transnational citizenship.* Princeton, NJ: Princeton University Press.

Bass, F., & Vekshin, A. (2013). Soaring rate of immigrant parents imperils overhaul boon. In *Bloomberg Report.* New York, NY: Bloomberg, L.P.

Batalova, J. (2012, May 30). *Senior immigrants in the United States.* Washington, DC: Migration Policy Institute. Retrieved May 1, 2014, from www.migrationpolicy.org/article/senior-immigrants-united-states.

Beaverstock, J. V. (2012). Highly skilled international labor migration and world cities: Expatriates, executives and entrepreneurs. In B. Derudder, M. Hoyler, P. J. Taylor, & F. Witlox (Eds.), *International handbook of globalization and world cities.* Cheltenham, UK: Edward Elgar Publishing Limited.

Benítez-Silva, H., Cárceles-Poveda, E., & Eren, S. (2011). *Effects of legal and unauthorized immigration on the U.S. Social Security system.* Ann Arbor, MI: Michigan Retirement Research Center, University of Michigan.

Borjas, G. J., & Katz, L. F. (2007). The evolution of the Mexican-born workforce in the United States. In G. J. Borjas (Ed.), *Mexican immigration to the United States* (pp. 13–55). Chicago, IL: University of Chicago Press.

Broder, T., & Blazer, J. (2011). *Overview of immigrant eligibility for federal programs.* Los Angeles, CA: National Immigration Law Center.

Brown, A., & Patten, E. (2013). *Hispanics of Mexican origin in the United States, 2011.* Washington, DC: Pew Research Hispanic Trends Project.

Brown, P. L. (2009, August 30). Invisible immigrants, old and left with "nobody to talk to." *New York Times.* Retrieved May 1, 2014, from www.nytimes.com/2009/08/31/us/31elder.html?pagewanted=all.

Bryceson, D. F., & Vuorela, U. (Eds.). (2002). *The transnational family: New European frontiers and global networks.* Oxford: Berg.

Caldwell, C. (2009). *Reflections on the revolution in Europe: Immigration, Islam, and the West.* New York, NY: Doubleday.

Carr, S., & Tienda, M. (2013). *Multiplying diversity: Family unification and the regional origins of late-age immigrants, 1981–2009.* Paper presented at the Population Association of America Annual Meeting, New Orleans, LA.

Castells, M. (2000). *The information age: Economy, society and culture, vol. I – The rise of the network society.* Oxford: Blackwell Publishers Ltd.

Castles, S. (2004). Why migration policies fail. *Ethnic and Racial Studies, 27*(2), 205–27.

Combs, S. (2006). *Undocumented immigrants in Texas: A financial analysis of the impact to the State Budget and economy.* Texas Comptroller of Public Accounts. Retrieved April 18, 2014, from www.window.state.tx.us/specialrpt/undocumented/.

Congressional Budget Office. (2007). The impact of unauthorized immigrants on the budgets of state and local governments. In *A Series on Immigration*. Washington, DC: Congressional Budget Office.

Congressional Budget Office. (2011). *Migrants' remittances and related economic flows*. Washington, DC: Congress of the United States.

D'Antonio, W. (2011). New survey offers portrait of U.S. Catholics. In *National Catholic Reporter*. Kansas City, MO: Catholics in America.

Ehrkamp, P., & Leitner, H. (2001). Beyond national citizenship: Turkish immigrants and the (re)construction of citizenship in Germany. *Urban Geography, 24*(2), 127–46.

Eschbach, K., Ostir, G. V., Patel, K. V., Markides, K. S., & Goodwin, J. S. (2004). Neighborhood context and mortality among older Mexican Americans: Is there a barrio advantage? *American Journal of Public Health, 94*, 1807–12.

Espenshade, T. J., Baraka, J. L., & Huber, G. A. (1997). Implication of the 1996 Welfare and Immigration Reform Acts for U.S. immigration. *Population and Development Review, 23*, 769–801.

Feinleib, J., & Warner, D. (2005). *The impact of immigration on Social Security and the national economy*. Washington, DC: Social Security Advisory Board.

Gerst, K., Miranda, P. Y., Eschbach, K., Sheffield, K. M., Peek, M. K., & Markides, K. S. (2011). Protective neighborhoods: Neighborhood proportion of Mexican Americans and depressive symptoms among very old Mexican Americans. *Journal of the American Geriatric Society, 59*(2), 353–8.

Guzmán, J. C., & Jara, R. C. (September 2012). *The economic benefits of passing the DREAM Act*. Washington D.C.: Center for American Progress.

Hirschman, C. (2004). The role of religion in the origins and adaptation of immigrant groups in the United States. *International Migration Review, 38*(3), 1206–33.

Huntington, S. P. (2004). The Hispanic challenge. *Foreign Policy, 141*, 30–45.

Joshi, N. (2013). *Federal Budget: Do immigrants drive up deficits? Immigrant-driven demographic trends can ease our long-term structural fiscal problems*. Washington, DC: Business Forward.

Kanaiaupuni, S. (2000). *Leaving parents behind: Migration and elderly living arrangements in Mexico*. Madison, WI: University of Wisconsin.

Kitroeff, N. (2013, April 27). Immigrants pay lower fees to send money home, helping to ease poverty. *New York Times*, p. 1.

Lee, R. D., & Miller, T. W. (1997). The current fiscal impact of immigrants and their descendants: Beyond the immigrant household. In J. P. Smith & B. Edmonston (Eds.), *Panel on the demographic and economic impacts of immigration* (pp. 182–204). Washington, DC: National Academies Press.

Maldonado, R., & Hayem, M. (2013). Remittances to Latin America and the Caribbean in 2012: Differing behavior across subregions. Washington, DC: Multilateral Investment Fund, Inter-American Development Bank.

Massey, D., Alarcón, R., Durand, J., & González, H. (1987). *Return to Aztlán: The social process of international migration from Western Mexico*. Berkeley, CA: University of California Press.

Massey, D. S., Durand, J., & Malone, N. J. (2003). *Beyond smoke and mirrors: Mexican immigration in an era of economic integration*. New York, NY: Russell Sage Foundation.

Massey, D. S., & Pren, K. A. (2012). Origins of the New Latino underclass. *Race and Social Problems, 4*(1), 5–17.

McNatt, R., & Benassi, F. (2006). Econ 101 on illegal immigrants. In *Bloomberg Businessweek*. New York, NY: Standard & Poor's RatingsDirect.

Miranda, C. O. (1998). United States Commission on Immigration Reform: The interim and final reports. *Santa Clara Law Review, 38*(3), 645–89.

Miranda, L. (2010). *Get the facts on the DREAM Act*. Washington, DC: The White House Blog.

Montes de Oca Zavala, V. (Ed.). (2008). Historias detenidas en el tiempo: El fenómeno migratorio desde la mirada de la vejez en Guanajuato. León, Guanajuato, México: Gobierno de Estado de Guanajuato.

Montes de Oca Zavala, V., Molina, A., & Avalos, R. (2008). *Migración, redes transacionales y envejecimiento: Estudio de las redes familiares transnacionales de la vejez en Guanajuato*. México, D.F.: Universidad Nacional Autónoma de México, Instituto de Investigaciones Sociales, Govierno del Estado de Guanajuato.

Nam, Y. (2008). Welfare reform and older immigrants' health insurance coverage. *American Journal of Public Health, 98*(11), 2029–34.

Nam, Y., & Jung, H. J. (2008). Welfare reform and older immigrants: Food Stamp program participation and food insecurity. *The Gerontologist, 48*(1), 42–50.

Nicholas, J., & Wiseman, M. (2009). Elderly poverty and Supplemental Security Income. In *Social Security bulletin*. Baltimore, MD: U.S. Social Security Administration.

Office of Immigration Statistics. (2009). *Persons obtaining legal permanent resident status by broad class of admission and selected demographic characteristics: Fiscal year 2008*. Washington, DC: U.S. Department of Homeland Security.

Pew Research Center for the People & the Press. (2013). "Borders first": A dividing line in immigration debate. Washington, DC: Pew Research Center.

Porter, E., & Malkin, E. (2005, August 4). Mexicans at home abroad. *New York Times*. Retrieved May 1, 2014, from www.nytimes.com/2005/08/04/business/worldbusiness/04retire.html?pagewanted=all.

Portes, A., & Rumbaut, R. G. (2006). *Immigrant America: A portrait*. Berkeley, CA: University of California Press.

Sassen, S. J. (2006). *Cities in a world economy*. Thousand Oaks, CA: Pine Forge Press.

Tareen, S. (2008, July 16). Officials hesitant to arrest immigrants who seek church sanctuary. *USA Today*. Retrieved April 18, 2014, from: http://usatoday30.usatoday.com/news/religion/2008-07-16-immigration-churches_N.htm.

Terrazas, A. (2009). Older immigrants in the United States. Washington, DC.

Torres-Gil, F., Suh, E. H., & Angel, J. L. (2013). Working across borders: The social and policy implications of aging in the Americas. *Journal of Cross-Cultural Gerontology, 28*(3), 215–22.

Treas, J. (2007). Older immigrants and U.S. welfare reform. *International Journal of Sociology and Social Policy, 17*(9/10), 8–33.

Treas, J., & Torres-Gil, F. (2009). Immigration and aging: The nexus of complexity and promise. *Generations, 32*(4), 6–10.

U.S. Bureau of Consular Affairs. (2013). *Immigrant investor visas*. Washington, DC: U.S. Department of State.

U.S. Census Bureau. (2012). *Native and foreign-born populations by selected characteristics*. Washington, DC: Statistical Abstracts of the United States.

U.S. Citizenship and Immigration Services. (2009). *Public charge*. Washington, DC: U.S. Department of Homeland Security.

U.S. Department of State. (2012). Immigrant and nonimmigrant visas issued at foreign service posts fiscal years 2008–2012. In *Multiyear report*. Washington, DC: Office of the Inspector General.

U.S. Department of State. (2013a). *Overview: Family-based immigrant visas.* Washington, DC: Office of the Inspector General.

U.S. Department of State. (2013b). *Statutory numbers*. Washington, DC: Office of the Inspector General.

Villagran, L. (2013). Slow U.S. growth, zero immigration hurt remittances to Mexico. *SmartPlanet*. Retrieved May 1, 2014, from www.smartplanet.com/blog/global-observer/slow-us-growth-zero-immigration-hurt-remittances-to-mexico/9904.

CHAPTER 5

Major Physical and Mental Health Conditions and Barriers to Care

HAUNTED BY DIABETES

Maria Gutierrez has arrived to pick up her father, Eliseo, from the dialysis center at 11 a.m., as she does three times a week. Maria works as a supervisor in the building in which she and her only son, Michael, live so she has some flexibility in her work schedule. Michael's father abandoned the family several years ago and Maria is raising the boy alone. Eliseo is 58 years old. He is a member of a group of friends who, if one saw them, one might imagine are veterans of some terrible war. Almost half are missing limbs and others are nearly blind. These are not war injuries, though; they are the result of amputations and diabetic retinopathy. The war these men have fought, and which most may well lose, is against an insidious foe that plagues Hispanics and other low-income populations. That enemy is diabetes. Hispanics are nearly twice as likely to be diagnosed with diabetes and they are one-and-a-half times as likely to die of the disease as non-Hispanic Whites. Eliseo does not have health insurance, but since he has contributed to Social Security for more than 20 years, Medicare pays for his dialysis treatments even though he is not yet 65.

Maria's son Michael, who is 12 years old but only in the fifth grade, was recently referred by the school nurse to the local clinic because of dark patches that had appeared on the back of his neck and on his groin. The doctor diagnosed the condition as *Acanthosis Nigricans*, a condition that is increasingly common among young Hispanics. Michael is 5 feet 2 inches tall and weighs over 160 pounds. Maria always realized that he was heavy, but then so are other members of the family, as well as most everyone in the Mexican neighborhood in which they live. The doctor explained to Maria that the skin condition is the result of Michael's obesity and indicates that he is "insulin resistant," which means that his body does not respond to insulin in the way that it should. Michael, like other individuals with this condition, is at elevated risk of Type II diabetes, a condition that until recently was extremely rare in children, but which is becoming more common among young Hispanics.

Each of Eliseo's dialysis sessions lasts for 4 hours and he finds them exhausting and demoralizing. He feels like a prisoner. The joviality Eliseo used to display at family events and with his friends at the local cantina are gone. He is clearly depressed and often speaks of stopping the treatment and moving on to the next life. Maria is also exhausted since, as the responsible sibling in her family, she is the one who usually takes Eliseo to treatment and picks him up when it is over. Her older brother is unemployed and spends his time with friends. Her younger sister is married to a man who does not let her interact with the family.

Eliseo is like many individuals who do not have health insurance and who, consequently, did not receive the preventive medical care that might have prevented the serious complications that he is experiencing. He saw a doctor a few times during his life, usually for acute illnesses or for injuries he suffered at his construction job. He was in his early 50s when his diabetes was diagnosed after he discovered that he had no feeling in his feet and a toe became seriously infected. He had clearly been diabetic for years. The doctors also discovered that Eliseo had seriously elevated blood pressure and high cholesterol. When he was diagnosed, Eliseo and his wife Carmen were given the name of a nutrition counselor whom they never contacted. He also immediately began insulin injections, and with Carmen's help he has been fairly diligent in taking the drug. Even so, he has ended up in the emergency room several times because of overdoses.

The dietary advice that the doctor gave the family was very difficult for Eliseo to follow. He had grown up with white flour tortillas and any number of delicious Mexican pastries. He loves tamales, chicharones (fried pork fat), refried beans (lard and mashed pinto beans), Mexican candies, and much else that is high in fat, sodium, calories, and carbohydrates. Sticking to the sort of diet that is necessary to control diabetes, which requires avoiding most of what gives Eliseo pleasure, has been very difficult. Despite medical intervention Eliseo's disease continues to progress and his doctor has told him that he may lose his feet in the not too distant future. That future is not bright for Eliseo or for his grandson.

A LONGER BUT SICKER LIFE?

Hispanics as a group enjoy remarkably long lives. Despite a socioeconomic profile that includes low levels of education and income and little wealth, Hispanics' life expectancy at birth and at older ages is similar and perhaps even superior to that of non-Hispanic Whites (Arias, Eschbach, Schauman, Backlund, & Sorlie, 2010; Markides & Eschbach, 2005). This advantage is clearly not the result of greater access to health care; Hispanics, and especially those of Mexican origin, are far less likely than non-Hispanic Whites to have health insurance or to receive preventive care (Escarce & Kapur, 2006; Parra & Espino, 1992; Schur, Albers, & Berk, 1995; Treviño & Coustasse, 2007). Of course, not all Hispanics lack health insurance. Middle-class Hispanics enjoy the same access to high-quality health care as any other citizen with sufficient resources (Quesnel-Vallée, Farrah, & Jenkins, 2011). Yet, as we document, at all ages Hispanics are at greater risk than non-Hispanic Whites of lacking adequate health insurance coverage. This risk begins in childhood, during which Hispanic children are particularly dependent on Medicaid since many Hispanic families lack private or group coverage. Even though many Hispanic children qualify for public health coverage on the basis of their family's low income, a substantial fraction do not participate (Angel, Lein, & Henrici, 2006).

The risk of lacking health insurance continues through the adult working years and after age 65, when all citizens become eligible for Medicare, because Hispanics are less likely than non-Hispanic Whites to have supplemental "Medigap" insurance (Angel, Angel, & Lein, 2007). For retirees, the lack of a Medigap policy, a label that refers to supplemental insurance that covers what Medicare does not pay, can have significant negative financial and health consequences. Medicare does not pay for long-term care, routine dental or eye care, hearing aids, or routine foot care. In addition, one must pay coinsurance for hospital stays, and a premium and deductible for basic medical care. These costs can be quite high for an older individual or couple with a limited income.

In this chapter we review the literature on the major health risks that Hispanics face as a result of the disadvantages they experience throughout life. As we shall see, a longer life does not necessarily mean a better or healthier life. Later in the chapter we present new data that shows that despite their relatively long average lifespans, Hispanics spend a large fraction of the years past 65 in poor health and plagued by functional limitations (Angel, Torres-Gil, & Markides, 2012; Angel, Angel, & Hill, 2013; Markides, Eschbach, Ray, & Peek, 2007; Palloni, 2007). This fact has important implications for individuals, their families, and society at large. A long period of poor health creates serious support and care needs and can result in large financial burdens for everyone. Faced by serious illness, an older person's or couple's assets can be rapidly depleted, leaving little to pass on to future generations. For adult children who assume even part of the financial burden of caring for an older infirm parent, the cost of acute and long-term care can undermine their ability to educate their children and prepare for their own retirements. Hospitals that provide uncompensated emergency care face serious losses and, ultimately, insured patients and taxpayers must pick up the tab.

Obviously many individuals live long and healthy lives and remain engaged and active until just before they die. Unfortunately, though, loss is inevitable and at some point that loss is total. The loss of one's physical vitality is serious in itself, but it is accompanied by other losses, including the death of friends, siblings, and others who were part of one's life. As one ages one is forced to witness the world in which one lived pass into history. The impact of these losses can be exacerbated by another important loss, the loss of cognitive ability. Neurons do not regenerate and the longer one lives the greater the risk that one loses important parts of the self, including memory, the ability to recognize others, and the ability to deal with the world. Declining cognitive ability, in addition to the other losses that one experiences as one enters the later years of life, can result in severe depression (Blazer, 2003). Cognitive decline and depression, which can be made worse by isolation, are the most common mental health problems among older populations. Dealing with cognitive impairment, depression, and isolation are major challenges in providing high-quality care to seriously impaired older people.

A major focus of recent research on the aging process has been on "active life expectancy," a label that refers to the fraction of life after age 65 in which one is healthy and active and capable of independent living. Ideally, this period of life should make up the majority of the years after age 65. We would all like to enjoy excellent health and remain vital and active well into our 90s and then die suddenly and painlessly. For some lucky individuals such a long and healthy life is a reality, but for others the reality is many years of poor health, functional limitation, and dependency. Before we examine active life expectancy, though, we begin with an examination of group differences in total life expectancy at birth and at age 65.

LIFE EXPECTANCY AT BIRTH AND 65

Over the last century life expectancy at birth has increased for all racial and ethnic groups. In the United States in 2010 average life expectancy for the population at large was 79, compared to slightly over 70 in 1970 (National Center for Health Statistics, 2013). Average life expectancy at birth is projected to climb to over 80 by 2030 and to 83 by 2050 (U.S. Census Bureau, 2008). The decreases in mortality that increased lifespans during the 19th and 20th centuries resulted from technological progress and productivity gains that improved standards of living. The health of the human population has also benefited greatly from improvements in public health and medical science (Bharmal, Tseng, Kaplan, & Wong, 2012; Easterlin, 2000; Elo, 2009; Morbidity and Mortality Weekly Report, 1999; Preston, 1996; Vaupel, 2010; Wilmoth, 1998). Yet, significant gender differences remain. As Figure 5.1 shows, men have not benefited to the same

2010   2050

76 Years   81 Years   81 Years   85 Years

FIGURE 5.1 *Projections of Gender Differences in Life Expectancy at Birth.*

Source: U.S. Census Bureau (2008, table 10).

degree as women. Between 2010 and 2050, life expectancy for males is projected to increase from just under 76 to nearly 81, while for females it is projected to increase from nearly 81 to over 85. Extreme old age, then, is female territory and the important question we must ask has to do with the quality of those additional years, a topic we address later.

Even though all groups have experienced declines in mortality and increases in life expectancy at birth and age 65, major racial and ethnic differences persist, some of which are counterintuitive (Olshansky et al., 2013). For both men and women, Asian Americans enjoy the longest life expectancy of any racial or ethnic group, although given their diversity we will not deal with them in any detail (Office of Minority Health, 2012a). We focus instead on Black and Hispanic patterns and compare those to the life expectancies of non-Hispanic Whites. In 2010 life expectancy at birth for non-Hispanic Black males was 71, while for non-Hispanic White males it was 76 (Murphy, Xu, & Kochanek, 2013). Life expectancy at birth is heavily influenced by infant mortality, which is higher among Blacks than among Whites. Lower life expectancy at birth among Blacks reflects higher infant mortality, as well as higher mortality at later ages (Xu, Kochanek, Murphy, & Tejada-Vera, 2010). A history of racism and exclusion, as well as high rates of other health risk factors including poverty and the stress associated with it, largely explain the lower life expectancy at birth among Blacks.

Given the fact that Hispanics share a similarly disadvantaged socioeconomic profile, and have low levels of education on average, we would expect their mortality experience to be similar to that of Blacks, but it is not. Among Hispanic males life expectancy at birth was 79 in 2010, 2 years longer than that of non-Hispanic Whites. This advantage, which has been referred to as the Hispanic "epidemiological paradox," has no obvious explanation, although there is evidence that it reflects lower rates of smoking among Hispanics (Markides, Coreil, & Ray, 1987; Pérez-Stable, Marín, Marín, Brody, & Benowitz, 1990). As we showed earlier, on average women live longer than men among all groups, but the racial and ethnic differences we find among men hold for women as well. This means that Hispanic females enjoy longer lives than non-Hispanic White or Black women (U.S. Census Bureau, 2008). In 2010, while non-Hispanic White women had a life expectancy at birth of 81, and Black women a life expectancy of 78, Hispanic females had a life expectancy of 84 (National Center for Health Statistics, 2013).

In addition to race, ethnicity, and gender, nativity status also affects longevity, as well as health in general, as we discuss later. In one study, Black and Hispanic immigrants had, respectively, a 52% and 26% lower chance of dying of any cause during a 10-year period than their U.S.-born counterparts (Singh & Siahpush, 2002). Age-adjusted mortality is lower in foreign-born than American-born Mexican-origin elders (Markides & Eschbach, 2005). This advantage dissipates the longer one lives in the United States (Angel, Angel, Díaz Venegas, & Bonazzo, 2010; Hummer, Powers, Pullum, Gossman, & Frisbie, 2007; Landale, Oropesa, & Gorman, 2000). For example, in a study of Mexican immigrants aged 60 and older, those who arrived in the United States before the age of 20 had higher cardiovascular mortality than those who came at older ages (Eschbach, Stimpson, Kuo, & Goodwin, 2007).

As we mentioned, life expectancy at birth is heavily influenced by infant mortality, so life expectancy at later ages tells us more about survival into old age. As Figure 5.2 shows, among men who survive to age 65, Hispanics can expect to live an additional 19 years, while non-Hispanic Whites can expect to live 18 years longer and Blacks 16 years longer (National Center for Health Statistics, 2013). Among women who survive to 65, Hispanics can expect to live 22 years longer, while non-Hispanic Whites can expect to live 20 years longer and Blacks 19 years longer (National Center for Health Statistics, 2013).

Although it is possible that the Hispanic advantage in life expectancy reflects data problems, such as the potential underreporting of deaths among Hispanics, analyses from the National Center for Health Statistics indicate that the

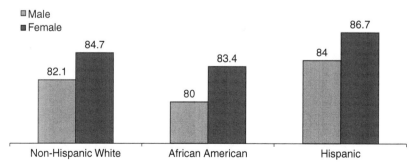

FIGURE 5.2 *U.S. Life Expectancy at Age 65 by Race/Ethnicty and Gender: 2006.*
Source: Arias et al. (2010).

data is largely accurate (Arias et al., 2010). Others reach a similar conclusion (Eschbach, Kuo, & Goodwin, 2006). What the evidence consistently reveals, then, is a Hispanic mortality advantage at birth (Hummer et al., 2007) and later in life (Hummer, Benjamins, & Rogers, 2004; Markides & Eschbach, 2005). This relatively consistent finding remains enigmatic, though, given the relative low levels of income and wealth, as well as the low levels of education among this population.

Although no single factor explains these racial, ethnic, and nativity differences in mortality, it is clear that achieved characteristics such as income, education, and marital status contribute to the gap (Crimmins, Hayward, & Seeman, 2004; Williams & Collins, 1995). Higher levels of education are associated with a lower risk of premature death for all groups, but the educational advantage differs among groups. Differentials in life expectancy between those with the highest levels of education and those with the lowest levels are greatest for non-Hispanic Whites and lowest for Hispanics (Olshansky et al., 2013). As we discussed in Chapter 2, average educational levels are extremely low among Hispanics and there may simply be less variation to give rise to large educational differences (Geruso, 2013).

As we discuss in the next section, even though Hispanics live longer than non-Hispanics, those extra years are often characterized by ill health. Among Hispanics, the illness profile of those of Mexican origin, the largest subgroup, reflects the paradox of longer lifespans but poorer health. Mexican-origin Hispanics suffer from higher rates of various chronic physical health conditions, including diabetes, than non-Hispanic Whites, whom they nonetheless outlive (Ionnatta, 2002).

ACTIVE LIFE EXPECTANCY

The objective of public health and medicine generally is to keep individuals as healthy as possible for as long as possible. Among health researchers and medical professionals the objective is to increase what is termed "active life expectancy." This label refers to the fraction of years one survives after some particular age, usually 65, in good health and with a high level of functioning. A preliminary step in increasing active life expectancy is to understand those factors associated with optimal active life expectancy, a number of which are associated with race and Hispanic ethnicity (Crimmins & Beltran-Sanchez, 2011; Eschbach, Al-Snih, Markides, & Goodwin, 2007; Hayward, Warner, Crimmins, & Hidajat, 2007).

Before discussing racial and ethnic differences in morbidity, we must note that a new study of active life expectancy among Mexican-origin elders provides sobering news concerning the possibility of increasing active life expectancy. Although Mexican-origin Hispanics' life expectancy at birth and at age 65 is comparable to or better than that of non-Hispanic Whites, almost half of the years past 65 are lived with serious physical impairment (Angel et al., 2013a,b). As in the determination of overall life expectancy, gender and nativity interact to affect active life expectancy, often in some unexpected ways. For example, although overall life expectancy at age 65 is highest for foreign-born Mexican-origin women and lowest for native-born males, foreign-born women on average spend close to two-thirds of their additional life in a functionally impaired state (Angel, Angel, & Hill, 2013a,b). Protracted periods of functional impairment characterize the other gender and nativity groups as well.

RACIAL AND ETHNIC DIFFERENTIALS IN ILLNESS AND DISABILITY

Mortality is just one indicator of a group's health and quality of life. As the above-mentioned study of active life expectancy demonstrates, one can spend many years with significant illness. The distribution of disease and chronic illness reveals a great deal about the general health of a population, as well as its system of social stratification. As we have shown in earlier chapters, economic, political, and institutional factors that perpetuate poverty and disadvantage among certain groups can give rise to a lifetime of stigma, financial hardship, and helplessness. These factors also exacerbate well-documented racial and ethnic health differentials in the latter part of the life course. Let us summarize the major physical and mental health problems among Hispanics and their implications for later life.

DIABETES

Type II diabetes, which is also referred to as adult-onset diabetes to differentiate it from juvenile diabetes, is a major cause of illness and death among Hispanics (Office of Minority Health, 2013). Diabetes, of course, is also a major problem among Blacks and individuals with low incomes in general, although it afflicts affluent non-minority adults as well (Abraham & Rozmus, 2012; Office of Minority Health, 2012b). Diabetes can result in blindness, amputations, and kidney disease, and is a major risk factor for cardiovascular disease (Katon et al., 2004). Diabetes contributes to a large fraction of deaths from heart disease and stroke (Centers for Disease Control and Prevention, 2011). Hispanic adults are nearly twice as likely as non-Hispanic White adults to develop diabetes and they develop it earlier (Office of Minority Health, 2013; Song, 2008).

Within the Hispanic population diabetes appears to affect certain areas and groups more than others. Mexican-origin individuals experience particularly high rates (Black, Ray, & Markides, 1999). The disease is two to three times more prevalent along the U.S./Mexico border area than in the general U.S. population or in Mexico (Bliss, 2010). Nearly 16% of the adult population, or about 1.2 million people, who live along the border report diabetes, compared to slightly over 8% in Mexico and approximately 5% in the United States as a whole (Bliss, 2010; Pan American Health Organization, 2010). As in other groups, among Mexican-origin adults on the border, diabetes is linked to low socio-economic status and low levels of education (Martinez & Bader, 2007). In a study of the lower Rio Grande Valley both diagnosed and undiagnosed diabetes occurred at significantly higher rates among those who earned less than the median annual household income than among those with higher incomes (Fisher-Hoch et al., 2010). Long-standing diabetes has been associated with an increase of disability and a more rapid decline in functional capacity among Mexican Americans aged 60 and older (Wu et al., 2003) and among African Americans aged 65 and older (Blazer, Moody-Ayers, Craft-Morgan, & Burchett, 2002).

A major indicator of the growing magnitude of the problem of diabetes among Hispanics and other low-income groups is the increase in the prevalence of Type II diabetes among adolescents and young adults (Abraham & Rozmus, 2012). Type I diabetes, or juvenile-onset diabetes, is a congenital illness, meaning it is present from birth. Type II diabetes occurs later in life, usually in later adulthood, and is associated with obesity. Until recently, Type II diabetes was thought not to occur in children or adolescents. As in our opening vignette, though, Type II illness is becoming more prevalent among adolescents, and is often associated with minority group status and obesity (Brickman, Huang, Silverman, & Metzger, 2010; Hu, 2011; Kong et al., 2007).

Historically, poor populations have been underweight as they struggled to get enough food to survive. In earlier centuries, the wealthy were overweight and suffered from gout and the other diseases that result from a rich diet. Today, obesity is a scourge of low-income populations (Hu, 2011). Shopping at organic and specialty markets, or even purchasing fruits and vegetables at the supermarket, can be more expensive than buying fast food or foods high in calories, fats, salt, and carbohydrates. What is clear, though, is that high-calorie diets are associated with higher rates of hypertension and diabetes. What makes the situation worse is the fact that among Hispanics Type II diabetes is manifesting earlier in life (Song, 2008). Given their high rates of diabetes and the earlier age at onset of the disease, the Mexican-origin advantage in life expectancy that is common today may decrease in years to come and compromise the quality of life of older Mexican-origin individuals.

The ravages of diabetes can be controlled or at least minimized through aggressive and continuous management. One must carefully watch one's diet and take one's medication. Compliance with diabetes control regimes, though, differs among racial and ethnic groups. Compared to non-Hispanic Whites Hispanics with diabetes engage in less self-monitoring to keep track of their blood sugar levels (Morrow, Haidet, Skinner, & Naik, 2008). Less aggressive monitoring can lead one to be less careful with medication adherence (Herrera et al., 2011). It is also associated with less intensive use of preventive health measures, which increases the risk of complications and disability (Fitten et al., 2008; Katon et al., 2004).

DEPRESSION

Mental illness is a common and serious problem in all nations of the world (Kessler & Ustun, 2008). Certain mental health specialists estimate that over one-half of adults in the United States will suffer from a serious mental illness at some point in their life (Hyde, 2011). Depression is perhaps the most common mental health problem that compromises the quality of life and the productivity of a large number of people. Major depressive disorder affects approximately 14.8 million American adults, or nearly 7%

of the population aged 18 and older, each year (Kessler, Chiu, Demler, & Walters, 2005; National Institute of Mental Health, 2013). The prevalence of depression is higher among Latinos than among non-Hispanic Whites, but lower than among Blacks (Centers for Disease Control, 2010). Mexican-origin women have higher rates of depression than men (Vega & Amaro, 1998). Aging magnifies these ethnic-based disparities in depression. Older Mexican-origin individuals suffer from higher rates of depression than older non-Hispanics (González, Haan, & Hinton, 2001).

Despite a high prevalence of mental illness, less than one-third of American adults with mental disorders that affect their daily functioning receive treatment (Messias, Eaton, Nestadt, Bienvenu, & Samuels, 2007; National Institute of Mental Health, 2013). Some of these individuals may self-medicate. Almost 90% of individuals who need substance abuse treatment do not receive it (Hyde, 2011). Hispanics and African Americans face many barriers to the recognition and treatment of major depression in clinical settings and consequently seriously underutilize mental health services (Cabassa, Zayas, & Hansen, 2006). In one study that evaluated differences in access to treatment for depression among adults from different racial and ethnic groups, as well as the quality of the treatment they received, researchers found that almost two-thirds of Latinos and over half of African Americans, as opposed to 40% of non-Latino Whites, did not receive treatment, and the treatment they received was of lower quality (Alegría et al., 2008).

Many factors are associated with the lack of access to appropriate mental health care. Underrecognition of depression in adult Hispanic Americans may be related to lack of insurance, a lack of English ability, a lack of health literacy, a tendency to somatize, that is to present psychological problems physically, and culturally specific ways of expressing emotional distress (Angel & Williams, 2013). Lower acculturation is associated with higher rates of depressive affect, which may be the result of cultural barriers to treatment encountered by immigrants and less-acculturated older Mexican-origin individuals, as well as to their poorer health status (González et al., 2001). Many Latinos are hesitant to accept help from a mental health care provider because of the stigma surrounding mental illness. The stigma of mental illness and the reluctance to get treatment are not unique to Latinos, of course. However, research suggests that it may represent a more serious barrier to care among Latinos. In a recent study, 200 low-income, Spanish-speaking Hispanic patients in Los Angeles who were being treated for depression in primary care clinics were screened for depression using Patient Health Questionnaires. Those patients who reported higher levels of perceived stigma associated with mental illness were less likely than those who perceived less stigma to disclose their diagnosis to their family and friends. They were also less likely to take prescribed medication or to keep scheduled appointments with primary care physicians (Vega, Rodriguez, & Ang, 2010).

Other studies indicate that primary care physicians frequently miss or misdiagnose symptoms of depression and anxiety (Eisenberg, 1992).

DEMENTIA AND DISABILITY

As we see, then, as they age Hispanics suffer disproportionately from a number of psychiatric and physical conditions that seriously compromise functioning (Markides, Rudkin, Angel, & Espino, 1997; National Institute on Aging, 2012). Among the most significant of these are cognitive impairments. Compared to non-Hispanic Whites, Hispanics are more likely to develop mild cognitive impairment, as well as Alzheimer's disease (Manly & Mayeux, 2004). Hispanics are at least one-and-a-half times more likely than non-Hispanic Whites to develop Alzheimer's disease or other serious dementias (Alzheimer's Association, 2010; Gurland et al., 1999). In a study of older Latinos in Sacramento, California, researchers found that the rate of cognitive impairment was higher in Mexican Americans than other racial and ethnic groups (Wu, Haan, Liang, Gonzalez, & Herman, 2003).

As with diabetes, Hispanics manifest cognitive impairments at earlier ages. Among Hispanics the onset of Alzheimer's disease occurs an average of almost 7 years earlier than among non-Hispanic Whites (Clark et al., 2005). In clinical settings Puerto Rican immigrants had an earlier age of onset of Alzheimer's disease, more cognitive impairment generally, and more serious impairment than non-Hispanic Whites and Blacks (Livney et al., 2011). Among elderly Hispanics, cognitive impairment often occurs in conjunction with physical conditions. Diabetic complications, for example, accompanies serious cognitive decline among Mexican-origin elders (Wu et al., 2003; Mayeda, Haan,

Kanaya, Yaffe, & Neuhaus, 2013; Samper-Ternent, Snih, Raji, Markides, & Ottenbacher, 2008). Circulation problems, kidney impairment, and depression are the major factors associated with cognitive decline in older Mexican Americans with diabetes (Rotkiewicz-Piorun, Snih, Raji, Kuo, & Markides, 2006).

Cognitive impairment is also associated with frailty and physical disability among older Latinos (González, 2012; Ottenbacher et al., 2009). Although no firm definition of frailty exists, the term refers to a general loss of strength and control, which can result in falls, disability, and mortality. Cognitive impairment, then, accompanies and is a marker for serious physical and mental decline. The condition has serious cost implications for families and for society at large. Impaired elders require ongoing care and many deplete whatever resources they have. Hispanics have, on average, lower levels of education, a risk factor for Alzheimer's disease, which may be one explanation for their higher rates compared to non-Hispanic White elderly (Manly et al., 2008). Health care expenses for dementia in the United States, including nursing and home health care, were in excess of $156 billion in 2010.

SOCIAL AND BEHAVIORAL DETERMINANTS OF HEALTH AND ILLNESS

Although gender, race, and Hispanic ethnicity are independently associated with differential morbidity and mortality risks, they are also proxies for other correlated social and economic risk factors. In explaining disparities in morbidity and mortality one's social location matters. As is the case for mortality, low educational levels, poverty, and other social class factors consistently emerge as significant individual risk factors for illness. Education is one of the strongest predictors of morbidity, as well as mortality outcomes, and differences in educational levels account for a substantial amount of the differences between groups in illness and death. Consistent findings of large racial and ethnic differentials in physical and mental illness, as well as cognitive functioning, have resulted in an increase in the number of bio-behavioral studies focused on the unique risk factors associated with race and Hispanic ethnicity (Ferraro, 2011). In general these studies show that low social standing, economic hardship, and high levels of stress during crucial developmental states affect one's brain and body to increases one's vulnerability to infection and illness later in life (Williams & Sternthal, 2010).

This research provides insights into how a growing range of social factors can affect physiological processes to undermine health and cause illness. These include social and economic status, poverty, deprivation at critical developmental stages, and inequality. Other factors related to gender and sex roles, immigration history and acculturation, social ties and social support, and factors related to the quality of the physical and social environment also affect health. Psychosocial processes, including social cohesion, social capital, and collective efficacy are also important (Hernandez, 2006). The psychological and physiological mechanisms through which these social factors affect health are as yet poorly understood, but progress is being made. Scientists have, for example, identified markers of chronic inflammation, a serious risk factor for heart disease and diabetes, in individuals who have experienced chronic social stress in childhood and adolescence (Gianaros & Manuck, 2010).

This evidence suggests that low social status increases chronic stress that can magnify group-based disparities in health at older ages (Ferraro, 2011). Children whose families experience serious financial hardship while they are young and vulnerable can suffer life-long health consequences. The cause of these negative effects may operate through subjective mechanisms. The lack of material security can increase feelings of powerlessness and a lack of control that place one at increased risk of premature death (Hayward & Gorman, 2004). These findings are buttressed by classic research that demonstrated that a lack of a sense of control over one's life and the hopelessness it fosters can undermine mental and physical health (Seligman, 1975, 1991).

More recent evidence for the importance of perceptions is provided by research that suggests that the subjective experience of racism experienced by African Americans has adverse health consequences (Williams & Sternthal, 2010). For several decades sociologists have comprehensively cataloged social stressors associated with racial disparities in health. This research has focused on how discrimination and racism affect the onset of disease (Williams & Mohammed, 2009). Understanding the links between racism, stigma, marginalization, and disease requires complex study designs. Stress, whatever its social source, can operate indirectly through physiological mechanisms that can mask the social aspects of the disease process. Stress and social marginalization, for example, can increase an individual's propensity to engage in unhealthy behaviors.

Race and Hispanic ethnicity are associated with differential rates of smoking, excessive drinking, and overeating, but not necessarily in consistently negative ways (Boardman, Barnes, Wilson, Evans, & Leon, 2013). Hispanics, for example, are less likely to smoke than other groups, which may be one important factor accounting for their favorable mortality. Researchers have also identified cultural and psychosocial resources that foster resilience. For example, certain researchers have found that religious involvement can protect health in the face of racial discrimination (Bierman, 2006). In general, though, it is increasingly clear that the harmful health effects of internalized racism can undermine health (Williams & Leavell, 2012).

CULTURAL DETERMINANTS OF HEALTH

A long tradition in medical anthropology and sociology demonstrates that the recognition of symptoms, the labeling of disease states, and the individual and social response to them are affected by culturally based cognitive schemata. This term "schemata" or "schema" refers to structured conceptions about disease processes, their causes, and the appropriate response to them that one shares with one's cultural group (Angel & Williams, 2013). These schemata influence how one responds to symptoms and disease and also how others react to an ill individual. Western societies, for example, tend to differentiate between the mind and the body, or the psyche and the soma to use their Greek and Latin roots. In Western cultures, mental illness is often dealt with as if it is independent of physical illness, an assumption that our earlier discussion of the co-occurrence of depression and diseases like diabetes leads us to question. Other cultures do not differentiate as clearly between physical and mental illness and view both as part of the same disease processes.

What is of relevance in the current discussion is the existence of what are termed "culture-bound syndromes." This label refers to illnesses that are recognized by members of a particular cultural group, and that may have culturally unique explanations and treatments. Exhibit 5.1 illustrates examples of culture-bound syndromes in various cultural groups. We do not wish to suggest that

Exhibit 5.1 Examples of Culture-bound Syndromes

CONDITION	RACE/ETHNIC GROUP	DESCRIPTION
Ataque de Nervios	Hispanic	Out-of-consciousness state resulting from evil spirits. Symptoms include attacks of crying, trembling, uncontrollable shouting, physical or verbal aggression, and intense heat in the chest moving to the head. These *ataques* are often associated with stressful events (e.g., death of a loved one, divorce or separation, or witnessing an accident including a family member).
Falling Out	African American	Seizure-like symptoms resulting from traumatic events, such as robberies.
Ghost Sickness	American Indians	Weakness, dizziness, fainting, anxiety, hallucinations, confusion, and loss of appetite resulting from the action of witches and evil forces.
Mal de ojo	Hispanics	Medical problems, such as vomiting, fever, diarrhea, and mental problems (e.g., anxiety, depression), could result from the *mal de ojo* (evil eye) the individual experienced from another person. The condition is common among infants and children; adults might also experience similar symptoms resulting from this *mal de ojo*.
Wind or Cold Illness	Hispanics Asians	A fear of cold and the wind; feeling weakness and susceptibility to illness resulting from the belief that natural and supernatural elements are not balanced.

Source: Modified from Paniagua (2000)

Hispanics or other racial or ethnic groups are particularly superstitious or that folk medicine is practiced by large numbers of individuals. Most of us have conceptions of disease causation that we receive from our culture and we act in accordance with those beliefs. Almost everyone self-medicates or engages in practices that they believe will maintain optimal health like exercising or eating a particular diet. Even practices and behaviors that are based on scientific medicine makes them no less cultural. We raise the issue of cultural influences on conceptions of health simply because individuals must understand health and disease from some perspective. Older individuals and immigrants may retain more traditional conceptions of the causes of illness and the appropriate treatments than younger people or the native-born.

ACCULTURATION: HEALTH RISK OR PROTECTIVE FACTOR?

As we have noted, in addition to education and income, nativity is associated with differential mortality and health levels. Assimilation and acculturation are important and well-studied aspects of the immigrant experience and help explain why the health of foreign-born and U.S.-born Hispanics differs (Thomson & Hoffman-Goetz, 2009). Although the term "acculturation" refers to the adoption of aspects of the host culture, that process is correlated with economic and social incorporation, which might be referred to as assimilation.

In earlier chapters we introduced the concept of segmented assimilation to emphasize the fact that while some immigrants move into the middle class within one or two generations, others do not (Portes & Zhou, 1993). These different patterns of assimilation could result in different health profiles. Those immigrants who remain at the bottom of the socioeconomic ladder continue to be exposed to the health risks associated with poverty and may even adopt more unhealthful coping behaviors. These less successful immigrants could suffer health declines whereas more successful immigrants do not (Lara, Gamboa, Kahramanian, Morales, & Hayes-Bautista, 2005). Acculturation is a complex concept and process that reflects many other factors that make it sensitive to the ways in which it is measured. It is often operationalized in terms of language proficiency, which is a reflection of one's ability to navigate a complex social and cultural environment. It is also reflected in the age at which an immigrant arrives, which also reflects one's life course stage at migration (Angel, Buckley, & Sakamoto, 2001; Burr & Mutchler, 2003; Cho, Frisbie, Hummer, & Rogers, 2004). Exhibit 5.2 shows a typical scale that measures acculturation in terms of its major theoretical dimensions, which include language, cultural beliefs and values, and social interaction with members from the majority group.

Exhibit 5.2 How do we measure acculturation?

Items in the Final Acculturation and Structural Assimilation Scales: San Antonio Heart Study, San Antonio, Texas, 1979–82
Dimensions Measured, Scale Items, and Scale Score Ranges

I.   Early childhood experience with English versus Spanish language
  1. What was the first language you learned to speak?
  2. What language was spoken in your home when you were a child?
  Scale range: 2–6 points

II. Adult proficiency in English
  1. In your opinion, how well do you understand spoken English?
  2. In your opinion, how well do you speak English?
  3. In your opinion, how well do you read English?
  Scale range: 3–12 points

III. Adult pattern of English versus Spanish language usage
  1. What language do you usually use with your spouse?
  2. What language do you usually use with your children?
  3. What language do you usually use with your parents?
  4. What language do you usually use at family gatherings, such as Christmas or other holidays?
  5. What language do you usually use with most of your friends?
  6. What language do you usually use with most of your neighbors?
  7. What language do you usually use with most of the people at work?
  8. In what language are the TV programs you watch?
  9. In what language are the radio stations you listen to?
  10. In what language are the books and magazines you read?
  Scale range: 10–50 points

IV. Value placed on preserving Mexican cultural origin

1. How important do you feel it is for your children to know something about the history of Mexico?
2. How important do you feel it is for your children to follow Mexican customs and ways of life?
3. How important do you feel it is for your children to celebrate Mexican holidays such as Cinco de Mayo or El Diez y seis de Septiembre?

Scale range: 3–15 points

V. Attitude toward traditional family structure and sex-role organization

1. Knowing your family ancestry or lineage, that is, tracing your family tree, is an important part of family life.
2. It is important to know your cousins, aunts, and uncles and to have a close relationship with them.
3. A person should remember other family members who have passed away on the anniversary of their death, All Soul's Day, or other special occasions.
4. Brothers have a responsibility to protect their sisters while they are growing up.
5. While they are growing up, sisters have an obligation to respect their brother's authority.
6. If they could live anywhere they wanted to, married children should live close to their parents so that they can help each other.
7. In the absence of the father, the most important decisions should be made by the eldest son rather than the mother, if the son is old enough.

Scale range: 7–35 points

Structural Assimilation

I. Childhood interaction with members of mainstream society

1. When you were growing up, were your neighbors mostly Mexican American, mostly Anglo, or about equal numbers of each?
2. When you were growing up, were your schoolmates mostly Mexican American, mostly Anglo, or about equal numbers of each?
3. When you were growing up, were your close, personal friends mostly Mexican American, mostly Anglo, or about equal numbers of each?

Scale range: 3–9 points

II. Adult interaction with members of mainstream society

1. Throughout your adult life, have your neighbors been mostly Mexican American, mostly Anglo, or about equal numbers of each?
2. Throughout your adult life, have your close, personal friends been mostly Mexican American, mostly Anglo, or about equal numbers of each?
3. (Are the people with whom you work closely on the job/ Are the people with whom you worked closely on your last job) mostly Mexican American, mostly Anglo, or about equal numbers of each?

Scale range: 3–9 points

Source: Hazuda, Stern, and Haffner (1988, table 3)

As we have pointed out earlier, immigrants who arrive early in life experience more complete acculturation than those who arrive later in life (Jasso, Massey, Rosenzweig, & Smith, 2004). Consequently, their health is more similar to that of the native-born population than that of the foreign-born (Abraido-Lanza, Chao, & Florez, 2005; Angel et al., 2001; Antecol & Bedard, 2006; Finch & Vega, 2003; Kaestner, Pearson, Keene, & Geronimus, 2009; Kimbro, 2009; Vega & Amaro, 1994). Among Hispanic immigrants certain studies find that longer residence in the United States is associated with poorer health (Cho et al., 2004; Markides et al., 1987). Findings from the Sacramento Area Latino Study of Aging demonstrate the adverse health consequences of "Americanization" in later life. In that study, more acculturated foreign-born Mexican-origin elderly individuals suffered higher rates of both mild and severe cognitive impairment than the native-born or those with lower acculturation scores (Haan et al., 2007).

Several explanations for this convergence have been offered. One relates to the potential effect of "acculturative stress," a term that refers to the stress of adapting to a new culture. For the immigrant adaptation includes the necessity of learning a new language at the same time that they often must work in dangerous and demanding jobs (Abraido-Lanza, Armbrister, Florez, & Aguirre, 2006). Traditionally, when they first arrive immigrants move into the substandard housing that has been abandoned by other groups (Kaestner et al., 2009). As we mentioned earlier, chronic stress has negative physiological and psychological effects that cause excessive wear and tear on the body that can result in illness (Kaestner et al., 2009). High levels of stress may encourage the adoption of risky health behaviors. The loss of the apparent immigrant advantage, then, may be partly attributed to increased rates of smoking, drinking, poor eating habits, and a lack of physical exercise, which we might label the unhealthy American lifestyle (Abraido-Lanza et al., 2005; Antecol & Bedard, 2006; Finch & Vega, 2003; Kaestner et al., 2009; Kimbro, 2009; Vega & Amaro, 1994). For older individuals migration and difficulties in adapting to a new environment can generate unique stresses. Certain evidence suggests that the stresses associated with late-life migration and insertion into a new and unfamiliar environment increases isolation and the risk of depression and poorer health (Angel & Angel, 1992; Angel et al., 2001).

Although migration is clearly stressful for both women and men, it may be especially challenging for women. Women may have less control over important aspects of the process, including the initial decision to migrate. Hispanic females are more likely than men to migrate with their husbands or with other members of their family, or they immigrate to rejoin a spouse who has come earlier (Donato, 2010). Given the fact that they are not in control of the process and are not fully autonomous agents, these women may be especially vulnerable to the negative health consequences of the stresses associated with the process of migration itself, as well as the need to adapt to a new environment (Donato, 2010; Kanaiaupuni, 2000; Salgado de Snyder, 1987).

Although most studies find that acculturation and late arrival have detrimental effects on health, a few studies produce contradictory or counterintuitive results of the negative effect of lifetime assimilation on healthful aging, such as exercise, dietary behaviors, and life satisfaction (Castro, Marsiglia, Kulis, & Kellison, 2010; Teitler, Hutto, & Reichman, 2012). Others have found that among older Mexican-origin immigrants longer residence results in better mental and physical health (González et al., 2009; González et al., 2001). The health advantage they find among longer-term residents may result from the higher socioeconomic status that a longer work history in the United States makes possible (González et al., 2009). The evidence is mixed, however, on the extent to which the retention of traditional behaviors protects health or undermines it. We do not know, for example, whether speaking Spanish at home adversely influences the acquisition of

English-language skills, how it affects educational attainment, or how it affects one's ability to navigate a new institutional environment.

SOCIAL ENGAGEMENT

One potential risk of late-life migration is the possibility that an individual might eventually find him- or herself isolated in a foreign environment as he or she loses the ability to work and interact with others. Far from a community of origin and one's extended family, and unfamiliar with the language of the host country, an older person can find him- or herself spending long hours alone. Migration, or any other disruption to long-standing networks, therefore poses risks. In addition to reducing social isolation and the risk of loneliness, supportive intimate relationships contribute to a strong self-identity that gives life meaning and purpose (Umberson & Montez, 2010). Marriage benefits both men and women at older ages for the simple reason that it increases the number of friends and family that one can turn to in times of need (Waite & Das, 2010). Marital and other sources of social support are crucial in preventing severe stress responses that can increase the risk of illness and death.

Social isolation and loneliness have been shown to increase the risk of physical and mental illnesses in later life (Berntson, 2002). Loneliness also undermines an individual's emotional health more generally. Researchers have found that individuals who score highly on the University of California Los Angeles Loneliness Scale – a widely used assessment scale that asks questions such as "[h]ow often do you feel alone?" or "[h]ow often do you have no one to talk to?" – have poorer diets than those who score low on the scale (Carr & Moorman, 2011; Ye Luo, Hawkley, Waite, & Cacioppo, 2012). As in the case of chronic stress, loneliness can lead to physiological changes that increase the risk of serious chronic conditions. Higher levels of inflammation-inducing substances have been found in the blood of lonely people. Chronic inflammation has been linked to heart disease, arthritis, Type II diabetes, and even suicide attempts. Older individuals who report that they are lonely react more strongly than those who are not lonely to negative events and perceive daily life as more stressful. Through inflammation and other biological avenues these negative affective states, especially when they become chronic, can depress the immune system (Jaremka et al., 2013). Take the loneliness test at 🌐 www.aarp.org/personal-growth/transitions/info-09-2010/How-Lonely-are-You.html.

Perhaps the most serious risk factor for loneliness and depression in later life is the loss of a spouse (Umberson, Wortman, & Kessler, 1992). Unfortunately the loss of a spouse is an age-graded life event that a surviving spouse must endure. Many older individuals must also deal with the loss of adult children. These losses increase the need for social support, but they come at a time when one's social network is inevitably shrinking as a result of the deaths of siblings and friends. Social ties are vitally important for older individuals because of the emotional and social support they provide (Fowler & Christakis, 2008). Even after a spouse dies, the network that couples build when they are together can be mobilized to help deal with the loss of a loved one (Umberson et al., 1992). As we discuss further in Chapter 7, a neighborhood that includes a large number of individuals from the same ethnic group can increase the amount of support available during times of loss. For individuals who outlive their families, non-family members assume a central role. Non-governmental and faith-based organizations are becoming increasingly important in this capacity. We discuss their potential role in eldercare more fully in Chapter 6.

In the case of older immigrants, linguistic isolation, which results when an older individual spends long periods of time without someone with whom he or she can converse because of language differences, can increase loneliness. Not having someone to talk to, and especially someone who not only knows one's language but also one's culture, means that one can be disconnected. Individuals with limited English-language proficiency are clearly at risk (Glymour & Manly, 2008; Woodward et al., 2012). Besides family, friends, and neighbors, the rich network of social interactions in the community are important for older individuals because of the emotional and social support they provide (Falcón, Todorova, & Tucker, 2009). Organizations, such as churches, community centers, and groups such as the Guanajuato clubs we described in Exhibit 4.3, that bring one into contact with others who speak one's language and understand one's culture are especially important for older immigrants because they increase social engagement and reduce the risk of depression and its negative health outcomes (Hill, Burdette, Angel, & Angel, 2006; Hill, Angel, Ellison, & Angel, 2005).

Having greater social capital, in terms of intimate and more casual relationships with a constellation of people, is vital for older individuals because of the emotional and social support they may provide (Christakis & Fowler, 2009; Dilworth-Anderson, Williams, & Gibson, 2002).

THE U.S./MEXICO BORDER: THE MEETING OF TWO WORLDS

All over the world international borders represent unique environments in which different nation states meet. For the most part those borders are political entities rather than physical barriers, and often they separate peoples with similar cultural roots, as in the case of East and West Germany. The southern border of the United States, which is the northern border of Mexico, is such a place. It may coincide with the Rio Grande, known as the Rio Bravo in Mexico, but it is not a physical barrier. The border is a historical and political reality that resulted from conflicts among various nations, including the Lone Star State of Texas in preceding centuries. Even though the line separating the United States from Mexico is in many ways arbitrary, it defines two very different worlds, one rich and one far poorer. It also marks distinct health environments even though the ecological environment on either side of the border is similar.

As we discuss more fully in Chapter 7, the place in which one lives can influence health. That physical location is of course related to numerous social factors that are themselves associated with health. As we mentioned earlier, ethnic enclaves have been shown to protect health, even if they are generally of low socioeconomic status. In addition to characteristics of the communities and neighborhoods in which they live, the larger geographic location also potentially affects health. Hispanics who live in New York, Boston, or Los Angeles are not only different in terms of national origin, they also have different levels of access to medical care and other social services as a result of different state economies and state policies.

The U.S./Mexico border is one of the few frontiers of the world that separates a very rich country from a much poorer one. Although Mexico is classified as a middle-income country its level of wealth and the dynamism of its economy have paled in comparison with those in the United States. Our southern border is quite different than our northern border, which is far less militarized. A large metal wall stands in the middle of a barren wasteland through much of the Rio Grande Valley and the region between Texas and California. At first sight it appears almost to be a war zone. Every day, though, thousands of Mexicans line up on the Mexican side of the border to make the crossing in places where they have a good chance of evading agents of the United States Citizen and Immigration Services (USCIS).

As an economic and social region the border region is both heavily Mexican and poor. Starr, Maverick, and Hidalgo counties in Texas are among the poorest in the nation. At the other end of the border area, Tijuana, Mexico is located across the border from San Diego, California, one of the richest cities in the country. Many other twin cities, such as El Paso, Texas and Juarez, Mexico juxtapose very different worlds. Drug cartels and gang violence make Juarez an internationally recognized murder capital. Violence, though, is only one of the health risks of the region, which is characterized by well-documented and serious public health problems.

Many of the most serious public health problems are related to the extreme poverty of large sections of the border, especially on the Mexican side. These interact with serious environmental and health threats, such as a shortage of clean water and high rates of tuberculosis, diabetes, and substance abuse. The problems of the border take on special importance in light of the fact that border counties continue to experience rapid population growth, despite their limited public health and social service infrastructures. In Texas, a state with a limited social safety network generally, welfare reforms and budget cuts motivated by a need to reduce expenditures on programs like Medicaid have reduced the availability of health care for the poorest residents (Combs, 1998). In 2013 two-and-a-half million people lived in 14 Texas counties along the U.S./Mexico border (Texas State Data Center, 2013). The area suffers from extreme poverty, and a large fraction of these counties have been designated as economically distressed (United States–Mexico Border Health Commission, 2010).

COLONIAS

The border region is also characterized by a unique form of land tenure and home ownership. It is dotted with several thousand "colonias," a Spanish word that means "colonies" and which refers to subdivisions without adequate access to clean water, sewage services, or other essential services. On both the Mexican and U.S. sides of the border adequate housing is in short supply and a large number of families live in substandard housing that they build themselves. (For the Directory of Colonias in Texas see 🌐 www.sos.state.tx. us/border/colonias/reg-colonias/index.shtml.)

Living conditions in colonias have often been likened to those of the Third World (Cisneros, 2001). The area has been plagued by dengue fever and other water-borne diseases (Ramshaw, 2011). Frequent traffic between the United States and Mexico allows any health problem to quickly spread from one side of the Rio Grande to the other (Davidhizar & Bechtel, 1999).

Despite these hardships, the area in South Texas is growing rapidly. In 2011 approximately 2,294 colonias were home to half a million residents (Grinberg, 2011). The population of Starr County, which contains an estimated 55 colonias, grew 13.8% between 1990 and 2000 from 53,597 to 60,968. Neighboring Hidalgo County, home to the largest number of colonias in the state, has grown 36% since 2000 from 569,471 to 774,769 residents.

The poverty and shortages of services in the border region, and especially in colonias, pose serious problems for eldercare. The area was traditionally largely rural and families cared for their elderly members at home. As in other areas, though, the family faces growing challenges in dealing with the problems of elder support alone (Ward, 2007). As the population ages, there is an increasing need for assistance with geriatric primary care services and the coordination of existing services. Standards of living and of health care that might have been inevitable in the past are increasingly unacceptable.

A major barrier to adequate health care in the border region results from relatively low rates of insurance coverage. Adults over the age of 65 are eligible for Medicare coverage if they have been employed in the United States and made payroll tax contributions for at least 10 years, which will cover a proportion of their health care expenditure (Cubanski, Huang, Damico, Jacobson, & Neuman, 2010). However, in the border region a significant number of people near retirement age (55 to 64 years) lack health insurance partly because of differences in exposure to lifelong disadvantages in the labor force. For example, in the Texas border region, about 50% of adults aged 55 to 64 report not having insurance, compared to 30% of the general population, with more women than men uninsured (Bastida, Brown, & Pagan, 2008).

In order to overcome the lack of coverage, older members of the border population resort to various strategies to ensure that they are able to support themselves and afford health care as they age. For many uninsured adults in the border region, one option is to cross the border into Mexico to seek health care, where the costs are cheaper compared to the United States and where those who retain Mexican citizenship will be eligible for subsidized health care. Research shows that among individuals under 65 in the Texas border region, uninsured individuals are three times more likely to use medical care in Mexico than insured individuals (Bastida et al., 2008).

A unique method of providing basic health care along the U.S./Mexico border is the use of "promotores de salud" (Health Promoters), lay health workers that provide services in Hispanic communities and colonias (Twombly, Stringer, & Holtz, 2009). As members of their communities, promotores are trained and funded by various non-profit organizations. Promotores organize educational activities such as information sessions on diabetes care, healthy eating, smoking cessation, and exercise. They also inform community members about available health care services and encourage healthy behaviors. Studies of the effectiveness of promotores indicate that they are of significant benefit to at-risk individuals, particularly in diabetes care (McCloskey, 2009) and for decreasing the risk of cardiovascular disease (Balcázar et al., 2010).

SUMMARY AND CONCLUSIONS

In this chapter we dealt with the health of the Hispanic population. We began with the observation that although Hispanics, and particularly Mexican-origin Hispanics, have low levels of education, as well as low incomes and limited wealth, they have life expectancies at birth and at 65 that are comparable to or more favorable than that of non-Hispanic Whites. They live far longer on average than African Americans, with whom they share a similarly disadvantaged socioeconomic profile. As in most matters related to health, men and women are very different. Women's life expectancy at birth and at 65 far exceeds that of men. Although this female advantage in longevity applies to all racial and ethnic groups, significant between-group differences emerge, such that Hispanic and Asian women have the longest lifespans at birth and at age 65, and African-American women the shortest.

In addition to race and ethnicity, nativity also influences life expectancy. Among Hispanics, foreign-born women have longer lifespans than native-born women. Although the reasons for these race/gender/nativity differentials in life expectancy are not fully understood, health-related behaviors are likely to play an important role. Many researchers have documented an immigrant advantage in longevity, which appears to be greater for later-life migrants than for early-life migrants. It appears that the immigrant advantage in health that may reflect migrant selectivity is largely lost for individuals who immigrate early in life. Such a finding may reflect the adoption of unhealthy lifestyles characteristic of the higher levels of consumption in the United States, and the loss of more beneficial behaviors, including lower rates of smoking and drinking, that are characteristic of Mexico.

Although Mexican-origin Hispanics enjoy a mortality advantage over non-Hispanics, they suffer from many serious diseases that can compromise their quality of life in the later years. Hispanics in general, and those of Mexican origin in particular, suffer from high rates of diabetes and depression, as well as high rates of dementia. Various studies indicate that the onset of diseases such as diabetes and dementia occurs earlier among Hispanics than non-Hispanics. New research that we reviewed indicates that although Mexican-origin Hispanics live longer than non-Hispanic Whites on average, almost half of the years that they live past the age of 65 are characterized by serious functional incapacity and a high level of dependency.

The immigrant advantage in health is related to the process of acculturation. We reviewed literature that suggests that, as in the case of longer residence in the United States, more acculturated individuals lose some of the protective factors associated with lower levels of acculturation. Of course, acculturation is correlated with many other factors related to social class in ways that make simple interpretation of associations difficult. In this chapter we also reviewed social and environmental factors associated with health. Recent research indicates that Hispanics who live in neighborhoods with high concentrations of other Hispanics report better health and less depression than individuals who live in neighborhoods with lower concentrations of Hispanics. This research suggests that ethnic enclaves, even when they are characterized by low socioeconomic profiles, can protect health. One potential explanation for this advantage is the greater opportunity for interaction and a lower probability of isolation for individuals who are able to interact on a regular basis with others who speak one's language and who understand one's culture.

Finally, we discussed the unique situation of the U.S./Mexico border region. Unlike the U.S./Canada border, which is sparsely inhabited and which does not separate two very different economies, the U.S./Mexico border defines two very different worlds. There are few other places in the world where a border separates such vastly different realms in terms of wealth. The difference between Tijuana, Mexico and San Diego, California illustrate the difference. We focused more, though, on the more rural and less affluent areas in which long-term residents live in colonias that are poorly served in terms of municipal services, such as electricity and water, and in which medical care is often inadequate. In many ways, the border exists in a previous era. In the isolated regions of the border health care is rare and many individuals seek care in Mexico. Given the problems of access and cultural barriers to care and compliance with medical regimes, lay advisors, or "promotores," provide advice and counseling to members of the community. In the end, the border region serves to dramatize the meeting of two worlds, one affluent and non-Hispanic and the other impoverished and largely Hispanic.

DISCUSSION QUESTIONS

1. In earlier centuries immigrants to the United States were primarily from Europe. Summarize some of the major commonalities and differences among immigrants from different European nations and list some ways in which they differed from immigrants today. Discuss whether the cultural and social differences characteristic of contemporary immigrants are likely to make their incorporation experiences more difficult and less complete than those of earlier European immigrants.

2. Professor Samuel P. Huntington, chairman of the Harvard Academy for International and Area Studies, published an article in *Foreign Policy* magazine in which

he claimed that Mexican immigrants refuse to assimilate and that because of their large numbers the cultural identity of the United States is threatened. According to Huntington, we are in danger of becoming two nations with two languages and cultures and he feels this change is dangerous. Discuss the proposition that Mexican immigration, because of its magnitude and the fact that a large number of immigrants are undocumented and poorly educated, poses a danger to our collective cultural identity. Discuss whether this proposition misrepresents the nature of Mexican immigration. Are Mexican immigrants in reality significantly different than earlier immigrant groups in terms of their ability and desire to assimilate and acculturate?

3. A large body of research suggests that racism is associated with poor mental and physical health. If the correlation exists, what might be some of the social and biological mechanisms through which perceptions that one is a victim of racism could affect health? How might minority groups and others compensate for their minority status to insure that negative stereotypes do not undermine their health?

4. Immigrants often come from parts of the world in which serious infectious diseases are common. As a consequence, legal immigrants to most countries must prove that they are healthy and do not pose a health threat to the country. In your opinion, should visitors and immigrants who come to developed countries from parts of the world with endemic infectious disease be barred from entry without an extensive medical examination? Discuss the ethical issues and the pros and cons of restricting international travel on the basis of the potential spread of disease.

5. The Affordable Care Act (ACA), often referred to as Obamacare, initially required states to extend Medicaid coverage to low-income adults. Prior to the ACA only children and pregnant women and a few very poor adults were eligible for coverage. The Supreme Court found that although the ACA itself is constitutional, the federal government cannot force states to expand Medicaid coverage. Medicaid, which provides physician and hospital coverage for poor families and impoverished old people who need long-term care, is a joint federal/state program that makes up a large fraction of state expenditures. Because of this fact, in addition to basic disagreements with government-mandated health

care, many states have chosen not to participate, even though the federal government would initially pay for all of the new enrollees and eventually cover 90% of the additional cost. Many of the states that have not extended coverage, like Texas, have large poor and Latino populations. Summarize the reasons that states might choose not to expand Medicaid. In your opinion, will the fact that the federal government will eventually pay most of the cost of expansion eventually convince them to participate? Does refusal to expand Medicaid represent discrimination or the unfair treatment of the poor and minorities or is it simply a reflection of genuine fiscal concerns? Would the expansion of Medicaid to poor adults benefit the Latino population?

6. Define acculturation. What are the dimensions of acculturation? To what extent does the measurement consist of anything other than socioeconomic incorporation?

LITERATURE CITED

Abraham, C., & Rozmus, C. L. (2012). Is Acanthosis Nigricans a reliable indicator for risk of Type 2 diabetes in obese children and adolescents? A systematic review. *The Journal of School Nursing, 28*(3), 195–205.

Abraido-Lanza, A. F., Armbrister, A. N., Florez, K. R., & Aguirre, A. N. (2006). Toward a theory-driven model of acculturation in public health research. *American Journal of Public Health, 96,* 1342–6.

Abraido-Lanza, A. F., Chao, M. T., & Florez, K. R. (2005). Do healthy behaviors decline with greater acculturation? Implications for the Latino mortality paradox. *Social Science and Medicine, 61,* 1243–55.

Alegría, M., Chatterji, P., Wells, K., Cao, Z., Chen, C. N., Takeuchi, D., et al. (2008). Disparity in depression treatment among racial and ethnic minority populations in the United States. *Psychiatric Services, 59*(11), 1264–72.

Alzheimer's Association. (2010). Alzheimer's disease: Facts and figures. from www.alz.org/documents_custom/report_alzfactsfigures2010.pdf.

Angel, J. L., & Angel, R. J. (1992). Age at migration, social connections, and well-being among elderly Hispanics. *Journal of Aging and Health, 4,* 480–99.

Angel, J. L., Buckley, C., & Sakamoto, A. (2001). Duration or disadvantage? Exploring nativity, ethnicity, and health in midlife. *Journal of Gerontology: Social Sciences, 56*(5), S275–84.

Angel, J. L., Torres-Gil, F., & Markides, K. (Eds.). (2012). *Aging, health and longevity in the Mexican-origin population.* New York, NY: Springer Sciences.

Angel, R. J., Angel, J. L., & Hill, T. (2013a). *The compression of morbidity among Mexican-origin elders in the United States: Social and political implications.* Paper presented at the International Association of Gerontology and Geriatrics, Seoul, Korea.

Angel, R. J., Angel, J. L., & Hill, T. (2013b). *Longer life, sicker life? The compression of morbidity in Mexican-American elders.* Paper presented at the Réseau Espérance de Vie en Santé (REVES), the University of Texas at Austin. http://nces.ed.gov/programs/digest/d07/tables/dt07_008.asp.

Angel, R. J., Angel, J. I.., & Lein, L. (2007). The health care safety net for Mexican American families. In D. R. Crane & T. B. Heaton (Eds.), *Handbook of families and poverty* (pp. 395–410). Thousand Oaks, CA: Sage Publications.

Angel, R. J., Angel, J. L., Díaz Venegas, C. D., & Bonazzo, C. (2010). Shorter stay, longer life: Age at migration and mortality among the older Mexican-origin population. *Journal of Aging and Health, 22*, 914–31.

Angel, R. J., Lein, L., & Henrici, J. (2006). *Poor families in America's health care crisis: How the other half pays.* New York, NY: Cambridge University Press.

Angel, R. J., & Williams, K. (2013). Cultural models of health and illness. In F. A. Paniagua & A.-M. Yamada (Eds.), *Handbook of multi-cultural mental health: Assessment and treatment of diverse populations* (pp. 49–68). New York, NY: Academic Press.

Antecol, H., & Bedard, K. (2006). Unhealthy assimilation: Why do immigrants converge to American health status levels? *Demography, 43*(2), 337–60.

Arias, E., Eschbach, K. E., Schauman, W. S., Backlund, E. L., & Sorlie, P. D. (2010). The Hispanic mortality advantage and ethnic misclassification on US death certificates. *American Journal of Public Health, 100*(April), S171–S177.

Balcázar, H. G., de Heer, H., Rosenthal, L., Aguirre, M., Flores, L., Puentes, F. A., et al. (2010). A *promotores de salud* intervention to reduce cardiovascular disease risk in a high-risk Hispanic border population, 2005–2008. *Preventing Chronic Disease, 7*(2), A28.

Bastida, E., Brown, H. S., & Pagan, J. A. (2008). Persistent disparities in the use of health care along the US–Mexico border: An ecological perspective. *American Journal of Public Health, 98*(11), 1987–95.

Berntson, G. G. (2002). Loneliness and health: Potential mechanisms. *Psychosomatic Medicine, 64*, 407–17.

Bharmal, N., Tseng, C.-H., Kaplan, R., & Wong, M. D. (2012). State-level variations in racial disparities in life expectancy. *Health Services Research, 47*(1pt2), 544–55.

Bierman, A. (2006). Does religion buffer the effects of discrimination on mental health? Differing effects by race. *Journal for the Scientific Study of Religion, 45*, 551–65.

Black, S. A., Ray, L. A., & Markides, K. S. (1999). The prevalence and health burden of self-reported diabetes in older Mexican Americans: findings from the Hispanic EPESE. *American Journal of Public Health, 89*, 546–52.

Blazer, D. (2003). Depression in late life: Review and commentary. *Journal of Gerontology: Medical Sciences, 58A*(3), 249–65.

Blazer, D. G., Moody-Ayers, S., Craft-Morgan, J., & Burchett, B. (2002). Depression in diabetes and obesity: Racial/ethnic/gender issues in older adults. *Journal of Psychosomatic Research, 53*, 913–16.

Bliss, K. E. (2010). The challenge of chronic diseases on the U.S.–Mexico border. *A Report of the CSIS Americas Program and the CSIS Global Health Policy Center.* Washington, DC: Center for Strategic and International Studies.

Boardman, J. D., Barnes, L. L., Wilson, R. S., Evans, D. A., & Leon, C. F. M. d. (2013). Social disorder, APOE-E4 genotype, and change cognitive function among older adults living in Chicago. *Social Science & Medicine, 74*(10), 1584–90.

Brickman, W. J., Huang, J., Silverman, B. L., & Metzger, B. E. (2010). Acanthosis Nigricans identifies youth at high risk for metabolic abnormalities. *J Pediatr, 156*(1), 87–92. doi: 10.1016/j.jpeds.2009.07.011.

Burr, J., & Mutchler, J. E. (2003). English language skills, ethnic concentration, and household composition: Older Mexican immigrants. *Journal of Gerontology: Social Sciences, 58B*, 83–92.

Cabassa, L. J., Zayas, L. H., & Hansen, M. C. (2006). Latino adults' access to mental health care: A review of epidemiological studies. *Administration and Policy in Mental Health and Mental Health Services Research, 33*(3), 316–30.

Carr, D., & Moorman, S. M. (2011). Social relations and aging. In J. Richard A. Settersten & J. L. Angel (Eds.), *Handbook of sociology of aging*. New York, NY: Springer Science.

Castro, F. G., Marsiglia, F. F., Kulis, S., & Kellison, J. G. (2010). Lifetime segmented assimilation trajectories and health outcomes in Latino and other community residents. *American Journal of Public Health, 100*(4), 669–76.

Centers for Disease Control. (2010). Current depression among adults: United States, 2006 and 2008. *Morbidity and Mortality Weekly Report (MMWR), 59*(38), 1229–35.

Centers for Disease Control and Prevention. (2011). *2011 National diabetes fact sheet: National estimates and general information on diabetes and prediabetes in the United States*. Retrieved from www.cdc.gov/diabetes/pubs/factsheet11.htm?loc=diabetes-statistics.

Cho, Y., Frisbie, P. W., Hummer, R. A., & Rogers, R. G. (2004). Nativity, duration of residence, and the health of Hispanic adults in the United States. *Immigration Migration Review, 38*(1), 184–211.

Christakis, N. A., & Fowler, J. H. (2009). *Connected: The surprising power of our social networks and how they shape our lives*. New York, NY: Little, Brown and Company.

Cisneros, A. (2001). *Texas colonias housing and infrastructure issues*. Dallas, TX: Federal Reserve Bank of Dallas.

Clark, C. M., DeCarli, C., Mungas, D., Chui, H. I., Higdon, R., Nuñez, J., et al. (2005). Earlier onset of Alzheimer disease symptoms in Latino individuals compared with Anglo individuals. *Archives of Neurology, 62*, 774–8.

Combs, S. (1998). Health: Chronic conditions. *Bordering the Future*. Retrieved from www.window.state.tx.us/border/ch08/ch08.html.

Crimmins, E. M., & Beltran-Sanchez, H. (2011). Mortality and morbidity trends: Is there compression of morbidity? *Journals of Gerontology Series B: Psychological Sciences and Social Sciences, 66*(1), 75–86.

Crimmins, E. M., Hayward, M. D., & Seeman, T. E. (2004). Race/ethnicity, socioeconomic status, and health. In N. B. Anderson, R. A. Bulatao, & B. Cohen (Eds.), *Critical perspectives on racial and ethnic differences in health in late life* (pp. 310–52). Washington, DC: National Academy Press.

Cubanski, J., Huang, J., Damico, A., Jacobson, G., & Neuman, T. (2010). *Medicare chartbook*. Retrieved from www.kff.org/medicare/upload/8103.pdf.

Davidhizar, R., & Bechtel, G. A. (1999). Health and quality of life within colonias settlements along the United States and Mexico border. *Public Health Nursing, 16*(4), 300–5.

Dilworth-Anderson, P., Williams, I. C., & Gibson, B. E. (2002). Issues of race, ethnicity, and culture in caregiving research: A twenty-year review (1980–2000). *The Gerontologist, 42*(2), 237–72.

Donato, K. (2010). U.S. migration from Latin America: Gendered patterns and shifts. *Annals of the American Academy of Political and Social Science, 630*(1), 78–92.

Easterlin, R. A. (2000). The worldwide standard of living since 1800. *Journal of Economic Perspectives, 14*(1), 7–26.

Eisenberg, L. (1992). Treating depression and anxiety in primary care: Closing the gap between knowledge and practice. *New England Journal of Medicine, 326*(16), 1080–4.

Elo, I. T. (2009). Social class differentials in health and mortality: Patterns and explanations in comparative perspective. In *Annual Review of Sociology* (Vol. 35, pp. 553–72). Palo Alto: Annual Reviews.

Escarce, J. J., & Kapur, K. (2006). Access to and quality of health care. In M. Tienda & F. Mitchell (Eds.), *Hispanics and the future of America* (pp. 410–46). Washington, DC: The National Academies Press.

Eschbach, K., Al-Snih, S., Markides, K. S., & Goodwin, J. S. (2007). Disability and active life expectancy of older U.S. and foreign-born Mexican Americans. In J. L. Angel & K. E. Whitfield (Eds.), *The health of aging Hispanics: The Mexican-origin population* (pp. 40–9). New York: Springer Publishing.

Eschbach, K., Kuo, Y. F., & Goodwin, J. S. (2006). Ascertainment of Hispanic ethnicity on California death certificates: Implications for the explanation of the Hispanic mortality advantage. *American Journal of Public Health, 96*(12), 2209–15.

Eschbach, K., Stimpson, J. P., Kuo, Y. F., & Goodwin, J. S. (2007). Mortality of foreign-born and US-born Hispanic adults at younger ages: A reexamination of recent patterns. *American Journal of Public Health, 9*(7), 1297–304.

Falcón, L. M., Todorova, I., & Tucker, K. L. (2009). Social support, life events, and psychological distress among the Puerto Rican population in the Boston area of the United States. *Aging and Mental Health, 6*(November), 863–73.

Ferraro, K. F. (2011). Health and aging: Early origins, persistent inequalities? In J. R. A. Settersten & J. L. Angel (Eds.), *Handbook of sociology of aging* (pp. 465–75). New York, NY: Springer Science.

Finch, B. K., & Vega, W. A. (2003). Acculturation, stress, social support, and self-rated health among Latinos in California. *Journal of Immigrant Health, 5*(3), 100–17.

Fisher-Hoch, S. P., Rentfro, A. R., Salinas, J. J., Pérez, A., Brown, H. S., Reininger, B. M., et al. (2010). Socioeconomic status and prevalence of obesity and diabetes in a Mexican American community, Cameron County, Texas, 2004–2007. *Preventing Chronic Disease, 7*(3), A53.

Fitten, L. J., Ortiz, F., Fairbanks, L., Rosenthal, M., Cole, G. N., Nourhashemi, F., & Sanchez, M. A. (2008). Depression, diabetes and metabolic-nutritional factors in elderly Hispanics. *Journal of Nutrition, Health and Aging, 12*, 634–40.

Fowler, J. H., & Christakis, N. A. (2008). Estimating peer effects on health in social networks. *Journal of Health Economics, 27*(5), 1400–5.

Geruso, M. (2013). Racial disparities in life expectancy: How much can the standard SES variables explain? *Demography, 49*(2), 553–74.

Gianaros, P. J., & Manuck, S. B. (2010). Neurobiological pathways linking socioeconomic position and health. *Psychosomatic Medicine, 72*, 450–61.

Glymour, M. M., & Manly, J. J. (2008). Lifecourse social conditions and racial and ethnic patterns of cognitive aging. *Neuropsychology Reviews, 3*, 223–54.

González, H. M. (2012). An overview of Latino aging: Risk of disability and chronic illness. In J. L. Angel, F. M. Torres-Gil, & K. Markides (Eds.), *Aging, health and longevity in the Mexican-origin population* (pp. 15–18). New York, NY: Springer Science.

González, H. M., Ceballos, M., Tarraf, W., West, B. T., Bowen, M. E., & Vega, W. A. (2009). The health of older Mexican Americans in the long run. *American Journal of Public Health, 99*(10), 1879–85.

González, H. M., Haan, M. N., & Hinton, L. (2001). Acculturation and the prevalence of depression in older Mexican Americans: Baseline results of the Sacramento Area Latino Study on Aging. *Journal of the American Geriatric Society, 49*(7), 948–53.

Grinberg, E. (Producer). (2011, July 9). Impoverished border town grows from shacks into community. CNN, *Defining America*.

Gurland, B. J., Wilder, D. E., Lantigua, R., Stern, Y., Chen, J., Killeffer, E. H. P., & Mayeux, R. (1999). Rates of dementia in three ethnoracial groups. *International Journal of Geriatric Psychiatry, 14*(6), 481–93.

Haan, M. N., Lopez, V. C., Moore, K. M., Gonzalez, H. M., Mehta, K., & Hinton, L. (2007). Predictors of decline in cognitive status, incidence of dementia/CIND and all-cause mortality in Older Latinos: The role of nativity and cultural orientation in the Sacramento Area Latino Study on Aging. In J. L.

Angel & K. E. Whitfield (Eds.), *The health of aging Hispanics: The Mexican-origin population* (pp. 50–64). New York: Springer Publishing.

Hayward, M., & Gorman, B. K. (2004). The long arm of childhood: The influence of early-life social conditions on men's mortality. *Demography, 41*(1), 87–107.

Hayward, M. D., Warner, D. F., Crimmins, E., M., & Hidajat, M. M. (2007). Does longer life mean better health? Not for native-born Mexican Americans in the Health and Retirement Survey. In J. L. Angel & K. E. Whitfield (Eds.), *The health of aging Hispanics: The Mexican-origin population* (pp. 85–95). New York: Springer Publishing.

Hazuda, H. P., Stern, M. P., Haffner, S. M. (1988). Acculturation and assimilation among Mexican Americans: Scales and population-based data. *Social Science Quarterly, 69*, 687–706.

Hernandez, L. M. (2006). The impact of social and cultural environment on health. In L. M. Hernandez & D. G. Blazer (Eds.), *Genes, behavior, and the social environment: Moving beyond the nature/nurture debate*. Washington, DC: National Academies Press.

Herrera, A. P., Smith, M. L., Ory, M. G., Rodriguez, H. P., Warre, R., Thompson, W. K., et al. (2011). The provision of diabetes-monitoring exams to older Latinos. *Journal of Aging and Health, 23*(7), 1075–100.

Hill, T. D., Angel, J. L., Ellison, C., & Angel, R. J. (2005). Religious attendance and mortality: An eight-year follow up of older Mexican Americans. *Journal of Gerontology: Social Sciences, 60B*, 102–9.

Hill, T., Burdette, A., Angel, J. L., & Angel, R. J. (2006). Religious attendance and cognitive functioning among older Mexican Americans. *Journal of Gerontology: Psychological Sciences, 61B*, P3–P9.

Hu, F. B. (2011). Globalization of diabetes: The role of diet, lifestyle, and genes. *Diabetes Care, 34*(6), 1249–57. doi: 10.2337/dc11-0442.

Hummer, R. A., Powers, D. A., Pullum, S. G., Gossman, G. L., & Frisbie, W. P. (2007). Paradox found (again): Infant mortality among the Mexican-origin population in the United States. *Demography, 44*(3), 441–57.

Hummer, R. M., Benjamins, M., & Rogers, R. (Eds.). (2004). *Race/ethnic disparities in health and mortality among the elderly: A documentation and examination of social factors.* Washington, DC: National Academies Press.

Hyde, P. S. (2011). *Behavioral health: Public health challenge public health opportunity.* Paper presented at the American Public Health Association, Washington, DC. Retrieved from http://store.samhsa.gov/product/Behavioral-Health-Public-Health-Challenge-Public-Health-Opportunity/SMA11-PHYDE10302011.

Ionnatta, J. (2002). *Emerging issues on Hispanic health: Summary of a workshop.* Washington, DC: National Academy Press.

Jaremka, L. M., Fagundes, C. P., Peng, J., Bennett, J. M., Glaser, R., Malarkey, W. B., & Kiecolt-Glaser, J. K. (2013). Loneliness promotes inflammation during acute stress. *Psychological Sciences, 24*(7), 1089–97.

Jasso, G., Massey, D. S., Rosenzweig, M. R., & Smith, J. P. (2004). Immigrant health: Selectivity and acculturation. In N. Anderson, R. A. Bulatao, & B. Cohen (Eds.), *Critical perspectives on racial and ethnic differences in health in late life* (pp. 227–66). Washington, DC: National Academies Press.

Kaestner, R., Pearson, J. A., Keene, D., & Geronimus, A. T. (2009). Stress, allostatic load, and health of Mexican immigrants. *Social Science Quarterly, 90*(5), 1089–111.

Kanaiaupuni, S. M. (2000). Reframing the migration question: Men, women, and gender in Mexico. *Social Forces, 78*(4), 1311–48.

Katon, W. J., Lin, E. H., Russo, J., Korff, M. V., Ciechanowski, P., Simon, G., & Young, B. (2004). Cardiac risk factors in patients with diabetes mellitus and major depression. *Journal of Internal Medicine, 19*, 1192–19.

Kessler, R. C., Chiu, W. T., Demler, O., & Walters, E. E. (2005). Prevalence, severity, and comorbidity of twelve-month DSM-IV disorders in the National Comorbidity Survey Replication (NCS-R). *Archives of General Psychiatry, 62*(6), 617–27.

Kessler, R. C., & Ustun, T. B. (Eds.). (2008). *The WHO world mental health surveys: Global perspectives on the epidemiology of mental disorders.* New York, NY: Cambridge University Press.

Kimbro, R. T. (2009). Acculturation in context: Gender, age at migration, neighborhood ethnicity, and health behaviors. *Social Science Quarterly, 90*(5), 1145–66.

Kong, A. S., Williams, R. L., Smith, M., Sussman, A. L., Skipper, B., Hsi, A. C., & Rhyne, R. L. (2007). Acanthosis Nigricans and diabetes risk factors: Prevalence in young persons seen in southwestern US primary care practices. *Ann Fam Med, 5*(3), 202–8. doi: 10.1370/afm.678.

Landale, N. S., Oropesa, R. S., & Gorman, B. K. (2000). Migration and infant death: Assimilation or selective migration among Puerto Ricans? *American Sociological Review, 65*, 888–909.

Lara, M., Gamboa, C., Kahramanian, M. I., Morales, L. S., & Hayes-Bautista, D. E. (2005). Acculturation and Latino health in the United States: A review of the literature and its sociopolitical context. *Annual Review of Public Health, 26*, 367–97.

Livney, M. G., Clark, C. M., Karlawish, J. H., Cartmell, S., Negrón, M., Nuñez, J., et al. (2011). Ethnoracial differences in the clinical characteristics of Alzheimer's disease at initial presentation at an urban Alzheimer's disease center. *American Journal of Geriatric Psychiatry, 19*(5), 430–9.

Manly, J. J., & Mayeux, R. (2004). Ethnic differences in dementia and Alzheimer's disease. In N. B. Anderson, R. A. Bulatao, & B. Cohen (Eds.), *Critical perspectives on racial and ethnic differences in health in late life* (pp. 95–142). Washington, DC: The National Academies Press.

Manly, J. J., Tang, M.-X., Schupf, N., Stern, Y., Vonsattel, J.-P. G., & Mayeux, R. (2008). Frequency and course of mild impairment in a multiethnic community. *Annuals of Neurology, 63*(4), 494–506.

Markides, K. S., Coreil, J., & Ray, L. A. (1987). Smoking among Mexican Americans: A three-generation study. *American Journal of Public Health, 77*(6), 708–11.

Markides, K. S., & Eschbach, K. (2005). Aging, migration, and mortality: Current status of research on the Hispanic paradox. *Journal of Gerontology: Social Sciences, 60*(October), S68–S75.

Markides, K. S., Eschbach, K., Ray, L. A., & Peek, M. K. (2007). Census disability rates among older people by race/ethnicity and type of Hispanic origin. In J. L. Angel & K. E. Whitfield (Eds.), *The health of aging Hispanics: The Mexican-origin population*. New York, NY: Springer.

Markides, K. S., Rudkin, L., Angel, R. J., & Espino, D. (1997). Health status of Hispanic elderly. In L. G. Martin & B. J. Soldo (Eds.), *Racial and ethnic differ-*

ences in the health of older Americans (pp. 285–300). Washington, DC: National Academy Press.

Martinez, N. C., & Bader, J. (2007). Analysis of behavioral risk factor surveillance system data to assess the health of Hispanic Americans with diabetes in El Paso County, Texas. *The Diabetes Educator, 33*(4), 691–99.

Mayeda, E., Haan, M. N., Kanaya, A. M., Yaffe, K., & Neuhaus, J. (2013). Type 2 diabetes and 10-year risk of dementia and cognitive impairment among older Mexican Americans. *Diabetes Care, 36*(9), 2600–6.

McCloskey, J. (2009). Promotores as partners in a community-based diabetes intervention program targeting Hispanics. *Family & Community Health, 32*, 48–57.

Messias, E., Eaton, W., Nestadt, G., Bienvenu, O. J., & Samuels, J. (2007). Psychiatrists' ascertained treatment needs for mental disorders in a population-based sample. *Psychiatric Services, 58*(3), 373–7.

Morbidity and Mortality Weekly Report. (1999). Ten great public health achievements: United States, 1900–1999. *Journal of the American Medical Association, 281*(16), 1481. doi: 10.1001/jama.281.16.1481.

Morrow, A. S., Haidet, P., Skinner, J., & Naik, A. D. (2008). Integrating diabetes self-management with the health goals of older adults: A qualitative exploration. *Patient Education and Counseling, 72*, 418–23.

Murphy, S. L., Xu, J., & Kochanek, K. D. (2013). Deaths: Final data for 2010 *National Vital Statistics Report* (Vol. 61). Hyattsville, MD: National Center for Health Statistics.

National Center for Health Statistics. (2013). *Health United States, 2012 special feature on socioeconomic status and health* (table 18). Hyattsville, MD: U.S. Department of Health and Human Services.

National Institute of Mental Health. (2013). Major depressive disorder. *The numbers count: Mental disorders in America.* Retrieved from www.nimh.nih.gov/health/publications/the-numbers-count-mental-disorders-in-america/index.shtml#MajorDepressive.

National Institute on Aging. (2012). *Health disparities and Alzheimer's disease.* Retrieved from www.nia.nih.gov/alzheimers/publication/2011-2012-alzheimers-disease-progress-report/health-disparities-and.

Office of Minority Health. (2012a). *Asian American/Pacific Islander profile.* Retrieved from http://minorityhealth.hhs.gov/templates/browse.aspx?lvl=2&lvlID=53.

Office of Minority Health. (2012b). *Diabetes and African Americans.* Washington, DC: U.S. Department of Health and Human Services.

Office of Minority Health. (2013). *Diabetes and Hispanic Americans.* Retrieved from http://minorityhealth.hhs.gov/templates/content.aspx?ID=3324.

Olshansky, S. J., Antonucci, T., Berkman, L., Binstock, R. H., Boersch-Supan, A., Cacioppo, J. T., et al. (2013). Differences in life expectancy due to race and educational differences are widening, and many may not catch up. *Health Affairs, 31*(8), 1803–13.

Ottenbacher, K. J., Graham, J. E., Snih, S. A., Raji, M., Samper-Ternent, R., Ostir, G. V., & Markides, K. S. (2009). Mexican Americans and frailty: Findings from the Hispanic Established Populations Epidemiologic Studies of the Elderly. *American Journal of Public Health, 99*(4), 673–9.

Palloni, A. (2007). Health status of elderly Hispanics in the United States. In J. L. Angel & K. E. Whitfield (Eds.), *The health of aging Hispanics: The Mexican-origin population* (pp. 1–14). New York: Springer.

Pan American Health Organization. (2010). Along U.S.–Mexico border, diabetes cases are the tip of the iceberg? *Pan American Journal of Public Health.* Retrieved May 1, 2014, www.pharmpro.com/news/2010/10/along-us-mexico-border-diabetes-cases-are-tip-iceberg.

Paniagua, F. A. (2000). Culture-bound syndromes, cultural variations, and psychopathology. In I. Cuéllar & F. A. Paniagua (Eds.), *Handbook of multicultural mental health: Assessment and treatment of diverse populations* (pp. 140–141). New York: Academic Press.

Parra, E. O., & Espino, D. V. (1992). Barriers to health care access faced by elderly Mexican Americans. *Clinical Gerontologist, 11,* 171–7.

Pérez-Stable, E. J., Marín, B. V., Marín, G., Brody, D. J., & Benowitz, N. L. (1990). Apparent underreporting of cigarette consumption among Mexican American smokers. *American Journal of Public Health, 80,* 1057–61.

Portes, A., & Zhou, M. (1993). The new second generation: Segmented assimilation and its variants. *Annals of the American Academy of Political and Social Sciences, 530,* 74–96.

Preston, S. H. (1996). *American longevity: Past, present, and future* (Policy Research Paper 36). Syracuse, NY: Syracuse University, Maxwell School of Citizenship and Public Affairs.

Quesnel-Vallée, A., Farrah, J.-S., & Jenkins, T. (2011). Population aging, health systems, and equity: Share challenges for the United States and Canada. In R. A. Settersten & J. L. Angel (Eds.), *Handbook of sociology of aging* (pp. 563–602). New York, NY: Springer Science.

Ramshaw, E. (2011, July 9). Many health problems linked to poverty. *New York Times*. Retrieved May 1, 2014, www.nytimes.com/2011/07/10/us/10tt health.html?ref=us.

Rotkiewicz-Piorun, A. M., Snih, S. A., Raji, M. A., Kuo, Y.-F., & Markides, K. S. (2006). Cognitive decline in older Mexican Americans with diabetes. *Journal of the National Medical Association, 98*(11), 1840–7.

Salgado de Snyder, V. N. (1987). Factors associated with acculturative stress and depressive symptomatology among married Mexican immigrant women *Psychology of Women Quarterly, 11*(Special Issue), 475–88.

Samper-Ternent, R., Snih, S. A., Raji, M. A., Markides, K. S., & Ottenbacher, K. J. (2008). Relation between frailty and cognitive decline in older Mexican Americans. *Journal of the American Geriatric Society, 56*(10), 1845–52.

Schur, C. L., Albers, L., & Berk, M. L. (1995). Health care use by Hispanic adults: Financial vs non-financial determinants. *Health Care Financing Review, 17*(2), 71–88.

Seligman, M. (1975). *Helplessness: On depression, development, and death*. San Francisco, CA: W. H. Freeman.

Seligman, M. (1991). *Helplessness: On depression, development, and death* (2nd ed.). New York, NY: W. H. Freeman.

Singh, G. K., & Siahpush, M. (2002). Ethnic-immigrant differentials in health behaviors, morbidity, and cause-specific mortality in the United States: An analysis of two national data bases. *Human Biology, 74*(1), 83–109.

Song, S. H. (2008). Early-onset Type 2 diabetes mellitus: A condition with elevated cardiovascular risk? *British Journal of Diabetes and Vascular Disease, 8*(2), 61–5.

Teitler, J. O., Hutto, N., & Reichman, N. E. (2012). Birthweight of children of immigrants by maternal duration of residence in the United States. *Social Science & Medicine, 75*(3), 459–68.

Texas State Data Center. (2013). *Texas population estimates by county*. San Antonio, TX: Texas Population Estimates Program.

Thomson, M. D., & Hoffman-Goetz, L. (2009). Defining and measuring acculturation: A systematic review of public health studies with Hispanic populations in the United States. *Social Science & Medicine, 69*(7), 983–91.

Treviño, F., & Coustasse, A. (2007). Disparities and access barriers to health care among Mexican American elders. In J. L. Angel & K. E. Whitfield (Eds.), *The health of aging Hispanics: The Mexican-origin population* (pp. 165–80). New York, NY: Springer.

Twombly, E. C., Stringer, K. A., & Holtz, K. D. (2009). *Using Promotores programs to improve Latino health outcomes: Implementation challenges for community-based nonprofit organizations*. Atlanta, GA: KDH Research & Communication, Inc.

Umberson, D., & Montez, J. K. (2010). Social relationships and health: A flashpoint for public policy. *Journal of Health and Social Behavior, 51*, S54–S66.

Umberson, D. J., Wortman, C. B., & Kessler, R. C. (1992). Widowhood and depression: Explaining gender differences in vulnerability. *Journal of Health and Social Behavior, 33*, 10–24.

United States–Mexico Border Health Commission. (2010). *Border lives: Health status in the United States–Mexico border region*. El Paso, TX: Border Health Commission.

U.S. Census Bureau. (2008). *Projected life expectancy at birth by sex, race, and Hispanic origin for the United States: 2010 to 2050* (NP2008-T10, Table 10). Washington, DC: Population Division.

Vaupel, J. (2010). Biodemography of human aging. *Nature, 464*(7288), 536–42.

Vega, W., & Amaro, H. (1998). Lifetime prevalence of DSM-III-R psychiatric disorders among rural and urban Mexican Americans in California. *Archives of General Psychiatry, 55,* 771–82.

Vega, W. A., & Amaro, H. (1994). Latino outlook: Good health, uncertain prognosis. *Annual Review of Public Health, 15,* 39–67.

Vega, W. A., Rodriguez, M. A., & Ang, A. (2010). Addressing stigma of depression in Latino primary care patients. *General Hospital Psychiatry, 32*(2), 182–91.

Waite, L. J., & Das, D. A. (2010). Families, social life and well-being at older ages. *Demography, 47*(Supplement), S87–S109.

Ward, P. M. (2007). Colonias, informal homestead subdivisions and self-help care for the elderly among Mexican populations in the United States. In J. L. Angel & K. E. Whitfield (Eds.), *The health of aging Hispanics: The Mexican-origin population* (pp. 141–62). New York, NY: Springer Science.

Williams, D. R., & Collins, C. (1995). US Socioeconomic and racial differences in health: Patterns and explanations. *Annual Review of Sociology, 21,* 349–86.

Williams, D. R., & Leavell, J. (2012). The social context of cardiovascular disease: challenges and opportunities for the Jackson Heart Study. *Ethnicity and Disease, 22*(3, Supplement), 15–21.

Williams, D. R., & Mohammed, S. A. (2009). Discrimination and racial disparities in health: Evidence and needed research. *Journal of Behavioral Medicine, 32*(1), 20–47.

Williams, D. R., & Sternthal, M. (2010). Understanding racial-ethnic disparities in health: Sociological contributions. *Journal of Health and Social Behavior, 51,* S15–S27.

Wilmoth, J. R. (1998). The future of human longevity: A demographer's perspective. *Science, 280*(5362), 395.

Woodward, A. T., Taylor, R. J., Bullard, K. M., Aranda, M. P., Lincoln, K. D., & Chatters, L. M. (2012). Prevalence of lifetime DSM-IV affective disorders among older African Americans, Black Caribbeans, Latinos, Asians and non-Hispanic White people. *International Journal of Geriatric Psychiatry, 27*(8), 816–27.

Wu, J. H., Haan, M. N., Liang, J., Ghosh, D., Gonzales, H. M., & Herman, W. H. (2003). Diabetes as a predictor of change in functional status among older Mexican Americans. *Diabetes Care, 26,* 314–19.

Wu, J. H., Haan, M. N., Liang, J. L., Gonzalez, H. M., & Herman, W. H. (2003). Impact of diabetes on cognitive function among older Latinos: A population-based cohort study. *Journal of Clinical Epidemiology, 56*(7), 686–93.

Xu, J., Kochanek, K. D., Murphy, S. L., & Tejada-Vera, B. (2010). *Deaths: Final data for 2007.* National Vital Statistics Reports (Vol. 58). Hyattsville, MD: National Center for Health Statistics.

Ye Luo, Hawkley, L. C., Waite, L. J., & Cacioppo, J. T. (2012). Loneliness, health, and mortality in old age: A national longitudinal study. *Social Science and Medicine, 74*(6), 907–14.

CHAPTER 6

Changing Eldercare Options

WORLDS APART: ELDERCARE THEN AND NOW

Tonie took the first of her many daily walks around the assisted living facility just after breakfast. At 95 she was physically healthy and even fit. She had trouble remembering things, though, and had even begun to confuse events that happened long ago. She could no longer remember her elder sister's husband, whom she had known very well. Her cognitive decline was clearly accelerating. Tonie had been born and lived her life in the Albuquerque barrio. She was born and grew up in the house her father, Crecenciano, had built when New Mexico was still a territory. She had earned a Master's in Education at the University of New Mexico and had been a school teacher for many years, before becoming an elementary school principal. Tonie recently moved to Austin, Texas where her son and daughter-in-law live. They are professionals who had settled in Austin for career reasons. Tonie was the last surviving member of her family and her only daughter had died of cancer at age 50. There was nobody left in Albuquerque.

Tonie's mother, Candelaria, had 13 children. Their names are recorded in household census records. Only five girls and one boy survived to adulthood, though; such were the harsh conditions in territorial New Mexico in which vaccination and antibiotics were unknown. By her early 80s Candelaria was worn out and could no longer care for herself. Since her five daughters lived in the same city and very close by, caring for their mother was not only something they were able to do, it was something they could never have imagined not doing. Candelaria lived with one or another of her daughters for the next few years. When she died at 87 it was in the home of one of her daughters with all of her family present.

With only one surviving son, Tonie's situation was very different than that of her mother. At 93 Tonie realized she could no longer live alone. She was forgetting things and could not deal with her finances or care for her home. She, her son, and daughter-in-law decided to sell the Albuquerque house and move Tonie to Austin. Since both her son and his wife had careers, bringing Tonie to live with them in their home was not possible. Someone would have to have quit their job. Although Tonie was physically healthy, her cognitive decline and the fact that she did not know the city or neighborhood and could not drive meant that she needed constant supervision to make sure she ate properly and did not hurt herself. The solution was the assisted living facility that was within two miles of the couple's home.

The personality traits that had made Tonie a successful school principal meant that she adapted well to the assisted living facility, where she was socially active. She made friends with another Spanish-speaking client and helped others who were wheelchair bound with daily tasks. She saw her son and daughter-in-law almost every day or at least talked on the phone. Her daughter-in-law took her to Mass every Sunday and prepared Sunday dinner. Tonie occasionally became confused and a few times said that she wanted to go back to Albuquerque and "get her old life back." Those episodes passed, though. When she died at 97 it was in a different city and far from the home in which she was born.

THE CHANGING FAMILY AND SOCIAL CONTEXT OF ELDERCARE

This vignette is based on the experiences of several older people we have known, and it is typical of the situation of many older individuals today. The reader may even recognize the story as his or her own. Although individuals have always migrated and some women have remained childless, it was fairly common in previous decades for older individuals to enter their later years with at least some of their children living close by (Ruggles, 1987). It was even fairly common for older parents, especially women, to live with one of their children, largely because there were few alternatives (Thane, 2005). In that world the family was the primary caregiving institution and solidarity between generations was reflected in mutual care and assistance (Bengtson & Achenbaum, 1993). Even today children provide a great deal of material, emotional, and practical assistance to older parents (Silverstein, Gans, & Yang, 2006). Often that help is the only thing that allows an older individual to remain in the community (Herrera, Angel, Díaz-Venegas, & Angel, 2012).

Nonetheless, for better or worse the traditional world of family-based support systems is changing rapidly (Silverstein & Giarrusso, 2010). As in Tonie's case, in the developed world older individuals have fewer children living close by on whom they can rely. Adult children, including daughters, have careers and must work to support themselves and others. Rather than setting up households close to their parents, children often move far away. The simple advantage of numbers is gone. Older Latinos are especially reliant on their children for care and support because of the low levels of asset accumulation we have documented in previous chapters. The problem is greatly exacerbated by the rapid increase in life expectancy at older ages. Despite the "familistic" cultural orientation that supposedly characterizes the Latino family, changing social practices, female labor force participation, migration, and changing demographics are affecting Latino families and their eldercare capacities in the same way that they are affecting other groups. As a consequence, older Latinos are having to adjust their expectations and finding that they must often turn to non-family sources of assistance (Ruiz & Ransford, 2012).

In this chapter we examine the family situations and living arrangements of older Latinos in the larger context of the options in living and care arrangements for older people generally. A major focus is on the changing nature of families' eldercare roles and an examination of the social, economic, and cultural forces that affect both the desire and capacity of adult children to contribute to their parents' care. We begin with the perhaps unsurprising observation that most older individuals prefer to stay in their own homes for as long as possible, even when their health deteriorates and even after their spouse is gone (Angel, 1991). Living alone, though, involves risks, especially for individuals in poor health who are frail and have problems carrying out basic activities of daily living, such as preparing meals and bathing. Falls are a major threat in old age, and unfortunately they are common (World Health Organization, 2007; Zecevic, Salmoni, Speechley, & Vandervoort, 2006). If no one is around to call for help, falls and other injuries can be life threatening. Older individuals who live alone are also at risk of malnutrition if they do not prepare meals for themselves or eat a balanced diet, and of course they are at elevated risk of the negative consequences of isolation, which can seriously undermine the quality of anyone's life (Elliott, Painter, & Hudson, 2009). As we discuss in greater detail later, dealing with isolation requires new approaches in which non-governmental and faith-based organizations (NGOs and FBOs) play an increasingly important role.

Before proceeding, though, we must note that one must be careful not to overemphasize the role of culture in the decisions Hispanic families make regarding long-term care. In any discussion of culture one runs the risk of granting too much influence to tradition, beliefs, and practices. Culture is not an unchanging set of inflexible rules. Rather, culture can be seen as a set of malleable and changing cognitive options from which individuals can pick and choose (Angel & Williams, 2013). Cultures also become less coercive with time as tradition becomes less binding (Giddens, 1991). Cultural change is affecting Latino families in ways that alter expectations and norms concerning one's duty toward parents, the virtue of self-sacrifice, and the need to foster one's own well-being and that of one's children. Such social forces as intermarriage, acculturation, and more perhaps render any reference to the cultural category "Latino" suspect. Many Latinos are indistinguishable from European Americans.

Latinos, like all other human beings, are also rational actors whose choices and behaviors are constrained by financial and other practical concerns. Long-term care is extremely expensive and the decision to institutionalize a frail parent is as much an economic decision as one based on values and norms (Herrera et al., 2013). In the end it is impossible to isolate the effects of cultural, economic, and access factors on the choice of living arrangements for an aging parent (e.g., De Vos & Arias, 2003). As Zsembik, (1996, p. 70) notes, "preferences are shaped not only by social norms embedded in ethnic heritage, the effect of which attenuates with acculturation, but are also outcomes of residential alternatives, and economic and noneconomic resources."

NURSING HOME CARE

The desire to stay in one's familiar surroundings is a basic human trait, but for many of us that desire eventually gives way to the reality of physical and cognitive decline. At that point older individuals and their families are faced with difficult and potentially financially ruinous decisions. Many options exist for individuals with different levels of need, such as those listed in Table 6.1 that range from staying in one's home to entering a nursing facility. Let us begin with the most intensive form of care, which is designed for individuals who need high-level or extensive assistance. Nursing homes and other residential facilities provide care to individuals who cannot care for themselves and who are often close to the end of life. They share characteristics of what sociologist Erving Goffman has characterized as "total institutions" (Goffman, 1961). These are places, like asylums and prisons, in which many individuals with similar characteristics live together isolated from the larger society, often involuntarily. In such institutions one's individuality and one's personal identity are replaced by an institutional identity. Clearly, this is a very negative image and the analogy no doubt somewhat strained since most nursing homes are far more open than asylums or prisons. Nonetheless, the comparison points out the fact that even if the elderly inhabitants are not inmates, they lose at least some degree of autonomy and become dependent on others.

Entering a long-term care facility involves several negative psychological and social losses. Leaving one's home in which one has often spent many years and entering a new and strange environment can be highly distressing. Research reveals that changes in living arrangements in the later years can have serious physical and mental health consequences (Grundy, 2010; Hughes & Waite, 2002; Robards, Evandrou, Falkingham, & Vlachantonia, 2012). A move to a nursing home also requires an acceptance of the fact that one is no longer able to care for oneself. In the most serious cases it forces one into a totally dependent role. Consequently, most older individuals resist the move and are basically forced into it by children who recognize that their aging parent can no longer live alone (Henry, 2006).

TABLE 6.1 *Options in Long-term Care*

Home Care	Community-based Care	Residential Care
Skilled Care	Adult Day Care	Nursing Home
Personal Care	Companion	Assisted Living
I-ADL Assistance		Continuing Care Retirement Community

Most of us can probably remember how stressful leaving home was for the first time when we were young. For young people moving to a dorm or an apartment is part of launching into autonomous adulthood. Despite the trepidation and homesickness that one might feel, the move is part of an adventure and one looks forward to a future filled with possibilities. For an older person a move to a nursing home is not the beginning of a new and more productive phase of life. However pleasant the nursing home environment might be, for most people life in the community is preferable. The challenge facing older individuals and their families, as well as formal eldercare organizations and NGOs and FBOs, then, is postponing the move to a nursing home for as long as possible, a topic we will discuss in a later section.

REASONS FOR THE UNDERUTILIZATION OF NURSING HOMES

Not surprisingly, need and the inability to care for oneself are among the strongest predictors of the use of nursing home and in-home health care services. The services that dependent elderly individuals need can be extensive and often complicated. They include medical care at different levels, as well as assistance with personal hygiene, dressing, and getting in and out of a bed or a chair. Individuals who are not self-sufficient need help bathing and using the toilet. They often need physical and other rehabilitative therapy, and someone must monitor what can be complex drug regimens (Wallace & Lew-Ting, 1992). When an individual becomes seriously cognitively impaired or incontinent, living alone or even with family becomes difficult if not impossible. Yet for populations with low incomes and little wealth other factors affect a family's decision to institutionalize an aging parent. The low use of long-term care by Hispanics reflects factors that are common to all groups, as well as certain factors that are unique to the Mexican-origin population. We might describe these sets of barriers as the three "A's": affordability, availability, and acceptability (Goldscheider & Jones, 1989). These encompass structural as well as cultural factors. Let us examine how each is related to low levels of nursing home use by Hispanics.

First, in terms of affordability nursing home care is expensive. The cost of a year of basic nursing home care can be very high. In 2013 the median annual cost of nursing home care was over $80,000 (Ellis, 2013). Of course costs vary greatly depending on location, the amenities provided, and the level of care required. For families with modest incomes and few resources the best care is prohibitive. Exhibit 6.1 presents the average cost of a year of nursing home care compared to the cost of other types of long-term care. For an affluent family the cost may be well within their means, given that the average stay is just over two-and-a-half years (Jones, Dwyer, Bercovitz, & Strahan, 2009). For a family with few resources paying for the average stay is probably impossible. For an older individual with few resources who can no longer live independently, the only options are moving in with someone else or entering a long-term care facility. In this case the payer of last resort is Medicaid. One can, of course, purchase long-term care insurance on the private market, which we discuss further below, but for individuals with few resources and no estate to preserve for their heirs, purchasing such a policy probably makes little sense.

Exhibit 6.1 Average Costs for Long-Term Care in the United States: 2010

- $205 per day or $6,235 per month for a semi-private room in a nursing home or $76,200 per year
- $229 per day or $6,965 per month for a private room in a nursing home or $83,840 per year
- $3,293 per month for care in an assisted living facility (for a one-bedroom unit) or $39,516 per year
- $21 per hour for a home health aide
- $19 per hour for homemaker services
- $67 per day for services in an adult day health care center

Source: U.S. Department of Health and Human Services, http://longtermcare.gov/costs-how-to-pay/costs-of-care

---

One might ask why families do not just use Medicare to pay for the nursing home care. The basic problem arises from the fact that Medicare does not pay for nursing home or long-term care. It only pays for 100 days of post-acute care after one is discharged from a hospital and in need of less intensive medical care than that provided in a hospital. If one cannot go home and needs longer-term care, either in an institution or in the community, one must pay for it oneself or turn to Medicaid. Medicaid is the program for low-income individuals and families.

Although most of the enrollees are children in poor families, most of the money paid out goes to financing long-term care for impoverished elderly persons and the disabled (Congressional Budget Office, 2013). Approximately 20% of Medicaid enrollees are seniors or persons with disabilities, but because these individuals need expensive health care and personal care services they account for nearly two-thirds of all Medicaid spending (Center for Budget and Policy Priorities, 2013). In 2013 the average per capita Medicaid expenditure was $11,350 for older individuals and $1,640 for children (Congressional Budget Office, 2013).

For older individuals with extremely low incomes and wealth Medicaid is the insurer of last resort and pays for what Medicare does not cover. In order to be truly secure in retirement, one must own a "Medigap" policy, a term that refers to a supplemental insurance plan that covers what Medicare does not pay for. More affluent seniors purchase Medigap policies through organizations such as the American Association of Retired Persons (AARP) or other private company, or they receive coverage as part of a retirement package. Seniors with low incomes cannot afford private coverage. Yet the costs that are not covered by Medicare can be substantial. Medicare does not cover dental or eye care, nor does it pay for dentures or hearing aids. It includes a substantial deductible for hospital stays and individuals must pay a premium and deductible for Medicare Part B medical insurance. In 2010 nearly nine million low-income frail, elderly, and disabled Medicare beneficiaries received Medicaid to cover these additional costs.

Many low-income Hispanics and others who might wish to participate in Medicaid cannot because of the highly restrictive financial eligibility criteria. These require that one qualify for the federal income maintenance program called Supplemental Security Income (SSI) for poor and disabled elderly or have extremely low income and few resources. Eligibility for SSI and Medicaid differ by state. In 2009, 24 states set the guidelines for eligibility below 75% of the federal poverty level (FPL); 9 states between 79 and 99% of the FPL, and 18 states, including the nation's capital, at 100% of the FPL (Henry J. Kaiser Foundation, 2010). Most states limit the amount of assets for a single person to less than $2,000. Medicaid is particularly important in states like Texas, New Mexico, and Colorado, which have a large fraction of older Hispanics. These states also have the most strict eligibility criteria that limit the participation of individuals who are poor but earn slightly over the eligibility threshold.

In order to qualify for Medicaid, then, an older person and his or her spouse must have almost no resources or income left. If they do they must "spend down" to the eligibility level, which means that they must deplete almost all of their personal resources before Medicaid will begin paying (Banerjee, 2012). In order to qualify, an older adult typically can have no more than $2,000 and a couple $3,000 in non-exempt assets. These amounts are set by individual states and can vary, although the objective is the same, to insure that individuals pay as much as possible for their own long-term care (Thomson/MEDSTAT, 2005). This requirement can leave the spouse who remains in the community with very little to live on. Exhibit 6.2 illustrates the consequences of having to "spend down" to Medicaid eligibility.

Exhibit 6.2 Losing one's nest egg

Ernesto and Lupe had been looking forward to a comfortable retirement. Five years after he retired at 62, Ernesto developed Alzheimer's disease and after a year had to be institutionalized. The family received a shock when they found out that Medicare does not pay for long-term care. When a lawyer suggested that Lupe apply for Medicaid, he also told her that she had to "spend down" to qualify. That meant that she would have to pay the over $100,000 per year that Ernesto's care cost. The cruel reality was that, even though she could keep her home and car, the savings and assets that she and Ernesto had worked so hard for all their lives would be nearly gone. Helping her children buy homes and educate their children was now a dream that would never become a reality.

Exhibit 6.3 provides an example of the income and assets that a spouse can retain when their partner must turn to Medicaid for long-term care.

Because of the high cost of nursing home care, and the fact that neither Medicare nor most health insurance policies pay for it, a relatively new insurance product has come on the market, long-term care insurance (U.S. Office of Personnel Management, 2008). Such plans potentially allow an individual to protect assets that they might wish to pass on to their children. Typically such policies provide a certain amount per year for a set period. They can be purchased by individuals or by couples and the total amount of coverage is split. The payout can cover a large fraction of the cost of care for a limited time or less of the cost for a longer time. As we mentioned earlier, given the high cost of such plans

Exhibit 6.3 Income and/or Assets That a Spouse Can Retain

- The home and its contents
- One car (per family)
- One burial plot, casket, etc. (per person)
- A funeral plan within certain limits
- The share of property allowed to the at-home spouse by the Spousal Impoverishment Law
- Personal possessions, such as wedding rings and clothes
- In some situations, property used in an ongoing business
- The community spouse keeps all of his or her own income plus half of any shared income.

Sources: The Medicare Catastrophic Coverage Act (MCCA) of 1988 (P.L. 100–360) added Section 1924 to Title XIX of the Social Security Act, www.ssa.gov/OP_ Home/ssact/title19/1924.htm. Detailed Federal guidance is in chapter 3 of the State Medicaid Manual, www.cms.hhs.gov/manuals/45_smm/sm_03_3_toc.asp (see Sections 3260–3263, 3702, and 3710–3714) and Thomson/MEDSTAT (2005)

they probably make little sense for older people or couples with few assets. They have relatively few assets to shelter, and will almost inevitably be forced onto Medicaid. Although one might wish to avoid having to go on Medicaid, it is unclear that long-term care insurance is the option. It simply makes no sense for older Hispanics with only limited real estate and financial assets.

The second barrier, availability, refers to the presence of a facility close enough for family members to remain in contact with the older person. A lengthy drive may mean that family members can visit only infrequently, and they probably cannot take the older person shopping, to the doctor, or out to eat as often as they might wish. For older individuals who live in rural areas or in the extremely poor counties along the U.S./Mexico border the lack of geographically convenient high-quality nursing homes that offer culturally and linguistically appropriate supportive services represents a major barrier to care (Feng, Fennell, Tyler, Clark, & Mor, 2011; Fennell, Zhang, Clark, & Mor, 2010).

The third set of barriers has to do with acceptability, which relates to the entire range of factors that reflect cultural preferences, from the ethnic composition of the facility, to the language spoken by senior staff, to the food that is offered, and the entertainment available. A strange environment in which one feels like a cultural outsider is undesirable and will in all likelihood be rejected by the older person and his or her family (Burr & Mutchler, 1992). Some research suggests that a major reason that Hispanics avoid nursing homes is because they do not view them as culturally acceptable alternatives (Baxter, Bryant, Scarbro, & Shetterly, 2001; Eribes & Bradley-Rawls, 1978; Espino, Neufeld, Mulvihill, & Libow, 1988; Griffith & Villavicencio, 1985). The rejection of nursing homes also appears to reflect cultural norms concerning family responsibility for elders (Abraido-Lanza, Armbrister, Florez, & Aguirre, 2006; Herrera et al., 2012; Weeks & Cuellar, 1981). In a small clinical sample that included Mexican Americans, researchers found that Hispanics kept their older parents at home even when they were far sicker than was the case for non-Hispanics (Espino & Burge, 1989).

Staff behavior can also contribute to the rejection of nursing homes. Research shows that Hispanic residents and their families often view service providers as culturally insensitive and lacking warmth, empathy, and respect (Gorek, Martin, White, Peters, & Hummel, 2002; Rhodes & Weatherspoon, 2009). For an older Latino who is used to a particular diet, the food provided in a nursing home or even that delivered to one's own home can be quite foreign. Affordability, availability, and acceptability are clearly highly correlated. The presence of facilities that are too expensive and that are culturally foreign means that no culturally acceptable option is locally available (Wallace, Levy-Storms, Kington, & Andersen, 1998).

AN IMPORTANT STUDY OF VERY OLD HISPANICS

The low use of nursing home and long-term care by older Mexican-origin adults is revealed in a major longitudinal study of older Mexican-origin men and women who live in the Southwestern United States, the Hispanic-EPESE that we have mentioned before. These individuals were followed for 18 years and their changes in living arrangements observed. Relatively few of these older Mexican-origin individuals entered a nursing home at any time during the study (Espino, Angel, Wood, Finely, & Ye, 2013). Since many of these individuals were very old at the beginning of the study the low use of nursing homes is notable. The oldest was actually over 100 and by the end of the study the average age of survivors was 86, yet during the 12 years in which the sample was followed less than 4% ever used a nursing home (Espino et al., 2013).

Those who did were older and were more likely to be functionally impaired. They were also more likely to speak English on a regular basis, suggesting that they were more acculturated and likely to be more open to nursing home use than those who spoke primarily Spanish (Espino et al., 2013). These individuals were more traditionally Mexican and had almost no personal resources. Cultural and need factors are also reflected in the fact that the foreign-born who migrated to the United States in late adulthood were far more likely than those who migrated earlier in life or than the native-born to live with their families and rely on them for help instead of using formal long-term care services (Angel, Angel, Lee, & Markides, 1999). Although it is impossible to derive exact reasons for the low use of nursing home care in this study, they suggest that, as seemed to be the case in the studies we mentioned before, several factors, including cultural norms, large families with the capacity to care for aging parents, the inability to afford expensive long-term care, and the desire to avoid the stigma of Medicaid or a lack of knowledge of its availability, account for the propensity to rely on informal care (Herrera et al., 2012).

The low use of nursing homes by seriously impaired older Hispanics leads us to ask about the alternatives they employ in the event they are unable to care for themselves. Traditionally, they moved in with their children or their children moved in with them. This was a period in which families were larger and when children tended not to move far away. It was also a time when people did not live as long as they do today. Although the old world is gone, most older individuals continue to live in the community. If they are less likely to look to family for all of the financial and practical care they need, we might ask who they turn to in the community. Figure 6.1 summarizes the community-based living arrangements of the survivors in 2010 of the Hispanic Established Populations for Epidemiologic Studies of the Elderly (H-EPESE) when the sample was 85 and older. Over 30% lived alone, and approximately 20% lived with a surviving spouse. Over one-half of the sample, though, lived with others, primarily with children. The vast majority were unmarried and widowed. Perhaps because of the fact that the sample was extremely old, this statistic is higher than for the population as a whole. National data on non-institutionalized older populations shows that approximately one-third of Latino elderly individuals lived with someone other than a spouse (U.S. Statistical Abstracts of the United States, 2012).

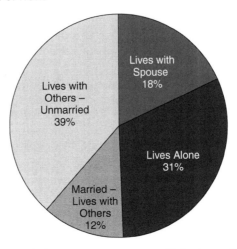

FIGURE 6.1 *Living Arrangements of Mexican-Origin Adults 85 and Older.*
Source: H-EPESE: 2010.

Table 6.2 shows the same living arrangements by health status. What these data reveal is that among the unmarried, an important source of support for the infirm and disabled are children and other family members. Married couples can rely on each other for emotional and instrumental support. Individuals who live alone are not as disabled as the unmarried who live with other kin. The baseline data from the study also show that married couples who co-reside with family were the most likely to do so for economic reasons as opposed to health problems.

TABLE 6.2 *Living Arrangements by Health and Disability among Older Individuals of Mexican Origin: 2010*

HEALTH/DISABILITY	SPOUSE ONLY	LIVE ALONE	UNMARRIED – LIVE WITH OTHERS	MARRIED – LIVE WITH OTHERS
At Least One ADL	34.5	50.2	57.0	44.4
At Least One I-ADL	92.9	92.1	79.3	82.7
Poor Physical Mobility (POMA)	32.8	48.7	50.3	36.7
Psychological Distress (CES-D)	16.8	30.8	33.7	12.9
Cognitive Impairment (MMSE)	13.2	19.8	33.6	25.4
Percent (N = 1,078)	18.6 (197)	30.8 (327)	38.1 (405)	12.5 (133)

Source: H-EPESE, 2010.

COMMUNITY OPTIONS IN LONG-TERM CARE

As much as an aging parent may wish to stay in his or her home, for many that would not be possible without at least some assistance. Some individuals need a great deal of assistance. Although fewer older individuals live with their children than in the past, as we have noted families continue to provide a large amount of support and care to older parents, but despite their best intentions, families face serious challenges in caring for parents who live longer, but often with serious physical and cognitive problems (Silverstein & Giarrusso, 2010). For most middle-aged adults financial as well as time resources are limited. Responsibilities for their own children create conflicting demands for time and money (Fingerman, VanderDrift, Dotterer, Birditt, & Zarit, 2011). Middle-aged adults who have children and aging parents are members of what has been termed the "sandwich generation," a colorful image that emphasizes the fact that these working-age adults are caught between the needs of both the younger and older generations (Spillman & Pezzin, 2000). With limited time and money, these sandwiched adults face difficult choices in deciding what resources to devote to the education and needs of children, their own savings and retirement plans as well as their careers, and supporting and caring for aging parents.

Affluent elderly individuals and couples can choose from among many options in long-term care, especially when they are relatively healthy. Retirement communities, assisted living at various levels, and community-based care are options for older individuals and couples with sufficient resources who need or desire some assistance but who are not fully disabled (Stone, 2011). Among the frail and disabled, one million Americans live in assisted-living facilities (ALFs) (Ortiz, 2013). This constitutes a small but growing segment of the elderly population, with 2.4% of the elderly lived in senior housing with at least one supportive service available to their residents (Administration on Aging, 2012). This population of elders that are housed in these institutionalized alternatives, which encompass a variety of services and housing supports for persons unable to live independently, has grown swiftly since 1985. In the last decade, ALFs grew significantly in popularity to number more than 38,000 nationwide in 2007 (Mollica, Houser, & Ujvari, 2012). The increase in the number of older people with disabilities living in community residential care facilities like ALFs offset the decline in the institutional population in the last two decades, which points to the fact that assisted living may be replacing nursing home care for a segment of the older population with disabilities (Redfoot & Houser, 2010). Designed to assist the frail elderly with performing activities of daily life, residents in ALFs are less impaired than most nursing home residents (Hawes, Rose, & Phillips, 1999).

Some individuals choose to move to retirement communities while they are still relatively young and in excellent health. The media are full of images of snowbirds who have moved to Florida or Arizona to spend their days on the golf course or by the pool socializing with other retirees. One can easily imagine that one can arrive at a point at which one is tired of dealing with the upkeep of a household and would rather live in a condo where someone else mows the lawn and sees to repairs. For those with enough money, such leisurely arrangements are a clear possibility. For those who cannot afford such living arrangements, other options are necessary.

The need for home- and community-based long-term care arrives when an older individual or couple cannot maintain their own home or care for themselves without assistance. At that point children or someone else must step in. Family members can provide informal support, but formal support is usually provided by agencies paid for by the family or Medicaid, or by NGOs and volunteers. Maintaining an impaired older person in the community can be a daunting task that requires a combination of informal and formal care. Medical needs mean that the older person must be taken to the doctor, or that home health care workers provide basic care in the individual's home. Much of what an older person needs, though, is assistance with basic housekeeping and personal care. Non-medical services and home support can include case management, which refers to the involvement of a professional to coordinate services. These services can include housekeeping assistance, home health aides, personal care services, adult day health services, home repair, food and nutrition, money management, education and respite for caregivers, and more.

Given the desire of most individuals to remain in their own homes and in the community, several community-based options designed to replace or supplement family efforts to provide care have been developed. These are particularly appropriate for individuals who are less impaired. Nursing homes and skilled care facilities represent the most comprehensive and usually the most expensive options for older individuals who need intensive and ongoing assistance. The question that arises is whether community-based care can be provided efficiently and economically, and perhaps in a more culturally appropriate manner than institutional care. Although other services are available, we mention three options in community care that are of particular interest for our purposes since they are widely available and hold out the possibility of greatly improving an older person's quality of life and providing respite to caregivers. These include adult day care centers, nutrition services, and visiting home health care providers. Let us examine what each offers. Exhibit 6.4 presents details of more comprehensive community-based long-term care services.

Exhibit 6.4 Comprehensive Community-based Long-term Care Services

Information and referral	Service management/case management
Assessment, planning and evaluation	Transportation
Access to legal assistance	Community integration
Adult day care	Housing, shelter, and home modifications
Foster care	Emergency response systems
Homemaker and chore services	Personal assistance services
Food, meal services, and nutrition counseling	Durable medical equipment
Nursing care	Habilitative and restorative therapies
Medical supplies	General medical services
Hospice care	Respite care
Individual, group, and family counseling	Assistive devices
Caregiver training and support	

ADULT DAY CARE

South Texas, which is primarily Mexican in origin, includes hundreds of adult day care centers (Ustinova, 2007). See the directory of the 190 adult day care programs in the Lower Rio Grande Valley at 🌐 http://lrgv.tx.networkofcare.org/aging/services/subcategory.aspx?tax=PH-0320. Caregivers who might initially be reluctant to use adult day care are usually relieved when they do, especially when they find out that Medicaid covers the cost of the services. These adult day centers have pleasant uplifting names such as Mi Nuevo Mundo (My New World), Amor y Paz (Love and Peace), and Un Dia a la Vez (One Day at a Time) and provide social, recreational, and educational services to seniors as well as a much-needed break for Latino family caregivers. In addition to offering Latino cuisine, elderly clients can take exercise classes, make arts and crafts, listen to musical entertainment with familiar Tejano bands, garden, play bingo, take regular local outings to the mall as well as occasional field trips to South Padre Island, celebrate holidays, and attend birthday parties. Some seniors arrive at a center early in the morning and return home in time for dinner, which allows families to avoid institutionalizing the older person while continuing to work and tending to their other responsibilities. Other seniors stay for only part of the day, during which they share a meal with others and enjoy their company. Such centers help avoid the isolation that many older individuals in the community experience.

Culturally appropriate services for the growing Hispanic elderly population are increasingly provided nationwide. In New Jersey the Adult Day Care Program (ADCP) provided through the Hispanic Family Center in Camden is specifically designed for Hispanic seniors and provides culturally sensitive and appropriate physical, social, and recreational activities to reduce the risk of social isolation. According to the program's website, 🌐 www.hispanicfamilycenter.com/wp/services/seniors/, the program provides services in a completely bilingual environment that is designed to be sensitive to the cultural needs of the clientele, who attend three times a week. The program offers several workshops on various topics of importance and interest to Hispanic seniors, and offers health screenings and recreational activities to promote healthful aging. Nutritious meals are also provided.

NUTRITION PROGRAMS

Community care takes other, less intensive, but important forms as well. Most Americans are familiar with Meals on Wheels, a nutrition program in which volunteers deliver nutritious meals to individuals who would otherwise be at risk of malnutrition. The Meals on Wheels Association of America is the nation's oldest nutrition program for the elderly and was founded during World War II (Meals on Wheels Association of America, 2013). It was founded to address what were at the time serious nutritional deficiencies among elders. The program is funded through grants from the federal to state governments as part of the Older Americans Act (OAA). The meals are required to be appealing to older adults and to take into account any special dietary needs that result from health or medical conditions, cultural preferences, or religious beliefs. Meals are delivered at home and also provided at central sites where older individuals can be brought (Weddle, Wellman, Marra, & Pan, 2007). See Exhibit 6.5 for an example of Meals-on-Wheels menu options designed for Latino seniors of San Diego.

Exhibit 6.5 Senior Latin Healthy Recipe

Flank Steak with Sweet Potatoes, Cherry Tomatoes, and Green Onions
4 servings

$\frac{1}{4}$ cup plus 3 tablespoons olive oil
$\frac{1}{4}$ cup red wine vinegar
1 teaspoon ground cumin
1 tablespoon dried oregano
$\frac{1}{8}$ teaspoon kosher salt
1 flank steak (about $1\frac{1}{2}$ pounds)
2 large sweet potatoes, peeled and cut into 1-inch cubes
1 pint cherry tomatoes
2 bundles green onions, green parts only, cut into $1\frac{1}{2}$ inch pieces
Freshly ground black pepper
$\frac{1}{2}$ cup guava sauce

Preparation:
Whisk the $\frac{1}{4}$ cup oil, the vinegar, cumin, oregano, and $\frac{1}{8}$ teaspoon salt together in a glass baking dish. Add the flank steak, turn so the meat is well coated, and then cover with plastic wrap. Refrigerate for at least 3 hours or overnight.

Place the sweet potatoes in a medium saucepan and cover with salted water. Bring to a boil over medium heat and cook until the sweet potatoes are tender when easily pierced with the tip of a knife but still hold their shape, about 5 minutes. Drain and set aside.

Remove the steak from the refrigerator 15 to 30 minutes before cooking.

Preheat your grill to high or heat a grill pan over medium-high heat.

Place the steak on the hot grill and cook for about 4 minutes, or until browned, before turning. Cook the second side for about 3 minutes for medium-rare. Transfer the flank steak to a cutting board and let it rest while you finish the garnish.

Heat the 3 tablespoons olive oil in a large sauté pan over medium-high heat until hot but not smoking. Add the sweet potatoes and let them cook, undisturbed, for about 2 minutes before turning them. Cook for about 2 minutes more, or until golden brown and crisp. Add the cherry tomatoes and sauté until they begin to blacken, about 2 minutes. Add the green onions and stir for about 1 minute; they should soften but retain their bright green color. Season with salt and pepper and transfer to a large platter.

Slice the steak against the grain into $\frac{1}{2}$ inch slices. Fan the slices of steak around the vegetables and drizzle the guava sauce over the steak. Season with a sprinkling of salt and some pepper.

Guava Sauce

Makes about 1 cup

$\frac{1}{3}$ cup cubed guava paste
1 garlic clove, minced
2 tablespoons olive oil
2 tablespoons dry white wine
$\frac{1}{8}$ tsp. kosher salt

Source: Isabel Cruz's Healthy Latin Cuisine Recipes developed for Meals-on-Wheels Greater San Diego, www.meals-on-wheels.org/blog/community/healthy-latin-cuisine-yes-indeed

HOME AND COMMUNITY-BASED HEALTH SERVICES

Various NGOs and FBOs are potentially important sources of care for elderly individuals in the community. They are in a unique position to provide companionship to isolated elders who might otherwise have no contact with others for long periods. Such organizations rely heavily on volunteers who are often local community members who can relate to the older person. Religious groups play an important role in providing a wide range of assistance, including transportation and emotional and spiritual support to older parishioners. Before discussing NGOs' and FBOs' eldercare roles, let us examine federal and state experiments in community care.

Several experiments in community-based long-term care have been carried out in recent years and provide useful information on ways in which frail elderly individuals can be supported in the community. The objective of such experiments is to optimize older individuals' mental health and well-being and to reduce the burden placed on families. Many of these programs, like On Lok, which provides extensive community-based support to Chinese-origin elders in the San Francisco Bay Area, and which we discuss further below, were begun as non-governmental programs. On Lok is an important example of a highly successful experiment that served as a model for the federal Program of All-Inclusive Care for the Elderly (PACE), which we also mention further below. Other local initiatives, such as the use of "promotores" or community health outreach workers, which we discussed in Chapter 5, are potentially important to Latino and other minority elders.

In addition to improving an older person's quality of life, community alternatives may be less expensive than high-level nursing homes. In order to determine the benefits of community options many states have applied for and received home- and community-based Medicaid waivers that allow them to experiment with new ways of providing long-term care on a cost-neutral basis. These are largely motivated by research that shows that community care services can prevent or at least delay institutionalization (Pande, Laditka, Laditka, & Davis, 2007). Exhibit 6.6 describes three types of Medicaid community-waiver programs now available to elderly persons with disabilities who qualify. These community-based programs encompass a wide array of services that help meet the needs of low-income older Americans with disabilities, including but not limited to adult foster care, home delivered meals, respite care, primary home care, and day activity and health services.

Evaluations of these programs suggest that they are more economical, or at least no more expensive, than institutional care (Lewin Group, 2004; Rudolph & Lubitz, 1999). Unfortunately, since they are primarily waiver experiments, they are unavailable in many areas and long waiting lists are common (Gleckman, 2012). In 2011 at least 1,300 aged and disabled Medicaid nursing home residents in California

Exhibit 6.6 Type of Medicaid Home and Community-based Waiver Services

TYPE	DESCRIPTION
1. *The Community-based Alternative Waiver Program*	Allows elderly persons (65+) with a disability, who meet nursing facility level of care, to live in the community. Services offered under this waiver include: adaptive aids, medical supplies, adult foster care, assisted living/residential care, consumer directed services, and emergency response.
2. The *STAR+PLUS Waiver Program*	Provides home and community-based care through managed care organizations. The waiver attempts to manage prospectively the cost of Medicaid long-term care services. STAR+PLUS is similar to the CBA waiver except that services are provided by health maintenance organizations or managed care. This program is designed to integrate acute (Medicare) and long-term care (Medicaid) financing and service delivery for elders with disabilities. Enrollment is required for Medicaid elderly beneficiaries. Evaluation of the managed long-term care model has proven cost effective, saving the state money and providing better care (Kitchener, Ng, Willmott, & Harrington, 2006).
3. The *Program of All-Inclusive Care for the Elderly (PACE)*	A capitated benefit authorized by the Balanced Budget Act of 1997 (BBA) that provides all acute, primary, and long-term care needs of the individual. The comprehensive health service delivery system integrates Medicare and Medicaid financing (Centers for Medicare and Medicaid Services, 2005). The program is designed for individuals 55 and over who meet the nursing facility level of care requirement.

Source: www.medicaid.gov/Medicaid-CHIP-Program-Information/By-Topics/Waivers/Waivers.html were on waiting lists for community care, and in Texas almost 44,000 were waiting to receive home care benefits (Kaiser Commission on Medicaid and the Uninsured, 2012).

Let us return to the San Francisco experiment we mentioned above and examine how it operates. *On Lok* is a Cantonese term that means "peaceful, happy abode." The experiment is an example of a culturally sensitive and focused initiative based in the Asian community. It began in 1971 as an NGO to provide a wide range of assistance to frail Asian elderly individuals in the San Francisco Bay Area (Hansen & Hewitt, 2012). The objective was to allow them to remain in their own homes and avoid institutionalization (Bodenheimer, 1999). As we discuss later, such civil society organizations hold great promise for providing assistance and services that formal organizations may not be well suited to provide. The success of this program led to its formal adoption by Congress in 1979 as a model for the PACE program to be replicated in other cities (Brinker, 2013).

As with On Lok the objective of PACE is to allow individuals to remain in the community. The services are designed for high-need frail elderly individuals aged 55 or older who would otherwise need a nursing home (Gross, Temkin-Greener, Kunitz, & Mukamel, 2004). A comprehensive service plan for each client is developed by an interdisciplinary team of health professionals, including doctors, nurses, nutritionists, and social workers, among others. PACE may also include other services that are available in the caregiver's area. To do this, the social services arm of the comprehensive case management team works very closely with the family to make sure everything happens on a timely basis to assist in the care of a loved one. PACE services are paid for primarily by Medicare and Medicaid and they are available in 31 states. See the PACE directory at www.npaonline.org/website/article.asp?id=12&title=Who,_What_and_Where_Is_PACE.

The PACE model boasts clearly measurable success, with substantial Medicaid savings compared to nursing homes. Nationally, the average estimated cost of providing care for PACE patients in traditional long-term care arrangements is $36,620, far higher than PACE's maximum cost of $27,648 (Wieland, Kinosian, Stallard, & Boland, 2013). Participants enjoy a significantly favorable survival rate. On average, they live three-and-a-half years longer than nursing home residents (Wieland, Boland, Baskins, & Kinosian, 2010). As potentially useful as PACE services might be to caregivers and the older individuals they care for, however, over 70% of low-income seniors who are eligible do not participate (National Council on Aging, 2012).

The PACE program in El Paso, Texas provides an interesting example of adaptations that address the unique needs of the local Hispanic community (Bodenheimer, 1999). Established in 1986, the program operates Bienvivir ("live well" in Spanish). The program provides services to almost 600 financially disadvantaged residents of El Paso, the majority of whom are of Hispanic origin (Levkoff, Chen, & Norton, 2013). Given the fact that this population needs services at relatively young ages, PACE's age-eligibility criterion of 55 is important. A major objective of the program is to involve families. Family members are included in all aspects of care delivery. In Texas the ultimate objective is to save money and to provide needed community services to the growing older Mexican-origin population. Initial data seem promising. The average monthly state expenditure in 2006 was $2,028 per participant for PACE community care, compared to $2,817 for nursing home care in Houston and $2,817 in Dallas/Fort Worth (Levkoff et al., 2013; U.S. Office of Personnel Management, 2008). For more information about Bienvivir, visit www.bienvivir.org.

Although Bienvivir has proven to be very successful in addressing primarily social and physical health care needs, only a small fraction of enrollees receive treatment for mental health problems (Levkoff et al., 2013). In order to improve access to mental health services, the City of El Paso created a new initiative called Project Focus for the Optimal Care of Underserved Seniors (FOCUS). Project Focus is one of nine Substance Abuse and Mental Health Services Administration (SAMHSA) funded model service programs designed to meet the mental health care needs of older adults (City of El Paso, 2014).

NON-GOVERNMENTAL AND FAITH-BASED ORGANIZATIONS

Although the welfare state provides the basic social safety net for citizens of all ages, informal organizations and social movements have always been important in furthering the well-being of individuals and groups (Angel, 2011; Keck & Sikkink, 1998). Religious groups have historically assumed a major role in caring for the poor and infirm (Idler, 2006). Given their grounding in spiritual matters and their mission of charity, these organizations are in many ways ideal for providing assistance to the elderly in the community. International FBOs, such as CARITAS, Catholic Charities, and Lutheran Social Services, provide assistance to the elderly as part of their missions. There are far too many NGOs involved in eldercare to provide even a partial list, but we mention a few to show how central they are becoming to the mission of eldercare.

An example of a local NGO that assists community-dwelling older individuals to live at home is Family Eldercare in Austin, Texas. This 501(c) 3 charitable organization was founded in 1982 by a group of professionals whose objective was to assist families to care for elders through training and information. The agency soon expanded to include a variety of services including guardianship, consultation and referral, a summer fan drive, money management, in-home care, respite care for Alzheimer's patients, and emergency subsidized housing to clients in Travis and Williamson Counties. In 2008, 17% of the 6,600 clients they served were Latino, 18% were African American, and 64% were non-Latino White (Family Eldercare, 2008). In addition to social services, Family Eldercare addresses the need for affordable and independent senior living. In 2004, the organization raised $5.6 million in private and public funding and opened Lyons Garden, which is located in a predominantly minority neighborhood in East Austin. This 54-unit senior housing community, one of which is reserved for the apartment manager, offers housing and social services to low-income seniors aged 62 and older. Residents live independently in one-bedroom apartments and have access to a large community building and an expansive interior courtyard that includes a meditation garden, club house, and play-scape for young visitors. The complex is located near a large grocery store, a neighborhood center that includes a medical facility, two bus lines, a senior activity center, churches, a community college, and other amenities.

Little Brothers – Friends of the Elderly (LBFE) (🐾 www.littlebrothers.org) is an international network of volunteer organizations with branches in the United States that addresses the problem of isolation and loneliness by providing volunteers to visit older people in the community and offer companionship. Even an hour or two with a visitor allows an older person to confide in someone or simply engage in social interaction. During such visits the volunteer can get some idea of how well the older person is functioning and possibly identify problems to be referred to a professional agency. Little Brothers is part of a larger international organization, the Fédération Internationale des petits frères des Pauvres (International Federation of little brothers of the Poor, 🐾 www.petitsfreres.org). Another international NGO that provides similar services is the Fédération Internationale des Associations de Personnes Agées (International Federation of Associations of Older Persons, FIAPA: 🐾 www.fiapa.net), headquartered in Paris. Its mission is also to address the problem of isolation and improve the quality of life of older individuals.

As these two examples show, the need to provide assistance and support to the elderly in the community is universal. In India, for example, NGOs are assuming a larger role as advocates for and providers of services to the elderly (Sawhney, 2003). The governments of developing nations with massive populations will clearly never be able to directly provide all of the services their aging populations require. *Dignity Foundation* (🐾 www.dignityfoundation.com), which is a member of the AARP Global Network, provides housing, companionship, recreation, and other services to elderly individuals in several Indian cities. *HelpAge India* (🐾 www.helpageindia.org) is yet another NGO that provides financial, medical, and emotional support to poor elderly Indians. These are examples of eldercare NGOs filling voids in contexts in which formal supports are rare. Given the fact that even in more developed nations governments are not able to address many of the needs of community-dwelling older persons, NGOs and FBOs assume the role of vital partners.

ADVOCATING FOR THE AGED

Long-term care policy and its implementation, like all other aspects of the political process, are influenced by various interested parties who lobby and engage in other activities to further their own interests. The major interests include the nursing home industry, consumers of long-term care services and their families, and governmental agencies that are responsible for operating within limited budgets. The nursing home industry is clearly interested in ensuring funding streams from Medicaid and other sources. Consumer groups are interested in lobbying for programs that satisfy their membership's preferences. Often these reflect the desire to further community-based options since older individuals prefer to remain in their own homes as long as possible. Yet, as in other areas of public policy, rapid paradigm shifts are rare given inertia and path dependence, as well as the fact that entrenched interest groups resist change (Margolis & Liebowitz, 1995). A major shift from nursing home to community-based care, for example, faces serious resistance from the nursing home industry.

The main lobbying organization of the for-profit nursing home industry in Texas is the Texas Health Care Association (THCA). Its counterpart, which represents the non-profit sector, is the Texas Association of Homes and Services for the Aging (TAHSA). These two organizations are powerful and effective special-interest groups that lobby for the interests of the nursing home industry. Their agenda includes higher nursing home reimbursement rates and greater availability of affordable liability insurance for long-term care providers. They also view the regulatory policy environment as much too restrictive and lobby for its liberalization (Wiener, Stevenson, & Goldenson, 1998).

Consumer interest groups, including the AARP and its state chapter, have made their presence known at the State Capitol. These age-based interest groups lobby the state legislature on a wide variety of issues. In contrast to the nursing home industry, they view the regulatory apparatus as relatively weak and ineffective and lobby for legislation that would provide greater protection to vulnerable residents of ALFs and nursing homes. The AARP has opposed reductions in Medicaid expenditures even in the face of state budget shortfalls. The organization resists cuts in Medicaid since the resulting increases in premiums and co-pays and greater cost sharing might reduce health care access to older individuals with limited incomes (Hudson, 2007).

Other national lobbying groups that act specifically on behalf of elderly Mexican-origin individuals include the National Alliance for Hispanic Health, the National Hispanic Council on Aging, the National Council of La Raza, and the Mexican American Legal Defense and Educational Fund (MALDEF) (Angel & Angel, 2008). For the most part, these organizations have been ineffective in promoting older Mexican-origin health and long-term care interests. One potential reason that they have not been able to put an aging agenda on the legislative table is that other important issues, such as education, immigration, and poverty among working-age families and children, take priority over long-term care. Although consumer and industry groups advocate on behalf of different parties, their interests overlap. They are all interested in ensuring adequate government funding for long-term care programs that address the needs of their specific clienteles.

ADVOCACY AND THE ROLE OF MUNICIPAL GOVERNMENT IN THE HISPANIC COMMUNITY

In 1965, the same year that Medicare was introduced, President Johnson signed the Older Americans Act (OAA) into law in response to concern by policy makers about a lack of community services for older adults (Hudson, 2005). The situation was particularly worrisome because at that time almost 30% of elderly Americans aged 60 and older were in poverty, a percentage that Congress recognized as intolerable. The objectives of the Act were to improve the lives of America's older individuals aged 60 and above in relation to income, health, housing, employment, long-term care, retirement, and community services (Administration on Aging, 2010). The original legislation established the Administration on Aging (AoA) to administer small grants to states for community planning and services programs. In 1973, Area Agencies on Aging were established to help low-income minority elders and their families remain in their homes (Administration on Aging, 2010). Today, the AoA provides funding for food programs, such as meals on wheels, and for supportive home and community-based services through a national aging network that includes 56 State Units on Aging (SUAs), 629 Area Agencies on Aging, 244 Tribal organizations, and two Native Hawaiian organizations. The National Association of Area Agencies on Aging is the leading advocacy organization and voice on aging issues for the Area Agencies on Aging.

In Texas, which has a large Hispanic population, the Texas Department of Disability and Aging Services (DADS) administers the OAA. The OAA has been reauthorized several times since it was first passed and in 2000 Congress established the National Family Caregiver Support Program (NFCSP). As we will discuss further in Chapter 8, the NFCSP funds a range of support services that assist families to care for their loved ones at home for as long as possible (Feinberg, Newman, & Steenberg, 2002).

The Bexar Area Agency on Aging, which includes San Antonio, the seventh-largest city in the United States, provides a good example of the services that will be increasingly necessary to address the growing need for eldercare services in the Mexican-origin community. The agency's clientele is 56% Mexican origin (Alamo Area Council of Governments, 2007). As we have documented, the Hispanic population, and especially in Texas, is on average poor and has little education. In order to make ends meet family members must work. For working families, caring for an infirm elderly parent can cause significant hardship and financial sacrifice (Lim et al., 1996). For these families the comprehensive services, including assistance with modifying the older person's dwelling to accommodate disabilities, that the agency offers are vital.

Unfortunately, the growing need places serious strains on the agency's ability to respond. The projected growth in the age 60 and older and minority population in this area may strain resources to the limit, resulting in a reduction of services. Although many older people need modifications to their dwellings to accommodate disabilities, because of the high cost it is increasingly difficult for the agency to build ramps and perform other minor home modifications. Homemaker services are another key service in the community that is increasingly difficult to provide.

SUMMARY AND CONCLUSIONS

In this chapter we reviewed options in long-term care for older individuals and examined patterns of use of various options by older Hispanics. Although most individuals would prefer to remain in the community and in their own homes as they age, the reality is that at some point independent living can become impossible. At that point institutionalization becomes almost inevitable, unless the family can assume the full-time care of the older person. A consistent finding in the literature is that Hispanics enter nursing homes at far lower rates than non-Hispanic Whites. Some evidence suggests that they stay in the community until they are far more impaired than is the case for non-Hispanics. There are clearly many reasons for this low use of nursing homes, some related to cultural expectations concerning the duty of children to care for aging parents, and others to financial and social factors, including the cost and availability of culturally appropriate care. We categorized the major barriers to the use of nursing homes by Hispanics into three large categories, affordability, availability, and acceptability.

Affordability is clearly a major barrier to long-term care for everyone and given the low levels of assets and income among Hispanics, this barrier is even more serious. Nursing home care is extremely expensive and all but the most affluent individuals and families can afford to pay for it out-of-pocket. Neither Medicare nor ordinary health insurance cover long-term care. The only option available to a family with limited resources is to turn to Medicaid, the governmental program for the poor. Unlike Medicare, Medicaid is a jointly funded federal and state program that places tremendous financial burdens on states. The cost of Medicaid is one of the major reasons that several states have refused to extend coverage to low-income adults as part of Obamacare. Although most of the enrollees in Medicaid are children in poor families, over half of the funding goes to the support of disabled and elderly individuals. Because of the cost and the fact that half or more must be paid by states, the program is limited and older individuals must have essentially no assets in order to qualify. Given their low levels of assets Medicaid is a clear funding alternative for older Hispanics.

Even if Medicaid is available, an acceptable long-term care facility may not be. Given the fact that there are relatively few nursing homes in Hispanic communities or even within a reasonable distance, availability remains a problem. If families are unable to see an aging parent on a fairly regular basis, they may feel that they have abandoned the older person, a serious violation of norms of love and respect for elders. We presented the example of the colonias of the border region as an example of low availability, in addition to extreme poverty. The border region is vast and seriously underserved in terms of health care generally, but especially in terms of long-term care.

The third group of barriers to the use of long-term care is related to acceptability, which refers to the cultural and social acceptability of long-term care facilities. Often long-term care facilities and their staffs are viewed as foreign and disrespectful of older Hispanics. In combination, the lack of availability, affordability, and acceptability seriously reduce nursing home use by Hispanics. We note, though, that given Hispanics' increasing lifespans and the demographic and social changes that are affecting the family's ability to provide care to seriously impaired elders, higher rates of nursing home use in the future may be inevitable.

Before institutionalization becomes necessary, other options are available to assist individuals with moderate to severe impairments remain in their own homes. We reviewed several of these options, including adult day care and home health care services. Depending on what is available in the community, home care and related supplemental services can include health care, personal care, meal preparation in the home, meal delivery, or meals at an outside facility. Other services include housekeeping, shopping, home repair, money management, transportation, companionship, as well as respite services for caregivers, and more.

The populations of most nations are aging rapidly, especially in the developed regions. Aging populations mean that for all nations maximizing the independence and preserving the quality of life of older citizens present major challenges. As the baby boom generation enters its later years, the demand for eldercare will grow and it is clear that the state cannot provide everything older individuals need. Dealing with problems of isolation and depression and issues of the quality of life are not tasks solely for bureaucrats in Washington or in state capitals. These problems must be dealt with closer to home. The growing need for care will require new experiments in providing support and care to older individuals in the community. Our review of the literature suggests that the best solution involves a combination of informal family support, formal governmental programs, and the participation of non-governmental and faith-based organizations.

DISCUSSION QUESTIONS

1. Discuss the various options in long-term care. How does long-term care differ from acute care? What are some of the reasons for low uses of formal long-term care by Hispanics?
2. Discuss ways in which long-term care might be made more appealing and acceptable to different racial and ethnic groups. If you were designing a new long-term care program, what factors would you consider to be first priority? What factors are less important?
3. How is long-term care financed? In your opinion, should Medicare pay for long-term care? Why do you imagine that Medicare policy excludes services like long-term care and dental work?
4. Two ways of conceiving of medical care generally and of long-term care in particular are: (1) as rights that all citizens are entitled to regardless of ability to pay, or (2) as commodities like any other that one can purchase if one can afford to and that one does without if one cannot. Discuss the moral and practical bases for each position.

5. Summarize the major factors that influence an older individual's and a family's decision to place an older parent in a nursing home or to attempt to keep them in the community.
6. Do NGOs and FBOs play a major role in providing or obtaining care for older individuals who can no longer live independently? Discuss the potential role of such organizations and identify some long-term care tasks that they might be well suited to perform.

LITERATURE CITED

Abraido-Lanza, A. F., Armbrister, A. N., Florez, K. R., & Aguirre, A. N. (2006). Toward a theory-driven model of acculturation in public health research. *American Journal of Public Health, 96,* 1342–6.

Administration on Aging. (2010). *Statement by Assistant Secretary Greenlee on the 45th anniversary of the signing of the Older Americans Act.*

Administration on Aging. (2012). *A profile of older Americans: 2011 – Living arrangements.* Retrieved from www.aoa.gov/Aging_Statistics/Profile/2011/6.aspx.

Alamo Area Council of Governments. (2007). *Bexar County area plan: Fiscal years 2008–2010.* San Antonio, TX: Area Agency on Aging.

Angel, J. L. (1991). *Health and living arrangements of the elderly.* New York, NY: Garland Publishing.

Angel, J. L., & Angel, R. J. (2008). *Caring for the elderly Mexican-origin population in Texas: Where does the burden fall?* Paper presented at the Conference on Latinos and Public Policy in Texas, University of Texas at Austin.

Angel, R. J. (2011). Civil society and eldercare in post-traditional society. In R. A. Settersten & J. L. Angel (Eds.), *Handbook of sociology of aging* (pp. 549–81). New York, NY: Springer.

Angel, R. J., Angel, J. L., Lee, G.-Y., & Markides, K. S. (1999). Age at migration and family dependency among older Mexican immigrants: Recent evidence from the Mexican American EPESE. *The Gerontologist, 39,* 59–65.

Angel, R. J., & Williams, K. (2013). Cultural models of health and illness. In F. A. Paniagua & A.-M. Yamada (Eds.), *Handbook of multicultural mental health* (pp. 49–68). New York, NY: Elsevier Inc.

Banerjee, S. (2012). Effects of nursing home stays on household portfolios. *EBRI Issue Brief* (pp. 1–20). Washington, DC: Employee Benefit Research Institute.

Baxter, J., Bryant, L. L., Scarbro, S., & Shetterly, S. M. (2001). Patterns of rural Hispanic and non-Hispanic White health care use: The San Luis Valley health and aging study. *Research on Aging, 23,* 37–60.

Bengtson, V. L., & Achenbaum, W. A. (1993). *The changing contract across generations.* New York: de Gruyter.

Bodenheimer, T. (1999). Long-term care for frail elderly people: The On Lok model. *New England Journal of Medicine, 34*(17), 1324–8.

Brinker, J. (2013). PACE Program provides seniors with comprehensive in-home care. *Archdiocese of St. Louis.* Retrieved from www.onlok.org/About/AboutPACE.aspx.

Burr, J. A., & Mutchler, J. E. (1992). The living arrangements of unmarried elderly Hispanic females. *Demography, 29*, 93–112.

Center for Budget and Policy Priorities. (2013). *Policy basics: Introduction to Medicaid.* Washington, DC: Center for Budget and Policy Priorities.

City of El Paso. (2014). *Project FOCUS, City of El Paso, TX.* Retrieved from www.positiveaging.org/projectfocus.html.

Congressional Budget Office. (2013). *Spending and enrollment details for CBO's February 2013 baseline: Medicaid.* Washington, DC: Congressional Budget Office.

De Vos, S., & Arias, E. (2003). A note on the living arrangements of elders 1970–2000, with special emphasis on Hispanic sub-group differentials. *Population Research and Policy Review, 22*(1), 91–101.

Elliott, S., Painter, J., & Hudson, S. (2009). Living alone and fall risk factors in community-dwelling middle age and older adults. *Journal of Community Health, 34*(4), 301–10.

Ellis, B. (2013). Nursing home costs top $80,000 a year. *CNN Money.* Retrieved from http://money.cnn.com/2013/04/09/retirement/nursing-home-costs/index.html.

Eribes, R. A., & Bradley-Rawls, M. (1978). The underutilization of nursing home facilities by Mexican-American elderly in the Southwest. *The Gerontologist, 19*, 363–70.

Espino, D. V., Angel, J. L., Wood, R. C., Finely, M. R., & Ye, Y. (2013). Characteristics of Mexican American elders admitted to nursing facilities in the United States: Data from the Hispanic Established Populations for Epidemiologic Studies of the Elderly (EPESE) Study. *Journal of the America Director's Association, 14*(3), 226.e221–4.

Espino, D. V., & Burge, S. K. (1989). Comparisons of age of Mexican American and non-Hispanic white nursing home residents. *Family Medicine, 21*, 191–194.

Espino, D. V., Neufeld, R. R., Mulvihill, M., & Libow, L. S. (1988). Hispanic and non-Hispanic elderly on admission to the nursing home: A pilot study. *The Gerontologist, 28*, 821–4.

Family Eldercare, Inc. (2008). *Community care matters: Annual report.* Austin, TX: Family Eldercare, Inc.

Feinberg, L. F., Newman, S. L., & Steenberg, C. V. (2002). Family caregiver support: Policies, perceptions and practices in 10 states since passage of the National Family Caregiver Support Program. *Administration on Aging.* Washington, DC: Family Caregiver Alliance.

Feng, Z., Fennell, M. L., Tyler, D. A., Clark, M., & Mor, V. (2011). Growth of racial and ethnic minorities in US nursing homes driven by demographics and possible disparities in options. *Health Affairs, 30*(7), 1358–65.

Fennell, M. L., Zhang, F. Z., Clark, M. A., & Mor, V. (2010). Elderly Hispanics more likely to reside in poor-quality nursing homes. *Health Affairs, 29*, 65–73.

Fingerman, K. L., VanderDrift, L. E., Dotterer, A. M., Birditt, K. S., & Zarit, S. H. (2011). Support to aging parents and grown children in Black and White families. *The Gerontologist, 51*(4), 441–52. doi: 10.1093/geront/gnq114.

Giddens, A. (1991). *Modernity & self-identity: Self and society in the late modern age.* Stanford, CA: Stanford University Press.

Gleckman, H. (2012). States expand their Medicaid community-based services but their benefits vary widely. *Forbes Magazine.* Retrieved from www.forbes.com/sites/howardgleckman/2012/12/10/states-expand-their-medicaid-community-based-services-but-their-benefits-vary-widely.

Goffman, E. (1961). *Asylums: Essays on the social situation of mental patients and other inmates.* New York, NY: Anchor Books.

Goldscheider, C., & Jones, M. B. (1989). Living arrangements among the older population. In F. K. Goldscheider & C. Goldscheider (Eds.), *Ethnicity and the new family economy: Living arrangements and intergenerational financial flows* (pp. 75–91). Boulder, CO: Westview Press.

Gorek, B., Martin, J., White, N., Peters, D., & Hummel, F. (2002). Culturally competent care for Latino elders in long-term care settings. *Geriatric Nursing, 23*(5), 272–5.

Griffith, J., & Villavicencio, S. (1985). Relationships among acculturation, sociodemographic characteristics and social support in Mexican American adults. *Hispanic Journal of Behavioral Sciences, 7,* 75–92.

Gross, D. L., Temkin-Greener, H., Kunitz, S., & Mukamel, D. B. (2004). The growing pains of integrated health care for the elderly: Lessons from the expansion of PACE. *The Milbank Quarterly, 82*(2), 257–82.

Grundy, E. (2010). Household transitions and subsequent mortality among older people in England and Wales: Trends over three decades. *Journal of Epidemiology and Community Health, 65*(4), 353–9.

Hansen, J. C., & Hewitt, M. (2012). PACE provides a sense of belonging for elders. *Generations, 36*(1), 37–43.

Hawes, C., Rose, M., & Phillips, C. D. (1999). *National study of assisted living for the frail elderly: Results of a national survey of facilities.* Mayers Research Institute, U.S. Department of Health and Human Services. Retrieved from http://aspe.hhs.gov/daltcp/reports/facres.htm.

Henry J. Kaiser Foundation. (2010). Medicaid financial eligibility: Primary pathways for the elderly and people with disabilities. In *Medicaid and the uninsured.* Menlo Park, CA: The Kaiser Family Foundation.

Henry, S. M. (2006). *The eldercare handbook: Difficult choices, compassionate solutions.* New York, NY: HarperCollins.

Herrera, A. P., Angel, J. L., Díaz-Venegas, C., & Angel, R. J. (2012). Estimating the demand for long-term care among aging Mexican Americans: Cultural preferences versus economic realities. In J. L. Angel, F. Torres-Gil, & K. Markides (Eds.), *Aging, health, and longevity in the Mexican-origin population* (pp. 259–76). New York, NY: Springer Sciences.

Herrera, A. P., Mendez-Luck, C. A., Crist, J. D., Smith, M. L., Warre, R., Ory, M. G., & Markides, K. (2013). Psychosocial and cognitive health differences by caregiver status among older Mexican Americans. *Journal of Community Mental Health, 49*(1), 61–72.

Hudson, R. B. (2005). *The new politics of old-age policy.* Baltimore, MD: Johns Hopkins University.

Hudson, R. B. (2007). Politics and policy in the lives of older Americans. In K. P. Ferraro & J. Wilmoth (Eds.), *Gerontology: Perspectives and issues* (3rd ed., pp. 307–24.). New York, NY: Springer Publishing Co.

Hughes, M. E., & Waite, L. J. (2002). Health in household context: Living arrangements and health in late middle age. *Journal of Health and Social Behavior, 43*(1), 1–21.

Idler, E. (2006). Religion and aging. In R. H. Binstock & L. K. George (Eds.), *Handbook of aging and the social sciences* (6th ed., pp. 277–300). New York, NY: Academic Press.

Jones, A. L., Dwyer, L. L., Bercovitz, A. R., & Strahan, G. W. (2009). The National Nursing Home Survey: 2004 overview. *Vital health statistics, 13,* 1–155.

Kaiser Commission on Medicaid and the Uninsured. (2012). *Medicaid home and community-based service programs: 2009 data update*. Washington, DC: Kaiser Family Foundation.

Keck, M. E., & Sikkink, K. (1998). *Activists beyond borders: Advocacy networks in international politics*. Ithaca, NY: Cornell University Press.

Levkoff, S., Chen, H., & Norton, M. (2013). Two approaches to developing health interventions for ethnic minority elders: From science to practice and from practice to science. In K. E. Whitfield & T. Baker (Eds.), *Handbook of minority aging* (pp. 205–20). New York, NY: Springer Publishing.

Lewin Group. (2004). *Actuarial assessment of Medicaid managed care expansion options*. Austin, TX: Prepared for the Texas Health and Human Services Commission.

Lim, Y. M., Luna, I., Cromwell, S. L., Phillips, L. R., Russell, C. K., & Torres de Ardon, E. (1996). Toward a cross-cultural understanding of family caregiving burden, *Western Journal of Nursing Research, 18*, 252–266.

Margolis, S. E., & Liebowitz, S. J. (1995). Path dependence, lock-in and history. *Journal of Law, Economics, and Organization, 11*, 205–26.

Meals on Wheels Association of America. (2013). *The Meals on Wheels Association of America*. Retrieved from www.mowaa.org.

Mollica, R., Houser, A., & Ujvari, K. (2012). Assisted living and residential care in the States in 2010. *INSIGHT on the Issues*. Washington, DC: AARP Public Policy Institute.

National Council on Aging. (2012). The senior disconnect: Millions are losing billions in benefits. In *Data Brief*. Washington, DC: National Council On Aging.

Ortiz, J. (2013). *Assisted living facilities*. Retrieved from www.sbdcnet.org/small-business-research-reports/assisted-living-facilities.

Pande, E., Laditka, S. B., Laditka, J. N., & Davis, D. (2007). Aging in place? Evidence that a state Medicaid waiver program helps frail older persons avoid institutionalization. *Home Health Care Service Quarterly, 26*, 39–60.

Redfoot, D. L., & Houser, A. (2010). *More older people with disabilities living in the community: Trends from the National Long-Term Care Survey, 1984–2004*. Washington, DC: AARP Public Policy Institute.

Rhodes, D., & Weatherspoon, K. (2009). Chicago's Latinos face cultural, financial barriers to accessing quality nursing home care. Retrieved from http://news.medill.northwestern.edu/chicago/news.aspx?id=126713.

Robards, J., Evandrou, M., Falkingham, J., & Vlachantonia, A. (2012). Marital status, health and mortality. *Maturitas, 73*(4), 295–9.

Rudolph, N. V., & Lubitz, J. (1999). Capitated payment approaches for Medicaid-financed long-term care. *Health Care Financing Review, 21*(1), 51–64.

Ruggles, S. (1987). *Prolonged connections: The rise of the extended family in nineteenth-century England and America*. Madison, WI: University of Wisconsin Press.

Ruiz, M., & Ransford, H. (2012). Latino elders reframing familismo: Implications for health and caregiving support. *Journal of Cultural Diversity, 19*(2), 50–7.

Sawhney, M. (2003). The role of non-governmental organizations for the welfare of the elderly: The case of HelpAge India. In P. S. Liebig & S. I. Rajan (Eds.), *An aging India: Perspectives, prospects, and policies*. Binghamton, NY: The Hayworth Press.

Silverstein, M., Gans, D., & Yang, F. M. (2006). Intergenerational support to aging parents: The role of norms and needs. *Journal of Family Issues, 27*(8), 1068–84.

Silverstein, M., & Giarrusso, R. (2010). Aging and family life: A decade review. *Journal of Marriage and Family, 72*(5), 1039–58.

Spillman, B. C., & Pezzin, L. E. (2000). Potential and active family caregivers: Changing networks and the "sandwich generation." *Milbank Quarterly, 78*(3), 347–74. doi: 10.1111/1468-0009.00177.

Stone, R. (2011). *Long-term care for the elderly.* Washington, DC: Urban Institute Press.

Thane, P. (Ed.). (2005). *The long history of old age.* London: Thames & Hudson.

Thomson/MEDSTAT. (2005). *Spouses of Medicaid long-term care recipients.* Washington, DC: U.S. Department of Health and Human Services.

U.S. Office of Personnel Management, Federal Long-Term Care Insurance Program (2008). *Find the cost of care in your area.* Retrieved from www.ltcfeds.com/ltcWeb/do/assessing_your_needs/costofcare?action=costofcare.

U.S. Statistical Abstracts of the United States. (2012). *Table 58: Living arrangements of persons 15 years old and over by race and age: 2010.* Washington, DC: U.S. Census Bureau.

Ustinova, A. (2007). Adult day-care industry booming in South Texas. *San Antonio Express-News.* Retrieved from www.reporternews.com/news/2007/sep/02/adult-day-care-industry-booming-in-south-texas.

Wallace, S. P., Levy-Storms, L., Kington, R. S., & Andersen, R. M. (1998). The persistence of race and ethnicity in the use of long-term care. *Journal of Gerontology: Social Sciences, 53B*(2), S104–S112.

Wallace, S. P., & Lew-Ting, C.-Y. (1992). Getting by at home: Community-based long-term care of Latino elders. *Western Journal of Medicine, 157*, 337–44.

Weddle, D. O., Wellman, N. S., Marra, M. V., & Pan, Y. (2007). *The Older Americans Act Nutrition Program: Choices for independence.* Miami, FL: Florida International University.

Weeks, J. R., & Cuellar, J. B. (1981). The role of family members in the helping networks of older people. *The Gerontologist, 21*(4), 388–94.

Wieland, D., Boland, R., Baskins, J., & Kinosian, B. (2010). Five-year survival in a program of all-inclusive care for elderly compared with alternative institutional and home- and community-based care. *Journals of Gerontology: Series A, Biological Sciences and Medical Sciences, 65*(7), 721–6.

Wieland, D., Kinosian, B., Stallard, E., & Boland, R. (2013). Does Medicaid pay more to a program of all-inclusive care for the elderly (PACE) than for fee-for-service long-term care? *Journal of Gerontology: Medical Sciences, 68*(1), 47–55.

Wiener, J. M., Stevenson, D. G., & Goldenson, S. M. (1998). *Controlling the supply of long-term care providers at the state level.* Washington, DC: Urban Institute.

World Health Organization. (2007). WHO global report on falls prevention in older age. In *Ageing and life course, family and community health.* France: World Health Organization.

Zecevic, A. A., Salmoni, A. W., Speechley, M., & Vandervoort, A. A. (2006). Defining a fall and reasons for falling: Comparisons among the views of seniors, health care providers, and the research literature. *The Gerontologist, 46,* 367–76.

Zsembik, B. A. (1996). Preference for coresidence among older Latinos. *Journal of Aging Studies, 10*(1), 69–81.

CHAPTER 7

Neighborhood Affluence, Safety, and the Quality of Life

TRAPPED IN A DYING NEIGHBORHOOD

Caroline stepped out of the van that had taken her and several of her elderly neighbors to the grocery store. This service is part of a special city program that provides transportation services for older low-income residents who need to go to the doctor, shop for food and other necessities, and have no other or only limited means of getting around. The program has been functioning for 2 years with funds provided by a non-governmental organization. The program purchased two new vans and reimburses the city for the use of their handicapped-accessible vehicles. One has to schedule appointments a week in advance and it is not always possible to go to where one wishes. The service is a clear improvement, though, over what was available before. When she needed to go somewhere Caroline had to take taxis. For older people in Caroline's neighborhood, transportation is a major problem that clearly affects the quality of their lives.

Caroline's daughter lives in another city in the state and cannot deal with Caroline's daily needs. Her son is in the Army and serving in Afghanistan. His wife and two daughters live in a different state. Caroline has no car and lives in her own home in a transitional neighborhood. When she and her husband, who died 10 years ago of heart disease, moved into their house in their 20s, the neighborhood was working class and of mixed ethnicity. As a veteran, Caroline's husband was able to obtain a VA guarantee mortgage and they bought a small but comfortable house. Most fathers of families, including Caroline's husband, worked at a nearby window-frame manufacturing plant or at various other blue-collar jobs in the area. Twenty years ago the plant closed and Caroline's husband lost his job. He never worked again, and Caroline still lives on the surviving spouse's part of his union pension and Social Security. She is barely able to afford the house even though the mortgage has been paid off. She can only do so because of special property tax provisions that have capped what she owes, and help with upkeep by members of her church. Even with their help, though, the house is in need of many repairs that will probably never be done. The plumbing and wiring are not up to code and the heating system is on its last legs.

As the neighborhood has changed it has become more Hispanic and Black. Unemployment has increased and the walls are covered with gang graffiti. When she first moved into this neighborhood Caroline was not afraid to walk to the local bodega or to sit in the park with the other women in the neighborhood as they watched their children play. That has changed; Caroline no longer feels safe. A few years ago her son put bars on the windows to keep burglars from entering easily. There have been several break-ins in the neighborhood and there was a home invasion a month ago only two blocks away. There is an open drug trade in the community and individuals on Caroline's corner stand about waiting for customers. Caroline only goes out with others, which means that if someone does not come for her she is alone and isolated. The van that takes her shopping and to the daycare center she attends are godsends. The center is several blocks away, and there is no way Caroline could walk to it. The center provides transportation to and from the facility, but there is a small fee so Caroline cannot go every day. At the center Caroline talks to old and new friends and the major topic of their conversation is crime. Despite the fact that the older adults have a lower victimization rate than younger groups, surveys of older people show that crime is their major fear, more so than medical problems, and Caroline and the other visitors to the center are no exception.

The residents of the neighborhood feel trapped, and feel that nobody, including the schools or police, is doing enough to deal with crime and the unruly adolescents that roam the neighborhood. They also blame the single mothers who seem incapable of controlling their children. What they fear most is violent crime, although they are not aware of any specific violent crime against an older person in recent years. Whatever the sociological or economic explanations, the neighborhood has changed, and clearly for the worse. Physical decline and social decline have gone hand in hand. Abandoned buildings, graffiti, broken windows, empty lots filled with trash, and more are all signs of a dying neighborhood. The physical decay feeds upon and, in turn, fuels the social decay. Over the years the neighborhood was home to different racial and ethnic groups. When Caroline and her generation are gone it is unclear who will live here. It seems unlikely that it will become the vibrant, socially integrated place that it was. Only time will tell.

This chapter examines (1) the meaning of community; (2) how researchers assess neighborhood quality; (3) changing face of communities and new Hispanic destination and settlement areas; and (4) the impact of neighborhood quality and especially Hispanic enclaves on various physical and mental health outcomes, as well as what is known about the risk factors for isolation and depression.

THE MEANING OF COMMUNITY

The physical and social characteristics of one's neighborhood, or at least one's perceptions of them, can greatly influence the quality of one's life (Hill, Ross, & Angel, 2005). Those perceptions are influenced by many factors, including objective neighborhood characteristics such as the area's socioeconomic level, its racial and ethnic composition, its age structure, the condition of the buildings, streets, and sidewalks, general cleanliness, the presence of homeless individuals, the amount of air pollution, noise, and more (Rantakokko et al., 2010; Sampson & Groves, 1989; Yen, Michael, & Perdue, 2009). One's perceptions are also influenced by aspects of the social environment including crime rates, gang activity, the presence of open areas where neighborhood residents can mingle, the degree of physical insecurity that residents feel, the approachability and friendliness of the residents, and other factors that can reduce the risk of isolation (Kim, Nair, Knight, Roosa, & Updegraff, 2008; Loukaitou-Sideris & Eck, 2007; Stodolska, Acevedo, & Shinew, 2009).

Feeling safe in one's neighborhood and enjoying the company of friends and neighbors in parks and at restaurants, social clubs, political gatherings, churches, and similar community locations are desirable community characteristics in and of themselves, but the social interaction that they entail has other benefits: they can improve one's physical and emotional health and even increase one's lifespan (Gardner, 2011; Ross, 2000; Wilson-Genderson & Pruchno, 2013). Social interaction and participation in community activities also provide one with a social identity that can enhance self-esteem and foster a sense of belonging (Berkman & Syme, 1979; Putnam, 2000). These benefits of a cohesive and supportive neighborhood and community are not surprising. Human beings are not solitary creatures, but rather depend upon one another for more than just physical survival; humans need one another to give meaning to their lives and to define their social selves (Cooley, 1902; Mead, 1934).

We all have an instinctive sense of what the term "community" refers to. We use it often in such phrases as "the community of believers," or "the community of scholars." The online Merriam-Webster dictionary defines community as

> a unified body of individuals: as *a*: state, commonwealth; *b*: the people with common interests living in a particular area; *broadly*: the area itself <the problems of a large *community*>; *c*: an interacting population of various kinds of individuals (as species) in a common location. (www.merriam-webster.com/dictionary/community)

The definition goes on to more specifics and examples, but the core meaning is clear. As most of us understand, community consists of people with something in common, including a geographical location, a similar social class, a professional identity, common political views, shared religious practices, etc.

MEASURING NEIGHBORHOOD QUALITY

The assessments of the impact of neighborhood quality on various aspects of health and well-being are based largely on surveys. Exhibit 7.1 presents an example of a survey-based assessment of neighborhood quality. Respondents are asked about their perceptions of safety and other aspects of their neighborhoods (Ross & Britt, 1995). Clearly, personality characteristics and other factors such as gender can influence an individual's responses. One individual might feel safe in an environment in which another person does not. Most likely responses to such questions reflect a large and complex set of factors that are as yet poorly understood.

Exhibit 7.1 Wilkes Community Health Council Community Health Survey

The following questions ask you to share your opinions about the quality of life in Wilkes County

QUALITY OF LIFE STATEMENTS	CIRCLE ONE NUMBER FOR EACH STATEMENT BELOW			
	STRONGLY DISAGREE	DISAGREE	STRONGLY AGREE	AGREE
1. I am satisfied with the health care system in Wilkes County. (Consider health care options, access, cost, availability, quality, etc.)	1	2	3	4
2. Wilkes County is a good place to raise children. (Consider availability and quality of schools, day care, after school programs, recreation, etc.)	1	2	3	4
3. Wilkes County is a good place to grow old. (Consider elder-friendly housing, access/ transportation to medical services, elder day care, social support for the elderly living alone, meals on wheels, etc.)	1	2	3	4
4. There is plenty of economic opportunity in Wilkes County. (Consider availability and quality of jobs, job training/higher education opportunities, affordable housing, etc.)	1	2	3	4
5. Wilkes County is a safe place to live. (Consider safety at home, in the workplace, in schools, at playgrounds, parks, shopping centers, etc.)	1	2	3	4
6. There are networks of support for individuals and families during times of stress and need in Wilkes County. (Examples include neighbors, support groups, faith community outreach, agencies, organizations, etc.)	1	2	3	4

Thank you very much for completing the Community Health Survey!

For more information call (336) 651-7457
Wilkes County Health Department
306 College St
Wilkesboro, NC 28697 Wilkes County.

Source: Adapted from Wilkes County, North Carolina, Community Health Survey

Although surveys are perhaps the most common method of assessing neighborhood quality, other more objective methodologies are also used. Before proceeding it would be useful to briefly review the various ways in which neighborhood quality is operationalized. One approach, often referred to as the "broken windows" theory of neighborhood decay, has been developed by Robert Sampson and colleagues to explain the effect of urban disorder and vandalism on the risk of crime and the escalation of criminal activity in certain neighborhoods (Wilson & Kelling, 1982). In addition to collecting information on residents' perceptions, these researchers take pictures of buildings and houses in order to document their state of repair and the extent to which they are covered with gang graffiti, etc. The research underscores the importance of the physical as well as the social environment. This research informs strategies for preventing vandalism and turning unsafe and disorganized neighborhoods into safe and crime-free communities. The solution that this research suggests is to fix broken windows, remove graffiti, and clean up litter. These improvements increase a sense of community and help engage citizens in preventing further damage and antisocial behavior.

For many critics of the improved physical environment approach, the notion that simply cleaning up will solve complex social problems is unrealistic and perhaps naive. Disorganized neighborhoods are beset by serious social problems that even extensive physical renovation does not address. Certain critics point out that citizens in disorganized neighborhoods suffer from a lack of a sense of collective efficacy, a label that refers to a sense that there is really little one can do to improve matters. Instilling a sense of collective efficacy requires far more than simply repairing broken windows (Sampson & Raudenbush, 1999).

The research in reality focuses on far more than physical decay. The researchers employ various sources of data including census data to characterize key social characteristics, such as population size, the proportion of families in poverty, the number of individuals per square kilometer, and the proportion of Black and Latino. They also employ police records on crimes of various sorts, and they conduct neighborhood surveys to assess residents' perceptions of what is right and wrong with their neighborhood. (Sampson and Raudenbush, 2004). Although the term "community" seems straightforward, as the Sampson work shows, operationalizing community and neighborhood quality and their impact on crime rates and the quality of life of the inhabitants is not. See Exhibit 7.2 for dimensions of neighborhood quality.

Exhibit 7.2 Systematic Social Observation of Neighborhood

An SUV was driven down the street, a pair of video recorders, one located on each side of the SUV, captured social activities and physical features observed. They coded the presence or absence of:

Physical Disorder – a) cigarettes or cigars in the street or gutter, b) garbage or litter on street or sidewalk, c) empty beer bottles visible in the street, d) tagging graffiti, e) graffiti painted over, f) gang graffiti, g) abandoned cars, h) condoms on the sidewalk, 9) needles/syringes on the sidewalk, and 10) political message graffiti.

Physical Decay – conditions of vacant houses; burned-out, boarded-up, or abandoned commercial/industrial buildings; burned-out, boarded-up, or abandoned houses; badly deteriorated residential units; and badly deteriorated recreation facilities.

Social Disorder – whether adults were loitering or congregating, drinking alcohol in public, peer group with gang indicators, public intoxication, adults fighting or arguing in a hostile manner, selling drugs, and street prostitution.

Commercial Building Security – whether iron security gates or "pulldowns" were present on the building fronts and whether the windows were covered with security gates.

Alcohol/tobacco Advertising – whether there were signs advertising either substance.

Bars/liquor Stores is a two-item scale based on videotaped assessments of the presence or absence of bars and establishments with visible signs of alcohol sales.

Land Use – mixed land use.

Source: Sampson and Raudenbush (2004, pp. 326–7)

In this chapter, we use community to refer to the group of individuals with whom one has strong associations or ties, to use a term from network theory. Sociologist Mark Granovetter distinguishes between what he terms "strong" and "weak ties" and has developed a theory of their different functions (Granovetter, 1973). Strong ties are those that are emotionally supportive and that characterize one's relationship with spouses, family members, and close friends and associates. Weak ties, on the other hand, are those that are more formal and less emotionally rich, such as those with teachers, co-workers, and professionals such as doctors or lawyers from whom one receives services. Although weak ties are not as emotionally supportive as strong ties, they are information rich and can place one in contact with a larger network. Robert Putnam, a political scientist, also theorizes about the nature of such ties. He distinguishes between what he calls "bridging" and "bonding" ties (Putnam, 2000). Again, as for Granovetter, ties refer to relationships and bonding ties refer to those that bond individuals to one another. They are similar to Granovetter's "strong" ties. They define an in-group that is mutually supportive, but that does not necessarily reach out to others. "Bridging" ties, on the other hand, are similar to Granovetter's weak ties. They bridge across and among groups and refer to contacts outside one's immediate circle of family, friends, and associates. Perhaps we might think of bonding ties as a bit parochial and inward-looking, and bridging ties as more cosmopolitan and outward-looking.

Any definition of community must deal with both bonding and bridging relationships as well as strong and weak ties. Clearly bonding or strong ties can be exclusionary in the worst sense of what parochial means. They can characterize associations that are racist or sexist or that reject outsiders and that encourage a narrow outlook among their members. The Ku Klux Klan and the American Nazi Party serve as examples. On the other hand, they can be positive, especially when they are more open to others as in the case of ecumenical religious associations or charitable organizations. These later organizations are examples of the combination of both forms of association. Bonding ties clearly need not exclude bridging ties. One can be a member of a close and supportive family and community and maintain less intense contacts with a larger number of people. But without strong or bonding ties one is alone in a very real sense, especially as one ages. It is in this regard that community deserves an entire chapter in any treatment of the health and welfare of older persons of any race or ethnicity.

ESTABLISHED HISPANIC BARRIOS

In Spanish the term "barrio" refers to one's neighborhood or section of town. The term is neutral or positive and conveys a sense of neighborhood and home, but for many Americans who have heard the term it conveys much of the sense of "ghetto," a place with a captive low-income population that is plagued by social disorganization, crime, and drug use. The existence of barrios, just as in the case of ghettos, reflects both the choice to live with others of one's own group, and social exclusion and the inability to move to more affluent neighborhoods. There are several established Hispanic barrios and communities in the country, each occupied primarily by a specific national origin group. Although we cannot describe them all it is useful to get a basic feel for a few of the most well known. Like other neighborhoods they differ greatly in housing values, average educational and income levels, amenities, and more. Most are quite peaceful and desirable places to live and raise a family. Here, though, we focus on negative aspects of marginalization and ghettoization. As we noted earlier, one of the major fears expressed by elderly individuals is the fear of crime, and especially violent crime. The presence of gangs and open drug dealing along with the physical decay of many neighborhoods undermines the emotional and even the physical well-being of their elderly residents.

LOS ANGELES

Most Americans are aware of the fact that Los Angeles has a huge Hispanic, predominantly Mexican-origin, population. In fact, it is second only to Mexico City in the size of its Mexican-origin population. Although the Mexican-origin population is the largest, California is also home to Central and South Americans. Perhaps the best-known Hispanic community is East Los Angeles, an unincorporated area that lies to the east of downtown Los Angeles in Los Angeles County. It is bordered by the communities of Alhambra, Boyle Heights, Commerce, El Sereno, Montebello, Monterey Park, and Vernon. In 2010, this neighborhood covered nearly seven-and-a-half square miles and included over 125,000 residents at the time of the 2010 census, 97.1% of whom were Hispanic (U.S. Census Bureau, 2013a). In 2000, 85% were of Mexican origin and nearly half of the residents were foreign-born (*Los Angeles Times*, 2013). The area includes a large fraction (30.3%) of households with incomes of less than $20,000 and a population that has less than a high school education (29.4%) (Los Angeles City Planning Department, 2009).

Like the majority of large cities, Los Angeles is home to numerous street gangs, many of which are Hispanic. The Los Angeles Police Department estimates that there are over 450 active gangs in the County and City of Los Angeles with over 45,000 members (Los Angeles Police Department, 2013). Many of these gangs have been in existence for over 50 years and, in addition to battling over control of the lucrative narcotics trade, they have been involved in a large number of violent crimes. As Exhibit 7.3 shows, certain gangs are international with ties not only to other parts of the United States, but also to Latin American and other countries (Diaz, 2009; Vigil, 2002; Wolf, 2010). The presence of gangs and the crime and violence that is part of the narcotics trade clearly undermine the sense of safety that residents feel (Stodolska et al., 2009).

Exhibit 7.3 Transnational Gangs

Mara Salvatrucha, also known as MS-13, is a gang that traces its origins to the Salvadorean civil war of the 1980s (Diaz, 2009). Refugees from that conflict came to Los Angeles where they learned to stick together to protect Salvadoreans and battle Mexican gangs. There is disagreement over the origin of the name "Mara Salvatrucha." "La Mara" is a local street gang in El Salvador, and "Salvatrucha" is the local name for a vicious Salvadorean army ant. The name also refers to Salvadorean peasant guerrillas, the source of much of the gang's original membership. In U.S. and Central American prisons where many were deported they learned to be violent and ruthless. Even after they were deported there was no keeping them out of the United States and those who returned illegally according to the FBI are part of a growing national threat (Federal Bureau of Investigation, 2008). What is unique about this gang is that, although not a unified criminal enterprise like the Italian Cosa Nostra, it is transnational, with branches in Central America, the United States, and many other countries. According to the FBI, MS-13 operates in most states and the District of Columbia and has perhaps 10,000 members. MS-13 members engage in a wide variety of crimes, and they have demonstrated their capacity for extreme violence.

Sources: Diaz, T. (2009); Federal Bureau of Investigation (2011)

CHICAGO

As is the case in most American cities, in Chicago the movement of manufacturing jobs overseas means that the service sector accounts for a growing proportion of jobs, especially for the poor and those who have recently arrived. Migration of Mexicans to the Midwest has given Chicago a Mexican-origin population second only to that of Los Angeles. Between 2000 and 2010, the Latino population of the Northeast region of Illinois, including cities like Chicago and suburban Cook County, grew nearly 30%, mushrooming from 1.4 million to 1.8 million (Chicago Metropolitan Agency for Planning, 2011). The Latino population now makes up 21.6% of the region's population, up from 17.2% in 2000. Without this growth, many communities in the region would have lost population, which would have had a serious effect on their ability to attract and retain businesses and local tax dollars.

A large Puerto Rican population also calls Chicago home. The city has been characterized as an ethnic mosaic because of the clear distinctions among its many neighborhoods. As immigrant groups arrived they occupied particular parts of the city and gave each its unique identity, in addition to well-defined boundaries. Like the Poles, Croatians, Lithuanians, Italians, and other groups who in years past lived in the same neighborhoods, the relatively new Mexican arrivals have transformed Pilsen/Little Village, which stretches from the Chicago River on its eastern border to the city limits on its western edge, and from around 16th Street on its north side to the Stevenson Expressway on its southern edge. Today Chicago has a complex economy including manufacturing and service jobs. Given the clear dominance of local neighborhoods, in studies of Chicago we have found that many of the residents of specific neighborhoods never travel far from their neighborhoods. They leave only to obtain services that are not available close by.

Like all big cities Chicago has a growing and serious gang problem. The city is home to over 600 gang factions with more than 70,000 members (CBS News, 2013). Among these are factions of the Hispanic gangs of Los Angeles. The presence of these gangs clearly redefines public spaces and forces residents to act in defensive manners or avoid those places altogether. One study based on focus group interviews found that the participants reported that gang members are almost always present in parks, which have been taken over to be used as sites for the sale and use of narcotics (Stodolska et al., 2009). Gang activity in other parts of certain neighborhoods makes it difficult for residents to go out in order to get to safer places. As a result neighborhood residents must remain vigilant and develop defensive strategies, unfortunately including giving up outside recreational activity. Although the threat encouraged collective responses, it is clear that the presence of criminal street gangs undermines residents' sense of safety and their overall well-being.

Another challenge for the city of Chicago, especially in the suburbs, is an aging Latino population. Regionally, the Latino population's 65-and-older segment grew an astounding 69% between 2000 and 2010 (Chicago Metropolitan Agency for Planning, 2011). As some Latinos head for the suburbs and others age, some might worry that common destination cities like Pilsen will stop serving its traditional role as a center of the region's Mexican-American community.

NEW YORK

In 2010 nearly 30% of New York City's eight million-plus inhabitants were Hispanic (U.S. Census Bureau, 2013b). This Hispanic population, though, is highly diverse and includes individuals from 25 nations. For a complete list of nations of origin go to 🌐 www.nyc.gov/html/dcp/pdf/census/census2010/t_sf1_p8_nyc.pdf. The largest group is Puerto Ricans, followed by Dominicans and Mexicans. The Mexican-origin population is the fastest-growing Hispanic group and will soon outnumber Dominicans (Limonic, 2008). The Ecuadorean population numbers over 160,000. Although the other groups are smaller, their presence gives the New York Hispanic community a very cosmopolitan feel. The Hispanic population has moved into all five boroughs, although there is clustering by group in each. Nearly two-thirds of the city's Puerto Rican population live in the Bronx and Brooklyn, while approximately 40% of the Dominican population live in the Bronx and nearly 30% in Manhattan. Over 80% of the Mexican-origin population live in Queens and relatively few live in Manhattan. Ecuadoreans are heavily concentrated in Queens. This distribution means that there are no areas in New York City without some Hispanic entrée.

Perhaps the best-known Hispanic community in New York City is Spanish Harlem, also known as El Barrio or East Harlem. The neighborhood is on the east side of Manhattan and bounded on the north side by the Harlem River, the East River, East 96th Street to the south, and 5th Avenue to the west. The neighborhood is predominantly Puerto Rican, but with a growing number of Dominicans, Salvadoreans, and Mexicans.

SAN ANTONIO

San Antonio, Texas is smaller than Los Angeles, Chicago, or New York and has a smaller Hispanic population than any of those larger metropolises. Yet it is unique in the fact that 63% of its population, which totaled 1,327,407, is Hispanic (Ennis, Ríos-Vargas and Albert, 2011). Nearly 90% of San Antonio Hispanics are of Mexican origin (Rentería, 2011). This fact gives the city a very Mexican flavor and tourism is one of its major sources of income. Unlike its larger counterparts it sprawls over an immense area and is far less dense. Also unlike the other cities San Antonio and Texas were a part of Mexico until the 19th century, when Texas became a sovereign nation after defeating General Santa Ana. Many Mexican-origin families trace their lineage back to the time when the state was part of Mexico. For many, however, the middle-class dream has not materialized. As we have documented in earlier chapters, Mexican-American education levels, incomes, and personal wealth remain far below those of the majority non-Hispanic White population.

Even though the city is heavily Hispanic, it is segregated by income, race, and ethnicity (Potter, 2011). Many Mexican-origin residents spend much of their time in or close to their local barrios. In one study of poverty in the city we encountered families whose school-age children had never visited downtown. Public transportation is inadequate compared to the larger cities. The city has no commuter train or subway system and getting around the city is a constant problem for poor families. While San Antonio is home to a major university health science center, its health care resources are concentrated on the outskirts of the city, and families using them must take long trips on public transportation. Children attend neighborhood schools with one particularly large elementary school accommodating over 1,000 students. The only grocery store serving the same neighborhood is a small bodega, or what might be characterized as a mom and pop convenience store. At a somewhat greater distance, one could find a clinic that accepted Medicaid. To shop for major items or to obtain care for serious health problems residents have to travel beyond the immediate neighborhood, which almost always represents a major effort. For the most part only the most basic medical care is locally available and residents must use public transportation or find a ride to get to the doctor or clinic. Since most families do not own a car, their limited access to transportation also restricts the jobs they can take.

THE DISPERSION OF THE HISPANIC POPULATION

Historically, Hispanics have been concentrated in specific regions of the country. The Southwest has been traditionally Mexican; the Atlantic seaboard Puerto Rican, Caribbean, Central American, and Florida Cuban. The traditional Mexican-origin homeland consisted of what have been termed the "gateway" states of the Southwest (Arizona, California, New Mexico, and Texas). Many families in these states have lived on their lands, or at least in the same region, for centuries. Yet in recent years the residential patterns of new Mexican immigrants have changed in ways that are transforming the cultural mosaic of the South and Midwest (Weeks & Weeks, 2010). In rather large numbers they are moving to cities, suburbs, and rural communities outside the traditional homeland (Lichter, Parisi, Taquino, & Grice, 2010; Wahl, Breckenridge, & Gunkel, 2007). Between 1995 and 2000 one-third of Mexican immigrants settled outside the Southwest, a huge change in destinations compared to previous decades. Today Atlanta, Washington, DC, and smaller cities such as Winston-Salem, Durham, North Carolina, and Reno, Nevada are major destinations for Mexican immigrants (Lichter et al., 2010; McConnell, 2008).

Historically many Mexican immigrants, and especially the undocumented, have lived and worked in rural areas as agricultural workers. Today, however, a substantial fraction of immigrants move to suburbs and rural towns where they work not only in agriculture, but also in meat processing, construction, landscaping, and the service industry (Kandel & Parrado, 2005). Migration to such areas is so large, in fact, that it accounts for nearly half of non-metropolitan growth (Johnson & Lichter, 2008). A major question that arises with this rapid dispersion of the Hispanic population relates to the nature of the communities into which they move and the degree of residential segregation that they experience in the new destinations. Many of the areas to which the new immigrants have moved have a long history of anti-Black racism and rejection of outsiders (McConnell & Miraftab, 2009). If the new arrivals remain residentially and economically separate from the native population, the new migration does not hold out the hope of an increased level of assimilation and economic incorporation.

Unfortunately, this in fact appears to be the case. In many of the new locations in which they have settled Hispanics remain highly segregated from non-Hispanics (Lichter et al., 2010). Table 7.1 shows the growth in the number of Hispanics between 1990 and 2000 in the five most highly segregated central cities, suburbs, and non-metropolitan areas. Non-metropolitan areas consist of places with fewer than 10,000 residents (Lichter et al., 2010). In places with very small populations to begin with, an increase of a few hundred or 1,000 individuals represents a major change. As this table shows, in these small places the growth in the Hispanic population has been huge. In many places the population has grown from fewer than a hundred to several hundred or over 1,000. When new arrivals are culturally different than long-term residents they can be quite threatening to the longer-term residents, especially in places with racist and exclusionary histories (McConnell & Miraftab, 2009).

TABLE 7.1 *Hispanic Population Growth in Highly Segregated New Destinations*

CENTRAL CITIES	HISPANIC POPULATION, 1990	HISPANIC POPULATION, 2000
Winston–Salem, NC	1,236	16,043
Durham, NC	1,610	16,012
Decatur, AL	386	3,040
Morristown, TN	91	2,603
Concord, NC	150	4,369
SUBURBAN PLACES		
Tarboro, NC	49	662
Allgood, Al	39	273
Delphi, IN	29	367
Melrose, MN	16	381
St. Stephens, NC	71	921
NONMETROPOLITAN PLACES		
Yazoo City, MS	62	1,087
Wilson, NC	259	3,237
Sioux Center, IA	11	280
Forrest City, AR	93	1,221
Greenwood, SC	108	1,440

Source: Lichter et al. (2010).

LOW-QUALITY NEIGHBORHOODS

Numerous studies have documented the negative effects of low-quality neighborhoods on all aspects of residents' well-being (Hill & Maimon, 2013). By low-quality neighborhoods we refer to those that have few amenities, offer few opportunities for interaction with friends and neighbors, and in which individuals feel unsafe. Unfortunately, many older adults with little income or assets often do not have the opportunity to move out of such neighborhoods (Oswald, Jopp, Rott, & Wahl, 2011). If one owns a home and has lived in it for many years, leaving is not a simple option. In many cases the neighborhood has deteriorated over the years and selling and moving away would be diffi-cult. Researchers find, though, that being trapped in a neighborhood in which one perceives high levels of dis-order increases feelings of powerlessness, normlessness, mis-trust, and isolation that can result in depression and anxiety disorder (Ross & Mirowsky, 2009).

Herbert Gans (1972) argues that institutional disen-gagement, or the inability to participate in the social life of a vibrant neighborhood that can be exacerbated by degraded public spaces, disproportionately affects older adults because they are already dealing with declines in health and social support. Institutional disengagement can restrict basic activities of living and increase the risk of serious isolation. A neighborhood study of inner-city New York residents found that while younger individuals leave their local neighborhoods for work and other activ-ities on a daily basis, older individuals are more likely to spend most of their time at home (Newman, 2003). Neigh-borhoods without amenities and opportunities for older individuals to go out and socialize at places such as com-munity centers, clubs, restaurants, cultural exhibits, sports arenas, and shopping complexes increase the risk of such isolation.

Given the fact that older individuals who live in them are often trapped by low income and the inability to leave, low-quality neighborhoods can become age- and race-based ghettos (Rogers & Power, 2000). In such places the support-ive aspects of community are lost and residents placed at risk of adverse health outcomes (Hill et al., 2005). Daily exposure to negative stressors can result in high levels of stress, anxiety, anger, and depression (Gardner, 2011; Ross, 2000; Wilson-Genderson & Pruchno, 2013). Although one might cope with such conditions on a temporary basis, when they become chronic they can seriously undermine health (Hill et al., 2005; LaGrange, Ferraro, & Supancic, 1992).

A vibrant community is one that includes opportunities for shopping for food, clothing, and other necessities. Stores and shops provide places for social interaction. Poor-quality neighborhoods frequently do not include local commercial enterprises. Many are "food deserts" in which grocery stores, farmer's markets, and other outlets that provide fresh vegetables and other nutritious foods are unavailable (Ploeg et al., 2012). The United States Department of Agriculture defines a food desert as an urban area or a census tract in which at least 500 people or at least 33% of the population reside more than one mile from a supermarket or large grocery store. For rural census tracts the distance is more than 10 miles (http://apps.ams.usda.gov/fooddeserts/foodDeserts.aspx). The food desert problem along the Texas/Mexico border in the lower Rio Grande Valley is illustrated in Figure 7.1. The map shows that the area is literally starving for healthy food since in a large part of the region people do not have easy access to fresh produce, healthy grains, low-fat dairy, and other nutritious foods. The lack of places at which to shop presents older individuals with serious practical problems and increases their levels of stress and anxiety (Phillipson, 2011).

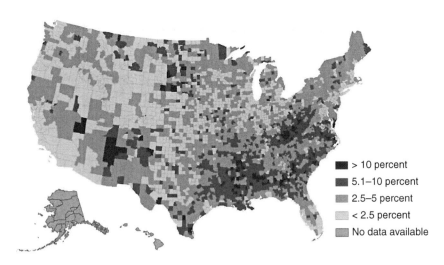

FIGURE 7.1 *No Car and No Supermarket Store Within a Mile.*

Source: http://americannutritionassociation.org/newsletter/usda-defines-food-deserts.

Crime and the fear it instills is a major contributor to the anxiety that the older residents of degraded neighborhoods feel. A recent Gallup poll found that individuals of all ages are concerned about crime. Nearly 4 in 10 Americans reported that they would be afraid to walk alone at night within a mile of their home (Gallup poll, 2010). Nearly half of the respondents felt that crime had gotten worse in their local area. The fear of robbery, sexual assault, murder, and other violent crime was common. Older adults living in violent and deteriorated urban areas tend to be particularly fearful. As a result, they are afraid to leave their homes and are at high risk of social isolation (Phillipson, 2011).

In the opening vignette for this chapter, Caroline was particularly afraid of crime in her neighborhood. This is not surprising since neighborhoods with high concentrations of Hispanics and Hispanic immigrants are poorer than more mixed or non-Hispanic White neighborhoods and suffer from much of the disorganization associated with poverty (Osypuk, Diez Roux, Hadley, & Kandul, 2009). Neighborhoods characterized by concentrated poverty and low rates of home ownership often lack the mechanisms of social control that more affluent and stable neighborhoods enjoy (Ross & Mirowsky, 2001; Sampson, Raudenbush, & Earls, 1997). As we discussed in Chapter 5, Hispanics who live in rural and economically stagnant areas along the Texas/ Mexico border experience high levels of stress that can ultimately undermine their health (Salinas, Abdelbary, Rocha, & Al-Snih, 2012). For older individuals this elevated risk results not only from the chronic exposure to threatening conditions, but also from the demographic stagnation common in areas of low economic opportunity where older persons age in place without an infusion of younger residents (Golant, 2009). Thus, growing old in a co-ethnic enclave ridden with neighborhood disruption, a lack of a sense of safety in a neighborhood, and overall low quality of the physical environment may exacerbate the already difficult challenges of coping with health and economic problems (Sampson, 2012; Wilson, 1990).

HEALTHY BARRIOS

A major complicating factor in the study of the impact of community and neighborhood factors on individual health outcomes relates to the potential contradictory or offsetting effects of racial or ethnic residential concentration. A rather large body of research, some of which we presented earlier, indicates that neighborhood disorganization contributes directly to negative social and health outcomes. However, other studies find that residing in an ethnically homogeneous neighborhood can be beneficial, at least among certain Hispanic samples. For Black Americans residential concentration is common at all social class levels and has clear negative social effects (Hobson-Prater & Leech, 2012; Sampson, Morenoff, & Gannon-Rowley, 2002). Middle-class Blacks live in very different neighborhoods than middle-class Whites (Massey, Fischer, Dickens, & Levy, 2003). Regardless of other factors, including average income, Black neighborhoods have low levels of social cohesion (Hobson-Prater & Leech, 2012). Assessing the independent impact of neighborhood on individual health outcomes presents serious methodological problems since many factors other than neighborhood characteristics interact in potentially complex ways to affect individual and group health levels (Sampson et al., 2002).

Many barrios and ghettos with high concentrations of minority individuals are poor, but not all are seriously beset by disorganization and crime. This raises the possibility that the health effects of concentration could be good, bad, or neutral depending not only on the specific characteristics of the neighborhood and community, but also on other factors, such as the availability of medical care and state welfare policies. Low-income Black and Hispanic neighborhoods may share certain common characteristics related to isolation, concentrated poverty, and more, but they differ in other ways by definition. The racism that Blacks have experienced historically is different than that experienced by Hispanics. How the specific history of each group combines with other aspects of neighborhoods to affect health and other factors such as social cohesion and trust remains poorly understood.

Ethnic enclaves are almost by definition characterized by strong bonding ties. In general the networks of individuals and families in low-income neighborhoods are smaller and less diverse than those of families in higher-income neighborhoods since they lack the weak bridging ties associated with affluence and professional activity (Campbell & Lee, 1992). The limited evidence we have, though, suggests that, at least for Hispanics, the strong bonding ties that high-concentration barrios foster may counteract the potentially negative effects of concentrated poverty. Common ethnicity represents one dimension of similarity, but other characteristics, such as immigration status, do as well. For immigrants, living in neighborhoods with high concentrations of other Hispanic immigrants has been identified as a source of resilience (Aranda, Ray, Al-Snih, Ottenbacher, & Markides, 2011; Eschbach, Ostir, Patel, Markides, & Goodwin, 2004). The concept of resilience refers to the ability of individuals to effectively adapt to the stresses associated with poverty and exposure to adverse events and to maintain their health. A neighborhood in which one feels safe and in which one interacts with individuals of the same ethnicity who have had similar experiences, as is the case in the Cuban neighborhoods of Miami, reduces the risk of isolation and potentially increases one's quality of life (Angel & Angel, 1992). The informal social ties that ethnic homogeneity creates might also help maintain social order, thereby improving the overall quality of the neighborhood (Sampson & Groves, 1989).

Given the complexity of the associations one must be cautious in interpreting findings based on surveys. Nonetheless, for Hispanics some data suggests that the negative impacts of poverty and limited social incorporation are mitigated, at least to some degree, by residential concentration. Data on Mexican-origin Hispanics over the age of 65 in the Southwestern United States indicates that those who live in barrios with high concentrations of Mexican-origin residents, which we refer to as ethnic enclaves, report less depression and better self-reported health than individuals who live in neighborhoods with lower concentrations of Mexican-origin residents (Eschbach et al., 2004). For Hispanics, ethnic enclaves provide a more familiar cultural environment for older individuals that appears to be beneficial. These neighborhoods are clearly different than Black ghettos despite their low average income and educational levels. Studies of other Hispanics also suggest that ethnic enclaves protect the psychological well-being, health, and physical functioning of individuals (Aranda & Knight, 1999; Aranda et al., 2011; Ostir, Eschbach, Markides, & Goodwin, 2003; Yen et al., 2009).

In one multiethnic study of atherosclerosis in adults aged 45 to 84, these beneficial effects measured in terms of lower depression levels benefited Hispanic men and women and African-American women, but not African-American men. The data suggest that for African-American males living in a neighborhood with a higher concentration of other African Americans actually undermines mental health (Mair et al., 2010). One characteristic of Hispanic ethnic enclaves is that older individuals are more likely to have family networks available. Those older individuals report lower financial strain, which may reflect very practical beneficial effects of having other family members close by (Díaz-Venegas, Eschbach, & Angel, 2012). The presence of family and engaged neighbors and friends enables older adults to age in place with dignity and contributes to the maintenance of an older person's health and welfare (Cantor, 1979).

CREATING THE AGE-FRIENDLY COMMUNITY

Cohesive, orderly, and safe neighborhoods with amenities and places for individuals to congregate and shop benefit all ages, but they are particularly vital to older individuals who rarely travel far from home. A major objective of urban and housing policy is of course to create such neighborhoods, which are referred to as age-friendly communities, but the challenge is daunting. The World Health Organization introduced an initiative, referred to as "Global Age-Friendly Cities," to promote active aging by developing communities that allow older people to remain socially engaged and physically active (World Health Organization, 2007). From our perspective one major aspect of creating the age-friendly community is to recognize the importance of local culture and history. As the research on ethnic enclaves we reviewed earlier suggests, older Hispanics who have lived their lives with other Hispanics benefit from continuing interaction with other Hispanics in their own neighborhoods. Continuity and familiarity, therefore, are important considerations in designing age-friendly communities, but such continuity can clash with the need for neighborhood renovation and infrastructure improvements.

In the context of our discussion of neighborhood quality it would be useful to speculate a bit about what an age-friendly community might look like. Such an exercise points out what needs to happen to create such neighborhoods, even if making such neighborhoods and communities a reality remains a major challenge. By age-friendly community we refer to a social and geographical area that is purposefully designed or redesigned to insure that older individuals feel safe and in which they can enjoy good health and remain socially engaged. For the elderly, specific aspects of neighborhood and community are central to optimal health and well-being. Major American cities are segregated to varying degrees on the basis of race, ethnicity, and age. The automobile has created a clear distinction between downtown neighborhoods, which are often Black, Hispanic, and old, and suburban communities that are more affluent.

An age-friendly community requires affordable housing and sidewalks and buildings that are suited for wheelchairs and provide easy access to individuals with limited mobility. An age-friendly community would provide the opportunity and means to take advantage of a city's amenities. Residents would be provided transportation to museums, libraries, civic centers, concert halls, and other locations at which public events are held. In an age-friendly community transportation to health facilities and to stores would be provided. Clearly, such a community would benefit everyone and allow optimal interaction among generations (Leon et al., 2009).

Unfortunately, most older adults live in places that are not well prepared for aging populations. Individuals who spent their prime adult years in a single-family home can find themselves stranded when they can no longer drive. The post-World War II migration of Americans to the suburbs was made possible by freeways and the automobile (AARP, 2012). America is a car culture and public transportation options can be limited in both the inner city and in suburbs. Inadequate public transportation can make suburban life isolating for infirm older residents. When one is young one hops in one's car and drives to the mall or the grocery store. When one can no longer do so the options are limited. Although most older Americans prefer to age in place, it is difficult to retrofit suburban communities to accommodate an older population's need for assistance. Aging populations, then, present municipal governments with major challenges. These challenges are even greater in ghetto and barrio communities in which residents have few economic resources or little political power.

A major part of the solution to the social isolation and lack of access to amenities in low-income neighborhoods is adequate public transportation (Kerschner & Harris, 2007; Murdock et al., 2008). With adequate transportation many communities would improve in terms of age friendliness, even if few other changes were made. A comprehensive and integrated public transportation system would have numerous benefits for all age groups, but especially for individuals who should no longer be driving. Each year approximately

600,000 drivers aged 70 and older give up driving (Foley, Heimovitz, Guralnik, & Brock, 2002). Many others continue to drive even though they should stop. Among drivers aged 75 to 84, fatality rates are equal to those of teenage drivers. Older individuals continue to drive because of a serious lack of public alternatives (Bailey, 2004). An adequate public transportation system would not only benefit elderly individuals, it would also relieve adult children and grandchildren from having to leave work to drive older parents to doctor's and other appointments (Robinson, Lucado, & Schur, 2012). Many major cities have introduced senior transit programs; see 🌐 www.cityofboston.gov/elderly/services/transportation.asp.

Yet, like all other aspects of the political process, planning for an age-integrated and age-friendly city is influenced by various interested parties who promote their own interests. Clearly a collaborative, citywide effort is needed to produce a plan for helping seniors continue to live active, healthy, independent lives. A major challenge arises from the fact of unequal power and political influence among different groups. Clearly the city cannot respond to everyone's needs and preferences. Even generous states like California and Massachusetts are finding that they must restrict certain services in order to deal with changing fiscal realities. Black and Latino communities are underrepresented in the policy-making process at all levels of government. This is perhaps one reason that public transportation remains inadequate. What is clear is that if neighborhoods and communities are to become more age friendly, the issue of inequality and inequity in decision-making power must be addressed. Many of the political challenges are illustrated by a Hispanic/Latino Quality of Life initiative carried out by the City of Austin, Texas, begun in 2008. Other concerted efforts to identify the needs of Hispanic communities, and especially the needs of aging Hispanics, should be carried out in different cities. The identification of need, though, is not enough. Cities must muster the political will to make meaningful changes. Clearly that possibility requires the mobilization of Hispanic communities. 🌐 www.austintexas.gov/sites/default/files/files/City_Manager/HispanicReport-ver_6-0901_13.pdf.

SUMMARY AND CONCLUSIONS

In this chapter we reviewed research on the role of community in determining the quality of individuals' lives. We began by defining community theoretically and operationally. Theoretically, and in common usage, the term "community" refers to a group of people with something in common that leads them to share certain points of view and objectives. We speak, for example, of the "community of scientists," which consists of individuals with an objective and analytic approach to the physical world, or the "community of believers," a label often used to refer to individuals who believe in the truth of a particular set of religious or spiritual teachings. Of course, when we use the label more locally we are referring to the individuals and families who live in a particular social area. Where one's community begins and ends is largely a subjective matter that might differ among individuals who live in the same geographic location. Nonetheless, a growing body of research demonstrates that aspects of community have important effects on one's sense of well-being and the quality of one's life. For older individuals who often feel vulnerable and whose neighborhoods are changing socially and physically, a sense of security and safety in one's neighborhood is especially important.

Assessing the health consequences of community requires that important aspects of the neighborhood be operationalized, that is, measured. In order to do so researchers must first identify important dimensions of community and neighborhood that they can assess. The most common way of measuring "neighborhood quality" is to employ surveys in which one asks individuals whether they feel safe in their neighborhoods, whether amenities such as health care are available, whether it is a good place to live, etc. More objective measures include assessments of the physical environment. We discussed the "broken windows" theory of neighborhood quality that holds that the decay of the physical environment contributes to the decay of the social environment and that repairing the physical environment can contribute to the social rehabilitation of the neighborhood. Although it is clear that the physical environment is closely tied to the social environment, many other factors, including the economic and employment opportunities in a neighborhood, the extent of policing, and the sense among neighborhood residents that they have control over activities that take place in the neighborhood, also affect the quality of life of residents. To use a psychoanalytic term, the neighborhood quality is "over determined," meaning that it has multiple interacting causes.

Communities are often characterized by high levels of racial and ethnic homogeneity. Often this reflects exclusionary practices by residents or the concentration of wealth in certain areas. Ethnic enclaves also arise for cultural and social as well as economic reasons. Traditionally Hispanics have been concentrated in certain parts of the country: Mexicans in the Southwest and the Midwest, Cubans in Florida, Puerto Ricans and Dominicans in the Northeast. Today Hispanics, and especially the Mexican-origin population, are more dispersed. From large cities to small rural towns, places that a few decades ago had no Hispanic residents find that they have dynamic and highly visible Hispanic communities. In many small Southern communities the Hispanic shift has been truly dramatic. The first Hispanics to make the move to these new areas were pioneers who established Latino communities that are attracting new immigrants. The Guanajuato clubs and the communities of individuals from this one state in Mexico who have formed communities in Chicago and Dallas, discussed in Chapter 4, are examples of the forces that draw similar individuals together to form new communities.

A growing body of research suggests that such "ethnic enclaves" are indeed supportive and that the residents of neighborhoods with high concentrations of co-ethnics enjoy better self-assessed health. Such neighborhoods reduce the risk of physical and linguistic isolation since residents can interact with individuals with whom they can communicate and who share a similar culture. A unique example of ethnic enclaves that combine both high concentrations of Hispanic residents and high concentrations of poverty are the colonias that dot the U.S./Mexico border region. These communities are ecological areas in which low-income Mexican-origin individuals are able to purchase land and build low-cost homes. These settlements are characterized by a lack of potable water and adequate roads, and have few services, including health care. In these colonias, the benefits of ethnic enclaves may be negated by the harsh reality of poverty and a lack of services.

DISCUSSION QUESTIONS

1. Look up the term "community" in a dictionary or online. How broad is the definition? Give some examples of the everyday use of the term.

2. Based on the dictionary definitions, identify the major dimensions of community; that is, what are the cultural, social, physical, and other components of the concept?
3. Based on the major dimensions of community you have identified, develop a short questionnaire that you could use to measure "neighborhood quality" using a survey or other methodologies.
4. Go to the Census Bureau webpage and search State and County Quickfacts (or you could just ask Google). Compare various counties in the United States and identify those with large concentrations of Hispanics. Which nationality groups are these likely to be? Find counties with few Hispanics.
5. Use the Web to find basic information on colonias. Describe these communities in terms of their cultural, social, and economic characteristics. What governmental or non-governmental efforts are being made to address the needs of colonia residents?

LITERATURE CITED

AARP. (2012). *AARP: Most baby boomers will age in suburbs, driving transportation needs*. Washington, DC: AARP.

Angel, J. L., & Angel, R. J. (1992). Age at migration, social connections, and well-being among elderly Hispanics. *Journal of Aging and Health, 4*, 480–99.

Aranda, M. P., & Knight, B. G. (1999). The influence of ethnicity and culture on the caregiver stress and coping process: A sociocultural review and analysis. *The Gerontologist, 37*(3), 342–54.

Aranda, M. P., Ray, L. A., Al-Snih, S., Ottenbacher, K. J., & Markides, K. S. (2011). The protective effect of the neighborhood composition on increasing frailty among older Mexican Americans: A barrio advantage? *Journal of Aging and Health, 23*(7), 1189–217.

Bailey, L. (2004). *Aging Americans: Stranded without options*. Washington, DC: Surface Transportation Policy Project.

Berkman, L. F., & Syme, L. S. (1979). Social networks, host resistance, and mortality: A nine-year follow-up study of Alameda County residents. *American Journal of Epidemiology, 109*(2), 186–204.

Campbell, K. E., & Lee, B. A. (1992). Sources of personal neighborhood networks: Social integration, need, or time? *Social Forces, 70*, 1077–100.

Cantor, M. H. (1979). Neighbors and friends: An overlooked resource in the informal support system. *Research on Aging, 1*(4), 434–63.

CBS News. (2013). By the numbers: Chicago-area gangs. Retrieved September 19, 2013, from www.cbsnews.com/8301-201_162-57584733/by-the-numbers-chicago-area-gangs.

Chicago Metropolitan Agency for Planning. (2011). Demographic and housing trends in Latino population. In *Policy Updates*. Chicago, IL: Author.

Cooley, C. H. (1902). *Human nature and the social order.* New York, NY: Charles Scribner's Sons.

Diaz, T. (2009). *No boundaries: Transnational Latino gangs and American law enforcement.* Ann Arbor, MI: University of Michigan Press.

Díaz-Venegas, C., Eschbach, K., & Angel, J. L. (2012). *Contextualizing financial strain in the older Hispanic population.* Paper presented at the American Sociological Association Annual Meeting, Denver, CO, August 16, 2012.

Ennis, S. R., Ríos-Vargas, M., & Albert, N. G. (2011). The Hispanic population: 2010. In *2010 Census Briefs.* Washington, DC: U.S. Census Bureau.

Eschbach, K., Ostir, G. V., Patel, K. V., Markides, K. S., & Goodwin, J. S. (2004). Neighborhood context and mortality among older Mexican Americans: Is there a barrio advantage? *American Journal of Public Health, 94*(10), 1807–12.

Federal Bureau of Investigation (2011). *National gang threat assessment: Emerging trends.* Retrieved from www.fbi.gov/stats-services/publications/2011-national-gang-threat-assessment.

Foley, D., Heimovitz, H., Guralnik, J., & Brock, D. B. (2002). Driving life expectancy of persons aged 70 years and older in the United States. *American Journal of Public Health, 82*(8), 1284–9.

Gallup. (2010, November 5). *Poll: Nearly 4 in 10 Americans still fear walking alone at night.* New York, NY: Gallup Inc. Retrieved from www.gallup.com/poll/144272/nearly-americans-fear-walking-alone-night.aspx.

Gans, H. (1972). *People and plans: Essays on urban problems and solutions.* London: Routledge.

Gardner, P. J. (2011). Natural neighborhood networks: Important social networks in the lives of older adults aging in place. *Journal of Aging Studies, 25*(3), 263–71.

Golant, S. M. (2009). Aging in place solutions for older Americans: Groupthink responses not always in their best interests. *Public Policy & Aging Report, 19*(1), 1, 33–9.

Granovetter, M. S. (1973). The strength of weak ties. *American Journal of Sociology, 78*(6), 1360–80.

Hill, T., & Maimon, D. (2013). Neighborhood context and mental health. In C. Aneshensel, A. Bierman, & J. Phelan (Eds.), *Neighborhood context and mental health* (pp. 479–501). New York, NY: Springer.

Hill, T., Ross, C., & Angel, R. (2005). Neighborhood disorder, psychophysiological distress and health. *Journal of Health and Social Behavior, 46*, 170–86.

Hobson-Prater, T., & Leech, T. G. J. (2012). The significance of race for neighborhood social cohesion: Perceived difficulty of collective action in majority Black neighborhoods. *Journal of Sociology & Social Welfare, 39*(1), 89–109.

Johnson, K. M., & Lichter, D. T. (2008). Natural increase: A new source of population growth in emerging Hispanic destinations in the United States. *Population and Development Review, 34*(2), 327–46.

Kandel, W., & Parrado, E. A. (2005). Restructuring of the US meat processing industry and new Hispanic migrant destinations. *Population and Development Review, 31*(3), 447–71.

Kerschner, H., & Harris, J. (2007). Better options for older adults. In *Public Roads.* Washington, DC: U.S. Department of Transportation.

Kim, S. Y., Nair, R., Knight, G. P., Roosa, M. W., & Updegraff, K. A. (2008). Measurement equivalence of neighborhood quality measures for European American and Mexican American families. *Journal of Community and Psychology, 37*(1), 1–20.

LaGrange, R. L., Ferraro, K. F., & Supancic, M. (1992). Perceived risk and fear of crime: Role of social and physical incivilities. *Journal of Research in Crime and Delinquency, 29*, 311–34.

Leon, C. F. M. de, Cagney, K. A., Bienias, J. L., Barnes, L. L., Skarupski, K. A., Scherr P. A., & Evans, D. A. (2009). Neighborhood conditions and walking in community-dwelling older adults: A multi-level analysis. *Journal of Aging and Health, 21*, 155–71.

Lichter, D. T., Parisi, D., Taquino, M. C., & Grice, S. M. (2010). Residential segregation in new Hispanic destinations: Cities, suburbs, and rural communities compared. *Social Science Research, 39*(2), 215–30.

Limonic, L. (2008). *The Latino population of New York City, 2007*. New York, NY: Center for Latin American, Caribbean and Latino Studies, Graduate Center, City University of New York. Retrieved September 9, 2013, from www.academia.edu/5929888/The_Latino_Population_of_New_York_City_2007_Latino_Data Project_-_Report_20_-_December_2008.

Los Angeles City Planning Department. (2009). *City of Los Angeles Area Planning Commission East*. Los Angeles, CA: Demographics Research Unit.

Los Angeles Police Department. (2013). *Gangs*. Retrieved September 14, 2013, from www.lapdonline.org/get_informed/content_basic_view/1396.

Los Angeles Times. (2013). Mapping L.A. > Eastside: East Los Angeles. Retrieved September 9, 2013, from http://maps.latimes.com/neighborhoods/neighborhood/east-los-angeles.

Loukaitou-Sideris, A., & Eck, J. E. (2007). Crime prevention and active living. *Am J Health Promot, 21*(4 Suppl), 380–9, iii.

Mair, C., Diez Roux, A. V., Osypuk, T. L., Rapp, S. R., Seeman, T., & Watson, K. E. (2010). Is neighborhood racial/ethnic composition associated with depressive symptoms? The multi-ethnic study of atherosclerosis. *Social Science & Medicine, 71*(3), 541–50.

Massey, D. S., Fischer, M. J., Dickens, W. T., & Levy, F. (2003). The geography of inequality in the United States, 1950–2000 [with Comments]. *Brookings-Wharton Papers on Urban Affairs*, 1–40.

McConnell, E. D. (2008). The U.S. destinations of contemporary Mexican immigrants. *International Migration Review, 42*(4), 767–802.

McConnell, E. D., & Miraftab, F. (2009). Sundown town to "Little Mexico": Old-timers and newcomers in an American small town. *Rural Sociology, 74*(4), 605–29.

Mead, G. H. (1934). *Mind, self, and society*. Chicago, IL: University of Chicago Press.

Murdock, S., Cline, M., Prozzi, J., Ramirez, R., Meers, A., McCray, J., & Harrison, R. (2008). *Impacts of current and future demographic change on transportation planning in Texas*. San Antonio, TX: University of Texas at San Antonio.

Newman, K. (2003). *A different shade of gray*. New York, NY: New Press.

Ostir, G. V., Eschbach, K., Markides, K. S., & Goodwin, J. S. (2003). Neighbourhood composition and depressive symptoms among older Mexican Americans. *Journal of Epidemiology & Community Health, 57*(12), 987e992.

Oswald, F., Jopp, D., Rott, C., & Wahl, H.-W. (2011). Is aging in place a resource for or risk to life satisfaction? *The Gerontologist, 51*(2), 238–50.

Osypuk, T. L., Diez Roux, A. V., Hadley, C., & Kandul, N. R. (2009). Are immigrant enclaves healthy places to live? The multi-ethnic study of atherosclerosis. *Social Science & Medicine, 60*(1), 110e120.

Phillipson, C. (2011). Developing age-friendly communities: New approaches to growing old in urban environments. In R. A. Settersten, Jr. & J. L. Angel (Eds.), *Handbook of sociology of aging* (pp. 279–93). New York, NY: Springer Science.

Ploeg, M. V., Breneman, V., Dutko, P., Williams, R., Snyder, S., Dicken, C., & Kaufman, P. (2012). Access to affordable and nutritious food: Updated estimates of distance to supermarkets using 2010 data. In *Economic Research Report* (p. 54). Washington, DC: United States Department of Agriculture.

Potter, L. (2011). *Texas & San Antonio: Characteristics and trends of the Hispanic population* (Presentation to KVDA Telemundo). San Antonio, TX: Office of the Texas State Demographer.

Putnam, R. (2000). *Bowling alone: The collapse and revival of American community*. New York, NY: Simon & Schuster.

Rantakokko, M., Iwarsson, S., Kauppinen, M., Leinonen, R., Heikkinen, E., & Rantanen, T. (2010). Quality of life and barriers in the urban outdoor environment in old age. *Journal of the American Geriatrics Society, 58*(11), 2154–9.

Rentería, M. (2011). *Hispanics in San Antonio*. San Antonio, TX: San Antonio Express-News.

Robinson, K., Lucado, J., & Schur, C. (2012). Use of transportation services among OAA Title III Program participants. In *Research Brief*. Washington, DC: Administration on Aging.

Rogers, R., & Power, A. (2000). *Cities for a small country*. London: Faber & Faber.

Ross, C. E. (2000). Neighborhood disadvantage and adult depression. *Journal of Health and Social Behavior, 41*(June), 177–87.

Ross, C. E., & Britt, C. (1995). *Survey of community, crime, and health, 1995, 1998* (ICPSR04381-v2). Ann Arbor, MI: Inter-university Consortium for Political and Social Research.

Ross, C. E., & Mirowsky, J. (2001). Neighborhood disadvantage, disorder, and health. *Journal of Health and Social Behavior, 42*(3), 258–76.

Ross, C. E., & Mirowsky, J. (2009). Neighborhood disorder, subjective alienation, and distress. *Journal of Health and Social Behavior, 50*(1), 49–64.

Salinas, J. J., Abdelbary, B. E., Rocha, E. A., & Al-Snih, S. (2012). Contextualizing the burden of chronic disease: Diabetes, mortality and disability in older Mexicans. In J. L. Angel, F. Torres-Gil, & K. S. Markides (Eds.), *Aging, health and longevity in the Mexican-origin population* (pp. 145–57). New York, NY: Springer Sciences.

Sampson, R. J. (2012). *Great American city: Chicago and the enduring neighborhood effect*. Chicago, IL: University of Chicago Press.

Sampson, R. J., & Groves, W. B. (1989). Community structure and crime: Testing social-disorganization theory. *American Journal of Sociology, 94*, 774–802.

Sampson, R. J., Morenoff, J. D., & Gannon-Rowley, T. (2002). Assessing "neighborhood effects": Social processes and new directions in research. *Annual Review of Sociology, 28*, 443–78.

Sampson, R. J., & Raudenbush, S. W. (1999). Systematic social observation of public spaces: A new look at disorder in urban neighborhoods. *American Journal of Sociology, 105*(3), 603–51.

Sampson, R. J., & Raudenbush, S. W. (2004). Seeing disorder: Neighborhood stigma and the social construction of "broken windows." *Social Psychology Quarterly, 67*(4), 319–42.

Sampson, R. J., Raudenbush, W., & Earls, F. (1997). Neighborhoods and violent crime: A multilevel study of collective efficacy. *Science, 277*, 918–24.

Stodolska, M., Acevedo, J. C., & Shinew, K. J. (2009). Gangs of Chicago: Perceptions of crime and its effect on the recreation behavior of Latino residents in urban communities. *Leisure Sciences, 31*(5), 466–82.

U.S. Census Bureau. (2013a). East Los Angeles CDP, California. In *State and county quickfacts*. Washington, DC: U.S. Census Bureau.

U.S. Census Bureau. (2013b). *State and county quickfacts*. Retrieved September 19, 2013, from http://quickfacts.census.gov/qfd/states/36/3651000.html.

Vigil, J. D. (2002). *A rainbow of gangs: Street cultures in the mega-city*. Austin, TX: University of Texas Press.

Wahl, A.-M. G., Breckenridge, R. S., & Gunkel, S. E. (2007). Latinos, residential segregation and spatial assimilation in micropolitan areas: Exploring the American dilemma on a new frontier. *Social Science Research, 36*(3), 995–1020.

Weeks, G. B., & Weeks, J. R. (2010). *Irresistible forces: Explaining Latin American migration to the United States*. Albuquerque, NM: University of New Mexico Press.

Wilson, J. Q., & Kelling, G. (1982). Broken windows: The police and neighborhood safety. *Atlantic Monthly*, March, 29–38.

Wilson, W. J. (1990). *The truly disadvantaged: The inner city, the underclass, and public policy*. Chicago, IL: University of Chicago Press.

Wilson-Genderson, M., & Pruchno, R. (2013). Effects of neighborhood violence and perceptions of neighborhood safety on depressive symptoms of older adults. *Social Science and Medicine, 85*, 43–9.

Wolf, S. (2010). Maras transnacionales: Origins and transformations of Central American street gangs. *Latin American Research Review, 45*(1), 256–65.

World Health Organization. (2007). *Global age-friendly cities: A guide*. Geneva: World Health Organization.

Yen, I. H., Michael, Y. L., & Perdue, L. (2009). Neighborhood environment in studies of health of older adults: A systematic review. *American Journal of Preventive Medicine, 37*(5), 455–63.

CHAPTER 8

Caregiver Burden and Burnout

LOVE IS NOT ENOUGH

Rosario, a 56-year-old elementary school teacher with a husband of 30 years, was looking forward to an empty nest after the couple's three children left home. The oldest, a son aged 35, became a career Army officer; the eldest of her two daughters, who is 32, became an elementary school teacher like her mother; and the youngest, 29, is a stay-at-home mom with two children of her own. Rosario and her husband get along well with their daughter-in-law and sons-in-law and see their grandchildren often. After 29 years of field hockey, orchestra, summer camp, and the inevitable adolescent crises, Rosario and her husband were ready to relax and spend more time together, even as they continued to work.

Their empty-nest period did not last long, though. A year ago Rosario's father, Edmundo, a retired machinist in his early 70s, suffered a major stroke. Even after months of rehabilitation and physical therapy, he is unable to speak or walk without assistance. Rosario's mother, who is also in her early 70s, suffers from serious osteoarthritis and cannot care for her husband or maintain a household. When Edmundo suffered his stroke, the older couple's options were limited. They owned their modest home in the Latino section of the city, but they had few other assets. Their income consisted of Edmundo's union pension and his Social Security. Buying a condo in a retirement community or paying for the sort of high-level nursing home care that Edmundo needed was simply impossible. The only solution was for the old couple to move in with Rosario and her husband. Rosario's sense of obligation and duty to her parents made the decision simple.

Rosario and her husband remodeled the children's rooms to accommodate the old couple. They removed walls and some stairs between two rooms that were at slightly different levels and replaced them with a ramp; they put safety bars in the bathroom and bought a special bed that allows Edmundo to get in and out with a little help. At first, Rosario kept working and was gone during school hours. Although she has two brothers, they live in a different state and are unable to help care for the old couple. When her parents first moved in Rosario paid a neighbor to prepare lunch for them while she was at work, and she would take time off when they needed to go to the doctor. Both parents required frequent doctor's visits. After a year of juggling lesson plans, work requirements, housekeeping, and dealing with her parents, Rosario decided to quit her job and devote all of her time to eldercare. She was becoming exhausted.

Even before she made the decision to quit working, Rosario had developed serious physical and emotional symptoms resembling those that doctors attribute to "Caregiver Syndrome." She was having trouble sleeping and felt exhausted during the day. She had frequent bouts of colitis that left her doubled up with pain. More recently she has been feeling depressed and after quitting her job, she feels like a failure and she is increasingly socially isolated. She spends most of her day at home interacting with her parents, but the experience is not rewarding. Although she loves and honors her parents, they are both becoming cognitively frail and their conversations are rambling and make little sense. Occasionally Rosario's mother thinks that Rosario is her sister and that neither have children. Rosario has become a prisoner in her own home and feels guilty about feeling somewhat resentful. She occasionally has the neighbor come over to watch the parents while she runs errands or does her shopping. She rarely sees her old friends at school.

Like many caregivers, Rosario was not aware of what would be involved when she decided to assume responsibility for her parents. Of course, there were very few alternatives. The only realistic option would have been to have put her father in a nursing home and let the couple "spend down" to Medicaid eligibility. The thought was unacceptable to Rosario. Unfortunately, after 2 years Rosario's mother became incontinent, and the level of care the old woman needed increased dramatically. When Rosario's grandmother grew old and needed constant attention, she had several daughters who lived close by and could provide care. Rosario is alone. She and her husband eventually hired a home health care service to provide hourly assistance for part of the time. They could not afford the amount of care that the two older people in fact needed.

As the old couple's physical health and cognitive capacities decline the amount of care and attention they will need will only increase. Eventually, they will be confined to their beds, if they survive. For Rosario the situation means no vacations, little relaxation, and few nights out. This is nothing like the empty nest that she and her husband had been looking forward to. The reality is that Rosario and her husband may eventually have no choice but to consider a nursing home for both parents if their health deteriorates further. Like many other children who feel a strong obligation to honor and care for their parents, Rosario had no idea what serious cognitive impairment and incontinence mean in terms of caregiving. Despite her strong commitment to assuming the responsibility she feels is hers, without extensive assistance of some sort Rosario will not be able to continue. The world has simply changed, and increasingly families must look to others, including the state and non-governmental agencies, for help.

FAMILY CAREGIVERS

Rosario's predicament is not unique. In fact, it is becoming more common as life expectancies increase and as aging parents require intensive assistance for longer periods of time. As we move into the 21st century, life is much different for American families than it was in the past, and the question of who will care for elderly parents is ever more difficult to answer. For Latino families, as for families from other racial and ethnic groups, the economic, medical, and practical needs of older parents who are living longer, but often with serious physical and cognitive disabilities, increasingly challenge traditional expectations concerning caregiving. The reality of the situation is that families increasingly will have to turn to other sources of assistance, including formal long-term care providers and non-governmental organizations. The days of taking a parent in and providing all of the financial and practical care that they might need are rapidly passing into history. Even so, adult children continue to play a central, if changing role in dealing with an older parent's care and support and in this chapter we investigate the consequences for the caregiver of different levels of caregiving responsibility.

Until we choose to or are forced to assume the task, most of us are unaware of how difficult and potentially exhausting the care of any highly dependent person, such as a disabled child, an ill spouse, or a cognitively impaired parent, can be. Caring for a dependent person often requires a team to deal with various aspects of care. Without such a team, or substantial assistance, the burden placed on an individual or even a family can become excessive. In this chapter we review research on the consequences for the caregiver of the burden of caring for someone with complex and extensive needs. We summarize research that shows that the ongoing strain of caring for a dependent family member can lead to caregiver burnout, a term that refers to the exhaustion that results from excessive caregiving demands that can seriously undermine the caregiver's own physical and mental health.

The subject is of particular salience in the context of our examination of the role of the Latino family in eldercare. Latinos of course differ greatly in their retention of tradition, and especially in terms of culturally based norms concerning filial piety, or one's duty to support and care for one's parents. All families, and not just Latinos, face difficult choices when a parent loses his or her capacity to live independently. Most families wish to optimize an older parent's autonomy and make it possible for the older person to stay in his or her home. Certain Latinos, though, perhaps like families from other traditional cultures, find themselves caught between two competing realities. On the one hand, they are motivated by the desire to care for an aging parent themselves. On the other hand, they are faced with the reality of other expectations and responsibilities, including the need to work, to care for one's own children, and the need to save for one's own retirement.

Conflicting expectations and norms can complicate the caregiving task and make seeking help difficult. Tita De La Garza, the youngest daughter in Laura Esquivel's poignant novel *Like Water for Chocolate* (1989), embodies an extreme version of the sacrifice that traditional Mexican culture called for in terms of caring for an aging parent. As the youngest daughter Tita was expected to remain single and sacrifice her own future and happiness to care for the old woman until she died. Such extreme expectations may be fictional or they may have characterized rural cultures of previous centuries, but the story reveals real expectations in traditional Mexican culture. Even short of such extreme self-sacrifice, caring for infirm aging parents means that one may have to give up aspects of one's own life.

Traditions fade, however, and today a more individualistic orientation that values greater self-actualization and a concern for one's own situation has displaced the norm of extreme self-sacrifice in the larger society (Wallace & Facio, 1987). A less familistic orientation means more of a rational approach that downplays total sacrifice and takes everyone's welfare into account (Sabogal, Marín, Otero-Sabogal, Marín, & Perez-Stable, 1987). Such an orientation implies a greater willingness to turn to formal sources of support (Rodríguez-Galán, 2013). Although a strong family orientation continues to characterize Latino culture, intermarriage, migration, higher levels of education, the media, and more will inevitably transform Latino culture (Schwartz, 2007).

THE HEALTH CONSEQUENCES OF TRADITION

Tradition, then, provides humans with an anchor based on a set of guiding principles. Tradition reduces the amount of uncertainty in life, but it also limits one's choices. Today, at least in the developed Western world, we live in what has been termed post-traditional society in which traditions are less binding, or in which we have the option of choosing among traditions (Giddens, 1991). Tradition can, therefore, protect health insofar as it provides security, but it also could conceivably undermine health if it traps one in unwanted roles. Several studies appear to confirm the potentially contradictory effects of traditional family values. As we have noted, traditional norms may discourage Latino caregivers from seeking help from outside the family (Flores, Hinton, Barker, Franz, & Velasquez, 2009). The caregiver may in fact feel that asking for such help is a sign of weakness or failure. As we noted, Latinos avoid institutionalizing demented relatives for longer periods than non-Latinos (Mausbach et al., 2004). A culturally coerced dependence on an adult child caregiver, especially if other family members are not available to help, combined with a long delay in seeking outside assistance may result both in inadequate care and undue stress on the caregiver (Rodríguez-Galán, 2013).

Small cross-ethnic caregiver studies suggest that this may indeed be the case. Several studies show that Mexican immigrant family caregivers are more likely than U.S.-born family caregivers to rely exclusively on the family network to care for functionally impaired parents rather than seek community-based services (Crist, García-Smith, & Phillips, 2006; Crist, Woo, & Choi, 2007). In a qualitative study of Puerto Rican family caregivers of older adults, a lack of perceived support from friends and neighbors combined with a reluctance to use social services was associated with greater stress and financial strain among caregivers (Aranda and Knight, 1997). Again, the closer one adheres to traditional cultural norms the greater the exclusive reliance on family caregivers. With greater acculturation such exclusivity declines. In previous research we have found that the children of native-born elders are more likely than the children of foreign-born elders to seek assistance from outside the family (Angel, Rote, & Markides, 2013).

THE SOURCES OF CAREGIVER STRESS

The stresses facing caregivers, then, arise from several sources. To begin with, the task can be objectively quite difficult in the case of a severely impaired older parent, but it is made potentially more difficult by the conflicting cultural and personal expectations that we have mentioned. The conflict between traditional respect for a mother's wishes and the desire to seek help from outside the family network creates stress (Flores et al., 2009). Flores et al. describe the dilemma faced by a traditional caregiver they interviewed by noting that she "alternates between accepting her caregiver role as an obligation, given her cultural upbringing, and wanting to run away and escape her mother's outbursts, which she sometimes does by locking herself in her room" (2009, p. 1063). The majority of Mexican-origin caregivers, like Flores's interviewee, are middle-aged women who face particularly serious inner conflicts due to traditional expectations and changing gender, work, and family roles (Aranda and Knight, 1997). Increased acculturation, which reflects a loss of a traditional orientation, weakens the norm of sacrificing oneself completely for a parent's care (Dilworth-Anderson, Williams, & Gibson, 2002).

We begin, then, with the observation that probably for most families, and especially for traditional Latinos, the expectation that children have a duty to care for their parents is still strong, but the changes that have affected the family's caregiving capacity may increase the burden on individual caregivers and take a serious toll on their health.

The caregiver role, like most other complex social roles, involves both rewards and costs. A responsible adult willingly assumes the duty of caring for others, including children and aging parents. As long as those responsibilities do not become excessive they can be rewarding and reinforce one's self-esteem and the sense that one is a responsible adult. The extent to which caring for a dependent person remains rewarding or becomes burdensome of course depends on the extent of the older person's needs, the nature of the relationship between the caregiver and the care receiver, and the personalities of both parties. Some caregivers have great stamina and patience and some care receivers are cooperative and pleasant. Other caregivers are easily stressed and some ill individuals are uncooperative and demanding.

It is also important to emphasize that caregiving occurs within different contexts, which can affect the level of burden placed on a caregiver. As the population ages new governmental programs are being introduced and old ones expanded to deal with the growing need. In what follows, we review the major federal programs that provide assistance to caregivers and discuss various experiments carried out at the state and local levels for providing assistance to reduce the burden of caregiving and to allow caregivers to attend to their other responsibilities. In Chapter 6 we discussed many of these programs in terms of the services they provide to older clients. Here we focus on the relief and assistance they provide to caregivers. The message we take away from the research is that in the future even groups with traditional orientations toward eldercare will have to turn to governmental programs and other non-governmental agencies for help. The family will always play an important role in eldercare, but the days of the family shouldering all of the responsibility are probably gone forever.

LATINOS AND CAREGIVING

The Latino family, like the rest of America, is undergoing changes that inevitably alter traditional family structures and living arrangements, as well as the family's capacity to care for aging parents (Herrera et al., 2013; Stone, 2011). As a result of greater need and fewer economic and social resources, Latino caregivers face serious challenges that place them at risk of financial and emotional stress (Ramos,

2004). As we have pointed out, older Mexican-origin Hispanics tend not to enter nursing homes (Espino, Angel,
Wood, Finely, & Ye, 2013). To a large extent this low use of
institutions reflects group norms and expectations concerning children's obligations to take their parents in, but it also
reflects economic realities. Nursing home care is extremely
expensive and it is not covered by Medicare. In reality low-
income Latino families simply have no choice but to keep
their aging parents at home. As a result, families are the
primary source of care among Hispanics, and in most cases
the responsibility for the care of aging parents and parents-
in-law falls to daughters and daughters-in-law (Angel,
Angel, McClellan, & Markides, 1996; Herrera, Angel, Díaz-
Venegas, & Angel, 2012). Latino family members currently
provide nearly 80% of the care that is provided at home, a
higher percentage than for African-Americans and non-
Latino Whites (Torres-Gil, 2005). According to the National
Alliance of Caregiving, over eight million Latinos provide
care to older individuals. One of every three Latino households reports that at least one family member provides care
to an older person.

THE REQUIREMENTS FOR INDEPENDENT LIVING

Most of us take for granted the routine activities and
responsibilities that we all deal with on a daily basis. They
are simply a part of everyday life that one carries out routinely, but when one loses the capacity to deal with these
activities and responsibilities their complexity becomes
obvious. At that point someone else must take over. These
routine responsibilities include such relatively high-order,
cognitively demanding activities as attending to financial
matters, obtaining health care, making decisions about
living arrangements, driving, shopping for food and clothing, and much more. Everyday life also includes lower-order
tasks such as eating, bathing, going to the bathroom, dressing, getting in and out of bed, and more. When one loses
the ability to carry out either the higher-order or the lower-
order tasks, independent living becomes difficult if not
impossible.

The barriers to independent living that an individual
who begins to lose his or her cognitive capacity faces are
obvious when we examine the complexity of what is
required to attend just to one's financial affairs. Dealing

competently with one's financial situation involves multiple complex tasks, including keeping track of income and expenses, paying property taxes on time, keeping records for federal and state income tax preparation, managing any investments one might have, supervising property that one might own, preparing a will, and more. Such complex tasks require that one's cognitive functioning be intact. Even younger individuals with high levels of education can fall victim to investment frauds, or get themselves into more debt than they can handle. An older person with some resources is at serious risk of exploitation or of making bad decisions concerning investments. When an older person becomes incapable of managing his or her own financial affairs, adult children must either assume the responsibility themselves or find a trustworthy and competent agent who can do so.

As long as they are in good health and mobile, most older individuals stay in their own home and provide for themselves. As people age, though, chronic medical conditions become more common. More often than not, an older person takes several prescription drugs for such conditions as hypertension, diabetes, heart disease, enlarged prostate, gastrointestinal problems, etc. As one ages, heart disease and cancer become more common and require frequent medical visits. Managing chronic conditions is time consuming and complicated. Someone must make appointments and make sure that the older person keeps them. Someone must monitor medication use and make sure that the older person takes it as prescribed.

If one lives long enough, at some point one is likely to lose the capacity to carry out basic household tasks such as cleaning, maintaining a yard, doing laundry, dealing with repairs, and the rest of what it takes to maintain a household. Personal hygiene can become a problem, and getting in and out of the bathtub or shower can pose a major challenge. Bathroom falls are a major risk for older individuals (National Institutes of Health, 2013). Often an older person does not realize that he or she can no longer deal with the basic activities of daily living and that he or she can no longer live alone. An older individual who lives alone has no one present to respond in the case of an emergency. Ads for services like Life Alert, which provides an emergency call button to seniors, present dramatic reminders that an older person who falls and who cannot get to a phone can go without help for hours or even days.

At the point at which it becomes clear that an older person can no longer live alone his or her adult children or someone else must assume the responsibility for their daily care, or the family must make the decision that institution-alization is the only realistic option. Serious cognitive decline and incontinence often mark the point at which institutionalization is necessary (Coward, Horne, & Peek, 1995; Lichter, Parisi, Taquino, & Grice, 2010; Sun et al., 2013). What is clear, though, is that Latinos continue to bear a large fraction of the burden of caring for older parents. On average, Latinos and African-American care-givers of relatives with dementia spend 30 hours per week providing care whereas non-Latino White caregivers of demented relatives spend only 20 hours per week in care-giving (Alzheimer's Association, 2013). Non-Latino Whites also tend to institutionalize family members with cognitive impairments sooner than Blacks or Latinos (Gaugler, Duval, Anderson, & Kane, 2007; Yaffe et al., 2002).

INSTITUTIONALIZATION: CAREGIVER FAILURE?

The decision to institutionalize an infirm parent occurs, then, when the family and the community system cannot provide all or a substantial portion of the care he or she needs. In cultures with a strong norm of filial piety and the expectation that the family should bear the burden, institu-tionalization of an aging parent could be seen as a failure on the part of adult children and even a mark of shame, espe-cially if one has to turn to Medicaid, which is almost inevit-able unless a family is quite affluent (Sun et al., 2013). Even in the face of a serious burden on caregivers, a constellation of factors work against placing a loved one in an institution (Luppa et al., 2010). Cultural norms against placing a parent in a nursing home remain particularly strong in rural Mexican-origin populations (Baxter, Bryant, Scarbro, & Shet-terly, 2009). Rural residents in general tend to be more tradi-tional than urban dwellers and cling to a philosophy of "taking care of our own" (Magilvy, Congdon, Martinez, Davis, & Averill, 2000). In traditional rural communities elders are treated with *respeto* (respect), which consists of valuing their wisdom and deferring to their authority. Certain researchers find that Latinas express more positive attitudes toward the caregiving role than Anglos (Mausbach et al., 2004). The strength of tradition is revealed by the fact that less acculturated Latinas express more positive views toward caregiving than more acculturated Latinas.

As we have mentioned in earlier chapters, it is important not to overemphasize cultural factors, and to bear in mind that financial and practical considerations influence a family's decisions in caring for an older parent. Many studies that find strong traditional orientations toward eldercare are based on rural samples from areas in which formal eldercare services are rare. Rural families, regardless of their race or ethnicity, have historically been self-sufficient of necessity. Hispanics in urban areas face a different set of constraints on their caregiving capacities and also have other sources of care available upon which to draw. Metropolitan areas offer other community-based options in caring for elderly parents, which we discuss shortly. What is clear, though, is that over time traditions weaken and social and economic changes inevitably alter institutions, including the institution of the family, in ways that alters the caregiving roles of adult children.

Although Latino family members, like the general population, would prefer to allow an aging parent to continue living in his or her own home, that option may simply become impossible. That option may require too much daily commitment by family members, or family members may simply live too far away to provide ongoing care. Although we have emphasized traditional cultural expectations concerning filial piety, Hispanics, like other groups, are shedding aspects of traditional culture as they move into the middle class. The focus on tradition, as we have noted, is based on observations in rural populations and provides a somewhat romantic view of family life as it was in previous decades. Although institutionalization remains fairly rare among Hispanics, the reality is that in the future the need for at least some assistance will drive Hispanic caregivers to seek help outside the family. We discuss these options in the remainder of the chapter.

Before reviewing community sources of caregiving assistance we must note that family networks are important in the decision to seek such assistance. For all racial and ethnic groups, decisions concerning parental care are made jointly by the older person's adult children. Interviews with the adult children of institutionalized elders reveal that the decision to finally institutionalize the parent was usually arrived at collectively (Sergeant, Ekerdt, & Chapin, 2010). Family networks are extremely important in decisions concerning all aspects of a parent's affairs and care. Siblings, in fact, have more influence on these collective decisions than physicians (Aneshensel, Pearlin, Mullan, Zarit, & Whitlach 1995).

THE STRESS OF NOT KNOWING WHERE TO TURN

Caring for an older parent who needs constant attention and supervision, then, would be stressful in any situation. When a caregiver or the family network finally decides that they cannot deal with the problem alone, another source of stress arises from not knowing what to do. A lack of knowledge of community-based options can prolong the period during which a family goes it alone. Even when a family decides that they must seek help they face what can be a confusing set of options (Feder, Komisar, & Niefeld, 2000). At least initially, caregivers are generally uninformed about the options, and social service agencies can be unresponsive and fail to provide useful information about services available (Abraham & Neese, 1993; Frieden, 2013; Stuen, 1985). Family caregivers, particularly those who do not live close to the older parent, often have only a vague or inaccurate idea of the health or functional status of a loved one. Without the ability to observe the older person in his or her daily context, a child who lives in a different city can imagine that everything is all right, when in fact it is not. When one begins to suspect that all is not right, one finds quickly that information on long-term alternative care arrangements is often not readily available nor easily understood. In an attempt to reach individuals in need of assistance social service agencies engage in outreach efforts to inform families about the services they offer or that are available elsewhere. Outreach involves identifying individuals who live alone or families with an older parent and informing them about available services. Outreach is necessary since most individuals do not know where to begin to locate what an older family member needs. A centralized webpage or information would clearly be useful. We discuss such efforts further below. A major problem facing effective outreach is that many individuals are not receptive. Racial or ethnic mismatch between agencies and potential clients create barriers. Other challenges to effective outreach to elderly clients and individuals with disabilities include the lack of adequate needs assessments, the failure to engage influential local leaders, and language and communication barriers (Aranda, Villa, Trejo, Ramirez, & Ranney, 2003; Frieden, 2013; Stuen, 1985).

Proponents of outreach efforts claim that various outreach models show great promise, but the lack of consistency across studies makes it difficult to generalize about the effectiveness of any given approach. Rarely is the term "outreach" operationally defined or empirically studied, making the assessment of best practices difficult. More empirical investigation will be necessary to identify the best way of disseminating information to those who need it. Outreach can include more than simply providing information. The most effective method of dissemination must be identified and implemented. To reach out to the rural elderly population, for example, programs must focus on building community networks of service providers, nongovernmental organizations including churches and community centers, and individuals that can facilitate the dissemination of such information (Abraham, 1993).

The lack of knowledge as to when and how to proceed is clearly a major barrier, but in the end, though, the decision to institutionalize an elderly parent is driven by the inability of the support network to cope. At that point the family begins the process of investigating the options. This realization that an aging individual must be institutionalized can arise from various sources. One study of caregivers of relatives with dementia found that the decision is driven by two major realizations concerning the status quo. The first is the recognition that the older person has become a potential threat to him- or herself or others. At this point the danger that the older person presents and the constant supervision that he or she requires is simply beyond any individual's or even a family's ability to provide in the community. The second realization arises from the recognition by the caregiver that they are burned out and can simply no longer deal with the demands of caregiving. At some point even the most committed caregiver can simply burn out (Aneshensel et al., 1995). As we noted earlier, cognitive impairment and incontinence result in levels of need that can simply overwhelm an informal care network.

SOURCES OF INFORMATION

Until one is confronted with the need to make decisions concerning a parent's long-term care, most individuals know almost nothing about it. In the beginning a parent's decline can be subtle and go unnoticed, especially if his or her children live far away. Events such as calls from collection agencies, the failure to file tax returns, confusion, the inability to make decisions, and other changes make it clear that something is wrong. Since long-term care is not a routine need, most of us know nothing about it until the need becomes obvious. Most of us are unaware of the options in home- and community-based care services nor do we have any knowledge of how to pay for such services. In a national telephone survey of a random sample of 1,456 adults, over half of respondents mistakenly believed that Medicare pays for assisted living facilities (AARP, 2006). Almost 60% erroneously believed that Medicare covers nursing home stays beyond 3 months for age-related or other chronic conditions. Caregivers often find it difficult to even begin locating information on home- and community-based services (Angel, 1999). To further complicate the problem, public and private agencies charged with helping caregivers often do not provide the information needed, or do so in manner that is confusing or not useful to caregivers (Herrera et al., 2013). Information concerning available services is often communicated in short messages and advertisements that do not provide sufficient information (Lucke, Hernando-Martinez, Mendez, & Arevalo-Flechas, 2013).

One potential solution, or at least partial solution, to this problem would be to have a state-based entry access point for long-term care services, perhaps similar to the health care exchanges that are part of the Affordable Care Act. In Texas such an information access program was proposed by the state legislature. The bill required the Texas Department on Aging to develop and annually update a statewide consumer guide for senior citizens designed to assist them and their families in making informed choices regarding senior services, but it was ultimately vetoed by the Governor on June 20, 1997 (Zaffirini, 1997). Such an access point, either online or offered in person, could provide more complete and useful information concerning long-term care options in the community and in institutions, provide information on financing, and help families navigate the complex system (Administration on Aging, 2012). The service could even offer advice on dealing with the everyday emotional burdens of caregiving.

Currently the Administration on Aging educates older people and their caregivers about the benefits and services available in their communities through an online search engine called Eldercarelocator. Caregivers either enter their zip code or select from numerous aging topics to help them connect to the appropriate resource. 🌐 www.eldercare. gov/Eldercare.NET/Public/Index.aspx. When the authors of this book entered their zip code they were given detailed contact information for the local Area Agency on Aging (AAA). AAAs are county-based agencies that are funded by the federal government and administered by states that provide information and referral services to promote community living, as well as information on public long-term support programs and benefits. Later in this chapter we discuss specific AAA programs for caregivers. Another outreach initiative by a federal agency is offered through Medicare. Medicare.gov is an online caregiver toolkit that provides useful information to ensure that family members and friends receive the best possible care. www.medicare.gov/campaigns/caregiver/caregiver-resource-kit.html.

CAREGIVER BURDEN

Even though caregiving is a noble task that can be rewarding, a large body of research shows that caring for someone with serious needs can have detrimental health and economic consequences for the caregiver. Traditionally, daughters and daughters-in-law have been the primary caregivers to their own and their husband's parents. In earlier eras a woman's primary responsibility was the family and adding the care of an infirm older adult to their daily tasks was a natural extension of that responsibility. Today women routinely work outside the home and unless one quits one's job to devote time to caregiving, assuming additional duties can cause serious strain, especially if one has a demanding full-time career. Time spent caring for elderly parents often results in lost wages and economic problems (Johnson & Sasso, 2006; Kane, Kane, & Ladd, 1998; Witters, 2011). Exhibit 8.1 shows the personal financial costs of elder caregiving. In 2007, full-time employed caregivers suffered an average loss of $5,625 in pre-tax wages (Evercare, 2007). Caregivers suffer significant reductions in retirement savings (MetLife Mature Market Institute, 2011). Although the Family Medical Leave Act allows employees to take unpaid time off to care for family members for limited periods, the intent is to allow workers to deal with temporary emergencies, but not to provide long-term care (Glass, 2009; Roog, Knight, Koob, & Kraus, 2004).

The economic burden represents only one of the potential burdens that caregivers assume. Perhaps even more serious are the potential negative mental and physical health consequences that arise from the stress that

Exhibit 8.1 Economics of Caregiving

Women who are family caregivers are 2.5 times more likely than non-caregivers to live in poverty and five times more likely to receive Supplemental Security Income (SSI).

In every state and DC the poverty rate is higher among families with members with a disability than among families without.

During the 2009 economic downturn, one in five family caregivers had to move into the same home with their loved ones to cut expenses.

Almost one half of working caregivers report an increase in caregiving expenses has caused them to use up all or most of their savings.

The average family caregiver for someone 50 years or older spent $5,531 per year on out-of-pocket caregiving expenses in 2007, which was more than 10% of the median income for a family caregiver that year.

Source: http://caregiveraction.org/statistics/#Economics of Caregiving

unassisted caregiving can bring. A recent Gallup survey of working adults found that approximately one-fifth of those who were caring for an elderly or disabled relative or friend report low levels of life satisfaction and suffer from emotional and physical health problems (Witters, 2010). Other studies of physical health and depression among caregivers report similar findings (Coughlin, 2010; Ho, Collins, Davis, & Doty, 2005). Poorly educated caregivers are at high risk of depression (Covinsky et al., 2003). Some research suggests that family caregivers who do not have enough money suffer emotional health problems (Bradley et al., 2009). In combination with ongoing responsibilities for their own children and households, the additional demands of dealing with an infirm family member can simply overwhelm a caregiver and undermine her physical and psychological health (Fortinsky, Tennen, Frank, & Affleck, 2007).

The extent of the negative health consequences depend, of course, on the magnitude of the burden. Caring for someone with a combination of dementia, depression, diabetes, and other chronic conditions clearly magnify the health threat to the caregiver (Hinton, Haan, Geller, & Mungas, 2003). As we mentioned earlier, incontinence and dementia often spell the end to attempts to keep an older person in the community. Although Latinos live longer on average than non-Hispanics, many suffer protracted periods of disability, as well as high rates of dementia at earlier ages. As caregiving demands increase, which can result in role overload, a caregiver's risk of depression also increases

(Gaugler, Davey, Pearlin, & Zarit, 2000). Among caregivers of individuals with Alzheimer's disease over 60% report emotional stress and over 40% report physical stress associated with caregiving (Alzheimer's Association, 2013). A lack of understanding of dementia symptoms often delays the decision to seek additional help (Neary & Mahoney, 2005). Poorly educated Hispanic caregivers are especially prone to misattributing dementia in their parent to mental disorders common in old age (Covinsky et al., 2003). This means that Latino caregivers can face a protracted period of demanding caregiving. The prohibitive cost of long-term care in combination with cultural norms against abandoning a parent place Latino caregivers in a catch-22 situation. They may feel overwhelmed by the addition of eldercare responsibilities to their own family responsibilities, but also feel that they cannot seek help. Exhibit 8.2 presents some facts concerning the particularly stressful and challenging role of caregiver for an elderly person with dementia. Caring for someone who is close to death may give rise to anticipatory grief and anxiety.

Exhibit 8.2 Facts: Caregiving for Elderly Relatives with Dementia

Disproportionately befalls women in families (Crist et al., 2007; Flores et al., 2009; Herrera et al., 2008).

Care recipients with dementia tend to be older than care recipients without Alzheimer's disease or dementia. They are more likely to be a parent or parent-in-law of the care providers (Bouldin & Andresen, 2010).

Caregivers of older persons with dementia report that they provide the most help with learning, remembering, or confusion (Bouldin & Andresen, 2010).

Although men also provide assistance, female caregivers ages 45–56 tend to spend more time providing care for parents than for children (Pierret, 2006).

Dementia caregivers spend more hours per week providing care than non-dementia caregivers and report more role strain and physical and mental health problems, as well as employment complications and family strain, than non-dementia caregivers (Bouldin & Andresen, 2010; Ory et al. 1999).

In various studies Latinos who are caring for older adults report feeling lonely, depressed, and that their overall health is poor (Crist et al., 2006; Gallagher-Thompson, Arean, Rivera, & Thompson, 2001; Herrera et al., 2013; Llanque & Enriquez, 2012). Given conflicting expectations and demands caregiver burdens are likely to be greater in families in which traditional norms are strongest, as in the case of families with immigrant parents. Although they live longer than the native-born, foreign-born Mexican-origin elders are far more likely than the native-born to suffer from cognitive impairment, mobility limitations, and disability, thereby increasing the demands placed on caregivers and potentially placing them at greater risk of negative health outcomes (Angel, Angel, Díaz-Venegas, & Bonazzo, 2010).

FACTORS THAT AFFECT THE ABILITY TO PROVIDE CARE

As we documented earlier, Latinos are moving far beyond their traditional areas of concentration and now live in communities all over the nation (Durand, Telles, & Flashman, 2006). Migration serves important positive functions for migrants, largely by enhancing their economic opportunities. Unfortunately, it can have negative consequences for those left behind. Inevitably, migration of any distance undermines adult children's ability to interact and provide even limited care for aging parents (Van Hook & Glick, 2007). In Chapter 4 we described the situations of older parents who are left behind in Mexico when their children, nieces, nephews, and other young community members move away in search of work. The older generations who are left behind can only long for the traditional extended families and communities that are now only memories. Adult children occasionally return home, but primarily to visit, and not to take care of their elderly parents.

Clearly, children who have moved to another city or state face unique barriers to providing care. They might perhaps assume responsibility for financial matters or for coordinating care, but daily assistance with dressing, bathing, meals, medications, transportation, shopping, etc., is clearly not possible. Those tasks must be dealt with by someone who lives close by, perhaps an adult child who has remained close to their parent's home. Studies of the caregiving burdens of adult children who live at least two hours or more away from parents with Alzheimer's reveal that they spend significant amounts of time coordinating care, especially when they are the only person available to do so, and they incur far higher out-of-pocket expenses for travel, communication, and paying for hired help than caregivers of individuals without Alzheimer's (Alzheimer's Association, 2013).

The possibilities for caregiving among transnational families can be severely limited. An adult child who lives and works in the United States is simply not available to care for an aging parent in Mexico. As we discussed in Chapter 4, even if they would like to bring an aging parent to live with them in this country, the fact that they must assume the full financial responsibility, including responsibility for medical and other care for the older person, means that such a move may simply be too burdensome. International migration is perhaps the most extreme case of family separation, but even internal migration causes problems for adult children with aging parents who lose their ability to care for themselves. Today, moving away from home is more the rule than the exception for adult children. Few of us remain on the family farm or join our parents in the family business. For adult children who live in a different city or state than their aging parents, interactions can be normalized with occasional visits and frequent electronic communication while the parents are still active and healthy. When a parent's health deteriorates, though, the situation can become seriously complicated.

With fewer children close by, there are fewer hands to share the burden of dealing with what can become complex and intensive caregiving tasks. The Waltons' solution to eldercare was simple, with several generations living together on the family farm, but increasingly for all groups such arrangements are a romantic myth. Given basic human psychology, an adult caregiver with siblings who must assume responsibility for a large part of the care of an older parent may come to feel that she is bearing an unfair burden and that the situation is inequitable. As among siblings generally, a sense of fairness depends upon the belief that one is not doing more than is reasonable or that one is not carrying an unfair share of the burden. One possibility results from the fact that caregiving involves different specific tasks. One sibling might, for example, assume more of the financial responsibility, while another, who perhaps does not have the same income or resources, might assume more of the responsibility for daily caregiving. If that sibling lives closer to the parent than the sibling who provides financial support a sense of equity might be fostered. As of yet we know little about family dynamics and their impact on a sense of equity, or the potential consequences of differential burdens on the physical and mental health of caregivers. Given the aging of the population, studies of these phenomena will be necessary in order to develop effective interventions to reduce excess burden.

Migration is only one of many social forces that are changing the family's capacity to assume the roles as sole or even primary caregiver to older parents. Single mothers who must raise children alone and couples in which both husband and wife work face particularly serious challenges. As Rosario's situation illustrates, having to quit work may create economic hardship for families and caregiver financial strain. Latinas must work today because their income is vital to the maintenance of household consumption (Meyer & Pavalko, 1996; Singley, 2008). As women find that they must enter the labor force these role strains become even greater (Herrera, Lee, Palos, & Torres-Vigil, 2008).

FORMAL CAREGIVING SUPPORTS: WHAT CAN BE DONE TO EASE THE BURDEN?

Despite the desire of aging parents to stay in their own homes, or at least in the community, and the desire of their children to allow them to do so, longer lives and high levels of disability, in conjunction with the social changes we have discussed, can eventually make that option unrealistic. Ultimately institutionalization may be inevitable, but before that point community options exist that can help decrease the burden placed on family members and increase the time that an older parent can avoid institutionalization. Unfortunately, as we will see, Latinos do not take full advantage of these options, perhaps because of a rejection of outside assistance, or perhaps because of a lack of awareness of their availability (Herrera, Benson, Angel, Markides, & Torres-Gil, 2013). Formal support refers to caregiving provided by formal agencies and organizations, such as home health care and visiting nurse services, transportation assistance provided by a municipal government, Meals on Wheels, etc. As we discussed in Chapter 6, caregivers can take advantage of various publicly funded long-term care services, including information and referral services, case management, and other services provided by municipalities, cities, states, and the federal government.

MEDICAID WAIVERS

States are beginning to shift resources toward community-based care to reduce costs while still providing sufficient services (Evans, Belyea, Coon, & Ume, 2012). Medicaid community waiver community-based programs encompass a wide array of services that help meet the needs of low-income adults with disabilities, including but not limited to adult foster care, home-delivered meals, respite care, primary home care, and day activity and health services. As we discussed in Chapter 6, one particularly important program for caregivers that is carried out under the waiver provisions of the Social Security Act is the Program of All-inclusive Care for the Elderly (PACE). PACE provides caregivers the flexibility to help an older person continue living in the community. In addition to paying for medical and dental care, PACE services include social services such as adult, day, and home care, recreational therapy, meals, nutritional counseling, social work counseling, and transportation. Over the past 20 years the PACE model has transformed options in long-term care for older adults by making it possible to intimately involve the family in the care of the elderly without forcing them to shoulder the entire burden. For more information about PACE's history, visit 🌐 www.npaonline.org/website/article. asp?id=12&title=Who,_What_and_Where_is_PACE?

Although the community-based waiver experiments offer states a unique opportunity to test new methods of providing services in non-institutional contexts, these experiments are not without potential dangers. In pursuing savings and economic efficiency, potential programs may introduce disincentives to enrollment, including long waiting lists (Ng, 2013). Nationwide, the average time on a waiting list for waiver services ranges from 13 months to almost 2 years, reflecting the high demand for these services and the difficulties that older adults experience accessing them (Kaiser Commission on Medicaid and the Uninsured, 2011; Ng, 2013).

Another problem is the cost of funding state Medicaid programs amid fiscal austerity. Community-based programs initiated under the waiver authority serve as laboratories for testing cost-neutral ways of packaging services and reimbursing providers. Yet, ongoing increases in the relative cost of health care for the elderly, especially prescription drugs, will affect legislative priorities for Medicaid financing and other funding in the future. For more information on the CMS-HCBS Waiver Program go to

⚉ www.medicaid.gov/Medicaid-CHIP-Program-Information/By-Topics/Waivers/Home-and-Community-Based-1915-c-Waivers.html.

AREA AGENCIES ON AGING

In addition to Medicaid waiver programs, the federal government provides funding to states for social services under the Older Americans Act (OAA). The law provides grants for a wide array of social services, food delivery, and nutrition programs as well as the Aging and Disability Resource Centers (ADRCs) (⚉ www.aoa.gov/AOA_programs/OAA/index.aspx). As we discussed in Chapter 6, the services are provided through the National Aging Network of 56 state agencies on aging, 629 Area Agencies on Aging (AAA), nearly 20,000 service providers, 244 Tribal organizations, and two Native Hawaiian organizations representing 400 tribes.

Among other OAA programs, one of the most important potential sources of caregiving assistance includes the National Family Caregiver Support Program (NFCSP). The NFCSP helps the caregivers of dependent family members, including grandchildren under the care of grandparents, avoid unnecessary institutionalization. The NFCSP provides training in respite services, day care, and hospice services (Administration on Aging, 2012). Services available to family caregivers include: assistance to caregivers in gaining access to supportive services, individual counseling, support groups, and caregiver training to assist caregivers in making decisions and solving problems relating to their roles, respite services to temporarily relieve caregivers of their responsibilities, and supplemental services, on a limited basis, to complement the care provided by caregivers.

As we discussed earlier, given that frail elderly Hispanics are likely to be taken care of by grown children at home this program is particularly useful for Hispanic family caregivers. The program can also relieve the stress placed on caregivers by providing counseling services and respite services and offering information and referral to help gain access to services and other health care providers (Administration on Aging, 2012). Exhibit 8.3 describes the five basic services offered by the AAA for family caregivers. In 2012, grants for the Family Caregiver Support Program amounted to almost $154 million (Napili & Colello, 2013).

Exhibit 8.4 outlines the specific characteristics of caregivers eligible for the program and Exhibit 8.5 discusses the number of clients served by program.

Exhibit 8.3 National Family Caregiver Support Program (OAA Title IIIE)

Authorizing Legislation: Section 371 of the Older Americans Act of 1965, as amended

1. Information to caregivers about available services;
2. Assistance to caregivers in gaining access to services;
3. Individual counseling, organization of support groups, and caregiver training to assist the caregivers in making decisions and solving problems relating to their caregiving roles;
4. Respite care to enable caregivers to be temporarily relieved from their caregiving responsibilities; and
5. Supplemental services, on a limited basis, to complement the care provided by family caregivers.

Source: Administration on Aging (2012)

Unfortunately, Latinos across the country tend to underutilize AAA services as well. A recent study revealed that low-income African Americans were most likely and Latinos least likely to avail themselves of services (Herrera et al., in press). Some observers suggest that this low participation rate by Latinos may be due to the lack of culturally tailored programs for ethnic minorities (Almendarez, 2007; Espino, Neufeld, Mulvihill, & Libow, 1988). Aside from the NFCSP the federal government funds an initiative designed specifically for family caregivers of persons with Alzheimer's disease. The caregiver intervention program called Resources for Enhancing Alzheimer's Caregiver Health (REACH) was established in 1995 in six cities – Boston, Birmingham, Memphis, Miami, Palo Alto, and Philadelphia – to help

Exhibit 8.4 Eligible Program Participants

✓ Adult family members or other informal caregivers age 18 and older providing care to individuals 60 years of age and older
✓ Adult family members or other informal caregivers age 18 and older providing care to individuals of any age with Alzheimer's disease and related disorders
✓ Grandparents and other relatives (not parents) 55 years of age and older providing care to children under the age of 18
✓ Grandparents and other relatives (not parents) 55 years of age and older providing care to adults age 18–59 with disabilities.

Source: Administration on Aging (2012)

Exhibit 8.5 Number of Clients Served

- Access Assistance Services provided over one million contacts to caregivers helping them locate services from a variety of private and voluntary agencies.
- Counseling and Training Services provided over **125,000** caregivers with counseling, peer-support groups, and training to help them better cope with the stresses of caregiving.
- Respite Care Services provided more than **64,000** caregivers with 6.8 million hours of temporary relief – at home, or in an adult day care or institutional setting – from their caregiving responsibilities.

Source: Administration on Aging (2012)

caregivers deal with stressors related to caregiving (Schulz et al., 2002). The type of stressors range from the nature of the disability and type of tasks, to the time dedicated to caregiving. For example, caring for a loved one with incontinence, dementia, or both requires constant supervision. Assisting with activities of daily living, such as bathing, dressing, and grooming, is the most burdensome. The time devoted to the tasks may restrict time for social activities and isolate the caregiver, leading to depression and exhaustion. Caregivers' lack of awareness of the expectations and obligations associated with the caregiver role can also create strain. For example, managing the tasks prior to impending death may give rise to anticipatory grief and anxiety. In addition, having to quit work, as Rosario did, may create economic hardship for families and caregiver financial strain.

The REACH program helps caregivers cope with dementia care by exposing participants to an intervention that consists of sessions providing information and support strategies, family therapy, education, and skill-based training. Hispanic family caregivers in the intervention experienced less depression than Hispanics who did not receive the treatment (Gallagher-Thompson et al., 2003).

ELDERCARE NGOS

To maximize the use of local community resources other organizations work to help connect family caregivers with services and support. As we discussed in Chapter 6, Family Eldercare of Austin, a private, not-for-profit agency, offers an information and referral service to senior citizens and families seeking alternatives to long-term care in nursing homes.

Adult child caregivers can ask for assistance in finding in-home care, housing alternatives, and other community-based services and support on behalf of their elderly parents. For example, Family Eldercare offers housing information and referrals in its home-sharing program. The program matches university students with frail older residents to help an elder stay in their home. The abundance of colleges and universities located in the city of Austin and the surrounding metropolitan area make this a viable option for many of the elders in Central Texas wishing to stay at home and for upper-class students who want and need affordable housing.

In addition, Family Eldercare provides in-home care services to reduce the risk of caregiver stress. The Caregiver Support Program lightens the caregiver's load with customized in-home care plans that offer the right mix of services to support independence, dignity, and safety. Services are offered on a sliding fee scale. The Homemaker plan provides assistance with tasks such as meal preparation, medication reminders, and transportation. In addition to the Homemaker plan, the Caregiver Support Program offers personal assistant services, such as bathing, toileting, skin and hair care, and exercise. 🌐 www.familyeldercare.org/in-home-care-overview.html#sthash.AG 91Wo37.dpuf.

SUMMARY AND CONCLUSIONS

In this chapter we dealt with the issue of caregiver burden, a label that refers to the exhaustion that can accompany caregiving, which in the extreme makes it impossible to continue. As we have noted in earlier chapters, once an individual becomes seriously cognitively impaired or incontinent, keeping him or her at home can become impossible. Given increased lifespans, today some caregivers are themselves quite old and may not be physically capable of carrying out the caregiving tasks required. Even for relatively young caregivers, though, the time and effort, as well as the emotional cost of intensive and ongoing caregiving, can cause stress that can undermine one's physical and mental health. Of course, the health and financial consequences of caring for a dependent individual depend on the context and circumstances in which the care is given, as well as the caregiver's expectations concerning their duty to their aging parents.

For Hispanics today traditional norms governing children's duty to care for their aging parents often conflict with newer orientations concerning the child's own self-interest. Traditional roles called for women to sacrifice their own lives in favor of their duties to family, including aging parents. Today such complete self-sacrifice is less common, and even disapproved of among more progressive groups. Modern orientations lead both men and women to seek education and to enter the labor force to better their own and their families' material well-being. At certain points traditional and more contemporary orientations collide, placing an individual and a family in a difficult situation. The problem has been made more serious by increasing lifespans, smaller families, and the fact that adult children often no longer live close to their parents' home.

For many older Hispanics the years after 65 are characterized by serious health problems and functional incapacity. We reviewed evidence that the onset of dementia and other disabling diseases occurs at earlier ages among Hispanics than among non-Hispanic Whites. As a consequence, many relatively young older Hispanics cannot care for themselves and require intensive assistance with activities of daily living, and with more complex matters related to finances, living arrangements, medical care, and more. In earlier chapters we reviewed new data that shows that although Hispanics live on average longer than non-Hispanic Whites, much of the life lived after 65 is characterized by serious functional impairment. Although both group norms and personal preference might be for children to care for families, the sheer magnitude of the task may make institutionalization more common in years to come.

In Chapter 6 we reviewed the various options in community-based care available to the families of parents with high levels of need. Clearly, the availability of such services as adult day care, nutrition services, transportation, and other services can greatly reduce the burden placed on caregivers and allow them the opportunity to continue working and to address their other responsibilities. Although rural residents, recent immigrants, and families with more traditional orientations may continue to keep aging parents at home, the use of community social services can clearly make the task easier and improve the lives of both caregivers and care receivers.

The caregiving role has changed dramatically as a result of the social and demographic changes that we have documented in previous chapters. Medical innovations in the control of conditions such as heart disease and diabetes that can result in early death have greatly increased longevity, even if they have not reduced the burden of disability. Longer lives with longer periods of illness and disability mean a greater need for medical care. They also mean that independent living is a challenge and may not be possible. For the adult children of infirm aging parents who need extensive and long-term care the task of providing all of that care alone may simply become unrealistic.

This changing world of caregiving means that the use of community and institutional long-term care will no doubt increase in the years to come. One major barrier to the use of available services arises from the fact that the families of individuals with disabilities usually lack adequate information on where to obtain such services. The need for eldercare assistance can occur quickly and without warning. When a family realizes that all is not well with an aging parent often they do not even know what questions to ask, let alone where to find the answers. Although many agencies and organizations provide information on the services they provide and refer families to appropriate care providers, there are few centralized sources of information. The Area Agencies on Aging and other organizations provide centralized webpages with information on sources of care in one's local area, but knowledge about the availability of the service is not widespread. As yet, outreach efforts are in their infancy and will have to be developed further in the future.

Eldercare is a dynamic and complex role due to a constellation of personal, social, and economic factors. As a parent grows old caregivers must adjust to the changing needs for greater assistance and knowing what to ask a professional is not always clear. Government and non-government programs such as the National Family Caregiver Act help caregivers meet those challenges. While state and local agencies provide much-needed information and referrals, resources, and solutions to help guide caregivers in dealing with role strain, gaps in knowledge still remain to effectively manage the responsibilities.

DISCUSSION QUESTIONS

1. Traditional Social Security systems are based on the principle of "intergenerational solidarity," a term that refers to the bond between generations that arises from the fact that younger workers support retired workers though payroll contributions, with the expectation that they will be supported in turn when they

retire. The fact that the number of workers relative to the number of retirees has declined dramatically since World War II means that this principle of solidarity has become strained. Retirement systems increasingly require workers to save for their own retirement and not look to younger workers to support them. Discuss the implications of this change in solidarity and expectations for intergenerational exchanges both for society and for the family. What are the implications of socializing the financial support of older parents through Social Security and Medicare?

2. Go to the Web and search the phrase "caregiver burnout." Compare some sites, including WebMD, to find out how the syndrome is defined, what its symptoms are, and how it might be treated. Discuss whether this is a real condition or perhaps only the complaints of caregivers who simply do not want the responsibility.

3. Caring for an older parent not only involves commitments of time and energy, it often includes significant financial costs for adult children if the parent does not have significant resources or income of their own. Discuss the extent of the obligations of adult children in paying for their parents' material needs. How might paying for these needs affect the adult child's obligations to his or her own children and his or her own future? Should adult children feel justified in placing an elderly parent in an institution on Medicaid?

4. Define the term "familism." You might use an online dictionary such as Merriam-Webster. What are the major dimensions, that is, components, of familism? How does the concept relate to the Latino family? Discuss whether or not the concept adds anything useful to our understanding of the Latino family, or whether it is merely a label with no substantive utility. Does the term describe or identify aspects of Latino culture that perhaps make aspects of the Latino family different than those of other groups, or does the concept really apply to most families?

5. Identify some possibilities for reducing the risk of caregiver burnout. How much of a burden can an individual or even a family assume for the care of elderly parents? It is conceivable, after all, that a couple could find that they must care for four or more older relatives at once. What other organizations might be called upon? Who should ultimately be responsible for the financial support of infirm elderly individuals?

LITERATURE CITED

AARP. (2006). *The costs of long-term care: Public perceptions versus reality in 2006* (report by GfK NOP). Washington, DC: AARP Public Policy Institute.

Abraham, I., & Neese, J. B. (1993). Outreach to the elderly and their families: Focus on the rural South. *Aging, 365*, 26–31.

Administration on Aging. (2012). *National Family Caregiver Support Program (OAA Title IIIE)*. Washington, DC: U.S. Department of Health and Human Services.

Almendarez, B. L. (2007). *Mexican American elders and nursing home transition*. San Antonio, TX: University of Texas Health Science Center at San Antonio.

Alzheimer's Association. (2013). *2013 Alzheimer's disease facts and figures*. Chicago, IL: The Alzheimer's Association.

Aneshensel, C. S., Pearlin, L. I., Mullan, J. T., Zarit, S. H., & Whitlatch, C. J. (1995). *Profiles in caregiving: The unexpected career* (1st ed.). San Diego, CA: Academic Press.

Angel, J. L. (1999). Helping families to navigate the system of long-term care alternatives: The role of information technology. *Journal of Family and Consumer Sciences, 91*, 116–23.

Angel, J. L., Angel, R. J., McClellan, J. L., & Markides, K. S. (1996). Nativity, declining health, and preferences in living arrangements among elderly Mexican Americans: Implications for long term care. *The Gerontologist, 36*(4), 464–73.

Angel, J. L., Rote, S., & Markides, K. (2013). *Nativity, late-life family caregiving, and the Mexican-origin population in the United States*. Paper presented at the Gerontological Society of America Annual Meeting. New Orleans, LA.

Angel, R. L., Angel, J. L., Díaz-Venegas, C., & Bonazzo, C. (2010). Shorter stay, longer life: Age at migration and mortality among the older Mexican-origin population. *Journal of Aging and Health, 22*, 914–31.

Aranda, M. P., & Knight, B. G. (1997). The influence of ethnicity and culture on the caregiver stress and coping process: A sociocultural review and analysis. *The Gerontologist, 37*(3), 342–54.

Aranda, M. P., Villa, V. M., Trejo, L., Ramirez, R., & Ranney, M. (2003). El Portal: Latino Alzheimer's project model program for Latino caregivers of Alzheimer's disease-affected people. *Social Work, 48*(2), 259–72.

Baxter, J., Bryant, L. L., Scarbro, S., & Shetterly, S. M. (2009). Patterns of rural Hispanic and non-Hispanic white health care use: The San Luis Valley Health and Aging Study. *Research on Aging, 23*(1), 37–60.

Bouldin, E. D., & Andresen, E. (2010). *Caregiving across the United States: Caregivers of persons with Alzheimer's disease or dementia in Connecticut, New Hampshire, New Jersey, New York, and Tennessee*. Chicago, IL: Alzheimer's Association.

Bradley, S. E., Sherwood, P. R., Kuo, J., Kammerer, C. M., Gettig, E. A., Ren, D., et al. (2009). Perceptions of economic hardship and emotional health in a pilot sample of family caregivers. *Journal of Neurooncology, 93*(3), 333–42.

Coughlin, J. (2010). Estimating the impact of caregiving and employment on well-being. *Outcomes and Insights in Health Management, 2*(1), 1–7.

Covinsky, K. E., Newcomer, R., Fox, P., Wood, J., Sands, L., Dane, K., & Yaffe, K. (2003). Patient and caregiver characteristics associated with depression in caregivers of patients with dementia. *Journal of General Internal Medicine, 18*(12), 1006–14.

Coward, R. T., Horne, C., & Peek, C. W. (1995). Predicting nursing home admissions among incontinent older adults: A comparison of residential differences across six years. *The Gerontologist, 35*(6), 732–43.

Crist, J. D., García-Smith, D., & Phillips, L. R. (2006). Accommodating the stranger en casa: How Mexican American elders and caregivers decide to use formal care. *Research and Theory for Nursing Practice: An International Journal, 20*(2), 109–26.

Crist, J. D., Woo, S. H., & Choi, M. (2007). Mexican American and Anglo elders' use of home care services. *Journal of Transcultural Nursing, 18*, 339–48.

Dilworth-Anderson, P., Williams, I. C., & Gibson, B. E. (2002). Issues of race, ethnicity, and culture in caregiving research: A 20-year review (1980–2000). *The Gerontologist, 42*(2), 237–72.

Durand, J., Telles, E., & Flashman, J. (2006). *The demographic foundations of the Latino population: Transforming our common destiny: Hispanics in the United States.* Washington, DC: National Academy of Sciences.

Espino, D. V., Angel, J. L., Wood, R. C., Finely, M. R., & Ye, Y. (2013). Characteristics of Mexican American elders admitted to nursing facilities in the United States: Data from the Hispanic Established Populations for Epidemiologic Studies of the Elderly (EPESE) study. *Journal of the American Medical Directors Association, 14*(3), 226.e1–4.

Espino, D. V., Neufeld, R. R., Mulvihill, M., & Libow, L. S. (1988). Hispanic and non-Hispanic elderly on admission to the nursing home: A pilot study. *The Gerontologist, 28*, 821–4.

Evans, B. C., Belyea, M. J., Coon, D. W., & Ume, E. (2012). Activities of daily living in Mexican American caregivers: The key to continuing informal care. *Journal of Family Nursing, 18*(4), 439–66.

Evercare. (2007). *Family caregivers: What they spend, what they sacrifice.* Bethesda, MD: National Alliance for Caregiving.

Feder, J., Komisar, H. L., & Niefeld, M. (2000). Long-term care in the United States: An overview. *Health Affairs, 19*(3), 40–56.

Flores, Y. G., Hinton, L., Barker, J. C., Franz, C. E., & Velasquez, A. (2009). Beyond familism: A case study of the ethics of care of a Latina caregiver of an elderly parent with dementia. *Health Care for Women International, 30*(12), 1055–72.

Fortinsky, R. H., Tennen, H., Frank, N., & Affleck, G. (2007). Health and psychological consequences of caregiving: I. In C. M. Aldwin, C. L. Park, III, A. Spiro, & R. P. Abeles (Eds.), *Handbook of health psychology and aging* (pp. 227–49). New York, NY: Guilford Publications, Inc.

Frieden, L. (2013). *Outreach and people with disabilities from diverse cultures: A review of the literature.* Washington, DC: National Council on Disability.

Gallagher-Thompson, D., Arean, P., Rivera, P., & Thompson, L. W. (2001). A psychoeducational intervention to reduce distress in Hispanic family caregivers: Results of a pilot study. *Clinical Gerontologist, 23*(1–2), 17–32.

Gallagher-Thompson, D., Coon, D. W., Solano, N., Ambler, C., Rabinowitz, Y., & Thompson, L. W. (2003). Change in indices of distress among Latino and Anglo female caregivers of elderly relatives with dementia: site-specific results from the REACH national collaborative study. *The Gerontologist, 43*, 589–91.

Gaugler, J. E., Davey, A., Pearlin, L. I., & Zarit, S. H. (2000). Modeling caregiver adaptation over time: The longitudinal impact of behavior problems. *Psychology and Aging, 15*(3), 437–50.

Gaugler, J., Duval, S., Anderson, K., & Kane, R. (2007). Predicting nursing home admission in the U.S.: A meta-analysis. *BMC Geriatrics, 7*(1), 13.

Giddens, A. (1991). *Modernity & self-identity: Self and society in the late modern age.* Stanford, CA: Stanford University Press.

Glass, J. (2009). Work-life policies: Future directions for research. In A. Booth & N. Crouter (Eds.), *Work life policies that make a difference* (pp. 231–50). New York, NY: Russell Sage.

Herrera, A. P., Angel, J. L., Díaz-Venegas, C., & Angel, R. J. (2012). Estimating the demand for long-term care among aging Mexican Americans: Cultural preferences versus economic realities. In J. L. Angel, F. Torres-Gil, & K. Markides (Eds.), *Aging, health, and longevity in the Mexican-origin population* (pp. 259–76). New York, NY: Springer Sciences.

Herrera, A., Benson, R., Angel, J. L., Markides, K., & Torres-Gil, F. (2013). Effectiveness and reach of caregiver services funded by the Older Americans Act to vulnerable older Hispanics and African Americans. *Home Health Care Services Quarterly.*

Herrera, A. P., Lee, J. W., Palos, G., & Torres-Vigil, I. (2008). Cultural influences in the patterns of long-term care use among Mexican-American family caregivers. *Journal of Applied Gerontology, 27*, 141–65.

Herrera, A. P., Mendez-Luck, C. A., Crist, J. D., Smith, M. L., Warre, R., Ory, M. G., & Markides, K. (2013). Psychosocial and cognitive health differences by caregiver status among older Mexican Americans. *Journal of Community Mental Health, 49*(1), 61–72.

Hinton, L., Haan, M., Geller, S., & Mungas, D. (2003). Neuropsychiatric symptoms in Latino elders with dementia or cognitive impairment without dementia and factors that modify their association with caregiver depression. *The Gerontologist, 43*(5), 669–77.

Ho, A., Collins, S. R., Davis, K., & Doty, M. M. (2005). A look at working-age caregivers' roles, health concerns, and need for support. In *Issue Brief.* New York, NY: The Commonwealth Fund.

Johnson, R., & Sasso, A. L. (2006). The impact of elder care on women's labor supply. *Inquiry, 43*, 195–210.

Kaiser Commission on Medicaid and the Uninsured. (2011). *Medicaid home and community-based service programs: Data update.* Menlo Park, CA: The Henry J. Kaiser Family Foundation.

Kane, R. A., Kane, R. L., & Ladd, R. C. (1998). *The heart of long-term care.* New York, NY: Oxford University Press.

Lichter, D. T., Parisi, D., Taquino, M. C., & Grice, S. M. (2010). Residential segregation in new Hispanic destinations: Cities, suburbs, and rural communities compared. *Social Science Research, 39*(2), 215–30.

Llanque, S. M., & Enriquez, M. (2012). Interventions for Hispanic caregivers of patients with dementia: A review of the literature. *American Journal of Alzheimer's Disease and Other Dementias, 27*(1), 23–32.

Lucke, K. T., Martinez, H., Mendez, T. B., & Arevalo-Flechas, L. C. (2013). Resolving to go forward: The experience of Latino/Hispanic family caregivers. *Qualitative Health Research, 23*(2), 218–30.

Luppa, M., Luck, T., Weyerer, S., König, H.-H., Brähler, E., & Riedel-Heller, S. G. (2010). Prediction of institutionalization in the elderly. A systematic review. *Age and Ageing, 39*(1), 31–8.

Magilvy, J. K., Congdon, J. G., Martinez, R. J., Davis, R., & Averill, J. (2000). Caring for our own: Health care experiences of rural Hispanic elders. *Journal of Aging Studies, 14*(2), 171–90.

Mausbach, B. T., Coon, D. W., Depp, C., Rabinowitz, Y. G., Wilson-Arias, E., Kraemer, H. C., et al. (2004). Ethnicity and time to institutionalization of dementia patients: A comparison of Latina and Caucasian female family caregivers. *Journal of the American Geriatrics Society, 52*(7), 1077–84.

MetLife Mature Market Institute. (2011). *The MetLife study of caregiving costs to working caregivers: Double jeopardy for baby boomers caring for their parents.* Westport, CT: MetLife Mature Market Institute.

Meyer, M. H., & Pavalko, E. K. (1996). Family, work, and access to health insurance among mature women. *Journal of Health and Social Behavior, 37*, 311–25.

Napili, A., & Colello, K. J. (2013). *Funding for the Older Americans Act and other aging service programs.* Washington, DC: Congressional Research Service.

National Institutes of Health. (2013). Falls and older adults: Causes and risk factors – many possible causes. In *NIH SeniorHealth.* Washington, DC: National Institutes of Health.

Neary, S. R., & Mahoney, D. F. (2005). Dementia caregiving: The experiences of Hispanic/Latino caregivers. *Journal of Transcultural Nursing, 16*(2), 163–70.

Ng, T. (2013). *HCBS wait lists: National estimates 2012.* Paper presented at HCBS Waiver Conference, Arlington, VA.

Ory, M. G., Hoffman, R. R., III, Yee, J. L., Tennstedt, S., & Schulz, R. (1999). Prevalence and impact of caregiving: A detailed comparison between dementia and nondementia caregivers. *The Gerontologist, 39*(2), 177–85.

Ramos, B. M. (2004). Culture ethnicity, and caregiver stress among Puerto Ricans. *Journal of Applied Gerontology, 23*(4), 469–86.

Rodríguez-Galán, M. (2013). The ethnography of ethnic minority families and aging: Familism and beyond. In K. E. Whitfield & T. Baker (Eds.), *Handbook of minority aging.* New York, NY: Springer.

Roog, S. A., Knight, T. A., Koob, J. J., & Kraus, M. J. (2004). The utilization and effectiveness of the Family and Medical Leave Act of 1993. *Journal of Health and Social Policy, 18*(4), 39–52.

Sabogal, F., Marín, G., Otero-Sabogal, R., Marín, B. V., & Perez-Stable, E. J. (1987). Hispanic familism and acculturation: What changes and what doesn't? *Hispanic Journal of Behavioral Sciences, 9*(4), 397–412.

Schulz, R., O'Brien, A., Czaja, S., Ory, M., Norris, R., Martire, L. M., et al. (2002). Dementia caregiver intervention research: In search of clinical significance. *The Gerontologist, 42*, 589–602.

Schwartz, S. J. (2007). The applicability of familism to diverse ethnic groups: A preliminary study. *Journal of Social Psychology, 147*(2), 101–18.

Sergeant, J. F., Ekerdt, D. J., & Chapin, R. K. (2010). Older adults' expectations to move: Do they predict actual community-based or nursing facility moves within 2 years? *Journal of Aging and Health, 22*, 1029–53.

Singley, C. (2008). *The status of Latinos in the labor force.* Washington, DC: National Council of La Raza.

Stone, R. (2011). *Long-term care for the elderly.* Washington, DC: Urban Institute Press.

Stuen, C. (1985). Outreach to the elderly: Community based services. *Journal of Gerontological Social Work, 8*(3–4), 85–96.

Sun, F., Durkin, D. W., Hilgeman, M. M., Harris, G., Gaugler, J. E., Wardian, J., et al. (2013). Predicting desire for institutional placement among racially diverse dementia family caregivers: The role of quality of care. *The Gerontologist, 53*(3), 418–29.

Torres-Gil, F. (2005). Aging and public policy in ethnically diverse societies. In V. Bengtson, P. Coleman, & T. Kirkwood (Eds.), *The Cambridge handbook of age and ageing* (pp. 670–81). New York, NY: Cambridge University Press.

Van Hook, J., & Glick, J. E. (2007). Immigration and living arrangements: Moving beyond the instrumental needs versus acculturation "dichotomy." *Demography, 44*, 225–49.

Wallace, S. P., & Facio, E. L. (1987). Moving beyond familism: Potential contributions of gerontological theory to studies of Chicano/Latino aging. *Journal of Aging Studies, 1*(4), 337–54.

Witters, D. (2010). In U.S., working caregivers face wellbeing challenges. *Gallup Wellbeing*. Retrieved from www.gallup.com/poll/145115/working-caregivers-face-wellbeing-challenges.aspx.

Witters, D. (2011, December 1). The cost of caregiving to the U.S. economy. *Gallup Business Journal*. Retrieved from http://businessjournal.gallup.com/content/151049/cost-caregiving-economy.aspx.

Yaffe, K., Fox, P., Newcomer, R., Sands, L., Lindquist, K., Dane, K., & Covinsky, K. E. (2002). Patient and caregiver characteristics and nursing home placement in patients with dementia. *JAMA, 287*(16), 2090–7.

Zaffirini, J. (1997). *SB 273 Last Action: 06/20/1997 E Vetoed by the Governor* (Council Document: 75R 2652 KKA-D). Austin, TX: Texas Legislature Online.

CHAPTER 9

Retirement Planning, Financial Literacy, and Savings

RETIREMENT ARRIVES BEFORE YOU KNOW IT

Fred Sandoval just turned 62 and has decided to apply for Social Security since he and his wife, Claudia, need the income now. However, since they will be receiving benefits early, Fred's benefits will be reduced by 20% and Claudia's spousal benefit by 25%. Claudia has no private retirement plan. Their total Social Security income will be under $1,500 per month. This will represent the lion's share of their income. The couple owns their home, in which they have approximately $124,000 in equity, but they still have 5 years on their mortgage, which will consume much of their monthly income. Fred has less than $70,000 in an individual retirement account, and the couple has $15,000 in personal savings and a checking account. They also have over $20,000 in high-interest credit card debt. Fred intends to continue working as a mechanic as long as he can, but given his age and a serious back problem he will only be able to work on a limited basis. The couple will not be among those who take cruises, contribute to charities, and help their children and grandchildren with college educations and home purchases. Their retirement years will be characterized by limited consumption. One wonders how they ended up in this predicament, which is, in fact, quite common. To answer that question we must go back a few years.

Fred joined the Army in 1956 at the age of 18 right out of high school. After basic training he received orders to Korea where the United States maintains a large force to insure the Armistice that was signed at Panmunjom on July 27, 1953. This was the first time Fred had ever been outside New Mexico. He spent his tour of duty at Camp Carroll near the city of Daegu where he was assigned to the motor pool. Fred had always enjoyed tinkering with cars and at Camp Carroll he learned to maintain and repair Jeeps and light trucks. There he discovered that he had a real aptitude as a mechanic. When he was discharged at the age of 20, he returned home to Albuquerque to carry on with his life. Almost immediately he married Claudia, his high school sweetheart, and within a year they had their first child, a healthy young daughter. Within 2 years they had two other sons.

After he and Claudia married Fred attempted to start his own auto repair shop in his parents' garage. Unfortunately, although he was a good mechanic he was a mediocre businessman. His old friends from high school would drop by during working hours and the group would drink and talk about the good old days. The few customers Fred had, mostly family members, became impatient when their repairs were not completed when promised. Within 6 months Fred closed the business and got a job at a local garage. Over the next 30 years Fred held several jobs at different service stations and repair shops, with one longer stable period at a major car dealership that we discuss later. His talent as a mechanic was well known, but so was his unreliability, part of which was the result of binge drinking. Most of the time Fred kept control of himself, but occasionally he had a "lost weekend" that lingered into the next week and he would fail to show up for work. He was fired from many jobs.

When he was a young man Fred, like so many others his age, never thought about retirement, nor did he think of planning and saving for future expenses like college educations for his children or helping them buy homes. The money that he earned today was spent today. Over the years Claudia worked at several clothing stores as a salesperson, but she never earned enough to allow the couple to save much. Claudia worked part-time and never participated in a retirement plan. Occasionally she would mention to Fred that perhaps they should save something for the children's education, but retirement was never a topic of conversation, and in the end they saved almost nothing. They never spoke to anyone about finances, retirement, or saving.

While he was working, Fred paid Social Security and had far more than the 10 years of contribution required to receive benefits. Most of the jobs he held, though, did not offer a retirement plan. At one point he got a job at a major dealership that offered a 401(k) plan. His supervisor and the human resources officer at the dealership explained that the employer would match his contribution and that he would be foolish not to take advantage of the opportunity. Fred signed up and contributed for nearly 7 years, after which he left the dealership and again bounced from repair shop to repair shop. He did not continue contributing to his 401(k). At one point he was tempted to borrow from the fund but found out that he would pay a substantial penalty for withdrawing before age 59-and-a-half and so resisted the temptation.

By his early 60s, Fred realized that he had not acted responsibly and that preparing for retirement is important. Of course it was far too late. He contacted a local non-governmental organization (NGO) that provides financial advice to the Hispanic community, but they could offer little by way of advice on increasing the couple's income. They offered some help with lowering Fred's credit card debt, and they explained rules concerning Medicare and provided information on sources of supplemental assistance with home repairs and other minor matters. Until they turn 65, Fred and Claudia will be at risk of bankruptcy in the case of serious illness since they have no health insurance. Because of the problems faced by so many of their clients, the NGO has applied for funding to provide financial literacy classes to younger individuals, but such a program would be too late for Fred and Claudia. The financial situation of older members of the community has negative consequences for everyone, including children and grandchildren who cannot turn to the older generations for help with education or starting businesses. Information on saving, investing, and the wise stewardship of financial resources is vitally important, but for Fred and Claudia that information was never available.

WILL MY MONEY LAST?

Financial security is important at all stages of the life course. Infants who are born into impoverished environments can suffer from malnutrition and a lack of basic health care that can have lifelong negative consequences. Early deprivation can undermine cognitive development and leave one less able to prosper even if the opportunities arise (Case, Fertig, & Paxson, 2005; Conroy, Sandel, & Zuckerman, 2010; Hayward & Gorman, 2004). Adults with few assets and income are unable to adequately provide for their children or address their own health care and other needs. These adults lack an essential part of what allows one to assert oneself and be a fully socially effective agent. Just as in earlier stages of the life course, an adequate income and assets are critical to older people's health and well-being, but low levels of education, labor force disadvantages, and lifelong deprivation means that many older minorities face a financially insecure old age. Many have nothing but Social Security to live on. Social Security was never meant to be one's only source of income; it was meant to supplement private pensions and savings, but the reality is very different for many older individuals, including a significant fraction of non-minority elders.

It is important to be clear that it is not only minority group members who do not have adequate savings to deal with short-term emergencies or the even larger amount that one needs for a secure retirement. Americans in general do not save enough money and many do not know how to invest for either the short or longer term. Given the importance of financial security for overall well-being, as well as for physical and mental health, in this chapter we review what is known of financial literacy, as well as the real financial options available to working-age and older minority Americans. We begin early in the life course since one's situation in later years depends on one's financial behavior earlier in life. We end with a discussion of the efforts of NGOs to provide financial assistance and education to low-income elders, but first let us review the retirement security situations of non-Hispanic Whites, African Americans, and Latinos.

Poverty, of course, is relative as well as an absolute. In the United States we do not witness the sorts of extreme poverty that result in starvation or severe protein malnutrition that one sees in much of the developing world. Few Americans have ever seen a case of rickets, a disease that results from Vitamin D deficiency, since most U.S. children drink milk and eat other foods that contain adequate amounts of essential vitamins and minerals. Yet the absence of the poverty-related diseases one might see in Somalia or Sudan does not mean that poverty does not have serious health and developmental effects in the developed world. In the United States those with the lowest levels of income and education have far poorer health than the wealthy, but even those with intermediate levels of income and education are less healthy than the most affluent (Braveman, Cubbin, Egerter, Williams, & Pamuk, 2010).

In previous chapters we documented the serious gap in income, and especially in wealth, between minority Americans and non-Hispanic White Americans. These gaps arise from differences in education, labor force disadvantages, and more. In this chapter we discuss another aspect of the problem related to how one manages one's finances. Financial literacy is every bit as important as the ability to read, write, and carry out basic mathematical calculations. We employ the term "financial literacy" to refer to knowledge of how best to manage what money and assets one has, and "financial capacity" or "financial capability" to refer to one's ability to act effectively on the basis of that knowledge. Knowledge is vital, but it clearly is not enough. One must have access to the financial institutions and tools that allow one to optimize one's economic situation. In this chapter we deal with basic issues related to managing money, especially in terms of the objective of saving for major purchases such as a home, paying for children's education, and providing for one's retirement. We also review basic income and other support programs for low-income individuals and families since these are a major source of economic security. We end by reviewing efforts by governmental agencies and NGOs to educate low-income individuals on how best to manage their resources and utilize public and private programs that compensate for the lack of an adequate income.

INADEQUATE INCOMES

We begin with the obvious by noting that the core of the financial difficulties that impoverished individuals and families face relates less to their lack of savings and money management skills and more to the fact that their incomes are inadequate. As we documented in earlier chapters, Hispanics and Blacks have far lower wages on average than non-Hispanic Whites. These income deficits translate directly into low rates of savings and investment. For these populations both income flows and asset stocks remain low. The result is that their ability to save for major purchases such as a home or children's college education remains limited, and their ability to take advantage of business opportunities or to contribute to a retirement fund is almost nonexistent. As we have documented in previous chapters, the reasons for low incomes are complex and operate interactively. Low educational levels mean that one is confined to the low-wage sectors of the economy in which one does not acquire either human or material capital. Workers with few job skills have lower lifetime earnings and are at higher risk of layoff than workers with higher-level skills.

Solutions to the problem of low wages and income are matters of ongoing debate and clearly separate the political left and right. The left traditionally favors greater redistribution of income from the rich to the poor, while the right favors encouraging individual responsibility. Each side has very different views concerning the causes of poverty and society's responsibility for the poor. As we are preparing this manuscript for press it appears that Democrats are planning to make raising the minimum wage a major part of their 2014 campaign strategy. Most states currently set their state minimum wages at the federal level of $7.25 per hour, but many Democrats propose raising federal and state minimum wages to $10 per hour or more. Raising the minimum wage by up to $3 dollars would clearly raise the incomes of individuals in jobs that pay minimum wage. Critics of increases in the minimum wage argue that the result would be an increase in unemployment since employers would simply not be willing to pay the increased wage for low-productivity workers. Others point out that the effect of an increase in the minimum wage could be relatively small since many workers in minimum wage jobs are young part-time workers or secondary earners who are not the sole support of a family.

Whatever the outcome of efforts to increase the minimum wage, the fact remains that even if it were raised the effect on the real ability of families to save and invest would probably remain limited. Even with wages that are a good bit above minimum wage the amount of extra income left after routine expenditures are paid is small. It is clearly better to save whatever one can than to save nothing at all. Unless one earns closer to the median income, though, one has little chance of saving the amount of money that is necessary for a secure and comfortable retirement. Enhancing financial literacy and capacity, then, requires concerted efforts to increase the productivity of low-wage workers by insuring that they do not become low-wage workers in the first place. Hispanics drop out of high school at alarming rates (Angel & Angel, 2009). Until the reality of low levels of education is addressed, their opportunities to earn substantially higher incomes remains limited.

Offering solutions to the problem of poverty is not our objective, though. Our objective in this chapter is more limited than proposing fundamental structural changes to enhance Hispanics' productivity, although it is imperative to point out that this is the core of the problem. Rather, our objective is to investigate what is possible to optimize individuals' and families' material welfare and long-term security given the current reality. For that reason, we include knowledge of governmental programs and other sources of material assistance as part of financial literacy since such knowledge is vital to survival for individuals with low incomes.

KNOWLEDGE OF BASIC FINANCIAL INSTITUTIONS AND TOOLS

It would be useful to briefly review the domains of financial literacy and capacity that are central to economic security for individuals at all income levels. Research shows that financial literacy can boost wealth accumulation by promoting retirement planning and savings (Van Rooij, Lusardi, & Alessie, 2012). Perhaps the most basic component of financial capacity is having knowledge of and access to banking and financial services, including checking and savings accounts, and credit and debit cards. Individuals without such knowledge and access can fall prey to potentially exploitative services that can undermine their credit and place them in serious debt. One sees such financial services advertised in most low-income areas and on radio and television. They include non-bank money orders, non-bank check-cashing services, non-bank remittances to Mexico, payday loans, rent-to-own services, pawn shops, and tax refund anticipation loans (Sherraden & Barr, 2005). Such services usually include extremely high fees or interest rates. In 2011 about 17 million adults lived in "unbanked households," meaning that they did not have access to basic banking services (Burhouse & Osaki, 2012).

At every level of income financial literacy refers to acquiring the financial knowledge and skills to make the most of what one has in terms of income and resources (Mitchell & Lusardi, 2008; Sherraden & McBride, 2010). Of course, what one needs to know related to finances depends greatly on what one has. If one inherits millions of dollars one needs the expert advice of estate lawyers, accountants, and investment advisors. Individuals with low incomes and few assets clearly do not need the services of experts on inheritance tax law or complex investment instruments. If one has nearly nothing, one needs advice on how to save whatever one can in a safe manner and information on tax credits, such as the Earned Income Tax Credit (EITC), and ways to budget effectively.

In the case of low-income families financial literacy and capacity mean something more. They refer to practical knowledge of means-tested municipal, county, state, and federal social support programs that are vital to survival. In the absence of an adequate income economic survival requires a street-level knowledge and simple rules of thumb that allow one to obtain goods and services that one may not be able to afford (Angel, Lein, & Henrici, 2006; Stack, 1974). If one cannot buy the services one's family needs one has to obtain them somewhere. Yet many individuals who qualify for various programs, from Medicaid and the Children's Health Insurance Program (CHIP) to EITC, do not take advantage of them, largely because of a lack of knowledge (Angel et al., 2006; Stoesz, 2013). The Internal Revenue Service estimates that up to 20% of the eligible working poor do not file for a refund (Finzel & Flores, 2013). In addition, the passage of the Affordable Care Act, or Obamacare, will require knowledge about how to apply for health insurance subsidies through the new health care exchanges or for Medicaid in those states that are expanding the program (Angel & Miles, 2014).

Unfortunately, we have relatively little empirical information on the extent or accuracy of knowledge of specific financial matters among Hispanics, and especially older Hispanics. The information available, though, indicates that many Hispanics do not take advantage of programs like the EITC. As a group, Hispanics are the least knowledgeable concerning this important program and consequently lose an important source of income (Robles, 2013). The National Survey of America's Families (NSAF), a survey of more than 40,000 families across the country carried out in 1997, 1999, and 2002 by the survey firm Westat, gathered information on the social and economic well-being of families; the data thus accumulated reveals large ethnic disparities in knowledge of EITC among low-income families. In the 2002 round of interviews only a small portion of low-income Hispanic working parents reported that they knew about the EITC program, a significantly lower proportion than among Black and non-Hispanic White respondents. Parents with the lowest levels of education were less aware of the program than parents with higher levels of education (Maag, 2005).

One important study sheds more light on the magnitude of the deficit of understanding of important financial matters among Hispanics (Robles, 2013). Members of the *Frontera* Family Asset Building Coalition (FABC) constitute a network of groups representing over 75 community-based organizations with ties to local, state, and federal government agencies in Texas, New Mexico, Arizona, and Texas, as well as corporate and non-profit sponsors. Various members of the coalition carried out surveys during the tax season from 2004 to 2008 at the participating border community-based organizations that offer either low-fee or free tax preparation services. About 32,694 adult respondents from low-income border families provided information about their financial behavior and knowledge. The study identified a constellation of serious shortcomings in respondents' financial knowledge that affected their capacity to optimize their financial situations. The key barrier to asset building was the lack of financial capability. Many respondents were unable to make informed decisions regarding financial affairs and had limited opportunities to engage in responsible financial activities. Factors such as seasonal employment, predatory lending practices, and the use of high-fee tax preparation services undermine financial capability for low-income families. (See Exhibit 9.4 later in the chapter for a comprehensive list of barriers.)

Regardless of race, ethnicity, or gender most individuals are less than financially sophisticated (Lusardi & Mitchell, 2013). Few of us have a clear understanding of compound interest; the differences between front-loaded, back-loaded, or no-load mutual funds; government, corporate, and municipal bonds of different types; equities; commodities; investing in precious metals; and more (Lusardi & Mitchell, 2013). For older minority adults, and especially minority women, many of whom have had little to save or invest, such sophisticated understanding is even rarer. Unfortunately, their children are also likely to be unsophisticated about finances and are often unable to provide good advice or to act as responsible guardians of their parents' assets.

Knowledge and the capacity to act on it are both necessary in order for one to prosper, or even to survive (Sherraden and McBride, 2010). A financial advisor would counsel that financial responsibility involves having a budget and following it carefully so that one knows where every penny goes, that one have a 6-month emergency fund, that one save for large expenses such as buying a house or sending children to college, and that one save for retirement (Butrica, Zedlewski, & Issa, 2010). But, in the absence of financial knowledge and capacity individuals and families are highly unlikely to meet their current financial obligations or to plan for the future. Even educated adults can be financially illiterate, meaning that they have no real sense of how much they need to save, how to invest, how much they need for retirement, how to avoid unnecessary debt, how much they can afford in housing, and more. Income and wealth are basic to our ability to control our lives and the responsible management of money is a basic component of being an effective agent for oneself and one's loved ones.

TWO WORLDS OF RETIREMENT SAVINGS

Almost everyone would like to be able to buy whatever one wants when one wants it, but what is far more important is that one has enough money to live a healthy and dignified life. From that perspective the difference between not having enough money and having enough is huge, while the difference between having enough and having more than enough is less important.

We are concerned with what can be done to make sure one has enough income, and preferably a bit more, at all points in the life cycle, and especially in old age when one's ability to earn diminishes, in order to live a dignified life and potentially to leave something to future generations. As we discussed earlier, the combined influence of financial literacy and the opportunity to take advantage of financial opportunities are both necessary. For younger families a core objective of financial behavior should be income maximization and asset building; for older individuals whose earning capacity is limited the objective is income maintenance (Sherraden, 2013).

In discussions of retirement security it is common to refer to the various sources of income one can draw on in retirement as pillars, such as those depicted in Exhibit 9.1. The pillars support the roof, which in this case represents financial security in old age. Obviously with only one pillar the roof is unstable, and one's financial security precarious, but with more pillars its strength and stability increases. Social Security is the first pillar and it is clearly important, although it was never meant to serve as the sole source of one's income. It simply does not provide enough for a truly

Exhibit 9.1 Five Pillars of Financial Security

Social Security	Employment Plans	Investments Savings	Inheritance	Wages

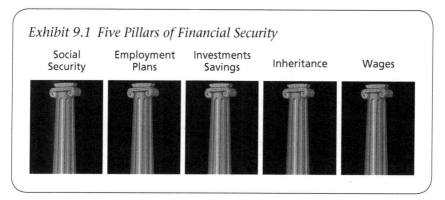

secure and comfortable retirement. Yet for 23% of married couples and 46% of unmarried persons Social Security accounts for 90% or more of their income (Social Security Administration, 2013a).

In order to enjoy a more secure retirement one must have a private retirement plan. Someone with several hundred thousand dollars in a 401(k) plan or a generous defined-benefit pension has a second pillar to support the roof of financial security. Yet in 2011 only two-thirds of workers in private industry had access to any sort of retirement plan (Wiatrowski, 2011). The savings and income from investments form a third pillar. With these three pillars one's chance of a comfortable retirement and one's ability to leave something to heirs increases.

Some very lucky individuals have a fourth pillar in the form of an inheritance. They are not really the subjects of our analysis, though, so we focus only on what one can acquire on one's own.

The final pillar consists of wages, since some individuals choose to or have no choice but to keep working. This group consists of individuals with rewarding occupations, such as Supreme Court justices and professors, who have no incentive to retire. Given the fact that most people have so little saved for retirement and given the shift from defined-benefit to 401(k) plans, many simply have no choice but to work well past the traditional retirement age even if they would rather not. Exhibit 9.2 outlines the differences between traditional defined-benefit pension plans that provided a guaranteed income for life and the newer defined-contribution plans that do not. Employers are increasingly dropping their defined-benefit pension plans for defined-contribution plans. This shift has profound implications for the financial security of seniors. In most cases, workers with

Exhibit 9.2 Defined-Benefit versus Defined-Contribution Retirement Plans

A **defined-benefit plan** promises a specified monthly benefit at retirement. The plan may state this promised benefit as an exact dollar amount, such as $100 per month at retirement. Or, more commonly, it may calculate a benefit through a plan formula that considers such factors as salary and service – for example, 1% of average salary for the last 5 years of employment for every year of service with an employer. The benefits in most traditional defined-benefit plans are protected, within certain limitations, by federal insurance provided through the Pension Benefit Guaranty Corporation (PBGC).

A **defined-contribution plan**, on the other hand, does not promise a specific amount of benefits at retirement. In these plans, the employee or the employer (or both) contribute to the employee's individual account under the plan, sometimes at a set rate, such as 5% of earnings annually. These contributions generally are invested on the employee's behalf. The employee will ultimately receive the balance in their account, which is based on contributions plus or minus investment gains or losses. The value of the account will fluctuate due to the changes in the value of the investments. Examples of defined contribution plans include 401(k) plans, 403(b) plans, employee stock-ownership plans, and profit-sharing plans.

A Simplified Employee Pension Plan (SEP) is a relatively uncomplicated retirement savings vehicle. A SEP allows employees to make contributions on a tax-favored basis to individual retirement accounts (IRAs) owned by the employees. SEPs are subject to minimal reporting and disclosure requirements. Under a SEP, an employee must set up an IRA to accept the employer's contributions. Employers may no longer set up Salary Reduction SEPs. However, employers are permitted to establish SIMPLE IRA plans with salary reduction contributions. If an employer had a salary reduction SEP, the employer may continue to allow salary reduction contributions to the plan.

A Profit Sharing Plan or Stock Bonus Plan is a defined contribution plan under which the plan may provide, or the employer may determine, annually, how much will be contributed to the plan (out of profits or otherwise). The plan contains a formula for allocating to each participant a portion of each annual contribution. A profit sharing plan or stock bonus plan include a 401(k) plan.

A 401(k) Plan is a defined-contribution plan that is a cash or deferred arrangement. Employees can elect to defer receiving a portion of their salary that is instead contributed on their behalf, before taxes, to the 401(k) plan. Sometimes the employer may match these contributions. There are special rules governing the operation of a 401(k) plan. For example, there is a dollar limit on the amount an employee may elect to defer each year. An employer must advise employees of any limits that may apply. Employees who participate in 401(k) plans assume responsibility for their retirement income by contributing part of their salary and, in many instances, by directing their own investments.

Source: U.S. Department of Labor, www.dol.gov/dol/topic/retirement/
typesofplans.htm

401(k) plans, including those who are close to retirement, have far too little saved to guarantee that their money will last through their retirement years (Fidelity Investments, 2013; VanDerhei, Holden, Alonso, & Bass, 2011).

Let us take a hypothetical example of a worker who has $150,000 in a 401(k) plan at the point of her retirement. If she were to annuitize the entire amount for 20 years and assume an optimistic 5% annual return she would receive $1,003.06 per month. After that the money would be gone and the income stream would stop. In 2012 the average 65-year-old female could expect to live 21 more years. Many will live much longer. The annuity income, which is clearly important, is not a major supplement to Social Security, which in 2013 amounted to $1,221.22 per month for the average retiree (Social Security Administration, 2013b). Unless this retiree has money from other sources, she will not have much for extras like vacations and helping children and grandchildren, and the likelihood of leaving much to her heirs is limited. Since the Fidelity amount presented in Exhibit 9.3 is an average and not a median it is upwardly biased by individuals with large 401(k)s. In reality, most individuals have far less in dedicated retirement savings.

For all of the reasons we have discussed in earlier chapters, minority group members are much less likely than non-Hispanic Whites to have all of the first three pillars, and those they do have are likely to be less adequate. Given the importance of employment-based retirement plans let us examine them a bit further. Almost by definition, a good job is one that offers not only a decent salary and health insurance, but a retirement plan as well (Crystal & Shea, 2002). Yet, Hispanics lag behind non-Hispanics in access to and participation in workplace retirement plans, based on data from the Survey of Consumer Finances (SCF). Only 38% of Hispanic workers aged 25–64 report coverage in employer-sponsored plans versus 62% for Whites and 54% for Blacks and Asians (Rhee, 2013). Racial disparities similarly persist in defined-benefit pension coverage, a program that guarantees lifetime income for retirees. Only half as many Hispanics are covered by defined benefits as non-Hispanics.

A private employer-based retirement plan represents one of the major sources of income for the middle-class elderly and, as the data in Figure 9.1 reveals, such plans can make the difference between a minimally adequate income and one that allows a person the freedom to enjoy his or her retirement. Figure 9.1 shows that race and ethnicity are

Exhibit 9.3 Getting Older, Growing Financially Insecure

Fidelity Investments, one of the nation's leading vendors of retirement plans, reports that in 2012 the average value of 401(k) plans of clients who were between 60 and 64 was $75,900 (Fidelity Investments, 2012). According to Fidelity Investments, the nation's largest 401(k) administrator, the average account balance increased by 12% up from $69,100 one year earlier (Fidelity Investments, 2013). Still this amount is inadequate for the typical middle-class retiree.

Perhaps because it includes a different group of savers, the Employment Benefit Research Institute (EBRI) Participant-Directed Retirement Plan Data Collection Project, the largest, most representative repository of information about individual 401(k) plan participant accounts, reports slightly different amounts.

> The 2010 EBRI/ICI database covered 46 percent of the universe of 401(k) plan participants, more than 10 percent of plans, and 47 percent of 401(k) plan assets. The EBRI/ICI project is unique because it includes data provided by a wide variety of plan record keepers and, therefore, portrays the activity of participants in 401(k) plans of varying sizes – from very large corporations to small businesses – with a variety of investment options.
>
> As of December 31, 2010, the EBRI/ICI database included statistical information about: 23.4 million 401(k) plan participants, in 64,455 employer-sponsored 401(k) plans, holding $1.414 trillion in assets.

In 2010, EBRI reported that the average value of 401(k) plans of all clients was $60,329 and the median balance was $17,686 (VanDerhei et al., 2011).

important determinants of having a retirement plan. The figure presents information on individuals aged 65 and older who have accounts and the approximate retirement plan payments by race, Hispanic ethnicity, and Mexican origin. This figure shows that while 72% of non-Hispanic White elderly households had retirement income accounts in 2010, only 39% of non-Hispanic Blacks and less than 37% of U.S.-born Mexican-American households had income from a retirement plan. Foreign-born elderly Mexican Americans were in the worst situation, with less than 15% receiving income from an employment-based retirement plan. This low rate of pension plan participation by Mexican-origin households means they are highly dependent on Social Security and that, if possible, they must continue working. As we have seen, though, serious disability is common among older Hispanics so continuing

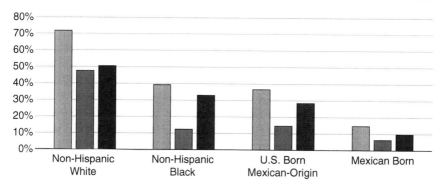

FIGURE 9.1 *Retirement Plans by Race, Hispanic Ethnicity, and Nativity: 2010.*
Source: Health and Retirement Study (2010).

to work may not be possible. The only other alternative is help from family and friends who are very likely not to have enough resources even for their own needs.

Figure 9.2 illustrates the crucial role that marriage plays in shaping retirement coverage for elderly minority group members. The figure shows the percentage of individuals aged 65 and older with coverage from any source, including a spouses plan. The data clearly show a substantial retirement advantage among married adults compared to unmarried adults. These data reveal an alarming disparity in retirement plan participation between unmarried and married female adults age 65 and older, as well as striking

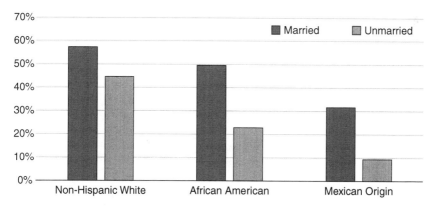

FIGURE 9.2 *Retirement Participation by Marital Status, Race, and Hispanic Ethnicity for Women Age 65 and Older: 2004–6.*
Source: Current Population Survey, 2004–6.

differences among women by race and Hispanic ethnicity. Among married women, 57.3% of non-Hispanic Whites in comparison to just 49.5% of African-American and 31.6% of Mexican-origin women participate in a retirement plan. Unmarried Mexican-origin women are the least likely to participate in a plan (9.4%) compared with 22.8% of African Americans and 44.6% of non-Hispanic Whites.

Figure 9.3 reveals major differences in retirement coverage among unmarried men by race and Hispanic ethnicity. Unmarried Mexican-origin males are less likely than unmarried African-American and non-Hispanic White males to report participation in a retirement plan. Similar racial and ethnic-based disparities in retirement plan participation occur among married men. Clearly, marriage matters in retirement to both men and women. Married couples can combine their incomes in later life, while single men and women must rely on themselves (Angel, Prickett, & Angel, forthcoming; Bricker, Kennickell, Moore, & Sabelhaus, 2012; Meschede, Sullivan, & Shapiro, 2011). Given women's less continuous labor force attachment, single women are particularly vulnerable to inadequate retirement income.

The large racial and Hispanic differences in sources of retirement income are partly due to difference in retirement behavior. Findings from a 2011 online retirement survey conducted by ING, a major corporation in the retirement plan industry, indicate that among employed individuals aged 25 to 69 with an annual household income of $40,000 or more, Hispanics felt the least prepared financially for

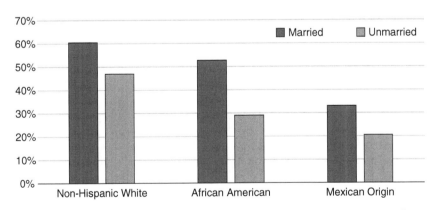

FIGURE 9.3 *Retirement Participation by Marital Status, Race, and Hispanic Ethnicity for Men Age 65 and Older: 2004–06.*
Source: Current Population Survey, 2004–6.

retirement of any group surveyed (ING, 2012). Slightly over half of Hispanic respondents reported that they were "not very" or "not at all" prepared financially for retirement. In addition, the researchers found that Hispanics tend to think less often about retirement than non-Hispanics. Fifty-seven percent of Hispanics have never calculated how much money they will need to maintain their current lifestyle, and 70% do not have a formal investment plan to save for retirement.

The lack of clear retirement goals affects savings behavior. In the 2010 SCF, among workers aged 24 to 65 four of every five Hispanics and three of every four African Americans report less than $10,000 in retirement savings compared to only one of every two non-Hispanic Whites (Rhee, 2013). In the ING survey, Hispanics reported the lowest average balances in their retirement plans, $54,000, considerably less than the average balance for all groups combined, $69,000. In contrast, Asian respondents reported the highest average plan balances, $81,000. Similar disparities in retirement savings are revealed in other data sets such as the SCF (Bricker et al., 2012).

Of course, the amount that one can save depends greatly on what one earns. In earlier chapters we documented low levels of education among Hispanics that means they are less likely than non-Hispanic Whites to hold high-paid professional positions. In the ING survey, approximately one-third of Hispanics reported that insufficient income prevented them from saving. More than one-quarter of Hispanic respondents also mentioned high levels of debt as a reason for inadequate savings. Other factors that contribute to low savings include a lack of knowledge about possible options in retirement savings, the inability to communicate with financial professionals, and the lack of Spanish-speaking financial advisors (Hannon, 2012).

Unique historical events, such as the major recession of 2008, can also seriously diminish savings. In addition, rapidly rising health care costs can undermine the ability to save at the same time that they consume what has been saved earlier. Inadequate savings can also be compounded by rapidly rising health care costs. The combined effects of economic shocks, rising health care costs, and other financial vulnerabilities put older Americans, and especially minority Americans, at risk of falling off a fiscal cliff. The SCF for 2010 reveals that while non-Hispanic White families have seen a 10% decline in their wealth since 2007, Hispanic families have seen their mean assets plunge by nearly 27% (Bricker et al., 2012). This is particularly devastating news since average Hispanic asset levels were far below those of non-Hispanic Whites to begin with.

As a consequence of low income, inadequate savings, and the lack of a retirement plan, elderly Hispanics, and especially women, rely on Social Security for the majority of their retirement income (Angel et al., forthcoming). Many unmarried or widowed retirees receive minimal Social Security or survivorship benefits (Social Security Administration, 2013a). The lower earnings capacity of many African-American and Hispanic husbands means that when a husband dies he leaves his wife little wealth and no long-term financial security. Divorced women often find themselves in a similar situation since they gain little from divorcing a husband with few assets. The situation only worsens over time since many widows and divorced women experience a considerable loss of assets and deterioration in their financial situation the longer they remain single (Angel, Jiménez, & Angel, 2007). In 2008, approximately 40% of African-American and Hispanic women aged 65 and older who lived alone were in poverty (U.S. Census Bureau, 2011).

POSTPONING RETIREMENT

If one does not have a defined-benefit pension, a well-funded 401(k), or substantial savings and assets, one faces the possibility of having to continue working after 65 (see Exhibit 9.2 for distinctions between defined-contribution and defined-benefit plans). Even if one needs the work, though, continuing in one's previous occupation or finding a new one may not be possible. Most men retire relatively early when they are eligible for reduced Social Security payments (Brown, 2013). If one retires 5 years before the normal retirement age one's annual payment is reduced by 30% (Social Security Administration, 2008). Individuals in white-collar occupations may find that they can continue working long past 65, but at some point hard manual labor becomes too demanding even if one needs the income, and finding a new job that pays well after age 60 is unlikely for an unskilled individual. We might ask, then, if working after age 65 is a realistic option and how common it is.

For individuals who are able to continue working, especially if they are in well-paying positions, later retirement is becoming more common. Older adults are now the fastest-growing segment of the American workforce. By 2020 workers aged 55 and over will make up one-fourth of the civilian labor force (Associated Press–NORC, 2013). In 1990 approximately 17.6% of men aged 65 and older worked. By 2010 that percentage had increased to 20.8% (Kromer & Howard, 2013). The proportion of men aged 65 to 74 who are still working is expected to rise to 30% over the next decade (Maestas & Zissimopoulos, 2010). Today, 12.5% of women aged 65 and older are working (Kromer & Howard, 2013). That number is expected to almost double to 22% in 2020 (Maestas & Zissimopoulos, 2010). Slightly over 10% of men and 8% of women will still be in the labor force past age 75 by 2030 (Maestas & Zissimopoulos, 2010). The basic question that concerns us, then, is whether employment after age 65 can substantially improve an individual's or household's long-term economic prospects.

Among older minority group men and women, the answer depends largely on health and income-related constraints (U.S. Administration on Aging, 2011). Findings from the 2004 and 2008 Health and Retirement Study reveal that Black and Hispanic men and women are far more likely than non-Hispanic Whites to delay retirement because of the lack of financial resources and the fact that they still had mortgage payments. Non-Hispanic Whites were more likely to report that they were continuing to work because of high job satisfaction (Choi, 2013). Even though they might wish to continue working, employment prospects for many Hispanics are bleak, especially for those with limited education. Research from the Center for Retirement at Boston College reveals that poorly educated older men and women have more limited job prospects than highly educated workers (Munnell & Jivan, 2005). Although many low-income workers may not be able to afford to stop working, they may be physically or mentally unable to continue.

The data on the early onset of dementia and functional incapacity that we documented in Chapter 8 suggest that many Hispanics could be forced out of the labor force for health reasons at relatively young ages. African-American and Hispanic blue-collar workers who rate their health as poor are far more likely than those in better health or white-collar employment to report a low probability that they will be able to continue working after 65. In the future it is possible that declining health rather than age will become the primary motivation for retirement.

The possibility of continuing to work is also affected by the business cycle and other economic shocks. Periods of high unemployment, such as that following the 2008 recession, can seriously derail the financial and work plans of even diligent workers (Van Horn, Corre, & Heidkamp, 2011). The recession left over two million workers aged 55 and older unemployed. Many of these workers joined the ranks of the long-term unemployed and many of those became discouraged and left the labor force (Van Horn et al., 2011). A prolonged absence from the workforce can have devastating economic and psychological effects and decrease the probability of ever finding employment. Even if they find work, many older workers must take jobs below their educational and experience levels at lower pay than they had been earning. They often accumulate serious credit card debt and can be forced to sell possessions to make ends meet. Many lose their homes and are forced to borrow from their retirement plans. For these individuals there is little opportunity to get back on their feet or to replenish depleted savings and retirement accounts.

REMOVING BARRIERS TO FINANCIAL CAPABILITY

In this section we discuss the efforts of government agencies and non-governmental organizations (NGOs) to provide financial assistance to low-income elders and to improve their financial literacy. Such assistance is vitally important since minority elders face several institutional barriers to the use of financial products (Sherraden, 2010). Unfortunately, although many sources of information and advice are available, not all are legitimate, honest, or accurate. Financial exploitation is a serious risk at all ages, but especially for older individuals who are often trusting and naive. Older individuals are often targeted by aggressive and unscrupulous vendors of dubious investments and products who take advantage of their limited financial knowledge (McCallion, Ferretti, & Park, 2013). The fiduciary dangers that older individuals face include the misappropriation of funds by others, being sold worthless investments, misrepresentation of a financial advisor's qualifications or experience, outright Ponzi schemes, and more. Many of the perpetrators of these incidents or schemes are difficult to identify and prosecute and the money lost almost impossible to recover. Some states define the financial exploitation of an older person as the intentional misuse of his or her resources, while other states define it to include negligent or reckless advice or conduct, such as failing to efficiently use an older person's resources for his or her care (Hafemeiste, 2003). Television shows such as *American Greed* illustrate the hardship that financial exploitation not only by unscrupulous strangers, but often also by church members, long-time associates, and even one's own children, can cause. An older person who loses a large portion of his or her life savings to financial fraud are rarely able to recover even a portion of the loss. The National Council on Aging goes so far as to label financial fraud aimed at seniors the crime of the 21st century (National Council on Aging, 2013).

Investing on one's own entails multiple risks and few individuals have the required knowledge, unless they are business majors or certified public accountants, and even then there are no guarantees. For ordinary investors the stock and bond markets can be treacherous. Investing one's 401(k) without competent advice places one at risk of losing all or a large part of one's savings. Most of us need financial advice and education, but honest and competent guidance can be hard to find. Anyone can offer a free seminar in which they present the latest no-risk, high-return investment or program. Financially naive elders are particularly vulnerable to such scams since they often have savings and wish to make a decent return. Unfortunately, promises of high returns can blind anyone, including older investors, into letting greed get the best of good judgment.

Besides the threat of financial abuse by institutions, older Americans are at risk of financial exploitation in domestic settings. Adult children, guardians, caregivers, and others who are in trusting relationships with an older person can violate that trust (Hafemeiste, 2003). The opportunity may be too easy and the temptation too great to keep some individuals from mismanaging or misappropriating an older person's funds. The problem of consumer fraud affects individuals of all ages and is serious enough that various governmental agencies are assigned the task of protecting consumers. The Board of Governors of the Federal Reserve System is responsible for implementing various federal laws intended to inform and protect consumers about credit and other financial fraud, and of ensuring that consumers receive comprehensive information and fair treatment in financial transactions. Given the fact that older individuals are particularly vulnerable, the Federal Consumer Financial Protection Bureau is responsible for helping older people, their caregivers, and others in the community to recognize and avoid frauds and scams (Hillebrand, 2013). In addition to consumer education and oversight, the Federal Reserve also promotes economic development and community lending in historically underserved areas (Board of Governors of the Federal Reserve System, 2013).

For most individuals financial advice is imperative in making investment decisions generally, and in preparing for retirement specifically. Financial advisors are easy to find, but it is often difficult to determine how qualified to offer advice they might be. Finding a certified financial planner is as important as finding a board-certified doctor. Organizations such as the National Association of Personal Financial Advisors, the Financial Planning Association, the Certified Financial Planner Board of Standards, and the

---

Exhibit 9.4 Barriers to Financial Capability

1. Securing identification documents
2. Securing social security and tax identification numbers
3. Reluctance to interact with official representatives for information on eligibility criteria for any governmental (official) services
4. Seasonal employment in the service sector paying cash wages (resulting in an intense cash-flow problem that creates opportunities for predatory lending)
5. Participation in the informal economy (engaging in economic activities outside the mainstream markets, for example, barter and cash transactions and self-employment non-reported income)
6. Spanish-language public, non-profit, and private sector outreach (especially documents related to tax and financial services) provide a direct translation of English documents without taking into account the lower educational attainment levels of many Southwest border residents, rendering much of the Spanish-version documents incomprehensible
7. Tax preparation services and the fees charged the EITC recipients pose a significant problem to the Latino working-poor community
8. Predatory lending along the Southwest border specifically targeting the Latino working poor by marketing payday loans and tax anticipation loans in Spanish and in English and
9. Commercial and seasonal tax preparation services and the fees charged for more complicated Self Employment and Schedule C tax forms for Latino microbusinesses and the self-employed who cannot use IRS Volunteer Individual Tax Assistance (VITA) tax-filing sites since volunteers are not trained in filing Schedule C and Schedule SE forms; being poor does not necessarily mean an automatic use of a 1040-EZ tax form.

Source: Robles (2013)

American Institute of Public Accountants can provide assistance in finding a certified financial advisor or retirement planner. Financial advice is imperative for individuals with large estates, but it may be even more important for individuals with modest estates who cannot afford to lose any of it. While a 35% loss for someone with a $2 million estate may be unfortunate, he or she still has $1,300,000. For someone with $200,000 in a retirement account the same percentage loss leaves him or her with $130,000, which can greatly undermine one's long-term prospects. Unfortunately, most people do not have even close to that amount.

IMPROVING FINANCIAL LITERACY ALONG THE BORDER

Earlier we discussed the *Frontera* Family Asset Building Coalition (FABC) study conducted in border communities to assess residents' financial literacy and capacity. The results clearly showed a lack of knowledge and ability to use financial instruments and institutions. In addition to assessing financial knowledge, a major objective of the FABC project was an intervention designed to improve financial literacy among Hispanics along the border. One aspect of that intervention was to encourage families to use free governmental tax preparation services. Because of the complexity in filing tax returns that include EITC claims, 62% of filers who qualify for EITC refunds use paid tax preparation services, compared to 53% of filers without an EITC claim (Stanfield, 2002). Other factors encourage the use of paid tax preparers. Many working-poor Latinos have self-employment income from seasonal and contractual work, which increases the complexity of their tax status if they file. Although the IRS provides free tax preparation services for low-income and elderly tax filers through the Volunteer Income Tax Assistance (VITA) and the Tax Counseling for the Elderly (TCE) programs, volunteers are not trained to complete complex forms (www.irs.gov/Individuals/Free-Tax-Return-Preparation-for-You-by-Volunteers). Unfortunately, the use of commercial tax preparation services that charge high fees takes precious resources from individuals who need them for other purposes. Latino workers who use such services are often pressured into rapid tax anticipation loans (RALs), high-interest loans based on one's expected federal income tax refund.

Based on the findings of this study, the researchers offer three recommendations. The first is that non-profit tax preparation services be provided at locations where other governmental and non-governmental community entities – such as affordable housing organizations, child care and health service organizations, and micro-lending organizations – are located. The second recommendation is that technical support be provided to local welfare-to-work programs so that they can assist with tax preparation and EITC claims. The third recommendation is the encouragement of bicultural economic activities in the Latino community that foster information sharing about financial products and services.

In addition to their recommendations for improving the financial knowledge of Latinos, the authors caution that while education is vital in reducing the probability that Latinos fall prey to predatory lenders in border communities, financial education alone is not enough to significantly improve families' economic situations. What is also required is that they have access to legitimate mainstream banking services so that they can avoid such fringe banking and financial services as payday loans, title loans, and the like. The authors note that mainstream banks and credit unions could serve the working poor in their communities by partnering with established community development financial institutions (CDFIs). CDFIs are financial institutions that economically empower underserved markets and populations by providing credit services and financial products, as well as community-based organizations (see www.cdfifund.gov/who_we_are/about_us.asp).

Clearly, outreach efforts by governmental agencies are important to inform families about the programs for which they might qualify. But other non-governmental actors are important as well, especially since governmental agencies are unlikely to provide all of the care and support or financial advice that a frail older person needs. NGOs have been addressing social problems for centuries, but since World War II their number has exploded (Angel, 2011). They operate in all countries and deal with all areas of need. These organizations, including faith-based organizations (FBOs), are part of what individuals refer to as "Civil Society," to emphasize the fact that it is not government, and often not-for-profit (Edwards, 2010). Given the nature of the needs of older individuals and their families, these organizations play a potentially important role in supplementing the efforts of governments and family. They are a potentially important third pillar in the support of older individuals in need.

Such organizations cannot, of course, replace government or even the family in addressing the needs of elderly individuals, but their potential flexibility and their proximity to the person in need makes them potentially important allies. Organizations such as Meals on Wheels rely on local volunteers to provide nutrition to older individuals who are at risk of malnutrition in the absence of the service. Other community-based organizations provide transportation, companionship, and counseling to older individuals who might otherwise become isolated. Some organizations, such as Family Eldercare of Austin, Texas, provide subsidized housing to a limited number of older individuals. Given the fact that the federal government does not provide adequate housing to poor families, local community-based organizations are increasingly important (Cisneros, 2012).

For the most part, though, the financial support of citizens remains a governmental and family matter. We have socialized the financial support of the elderly through Social Security. This is clearly a federal task, but dealing with the day-to-day needs of individuals living in the community calls for the voluntary contributions of neighbors and other citizens. Such involvement holds out the possibility of increasing participants' sense of community and mutual solidarity. Given the fact that the need for such daily care and support will only grow as the population ages, and since formal agencies will never be able to address all of that need, the potential contribution of NGOs and FBOs to the mix of services must be investigated.

Given their major role in social services, we end the chapter with a closer examination of the NGO world as it relates to eldercare and we address the question of what non-profit organizations do and what more they might do to help individuals and families in need. There are many programs that can assist clients in understanding assets and their options to help people connect daily budgets to long-term saving. But this first begins by creating public awareness of financial education programs that assist low-income individuals navigate the system.

NGOs are increasingly offering financial advice to low-income individuals and families, including older adults. The non-profit organization Earned Assets Resource Network (EARN), for example, attempts to increase the ability of individuals who have little financial sophistication and are often deeply in debt to become better money managers and get out of debt. This NGO educates clients on how to save money and build financial capability. EARN encourages saving by offering Individual Development Accounts (IDAs), which are savings accounts that include up to 300% matching contributions. The organization also offers financial coaching to low-income participants to manage their affairs more effectively in terms of how to invest in college education, micro-enterprises, and first homes and assets that will secure their futures, and the program teaches clients how to find goods and services at the lowest cost (Lapp, 2010). Research shows that financial self-efficacy, a label that refers to the subjective belief that one has the ability to handle one's own finances, increases savings and enhances one's actual effectiveness as a consumer.

EARN gives families the tools to build wealth and achieve life-changing goals such as saving for college, buying a first home, or starting a small business. Since 2001, the organization has assisted numerous low-wage families in the San Francisco Bay Area achieve these goals through innovative and essential financial products that, in addition to the matching savings accounts, include checking accounts for those who do not have one, and financial coaching. The organization has many success stories. One EARN client, Dametra Williams, shared her experience, in a video recording posted on the EARN website, of the lessons she learned on how to get out of debt and back on the road to financial stability, with the help of her Financial Coach, EARN's Saundra Davis, who was honored with the 2010 Heart of Financial Planning Award. Dametra reported that

> I knew that my expenses definitely outweighed my income. I was constantly asking my child care provider and landlord to hold on until next month. But, it created a vicious cycle of always having to worry, which put me in a stressful state all day. I did not know how to provide a quality existence for my daughter with the resources that I had. This was my challenge. I felt a great deal of shame. I found it difficult to find decent, safe and affordable housing and to make my child's life a good place. I was trying to figure out what to do. (www.youtube.com/watch?v=fAf-9F4sfrg)

Demetra slowly changed her attitude from focusing on why she could not make ends meet to starting a savings program and helping her daughter get the extra help she needed to prepare for college. She opened an Individual Development

Account (IDA) in which she received a two-dollar match for every one dollar that she saved for her daughter's higher education. Funded by the Assets for Independence Act (AFI), the federal anti-poverty program matches every dollar in savings deposited into an IDA from $1 to $8 (Administration for Children and Families, 2012). The IDA mechanism promotes savings and enables participants to acquire a lasting asset after saving for a few years. IDAs are simple and adaptable to different cultures and circumstances. Participation in this program enabled her both to receive a full college scholarship for her daughter and to plan on capitalizing on her own small business (EARN, 2013).

EARN, like other NGOs, seeks to promote financial empowerment through financial literacy education by protecting individuals from abusive financial practices and increasing knowledge of access to personal financial products that preserve household wealth and assets, such as micro-loans and money management advice (Perry & Morris, 2005). Individuals can acquire this information at technical assistance workshops, or in counseling and coaching sessions. With this information, clients increase control over their financial matters, which can transform their view of the future.

In Chapter 8 we discussed Family Eldercare of Austin, Texas, an NGO focused on the welfare of elders with which the authors have extensive experience. Family Eldercare's Money Management Program helps seniors and people with disabilities continue to live independently in their homes and in their neighborhoods by providing two types of money management services (Family Eldercare, n.d.). The Bill Payer Assistance Program is available to low-income elders and people with disabilities who need help with managing their financial affairs. Services include sorting mail, writing checks for the client to sign, balancing checkbooks, and making sure bills are paid in a timely manner. For individuals determined to be incapable of handling their own finances, the NGO provides certified representatives who are approved to directly manage their client's financial affairs. In addition to financial assistance, all clients receive additional case management services to ensure adequate food, shelter, and medical care. All bank accounts are insured through the American Association of Retired Persons (AARP) and are monitored by third-party volunteers who ensure accountability.

Some financial education programs are aimed at certain groups at risk for financial insecurity and they could serve as an important resource for young Hispanics. For example, there are financial literacy programs for survivors of intimate partner and domestic violence. These include: (1) the Hope and Power for Your Personal Finances program from the National Coalition Against Domestic Violence; (2) the Personal Economic Planning program used by the Iowa Coalition Against Domestic Violence (VonDeLinde & Correia, 2005); (3) Redevelopment Opportunities for Women's (ROW) Economic Action Program (REAP) in St. Louis, Missouri (Sanders, Weaver, & Schnabel, 2007); and (4) the Moving Ahead Through Financial Management program from the Allstate Foundation, implemented in partnership with the National Network to End Domestic Violence. These programs provide financial literacy content that focuses on helping IPV survivors reach individualized economic goals and on strengthening their financial management skills (Postmus, 2011).

For example, REAP offers training across the United States to help women develop skills in defining financial goals, preparing a monthly budget, accessing financial services and products, and financial confidence. The Oklahoma Native Assets Coalition develops local leadership to expand asset-building opportunities for Native American tribes and communities. A major goal is to promote FCAB initiatives by providing certification and training in financial skills for families. It partners with the First Nations Development Institute and its wholly owned subsidiary First Nations Oweesta Corporation (a community-development financial institution) to assist them in designing and administering financial and investor education programs (Oklahoma Native Assets Coalition, 2013).

SUMMARY AND CONCLUSIONS

In this chapter we dealt with financial literacy and financial capacity and examined differences among Hispanics and non-Hispanics in their knowledge of financial matters and their ability to manage their finances. We began with the observation that financial literacy is as important as the ability to read and write since the control of one's finances is vital to material well-being and ultimately to physical and mental health. Financial literacy refers to the possession of the knowledge of how to handle one's finances and optimize one's financial future. What one needs to know depends of course on how much one has. It is perhaps a truism to note that the basic cause of poverty is low income. However, the causes of chronic low income are complex. As we have documented in earlier chapters extremely low levels of education and employment in low-wage jobs limits economic mobility among Hispanics. These factors also limit the ability of Hispanic workers to save for retirement. Hispanics are at far higher risk than non-Hispanic Whites of not having a retirement plan of any sort and they have far less saved for retirement in 401(k) plans. A lack of assets limits the mobility chances of individuals and communities. Children in families with few assets receive far less in inheritances and assistance with education, home ownership, and business startups than children in more affluent families.

Given the fact that low-income families have less to save and spend than more affluent families, knowledge of how best to use their limited resources is crucial. For low-income families financial literacy also includes knowledge of and the ability to access means-tested social services, including medical, nutritional, housing, and cash assistance. We also noted that as important as knowledge of financial matters is, it is not enough to insure financial security. One must have access to and the ability to use financial instruments and institutions such as banks, credit unions, and legitimate financial services. Such services are not always available in minority communities and low-income individuals often fall prey to unscrupulous vendors of costly and risky financial services such as payday or title loans. Low-income individuals often have no choice but to use such services, even if they are aware of the high fees and interest rates involved.

The data available indicate that Hispanics, and especially low-income and poorly educated individuals and families, are unaware of ways in which to save and budget. They are also often unaware of opportunities for increasing their income, such as through the Earned Income Tax Credit (EITC), the federal program that reduces the tax liability of low-income workers. Workers with no tax liability can receive a credit if they file. Unfortunately, many working families who would qualify do not know that they are eligible or do not file for other reasons. The resulting loss in purchasing power can be substantial. Hispanics also fail to use other important and available services. Many Hispanic families whose children qualify for Medicaid are not enrolled. This failure to enroll in such an important program results from many barriers, including a complex bureaucracy and a lack of knowledge of how to apply for and maintain coverage.

Although all poor neighborhoods and communities share similar characteristics in terms of the presence of financial institutions, the U.S./Mexico border region represents a unique financial environment. It is an extremely poor region with limited services. We reviewed research that shows a serious lack of financial knowledge among residents. Because of seasonal work and other unique aspects of their financial situations, many do not file tax returns that would allow them to receive a tax refund or EITC credit. Given the complexity of the tax laws, others resort to paid tax preparers when free tax services are available.

We ended with a discussion of the role of NGOs in providing financial advice, services, and education. Many are funded from governmental sources to provide these services. It is clear that more needs to be done to improve the financial situations of Hispanic individuals, families, and communities. Clearly, a major step is to increase the productivity and earnings power of Hispanic workers. This requires far higher levels of education, including graduate and professional education, than is typical today. Such a change will take time and the reality of the situation of current workers and retirees calls for different approaches. These involve a combination of outreach by governmental agencies and the use of volunteers to assist families navigate the often treacherous financial environments in which they live.

DISCUSSION QUESTIONS

1. Find data on the Web related to average savings in 401(k) plans. The Fidelity webpage is one possibility but there are others. Also find sources that provide advice on how much one needs to maintain one's pre-retirement standard of living, or close to it. Are Americans saving enough? How do Hispanics compare to other groups? Discuss the consequences of inadequate retirement savings.

2. Go to the Social Security Administration's webpage and look up the average payment for Old-Age and Survivors Insurance, Survivor benefits, and Disability Insurance. Search the site to find out what each of these categories of recipient refers to. What are the major categories within these larger categories?

3. Search the Web for information on differences in assets (wealth) among racial and ethnic groups. Also find out how much the typical inheritance is. Discuss the implications for intergenerational transfers, either *inter vivos* transfers, which refers to gifts while the parent is still alive, or inheritances after the parent is dead, for the long-term economic prosperity of a group.

4. Discuss the meaning of "financial literacy" for different income groups. What do individuals with substantial assets and high incomes need to know? What do individuals with few assets and low incomes need to know? Is it possible for everyone to save at least a portion of their income? Discuss how that might be possible.

5. Find information on the Web related to the Earned Income Tax Credit (EITC). Describe how the program works. Conservatives favor this form of income support for low-income individuals and families over direct transfers, such as welfare. Identify potential reasons for this preference. Does the EITC conform more to American work values than such programs as Temporary Assistance to Needy Families (TANF)? Identify some shortcomings of this employment-based approach to income support.

LITERATURE CITED

Administration for Children and Families. (2012). *About Assets for Independence*. Washington, DC: U.S. Department of Health and Human Services, Office of Community Services: Asset Building.

Angel, J. L., Jiménez, M., & Angel, R. J. (2007). The economic consequences of widowhood for older minority women. *The Gerontologist, 47*(3), 222–34.

Angel, J. L., & Miles, T. P. (2014). Lessons learned from teaching the Affordable Care Act. *Journal of Public Affairs Education*.

Angel, J. L., Prickett, K., & Angel, R. J. (forthcoming). Sources of retirement security for Black, non-Hispanic White, and Mexican-origin women: The changing roles of marriage and work. *Journal of Women, Politics and Policy*.

Angel, R. J. (2011). Civil society and eldercare in post-traditional society. In R. A. Settersten & J. L. Angel (Eds.), *Handbook of sociology of aging* (pp. 549–81). New York, NY: Springer Science.

Angel, R. J., & Angel, J. L. (2009). *Hispanic families at risk: The new economy, work, and the welfare state*. New York, NY: Springer Sciences.

Angel, R. J., Lein, L., & Henrici, J. (2006). *Poor families in America's health care crisis*. New York: Cambridge University Press.

Associated Press–NORC. (2013). Working longer: Older Americans' attitudes toward work and retirement. In *Research Highlights*. Chicago, IL: Center for Public Affairs Research, University of Chicago.

Board of Governors of the Federal Reserve System. (2013). Consumer and community affairs. In B. J. Robles (Ed.), *The Economists*. Washington, DC: Board of Governors of the Federal Reserve System.

Braveman, P. A., Cubbin, C., Egerter, S., Williams, D. R., & Pamuk, E. (2010). Socioeconomic disparities in health in the United States: What the patterns tell us. *American Journal of Public Health, 100*(S1): S186–S96.

Bricker, J., Kennickell, A. B., Moore, K. B., & Sabelhaus, J. (2012). Changes in changes in U.S. family finances from 2007 to 2010: Evidence from the survey of consumer finances. In *Federal reserve bulletin*. Washington, DC: Board of Governors of the Federal Reserve System, Division of Research and Statistics.

Brown, A. (2013). In U.S., average retirement age up to 61: Younger nonretirees most likely to expect to retire at a younger age. In *Gallup Economy*. New York, NY: Gallup Inc.

Burhouse, S., & Osaki, Y. (2012). 2011 *FDIC national survey of unbanked and underbanked households*. Washington, DC: FDIC.

Butrica, B. A., Zedlewski, S. R., & Issa, P. (2010). Understanding early withdrawals from retirement accounts. In *Retirement Policy Program*. Washington, DC: The Urban Institute.

Case, A., Fertig, A., & Paxson, C. (2005). The lasting impact of childhood health and circumstance. *Journal of Health Economics, 24*(2), 365–89.

Choi, E. (2013). *Racial/ethnic inequality among older workers: Focusing on Whites, Blacks, and Latinos within the cumulative advantage/disadvantage framework*. Doctoral dissertation, University of Pittsburgh.

Cisneros, H. (Ed.). (2012). *Independent for life: Homes and neighborhoods for an aging America*. Austin, TX: The University of Texas Press.

Conroy, K., Sandel, M., & Zuckerman, B. (2010). Poverty grown up: How childhood socioeconomic status impacts adult health. *Journal of Developmental & Behavioral Pediatrics, 31*(2), 154–60.

Crystal, S., & Shea, D. G. (2002). Cumulative advantage, public policy, and inequality in later life. *Annual Review of Gerontology and Geriatrics, 22*, 1–13.

EARN. (2013). *What we do*. Retrieved August 6, 2013, from www.earn.org.

Edwards, M. (2010). *Civil society*. Malden, MA: Polity Press.

Family Eldercare, Inc. (n.d.). *Money management*. Austin, TX: Family Eldercare, Inc.

Fidelity Investments. (2013). *Fidelity average 401(k) balance climbs to record high at the end of 2012*. Smithfield, Rhode Island: Fidelity Investments Institutional Services Company, Inc.

Finzel, R., & Flores, Q. T. (2013). *Tax credits for working families: Earned Income Tax Credit (EITC)*. Washington, DC: National Conference of State Legislatures.

Hafemeiste, T. L. (2003). Financial abuse of the elderly in domestic settings. In R. J. Bonnie & R. B. Wallace (Eds.), *Elder mistreatment: Abuse, neglect, and exploitation in an aging America*. Washington, DC: National Academies Press.

Hannon, K. (2012, February 14). Why Latinos aren't saving for retirement. *Forbes Magazine*.

Hayward, M. D., & Gorman, B. K. (2004). The long arm of childhood: The influence of early-life social conditions on men's mortality. *Demography, 41*(1), 87–107.

Hillebrand, G. (2013). Financial capability across the life course: The role of the consumer. In *Financial capability across the life course: Focus on vulnerable populations*. St. Louis, MO: Washington University in St. Louis, George Warren Brown School of Social Work.

ING. (2012). *ING study: Cultural influences impact retirement planning and decision making*. Windsor, CT: ING.

Kromer, B., & Howard, D. (2013). Labor force participation and work status of people 65 years and older. In *American Community Survey Briefs*. Washington, DC: U.S. Census Bureau.

Lapp, W. M. (2010). *Financial self-efficacy's critical role in financial capability* (EARN White Paper). San Francisco, CA: Earn.

Lusardi, A., & Mitchell, O. S. (2013). *The economic importance of financial literacy: Theory and evidence*. Discussion Paper, Aging and Retirement Networks for Studies on Pensions. Tilburg, the Netherlands: Tilburg University Campus.

Maag, E. (2005). Disparities in knowledge of the EITC. In Tax Policy Center (Ed.), *Tax notes* (p. 1323). Washington, DC: Urban Institute.

Maestas, N., & Zissimopoulos, J. (2010). How longer work lives ease the crunch of population aging. *Journal of Economic Perspectives, 24*(1), 139–60.

McCallion, P., Ferretti, L. A., & Park, J. (2013). Financial issues and an aging population. In J. Birkenmaier, M. Sherraden, & J. Curley (Eds.), *Financial capability and asset development* (pp. 129–55). New York, NY: Oxford University Press.

Meschede, T., Sullivan, L., & Shapiro, T. (2011). The crisis of economic insecurity for African-American and Latino seniors. In *Living longer on less*. Waltham, MA: Brandeis University, Institute of Assets and Social Policy.

Mitchell, O. S. & Lusardi, A. (2008). *Financial literacy: Implications for retirement security and the financial marketplace*. New York: Oxford University Press.

Munnell, A. H., & Jivan, N. (2005). *What makes older women work?* Chestnut Hill, MA: Center for Retirement Research, Boston College.

National Council on Aging. (2013). *Top 10 scams targeting seniors*. Washington, DC.

Oklahoma Native Assets Coalition. (2013). *Our work: ONAC strategies*. St. Louis, MO: Oklahoma Native Assets Coalition.

Perry, V. G., & Morris, M. D. (2005). Who is in control? The role of self-perception, knowledge, and income in explaining consumer financial behavior. *Journal of Consumer Affairs, 39*(2), 299–313.

Postmus, J. L. (2011). *Understanding financial literacy with survivors of intimate partner violence*. Madison, WI: Center for Financial Security, University of Wisconsin.

Rhee, N. (2013). *Race and retirement security in the United States*. Washington, DC: National Institute on Retirement Security.

Robles, B. J. (2013). Financial and asset-building capabilities of Southwest Border working families: An action research approach to culturally responsive economic resiliency behaviors. In J. Birkenmaier, J. Curley, & M. Sherraden (Eds.), *Financial capability and asset development: Research, education, policy, and practice*. New York, NY: Oxford University Press.

Sanders, C. K., Weaver, T., & Schnabel, M. (2007). Economic education for battered women: An evaluation of outcomes. *AFFILIA: Journal of Women and Social Work, 22*(3), 240–54.

Sherraden, M. (2013). Building blocks of financial capability. In J. Birkenmaier, M. Sherraden, & J. Curley (Eds.), *Financial capability and asset development: Research, education, policy, and practice* (pp. 3–43). New York, NY: Oxford University Press.

Sherraden, M. S. (2010). *Financial capability: What is it, and how can it be created?* St. Louis, MO: University of Missouri – St. Louis, Center for Social Development.

Sherraden, M., & Barr, M. (2005). Institutions and inclusion in saving policy. In N. P. Retsinas & E. S. Belsky (Eds.), *Building assets, building wealth: Creating wealth in low-income communities* (pp. 286–315). Washington, DC: The Brookings Institute.

Sherraden, M. S., & McBride, A. M. (2010). *Striving to save: Creating policies for financial security of low-income families.* Ann Arbor, MI: University of Michigan Press.

Social Security Administration. (2008). Early or late retirement. In *Social Security benefits.* Washington, DC: Social Security Administration.

Social Security Administration. (2013a). *Social Security basic facts.* Washington, DC: Social Security Administration.

Social Security Administration. (2013b). *Table 2. Social Security benefits, June 2013.* Washington, DC: Social Security Administration.

Stack, C. (1974). *All our kin.* New York, NY: Basic Books.

Stanfield, R. (2002). *Social policy and the tax system: Tax policy research program.* Washington, DC: The Urban Institute.

Stoesz, P. (2013). Paradigms of anti-poverty policy. In J. Birkenmaier, M. Sherraden, & J. Curley (Eds.), *Financial capability and asset development: Research, education, policy, and practice* (pp. 62–82). New York, NY: Oxford University Press.

U.S. Administration on Aging. (2011). A profile of older Americans: 2011. In *Aging statistics.* Washington, DC: U.S. Department of Health and Human Services.

U.S. Census Bureau. (2011). *Table 3. Poverty status of people, by age, race, and Hispanic origin: 1959 to 2010.* Washington, DC: U.S. Census Bureau.

VanDerhei, J., Holden, S., Alonso, L., & Bass, S. (2011). 401(k) asset plan allocation, account balances and loan activity: 2010. In *Issues brief* (p. 52). Washington, DC: Employee Benefit Research Institute.

Van Horn, C. E., Corre, N., & Heidkamp, M. (2011). Older workers, the great recession, and the impact of long-term unemployment. *Public Policy and Aging Report, 21*(1), 1–48.

Van Rooij, M. C. J., Lusardi, A., & Alessie, R. J. M. (2012). Financial literacy, retirement planning and household wealth. *The Economic Journal, 122*(560), 449–78.

VonDeLinde, K. C., & Correia, A. (2005). *Economic education programs for battered women: Lessons learned from two settings* (Publication number 18). Harrisburg, PA: The National Resource Center on Domestic Violence.

Wiatrowski, W. J. (2011). *Changing landscape of employment-based retirement benefits.* Washington, DC: United States Department of Labor, Bureau of Labor Statistics.

CHAPTER 10

The New Pact between the Generations
Who Will Care for Us?

NEW SOCIAL RISKS AND THE WELFARE STATE

The traditional welfare state introduced by Otto Von Bismarck in Germany in the 19th century and most other developed and developing nations after World War II was designed to collectivize risks of such economic setbacks as illness, unemployment, disability, and poverty in old age. All of these risks were beyond the individual worker's control. The traditional welfare state was also founded on a "male breadwinner" model of social protection and income security. As long as the male breadwinner of a household had a good unionized job with protections against the loss of income, the entire family would remain secure (Huber & Stephens, 2006).

Today, although the risk of poverty in old age, disability, unemployment, and illness remain, political scientists, sociologists, and others identify a new set of risks associated with post-industrial and post-traditional societies. These include the loss of unpaid domestic labor as women enter the labor force in large numbers, the rise in single motherhood with the accompanying risk of poverty, longer lifespans that increase the need for formal long-term care, obsolete skills that undermine one's ability to earn an adequate income, a lack of adequate retirement income, and more (Armingeon & Bonoli, 2006; Giddens, 1994, 1998; Pierson, 2007). These are new social risks in the sense that they are products of the changing social, economic, demographic, and political realities we have dealt with in previous chapters. They are no doubt also the result of changing expectations concerning what government should provide. Once welfare states are established, citizens come to view the receipt of basic social services, including Social Security, unemployment insurance, and health care, as a right. The most important point, though, is that the new social risks present the welfare state with a new set of challenges that are accompanied by a very different, and often contentious, political discourse.

The concept of "new social risks" applies to elderly Hispanics, as well as to other racial and ethnic minorities, in the sense that the United States like other developed nations faces a new set of challenges related to addressing the needs of a large and diverse aging population during a time of fiscal retrenchment and growing public opposition to increases in social spending. A rapidly aging population presents new challenges related to the growing racial and ethnic variation among different age strata. Given their higher fertility and continuing high rates of immigration, younger age ranges will become increasingly Hispanic, while older age ranges will remain predominantly non-Hispanic and White. We end this book with an examination of the debate concerning the future of the welfare state and summarize how the various social changes that we have documented in earlier chapters may influence social policy, the welfare state, and ultimately the well-being of older Hispanics and other minority groups.

THE NEW MEANING OF SOLIDARITY

Along with health care, old age security is a defining component of the welfare state. Older individuals who have labored all of their lives to raise families and produce the goods and services that societies want and need have, at least in recent times, earned the right to some leisure in their later years. As we described in Chapter 9, in traditional pension schemes currently employed workers pay for the support of current retirees through payroll taxes. The rapid abandonment of such pension arrangements in favor of fully funded individual plans in which a worker is responsible for his or her own retirement security represents a profound change in the basic philosophy of old-age income security and solidarity between the young and the old. It would be useful in this closing chapter to review the basic philosophies, objectives, and funding of different retirement income schemes and discuss their social and intergenerational implications. We then examine other aspects of the new welfare state in terms of the basic principles that apply to pensions. These principles relate not only to practical fiscal considerations, but also to the philosophical and moral bases of how individuals conceive of individual responsibility and the nature of our mutual interdependence.

Traditional public or pay-as-you-go pension arrangements typically promise workers a guaranteed income based on some portion of their working life, often their highest-paid years, after they have contributed for a predetermined period (Orenstein, 2008). These pensions are typically paid from a pension fund into which current workers, employers, and perhaps the state contribute. The pension fund is usually invested in government bonds. Such plans are also referred to as "defined-benefit" plans since a worker is entitled to a specific payment for life, often with a cost-of-living adjustment. The fact that current retirees are supported by current workers creates an immediate bond of solidarity between generations since each worker contributes to the support of retired workers with the expectation that they will be supported in turn (United Nations Economic Conference for Europe, 2008; United Nations, 2002; Zaidi, Gasior, & Manchin, 2012). Although it may be possible to foster solidarity without collectivizing or socializing the risk of poverty in old age, the principle of solidarity is a major basis on which traditional publicly funded pension systems are based.

The problem that pay-as-you-go or defined-benefit systems face is solvency in the face of rapid population aging. Such plans can remain solvent as long as the population is young, with a large number of workers contributing to the support of relatively few retired individuals. They face serious fiscal problems, though, as the number of retirees relative to the number of workers increases. Given the rapid aging of the populations of developed and even developing nations, many observers feel that generous defined-benefit public systems are simply unsustainable in the long run (Piñera, 1995/6). These observers also fear that such systems ultimately undermine solidarity rather than promote it as younger generations find themselves seriously burdened by the need to support a growing elderly population. In light of the data we presented in earlier chapters, it seems clear that this danger may be even greater if that younger working-age population consists disproportionately of minority group members with low educational levels and the retired population consists of a demanding non-Hispanic White older population.

The obvious solution to the fiscal crisis faced by traditional public pension systems is to de-collectivize the risk of poverty and shift it to individuals. Such a transition is consistent with current neoliberal market-focused solutions for addressing social problems. Defined contribution retirement plans are tax-deferred individual savings or investment accounts in which employees, perhaps with an employer contribution, save toward their retirement. Such an arrangement ties a worker's retirement security directly to his or her saving and investment behavior during the working years. If one saves diligently, invests wisely, and is lucky one will enjoy a financially secure retirement. If one fails to save enough, or if the investment in which one's contributions are invested experience a low return or even a loss, one's financial situation in old age can be dire. In addition, such plans place the individual at the mercy of the market in terms of the timing of retirement. If one retires when the market is down one may be forced to annuitize at a depressed rate, whereas someone with the same nest egg who retires when the market is more favorable will find him- or herself in far better shape.

In 1981 Chile switched its retirement system from a defined-benefit to a fully funded individual defined-contribution plan in which new workers in the formal sector were required to assume responsibility for their own retirement savings. In subsequent years other nations in Latin America adopted such plans with the encouragement of the World Bank and other financial institutions (Mesa-Lago, 2008; Orenstein, 2008, 2011). Of course, in most Latin American nations rates of labor force informality are huge so private pensions are irrelevant to large segments of the population who have no retirement or savings plan of any sort. For this reason such systems often have a non-contributory public pillar for individuals with no other source of retirement income. The payments from such non-contributory pensions tend to be low. In Latin America and elsewhere these new pension systems have undergone subsequent reforms to correct initial problems, but few countries seem likely to return to the old defined-benefit arrangements. In Latin America the one exception is Argentina, which in 2008 completely abandoned its defined-contribution plan and moved all workers back to a public defined-benefit system (Ferro & Castagnolo, 2010). Although there was some discussion of partially privatizing Social Security in the United States during the second Bush Administration, those proposals were never adopted.

The important point for our discussion is that the shift from defined-benefit to defined-contribution plans intentionally shifts the burden for the support of retirees from the population of workers or taxpayers to the individual him- or herself. The justification is financial and actuarial and focused on long-term fiscal sustainability, but it has other implications and potential consequences, especially for individuals who are financially illiterate and who have little to save. Hispanics and other minority group members are disproportionately represented in this group. What is most salient to our discussion is that the new pension arrangements weaken or completely sever the tie between generations on which the solidarity principle of traditional pension systems is based. Largely because of these problems, the shift from public to private pension plans has been opposed by defenders of traditional systems, including groups such as the International Labour Organization (ILO) and the International Social Security Association (ISSA). These organizations, though, have not been as effective as the proponents and have not succeeded in slowing the trend toward privatization (Orenstein, 2008, 2011).

NO RIGHTS WITHOUT RESPONSIBILITIES

The example of pension reform illustrates a fairly dramatic change or evolution in the ways in which modern welfare states deal with social risks. We are a long way from World War II and the beginning of the modern welfare state. Today's welfare states are mature and expensive, especially in Europe in which social protections are more universal and extensive than they are in the United States. Some critics have always opposed the extensive social protections in principle and have preferred a focus on individual responsibility and the market (Hayek, 1944, 1959; Mead, 1986, 1997; Murray, 1994, 2006). Criticism has not just come from the right. Certain critics on the political left believe that capitalist welfare states suffer from basic contradictions that make them inherently unsustainable (O'Connor, 1973; Offe, 1982). Since at least 1973 when the Organization of Arab Petroleum Exporting Countries (OAPEC) imposed its oil embargo, concerns over the rising cost of social protections have increased. Subsequent energy price hikes and serious economic recessions, culminating in the 2007–8 worldwide slowdown, have only fueled those fears and led to the adoption of at least modest, but in certain countries rather severe, austerity programs.

Since the Reagan Administration in the United States, social policy has been guided by a desire to devolve government functions to local agencies and even non-governmental organizations (NGOs). Conservatives, communitarians, and anti-welfare-state free market purists strongly believe that local control and NGOs are superior to big government in providing social services (Etzioni, 1993, 1995, 2000; Hayek, 1944, 1976; Mead, 1986, 1997; Murray, 1994, 1996, 1999, 2006). Welfare reform in the United States and the New Third Way in Britain and elsewhere rejected the philosophy of social protection as a citizenship right and replaced it with a philosophy of "no rights without responsibilities" that made the receipt of social benefits conditional on accepting employment (Giddens, 1994, 1998).

A focus on employment is appealing to most everyone since work and a tie to the labor market provide important benefits in addition to money. Employment provides one with a social identity and it fosters routines and responsible parenting. Such benefits, however, require that one have decent work that pays a living wage, has reasonable and predictable hours, and is reasonably secure. Chapter 3 highlights how employment in the low-wage service sector makes it almost impossible for individuals to save and to prepare for any of life's major transitions, including retirement.

CHANGING RISK PROFILE OF INDIVIDUALS AND FAMILIES

It is clear that the new social reality and the risks it entails are complex and preclude simplistic explanations of the situation of Latinos and other minority groups. Although one might long for the certainty of traditional institutions and practices, today we live in what has been characterized as a "post-traditional" society or perhaps societies (Giddens, 1991, 1994). In traditional societies institutions and norms were strong and well-defined and they almost completely constrained the life choices one made. One married, had children, and worked at the same occupation probably for one's entire working life. Today such defined and constraining institutions no longer exist, or at least they do not constrain one's life choices to the same degree. Traditions clearly remain. Most individuals eventually marry, but they do not necessarily remain married to the same individual for life. Same-sex couples are changing the meaning of marriage. Today following traditions is more of a choice than an imperative. One can create one's own traditions and accept only those old traditions that one finds useful or satisfying; individuals increasingly reinterpret and modify traditions in light of changing circumstances and social realities. Daughters and daughters-in-law are not constrained by strong community expectations to stay at home to care for their aging parents or in-laws.

The arrival of post-traditional society changes the risk profile for individuals, families, and communities. A major change that we have documented that is affecting even supposedly familistic Hispanics is the decline of the male breadwinner model of family economic security and the growing need for women, and even the mothers of young children, to join the labor force. For women today work is often full-time and necessary in order to support a family. Yet women continue to bear the majority of responsibility for the care of children and the elderly even in post-traditional societies. Daughters and daughters-in-law have historically been the primary long-term care option for dependent parents and they continue to fill that role today, although the strains are growing. As we discussed in earlier chapters, with fewer children living nearby the remaining daughters are less able to provide all of the care that aging parents might need. The costs associated with caring for parents can strain family budgets, and women pay another price in terms of interrupted paid employment. When they work women tend to earn less than men, which means that they contribute less to retirement plans, even when they have them. In the language of pensions, they have lower contribution densities, meaning that they contribute to pension funds for fewer years on average than men, largely because of their child and eldercare responsibilities. As a consequence they are less likely than men to contribute for the number of years required for a basic pension. Yet they live longer and for many Latina women marriage has never guaranteed economic security in old age since Latino men do not earn enough to secure a couple's economic welfare (Angel, Prickett, & Angel, forthcoming).

LOW EDUCATIONAL LEVELS

Although we have identified the major social risks faced by Hispanics, and discussed their potential negative consequences for the Hispanic community itself and for the nation as a whole, it would be useful to summarize the major risk factors here, and end by calling for a new social investment state. We also investigate the potential for civil society organizations to complement government in defining new social arrangements that could provide a wider range of options in addressing the serious social needs of aging populations.

As we documented extensively in previous chapters, one of the most serious social risks for Latinos results from very low levels of education (Angel & Angel, 2009). Hispanics are at elevated risk of not completing high school, which blocks any chance of higher education for a large segment of the population. Without higher education the routes to graduate and professional education are blocked. Hispanics who obtain higher levels of education and become professionals do as well as similarly educated individuals from other groups, but a far smaller fraction of the Hispanic population obtains those vitally important higher levels of education than non-Hispanic Whites (Angel & Angel, 2009). The lack of education clearly represents an individual risk factor for limited occupational and economic opportunities, but it also handicaps entire communities and the Hispanic population at large.

Political and economic power derive from social capital, which we might define as interaction with individuals and groups who themselves enjoy social, political, and economic power. One frequently hears the adage that "it is not so much what you know, but who you know" that allows one to get ahead. Access to social capital depends on connections with influential people. Communities as a whole can be characterized in terms of their collective social capital (Angel, Bell, Beausoleil, & Lein, 2012). Low levels of average education represent a serious handicap for a group as a whole.

As we have noted throughout, though, low levels of education among Latinos are not only risk factors for those groups alone. Given the fact that the proportion of the labor force that is Hispanic is growing rapidly, the productivity of the nation as a whole will be heavily influenced by the productivity of these groups. In the future a growing Hispanic labor force will be called upon to support a predominantly non-Hispanic White retired population, at the same time that they will have to fund education, health care, the repair of our nation's decaying infrastructure, defense, scientific exploration, and more. If the productivity of this labor force is undermined by low levels of education, everyone will suffer. Insuring the highest level of education for all young people, therefore, is not only a generative and selfless act, it is a highly self-interested act. Today political discussions often focus on illegal immigration and the drain that undocumented workers supposedly place on our economy. In the United States, as in Europe, the reality of the future is that economic necessity and aging populations make immigration inevitable and also that the productive potential of young Hispanics must become a national priority.

DIFFICULTIES IN SAVING FOR RETIREMENT

High on the list of the new social risks facing Latinos and others that we discussed in Chapter 9, then, is the possibility that they will not save enough for retirement. This risk, of course, is affected by other risks such as low education, which limits one's employment and earnings potential. Poorly educated workers often work for small firms that do not offer health insurance or retirement plans. The fact that many workers have no retirement plan at all and the rapid shift by employers from defined-benefit to defined-contribution plans means that many Americans of all races and ethnicities will find that they are far short of what they need for a comfortable and dignified retirement. Saving is a virtue that should be fostered, but for most families, current needs, combined with a lack of financial sophistication, means that they do not start saving seriously early enough. The failure to plan means that a retired individual will be heavily dependent on Social Security, which seriously limits one's options for personal consumption and the possibility of helping children. Even in retirement one has to pay taxes, maintain a home, pay for medical bills that Medicare will not cover or pay premiums for a supplemental Medigap plan, buy clothing, pay car insurance or pay for public transportation, and more.

The greater risk of insufficient savings and low rates of pension plan participation we have documented mean that Latinos will remain disproportionately dependent on means-tested public programs, particularly Supplemental Security Income (SSI), which provides a basic income floor to individuals over 65 with few assets. The average monthly SSI payment is $423.00 (www.ssa.gov/policy/docs/quickfacts/stat_snapshot), an amount that clearly leaves one with little buying power. Programs like SSI, like similar basic public pensions in other nations, point out a basic problem with pension systems based on payroll taxes, as in the case of Social Security. Pension plans that rely on payroll taxes exempt income from assets, interest, and other sources. In addition the Social Security tax (FICA) is regressive since it only applies to the first $113,700 in 2013. Such a plan places most of the tax burden on individuals who depend on wages and exempts much of the income of richer individuals with capital gains and other income. Another possibility for funding Social Security that would increase the range of income sources on which the tax to support it is based would be to fund it from general revenues (Myles, 2002). Clearly, although such a possibility should be discussed, given the fact that programs like Social Security are "path dependent," a term used by political scientists to characterize the inertia in any established public program, such a change would be difficult to legislate.

In addition, such a suggestion is incompatible with current moves toward fully funded personal retirement plans in which each individual worker is responsible for his or her own retirement savings. The clear intention of such a shift is to address long-term fiscal problems by severing the solidaristic principles of collectivizing the risk of poverty in old age and privatizing the risk. Although there are real fiscal considerations to be taken into account, the evidence we have presented in previous chapters clearly shows that privatizing risk penalizes those individuals and groups that are most vulnerable and least able to deal with the risk. For the foreseeable future, and probably forever, some form of means-tested program like SSI and Medicaid will be necessary. A system that relies on payroll taxes and personal savings clearly favors individuals with high incomes and penalizes those with low incomes.

We should point out that the problem of inadequate savings is not just a problem associated with private defined-contribution retirement plans. Companies, municipalities, and states that offered and still offer defined-benefit pension plans never saved enough collectively either. Although we have reframed the problem as one of inadequate personal savings and a lack of financial sophistication, the problem is clearly far more collective. At some point we will have to revisit the politically sensitive issues related to income distribution in a world in which slower rates of economic growth may be a permanent reality of national economies (Pierson, 2001).

EARLY INVOLUNTARY RETIREMENT AND LONG-TERM UNEMPLOYMENT

The problems with a retirement system based on individual savings plans are made manifest during periods of economic downturns like the 2007/2008 global depression that destroyed trillions of dollars in wealth and decimated the retirement savings of workers and retirees all over the world. Many individuals were forced to borrow from their retirement savings as they experienced protracted periods of unemployment (Bernard, 2013). The increase in the number of long-term unemployed (a category that includes individuals who have been looking for work for 27 weeks or more) and discouraged workers (who have simply given up looking for work since they believe that jobs are not available) suggests a new reality in which the employment and labor force participation rates of the post-World War II years may be gone for good.

In December 2012, of the 12.2 million workers who were unemployed 4.7 million, or 39%, had been searching for work for 27 weeks or longer (Mitchell, 2013). Blacks and Latinos are far more likely to find themselves among this group than non-Hispanic Whites. Blacks make up nearly 23% of the long-term unemployed, and Hispanics 19%. Among discouraged workers, the group of workers who believe they will never find work and have basically given up, Blacks make up over a quarter and Hispanics over 20% (Mitchell, 2013). Clearly, these individuals' ability to save for retirement is seriously curtailed. Most of whatever income they obtain must go to dealing with daily needs.

THE LIMITED POWER OF UNIONS

A major social risk that affects Latinos that we have not discussed before arises from the fact that the United States has no labor party or strong unions that might serve to organize Latinos in an attempt to guarantee their social rights through collective action. Of course, unions can be racist and exclusionary and oppose immigration and the regularization of the undocumented whom they could see as potentially undermining wages. Nonetheless, as venues for collective action unions could offer some hope for group solidarity and political action. Historically Latinos, including Mexican-origin Latinos, have joined unions at similar rates as other groups (Rosenfeld & Kleykamp, 2009). But the fact that union membership has shrunk and their political power is limited means that unionization is not a promising avenue for furthering Latino interests. This is especially true given that Latinos are employed in the service sector into which unions have entered, and as day laborers in construction in which structural factors and skill segregation undermine collective behavior (Camou, 2012). Although some service sector unions have successfully fought for benefits for their membership, including those who are undocumented (Medina, 2013), for the most part unions have not demonstrated the ability to significantly change the rules of the game related to wages, hours, and working conditions for Latinos, nor are they particularly effective in dealing with immigration or citizenship rights. As participants in complex social debates, the power of contemporary unions is severely limited.

THE UNCOUPLING OF MARRIAGE AND FERTILITY

Even though Hispanic fertility remains higher than that of non-Hispanics, they too face the social risk of low fertility. Smaller families mean that there are fewer children to help care for elderly parents or to assist in paying for long-term care. Traditionally women have assumed the responsibility for caring for the young and the old. The fact that they increasingly must enter the labor force full-time means that they are not available to care for incapacitated parents or parents-in-law who can no longer care for themselves. If the family can no longer assume the full responsibility for elderly parents who are living longer, other alternatives will have to be developed. As we propose in our closing section, these possibilities will have to include non-governmental and faith-based organizations to supplement formal programs and the informal care provided by family members.

Another social risk related to fertility is the decline in the traditional family that has affected all groups, including Hispanics. As we showed in Chapter 2 fertility rates for Latinas and Black women are approaching those of non-Hispanic White and Asian women. In the past two decades, the Mexican-origin Latina fertility rate dropped sharply, from 2.9 births per woman in 1990 to 1.8 births per woman in 2010, with similar declines for Puerto Rican (2.2 to 1.5) and Cuban women (1.9 to 0.9), as well as for Black women (2.3 to 1.5) (Martin et al., 2012). Although Hispanics have higher marital rates than Blacks, their marital rate is lower than that of non-Hispanic Whites. Hispanics' divorce rate remains lower than that of non-Hispanic Whites or Blacks, but is significant.

Hispanics, like other groups, are being affected by those demographic and social forces associated with post-traditional society that are changing the meaning of marriage and the family. High rates of out-of-wedlock fertility among Blacks reflect problems in the marriage market that result in changing expectations and mores. A lack of marriageable men, which means men who are able and willing to contribute to the support of the family, means that marriage is not the route to economic security. In earlier eras if a woman became pregnant out of wedlock, family and community forces often forced a marriage. Today that is not the case and fertility and marriage are becoming uncoupled. In the future the same forces that have led to the uncoupling of fertility and marriage for Blacks may alter the Hispanic family, with profound implications for the welfare of single-parent families.

IMMIGRATION

For Latinos the difficulties associated with immigration are a major social risk. The situation of undocumented immigrants remains entirely precarious. Undocumented immigrants do not qualify for basic services, other than emergency medical services. Their situation, though, reflects more than just the legal transgressions of individuals who come seeking the opportunities for a better life. Undocumented labor is vital to the economies of most developed economies (Castles, 2004). Despite the strident anti-immigrant discourse that one hears in many nations, undocumented immigration is a reality that presents receiving countries with difficult dilemmas regarding the incorporation or regularization of the situations of immigrants.

Residents of developing nations migrate since their labor is needed in developed nations and in most receiving nations legal restrictions and economic reality are at odds. Africans, Eastern Europeans, and others see Western Europe as a land of opportunity, just as Latin Americans and Asians view the United States. Sealing borders seems not to work, but even if it did such a policy would not address the problem of those undocumented who are already in the country. After decades of immigration the reality of the new arrivals becomes a major political and social reality that cannot be ignored. Nations like Germany might prefer to bring Turkish immigrants as temporary laborers when they are needed and send them home when they are not. As the Germans found out, though, once in the country guest workers do not readily return home. After a generation or two those Turks have become German even if they remain incompletely incorporated. The Bracero program in the United States marked the beginning or continuation of a process that brought millions of Mexican nationals into the country to provide the labor that the agricultural, construction, and service sectors of the economy need.

The fact that the ties between Mexico and the United States are close and based on mutual economic need must inform public policy. Immigration has been a fact of life for generations. Many undocumented immigrants have been in the country for decades; in some cases they have been here all their lives. The DREAM Act that we mentioned in Chapter 4 is intended to deal with the poignant dilemma facing individuals who were brought into the country when they were infants and who know little or nothing of Mexico, but who are not legal residents of the United States. Since they are not refugees they do not qualify for special privileges, but this is the only home they have ever known. The situation of young people who have pursued the American dream and been good citizens only to find that they do not have access to college, legal employment, or other benefits because they are not citizens is not a problem that can be solved by inflammatory rhetoric or expulsion. These and other immigrants demand recognition for the labor and benefits they provide. Given the growing size of the Hispanic population, their demands will be difficult to ignore.

As we noted in Chapter 4, immigration law has its more humane aspects, especially in terms of family reunification. Under current law family members of immigrants who are already legal residents can immigrate without being subject to quotas. However, as we also discussed in Chapter 4, bringing a family member to the United States requires that the sponsors, which are almost always family members, agree to assume complete financial responsibility for that individual at least for a period of 5 years. While this may be a reasonable responsibility to assume in the case of a child or young adult, for an aging parent who is at risk of serious illness the potential financial burden could be huge. As we noted, although we do not have exact numbers, it must be the case that the potential burden discourages some families from bringing their older parents from Mexico. The result is family separation even with the family reunification provisions of U.S. immigration law.

A SOCIAL INVESTMENT STATE

The social risks faced by Hispanics and others, then, go beyond the traditional welfare state protections against old-age poverty, unemployment, disability, and ill health. Although the old risks clearly remain, the new social risks are part of a globalized economy, easy and rapid transportation, and the drastically unequal distribution of wealth among nations. Nations and local communities are no longer shielded by oceans, mountain ranges, or distance. As a result of these new realities the nations of the world are changing racially, ethnically, and culturally at the same time that they are aging. In most European nations fertility rates are below replacement level.

As a consequence, these societies are forced to confront the necessity of immigration, even as they fear the threat to their traditional forms of life and culture. In the United Sates, Latinos are the key to population stability, and they are rapidly becoming an important part of the labor market in parts of the country in which they were unknown just a few decades ago. A major threat to economic prosperity and social stability lies in the possibility that these new arrivals will remain apart from the mainstream. If immigrants are denied adequate educational and labor force opportunities the receiving nations will experience declining productivity and potentially ethnically and racially based intergenerational conflict. Immigration is a reality for the economies of the developed world and its necessity overrides all rhetoric aimed at stopping it or ejecting migrants who have already arrived (Castles, 2004).

While the fear of immigrants and immigration creates misunderstandings and distance between peoples, the new demographic and economic reality create interdependence. Immigrant labor is a reality that must be dealt with since the quality of that labor will determine the nation's productivity for decades to come. Rather than rejection, this reality calls for a new social investment state that optimizes investments in people not only to benefit individuals, but to benefit society at large (Giddens, 1998). By social investment state we mean one in which a core objective is to provide high-quality education to everyone, insure their basic material well-being, and to insure their physical and mental health. Clearly, not everyone agrees with such an objective, but the alternatives are a status quo that is unsustainable in the long run.

Achieving the objective of creating a social investment state of course means starting before birth. Women should be in peak health when they become pregnant; they should receive early and comprehensive prenatal care; their newborns should be well fed and receive the necessary vaccinations; they should live in high-quality housing in safe neighborhoods; and they and their children should receive as much education as possible to prepare them to succeed in the labor market and act as effective agents on their own behalf, as well as that of their families and communities. These are clearly not benefits from which only Latinos would benefit; everyone would. Currently middle-class individuals with social advantages enjoy enriched childhoods in good neighborhoods and receive high-quality educations. Extending similar opportunities to those to whom they are currently denied represents a major challenge, especially in the current period of austerity. As we have documented, though, given the status quo the probability that an individual benefits from our current system of social investments is greatly influenced by race and ethnicity.

AN IMPORTANT ROLE FOR CIVIL SOCIETY

The focus on the social investment state, by its very name, emphasizes government and there can be little doubt that a strong, efficient, and benevolent government that functions well at all levels is vital to democratic political processes, social order and justice, and an efficient economy. Yet in recent years interest in the role of civil society as a complement to the state has grown as the number of international, national, and local NGOs has exploded (Albrow, Anheier, Glasius, Price, & Kaldor, 2008; Boli & Thomas, 1997, 1999; Salamon, 2003). Some observers view the rapid growth of such international civil society organizations as part of the emergence of a new supranational global culture that is changing the international political order (Edwards & Sen, 2000; Grzybowski, 2000). In light of the fact that governments and formal state organizations will simply be unable to provide or even pay for all of the care and services that an aging population demands, experiments with other options and sources of care are rapidly becoming necessary (United Nations Economic Conference for Europe, 2008).

Latin America serves as a good example of the problem and the potential role of civil society. As in the United States the populations of the nations of Latin America are aging at historically unprecedented rates (CEPAL, 2007; Cotlear, 2011). The doubling of the population in the older age ranges in the countries of Europe took over 100 years. Although this demographic process began much later in Latin America, as a result of improved nutrition, better medical care, and other factors that doubling is taking slightly more than 20 years (CEPAL, 2007; Cotlear, 2011). Given the fact that these governments must deal with the needs of the young and working-age populations, rapidly aging populations pose major fiscal, political, and practical challenges (MIDES, 2012; Papadópulos & Falkin, 2011; WHO & Milbank Memorial Fund, 2000; World Health Organization, 2003).

Given this new demographic, economic, and social reality new models for institutional and community-based eldercare must be explored (Angel, 2011; Xu & Chow, 2011; World Health Organization, 2000, 2002). While decreasing fertility rates may reduce educational and child care expenditures, a growing older population increases the need for chronic medical and long-term custodial care (Cotlear, 2011; Lloyd-Sherlock, 2000). The problem is made more serious for developing nations since they have fewer resources with which to address the problem, and developing new institutional arrangements takes time. Although all Latin American nations have pension plans for workers in their formal sectors, individuals in the informal sector, which makes up large segments of the population, do not participate. These individuals will receive no or little income in old age. Nor will health systems be able to provide all of the care and support that older individuals need, especially in terms of companionship and assistance with activities of daily living.

In Chile, a faith-based organization known as Hogar de Cristo (Christ's Home), that began to provide the full range of support to poor Chileans in 1945, has become a major provider of institutional and community-based care to the elderly (Pereira, Angel, & Angel, 2007). This organization, which we discuss further below, serves as an example of how non-governmental and faith-based organizations can complement governmental and family efforts to provide essential but often hard-to-deliver services. Let us briefly explore some of the experiments in non-governmental eldercare that are being developed in various countries.

LOCAL KNOWLEDGE AND GREATER FLEXIBILITY

Non-governmental options are appealing to observers from all points on the political spectrum. For conservatives the reliance on local non-governmental options is more efficient and frees one from the oversight of big government. For those on the left civil society fosters self-help and provides venues in which individuals and groups can learn to act collectively to further their own ends. As service providers NGOs often have certain advantages in dealing with the more routine daily needs of specific populations (Pereira & Angel, 2009; Pereira et al., 2007). Although complex and expensive high-tech medicine may be beyond the capacity of most NGOs to provide, they are in a particularly advantageous position to provide routine and relatively inexpensive services, such as basic health monitoring, assistance with activities of daily living, and companionship. These services do not require expensive equipment or advanced technical knowledge. Ideally, the role of such groups would be to complement formal state agencies in supporting older individuals in the community and enhancing the quality of their lives. They should not be expected to function as substitutes for state efforts. Their potential role arises from that fact that because of their local knowledge of the legal, transportation, nutritional, and other needs of the elderly they could potentially act as both service providers and advocates.

Although relatively little formal research has been carried out focused on the role of civil society organizations in eldercare, a large body of research documents the importance of social networks and social support in later life for maintaining optimal physical and mental functioning and avoiding isolation (Krause, 2006; Moren-Cross & Lin, 2006). Social engagement is as important for the elderly as for younger individuals, but the elderly are at elevated risk of isolation as they age. For individuals with few surviving family members, non-family members may be able to provide basic companionship. Studies of volunteerism, including a recent study in Mexico, reveal that in situations of high need neighbors and community members provide assistance to those in need, either through formal groups such as churches or voluntary organizations, or informally as personal assistance (Burcher, 2008). Churches and congregations have historically cared for the poor and infirm and as part of that mission they provide much-needed companionship and care to the elderly (Idler, 2006).

NGOS AS SERVICE PROVIDERS

From a communitarian perspective, by fostering pro-social behavior civil society organizations not only assist individuals in need, but ultimately strengthen communities (Etzioni, 1993, 1995). Providing services, therefore, can be part of larger community development projects depending on the extent to which they facilitate local capacity building. Faith-based international organizations such as *CARITAS*, *Catholic Charities*, and *Lutheran Social Services* provide assistance to the elderly as part of their general missions. The Red Cross and many of the other major international and local relief agencies identify the elderly as a vulnerable population. An examination of NGO directories and the mission statements of the webpages of international and local organizations yields hundreds of such organizations in every country with some focus on the elderly as a uniquely vulnerable population. Although it is impossible to mention more than a tiny fraction of such organizations that operate internationally and locally in almost all countries of the world, let us mention a few and describe their eldercare missions.

In Chapter 6 we pointed out that most Americans are familiar with the *Meals on Wheels Association of America*, the oldest non-governmental nutrition program for the elderly in the country (Meals on Wheels Association of America, 2013). The Meals on Wheels program was begun during World War II and founded on the mission of ending hunger among the elderly. Clearly, providing the elderly with nutritious meals is important, but in the process of doing so they provide basic human contact and monitoring. Some local communities partner with Meals on Wheels to provide additional services. For example, in Austin, the Meals on Wheels program has expanded to include a multi-service organization of nearly 7,000 volunteers reaching more than 5,000 Greater Austin neighbors in need. In addition to delivering hot, nutritious meals to the elderly, disabled, and home-bound clients, Meals on Wheels and More (MOWAM) offers many other programs designed to keep people healthy and living in their own homes (Meals on Wheels and More, 2013). The organization provides specialty food services for the most vulnerable, including rural residents, veterans, and clients who are nutritionally at risk, such as individuals with Alzheimer's disease. Volunteers also buy groceries twice a month and help clients with minor home repairs related to health and safety, and pet visits and a monthly pet-food allotment. Services have expanded to non-elderly groups as well and include evening meals for low-income children.

Other NGOs that work with the elderly are less well-known than Meals on Wheels, but they provide services that clearly improve the lives of older people and reduce their risk of isolation *Little Brothers – Friends of the Elderly (LBFE)*, is an international network of non-profit, volunteer-based organizations with branches in the United States and several other countries (www.littlebrothers.org). These national organizations provide companionship and other services to isolated elderly individuals. Each chapter runs a friendly visiting program and related activities. The program involves matching a volunteer with an elderly friend in neighborhoods located in seven U.S. cities – Boston, Philadelphia, Cincinnati, Chicago, Upper Peninsula of Michigan, Minneapolis/St. Paul, and San Francisco. The goal of the program is to promote close relationships with elderly clients through friendship among generations. Volunteers meet with the elder once a week for about an hour in the privacy of their own home. The LBFE network participates in a larger international non-profit organization, the *Fédération Internationale des petits frères des Pauvres* (International Federation of Little Brothers of the Poor), which operates in Mexico and Canada and has chapters located in six European countries: France, Ireland, Spain, Germany, Poland, and Switzerland. Like the chapters in the United States, the LBFE volunteers provide services aimed at developing a close friendship and social contact to individuals age 65 and older (International Federation of the little brothers of the Poor, 2013). In Madrid, Spain, this elder NGO uses volunteers to help an elderly person in local neighborhoods to submit official paperwork, go to the doctor, or run errands (www.amigosdelosmayores.org). Aside from home visitation, the Medical Transportation program offers a round-trip ride to hospital and doctor's appointments. This includes operating wheelchair vans for those who use a wheelchair for mobility. Each chapter designs their own websites to target the unique needs of the community.

These are only a few of the hundreds of NGOs that one can find on the Internet that provide services to the poor as part of their overall missions. Often, as in the case of *Hogar de Cristo* in Chile, mentioned above, the growth in the number of elderly individuals in developing nations who have no retirement income and who are at risk of serious deprivation has led these organizations to redefine their missions to focus on this growing vulnerable population.

Given the limitations in the social security safety nets for the elderly in developing nations, NGOs are increasingly playing a vital role in providing nutritional, housing, medical, and other services that can make the difference between life and death. India, like most of the developing world, is facing a serious problem related to the care of an older population. Even though like other developing nations it is comparatively young because of high fertility, the older segments of the population are growing in absolute and relative sizes. As in Latin America, improvements in nutrition and greater access to basic medical care translate into significant increases in life expectancy at birth and at age 60. In India in 2013, life expectancy at birth was 67 (Central Intelligence Agency, 2013). At age 60 both men and women can expect to live an additional 17 years in 2011 (World Health Organization, 2013). In India NGOs are increasingly important advocates for the elderly and they directly provide basic services (Sawhney, 2003). *Dignity Foundation* (www.dignityfoundation.com), an Indian NGO, is also a member of the *American Association of Retired Persons* (AARP) Global Network. This organization provides housing, companionship, recreation, and other services to elderly individuals in several Indian cities. *HelpAge India* (www.helpageindia.org) has a similar service mission. It also provides financial, medical and emotional support to poor elderly Indians in underserved areas. One example highlighted on the organization's website is a Mobile Medicare Unit (MMU) program that provides basic health care, as well as new initiatives such as help lines, disability aids, shelter assistance, yoga, specialized home visits, and psychotherapy.

Dignity Foundation and HelpAge India are examples of eldercare NGOs operating in nations and regions in which formal services are rare and in which poverty rates are high. Hogar de Cristo is an example of a faith-based organization that operates in a fairly prosperous middle-income country, Chile, which still experiences problems of old-age poverty and isolation. Let us briefly discuss its mission and operation as an example of what a strong organization can accomplish in a highly Catholic country (Pereira et al., 2007). The fact that Hogar de Cristo is a Catholic organization in a highly Catholic country has no doubt contributed to its success. The organization was begun in 1944 by a Catholic priest named Alberto Hurtado to address the needs of poor Chileans. In Chile Father Hurtado is revered and is somewhat of a national hero. Although the organization continues to focus on vulnerable Chileans regardless of age, the growing population of older individuals, many of whom find themselves at serious risk of poverty, homelessness, and malnutrition, has made them a core focus of the organization's mission. The organization also stepped in to fill a void created by the serious cutbacks in social services that were part of the neoliberal reforms introduced during the Pinochet dictatorship. In recent years Hogar's mission has expanded to provide the full range of services to poor elderly individuals, including day care, nutritional programs, and even housing. In the absence of an adequate old-age welfare state, Hogar de Cristo fills a void that is created by limited government commitments or capacities to address serious old-age vulnerabilities.

NGOs, often supported by government grants, function in Europe and the United States. As we discussed in Chapter 6, one well-known example in the United States is an attempt to provide comprehensive care and support to elderly Asian individuals in the San Francisco Bay Area. The program is named *On Lok*, a Cantonese term that means "peaceful, happy abode." It was begun in the early 1970s to provide comprehensive services to frail Asian elderly individuals in order to allow them to remain in their own homes (www.onlok.org) (Bodenheimer, 1999). The success of the program led Congress to introduce the *PACE* program (Program of All-inclusive Care for the Elderly: www.cms.gov/Medicare/Health-Plans/pace/downloads/PACE FactSheet.pdf), which provides comprehensive services paid for primarily by Medicare and Medicaid to high-need frail elderly individuals (Gross, Temkin-Greener, Kunitz, & Mukamel, 2004).

The On Lok experience serves as an example of how private non-governmental initiatives can serve as laboratories in which best practices related to the care of older persons can be tried and eventually inform state initiatives. Currently 70 PACE programs employ interdisciplinary teams of care providers who develop care plans for each individual and monitor their progress with the objective of allowing them to enjoy the highest possible quality of life. In addition to primary care the programs offer specialist care, home health aides, transportation, recreation, and companionship (Gross et al., 2004).

PACE is a public–private partnership because government funding allows non-profit providers to deliver services (Bodenheimer, 1999). Even so the development of a PACE site requires substantial upfront investment. The early PACE demonstration sites received approximately 70% of their funding through grants from large national foundations. Since PACE is no longer a demonstration project, these grants are no longer available. Most PACE sites are sponsored by established non-profit hospitals or health care systems in order to expand their services. Given the substantial startup costs smaller community organizations are largely priced out of competition (Lynch, Hernandez, & Estes 2008). Many existing PACE sites do not have adequate funding to expand their facilities in order to enroll more individuals. Labor shortages pose an additional barrier to enrollment. A PACE team can only care for 120 to 150 individuals, after which a new team must be developed to care for additional enrollees. Most PACE sites are unable to provide competitive benefit packages to attract new staff during a labor shortage (Gross et al., 2004). Hundreds of other examples can be found in all nations of the world and it would be impossible to summarize the activities of even a few. As the PACE example shows, there is often a blurring of the distinction between non-governmental and governmental. PACE programs rely heavily on Medicaid and Medicare for financing their operations.

The category of non-governmental, therefore, includes many different degrees of government/civil society cooperation, which is a desirable aspect of the approach. Smaller local organizations, such as Family Eldercare of Austin, Texas (www.familyeldercare.org), which we have mentioned before and on whose Board of Directors one of the authors has served as President, provides important legal services to elderly clients. In addition it engages in case management to coordinate a wide range of services that the organization's poor and largely minority clientele needs. These services include assistance with housing, instrumental support, and legal and financial services. Since 1986, Family Eldercare has been operating the local guardianship program, the largest and most established in Travis County, Texas. The program uses both paid staff and volunteers, including pro bono attorneys, to provide services to elderly and disabled individuals who lack the mental capacity to make decisions for themselves and/or are at risk of abuse, neglect, and/or financial exploitation. The guardianship volunteers help establish budgets, bank accounts, and other systems that will assist in managing finances and provide for basic human needs. In addition to the Guardianship Program, Family Eldercare provides other financial services in the Bill Payer Program. The guardianship volunteers help older clients prepare budgets and manage their bank accounts. In addition, they assist with other potentially complex financial matters and provide help to the older person in paying bills. 🌐 www.familyeldercare.org/get-involved/volunteer-center/item/79-volunteer-to-be-a-bill-payer.html. The organization participates in a summer fan drive in which fans and money to purchase them are collected to provide vital cooling to older people who live in a part of the country in which the heat of summer can be life-threatening. These activities are replicated in various forms by any number of NGOs all over the country.

ADVOCACY

As we mentioned before, in addition to organizations focused specifically on the needs of the elderly, many other non-governmental and faith-based groups include assistance to the elderly as part of their missions. Service delivery, though, is not the only mission of NGOs. Addressing the legal and structural impediments that create large social class differences in opportunities and asset accumulation requires political action. In addition, securing the rights of specific individuals and communities requires mobilization in order to confront cumbersome bureaucracies. As important as services are for vulnerable elderly individuals especially in developing nations, basic assistance does not change the social structural factors that account for their vulnerabilities. In fact, as we discuss below, such assistance can be seen as palliative and a means of keeping the disadvantaged from asserting themselves. While basic assistance with food, medical care, and housing might alleviate some of the most immediate problems that older individuals face, they are no substitutes for more comprehensive and continuous social security programs (HelpAge International, 2009; Willimore, 2006).

In addition to service delivery, then, a major role of NGOs is advocacy for those who are unable to effectively demand their social rights. *Fédération Internationale des*

Associations de Personnes Agées (International Federation of Associations of Older Persons, FIAPA) is an international elder organization headquartered in Paris with a mission of preventing isolation and improving the quality of life among the elderly (🌐 www.fiapa.net). The World Health Organization (WHO) recognizes FIAPA as an international organization representing the interests of elderly people. In 2012, on the basis of chapter charters and many discussions a working group created an international convention relating to the application of human rights for older people, including those in need of long-term care, protection against discrimination based on age, as well as the inclusion of older adults in society (see 🌐 www.fiapa.net/wp-content/uploads/2013/03/Convention-version-6-An-Copy.pdf). To carry out the mission in Europe, FIAPA works in close collaboration with UNESCO in culture and education sectors as well as in medical and social programs for the elderly.

In the United States, the AARP is the most well-known and effective advocate for its membership, which includes individuals aged 50 and older (Binstock, 2004). Yet there are other, perhaps less well-known organizations engaged in advocacy (Hudson, 2005). The *National Committee to Preserve Social Security & Medicare* (NCPSSM; 🌐 www.ncpssm.org), the *Alliance for Retired Americans* (ARA; 🌐 www.retiredamericans.org), and the *National Hispanic Council on Aging* (NHCOA; 🌐 www.nhcoa.org) are three examples of organizations with general or specific missions and target populations.

The National Hispanic Council on Aging is an informative example. NHCOA was incorporated in 1980 to enhance the quality of life for older Hispanics. After four decades in operation, the organization's mission includes advocacy, the support of research, the funding of community-based projects, the creation of support networks, capacity-building in Hispanic communities, and the support and strengthening of Hispanic community-based organizations. The organization's core objective is to "empower Hispanic community organizations and agencies, as well as Hispanic older adults and their families." NHCOA offers educational programs focused on the major health risks faced by Hispanics, such as diabetes, and it has developed an e-course on cultural competence that educates health care professionals concerning culture of their patients (🌐 http://edu.nhcoa.org). Located in Washington, DC, NHCOA has independent affiliates throughout the country and holds annual national conferences in order to encourage information sharing and to develop solutions to problems in the Hispanic community. The organization sponsors a Business Advisory Council to provide strategic guidance in developing private-sector enterprises.

SUMMARY AND CONCLUSIONS

In this chapter we looked to the future and discussed problems that confront mature welfare states, including that in the United States. We were particularly interested in the implications of the retrenchment that fiscal crises make necessary for Hispanics and other minority groups. Given low levels of education and income, Hispanics are particularly dependent on social welfare state programs at all ages. Cuts in funding to medical, nutritional, housing, and other programs have potentially serious implications for Hispanics, and especially older Hispanics.

Hispanics' dependence on social welfare programs is exacerbated by various historical and group-specific issues. Given low levels of education, Hispanics are not employed in high-paying jobs, which means that they have a difficult time saving for any purpose, and they face particularly serious problems in saving for retirement, which requires that one put away a substantial fraction of one's income, beginning at an early age. For individuals with low levels of education bouts of unemployment are common and the needs of the moment too pressing to permit substantial saving. As we noted in earlier chapters, Hispanics are less likely than non-Hispanics to have any sort of retirement plan. Even when they have a plan, low levels of savings mean that they have less than non-Hispanic Whites in defined-contribution 401(k) plans. In earlier chapters we documented the low level of pension coverage among Hispanic workers and the dependence on Social Security alone among older Hispanics. Clearly, cuts to Social Security would have serious implications for this population.

Low educational levels clearly account for much of Hispanics' economic vulnerability earlier in life and in the later years. Individuals with low levels of education are at high risk of long-term unemployment. If one loses one's job after age 50 the chances of finding a new one can be small and unemployment can become involuntary early retirement. In this chapter we also documented the declining power and influence of unions, which might be one means through which Hispanics could improve their overall economic situation and improve their retirement prospects.

Historically, Hispanics have joined unions at the same rate as other groups, but the overall decline in union membership means that unions are probably not a promising source of economic or political power for Hispanics. Although some service sector unions have benefited Hispanics, including undocumented Hispanics, in general their influence has been limited.

Throughout the previous chapters we have noted the fact that Hispanics are being affected by the social forces that have resulted in the increasing uncoupling of marriage and fertility. Traditional Hispanic culture, regardless of the nation in question, was based on the family unit. Increasing rates of single motherhood, divorce, and family separation as the result of migration mean that the family is no longer the support system it once was. Older individuals have fewer children available to whom they can turn for assistance. As we noted, traditional norms of filial piety and the expectation that children will provide all of the care their aging and infirm parents need is giving way to more individualistic expectations in which children attend to their own needs and responsibilities as well. Given the reality of longer lives and high levels of disability and dementia, institutionalization and the greater use of community-based long-term care services will become inevitable.

We ended this chapter and the book by discussing various alternatives and solutions to the problems faced by the Hispanic community, and especially Hispanic elders. Many modern supporters of the welfare state realize that it must adapt to the new fiscal realities and the growth in the size of public programs. Criticisms of the welfare state include claims that it fosters dependency and provides support without a reasonable expectation that the recipients behave responsibly. The new philosophy of "no rights without responsibilities" calls for a greater expectation for responsible behavior, primarily involving welfare recipients' work effort. Yet expecting individuals to become self-sufficient when they lack basic skills is unrealistic. Alternative calls, therefore, are for a social investment state in which the expectation that one work and become a productive citizen are combined with education and training that make such an outcome realistic.

It seems clear that in the future civil society organizations, including non-governmental and faith-based organizations, will play an increasing role in providing services to and advocating for the elderly, including the Hispanic elderly. Such organizations are assuming a growing role in social services for individuals of all ages in all countries of the world. As important as they may be in improving the situation of Hispanics of all ages, they cannot function as substitutes for enlightened and effective governments. Local, non-governmental approaches to providing assistance to needy individuals are appealing because they are more personal, draw upon local knowledge, and employ local actors. The evidence we have presented in this book clearly suggests that addressing the needs of younger and older minority populations, including the older Hispanic community, will require political action and the concerted efforts of governmental agencies and a wide range of non-governmental actors.

DISCUSSION QUESTIONS

1. Define the term "solidarity." What are its major dimensions, that is, what areas of life does it apply to and how does it relate to the pact between generations? How might racial and ethnic differences influence a nation's level of solidarity?

2. Discuss the problems that defined-benefit retirement plans face in all nations that introduced them during the 20th century. Summarize the practical and moral dilemmas involved in supporting such systems in the long term. Do workers who were promised a specific pension when they were working have a right to expect that the amount of that pension will not be changed regardless of changing fiscal realities?

3. Has the welfare state grown beyond the ability of even developed economies to support it? Have citizens' expectations about what the state should provide in terms of health, education, housing, and more become excessive? Does a generous welfare state undermine individual initiative? Who would be harmed the most by reductions in welfare state services? Who would benefit from such reductions?

4. The traditional family was based on a "male breadwinner" model of household production and consumption. Describe key aspects of the male breadwinner model of household economy. How does it related to gender roles and the domestic and labor force activity of husbands, wives, and children? Summarize potential benefits as well as drawbacks of the male breadwinner model for various family members.

5. Define the "social investment state." How does it relate to or differ from the traditional welfare state?

6. What are some of the major reasons for the lack of adequate retirement savings among all groups, but especially among Hispanics? Are there any realistic solutions to the problem of inadequate personal retirement savings? What implications does the lack of adequate retirement savings have for proposals to privatize Social Security, that is, make it more of a defined-contribution scheme in which one is responsible for investing for his or her retirement?

LITERATURE CITED

Albrow, M., Anheier, H., Glasius, M., Price, M., & Kaldor, M. (Eds.). (2008). *Global civil society 2007/8*. Thousand Oaks, CA: Sage.

Angel, J. L., Prickett, K., & Angel, R. J. (forthcoming). Retirement security for Black, non-Hispanic white, and Mexican-origin women: The changing roles of marriage and work. *Journal of Women, Politics and Policy*.

Angel, R. J. (2011). Civil society and elder-care in post-traditional society. In R. A. Settersten & J. L. Angel (Eds.), *Handbook of sociology of aging* (pp. 549–81). New York, NY: Springer.

Angel, R. J., & Angel, J. L. (2009). *Hispanic families at risk: The new economy, work, and the welfare state*. New York, NY: Springer.

Angel, R. J., Bell, H., Beausoleil, J., & Lein, L. (2012). *Community lost: The state, civil society and displaced survivors of Hurricane Katrina*. New York, NY: Cambridge University Press.

Armingeon, K., & Bonoli, G. (Eds.). (2006). *The politics of postindustrial states: Adapting post-war social policies to new social risks*. London and New York: Routledge.

Bernard, T. S. (2013). One dip into a 401(k) often leads to another. *New York Times*. Retrieved October 4, 2013, from www.nytimes.com/2013/08/17/your-money/one-dip-into-401-k-savings-often-leads-to-another.html?pagewanted=all&_r=0.

Binstock, R. H. (2004). Advocacy in an era of neoconservatism: Responses of national aging organizations. *Generations, 28*(1), 49–54.

Bodenheimer, T. (1999). Long-term care for frail elderly people: The On Lok model. *N Engl J Med, 341*(17), 1324–8.

Boli, J., & Thomas, G. M. (1997). World culture in the world polity: A century of international non-governmental organization. *American Sociological Review, 62*(2), 171–90.

Boli, J. G., & Thomas, M. (Eds.). (1999). *Constructing world culture: International nongovernmental organizations since 1875*. Stanford, CA: Stanford University Press.

Burcher, J. (Ed.). (2008). *México solidario: Participación cudadana y voluntaiado*. Mexico, D.F.: Limusa.

Camou, M. (2012). Capacity and solidarity: Foundational elements in the unionization strategy for immigrant day labourers. *International Migration, 50*(2), 41–64.

Castles, S. (2004). Why migration policies fail. *Ethnic and Racial Studies, 27*(2), 205–27.

Central Intelligence Agency. (2013). Life expectancy at birth. In *The world fact book*. Washington, DC: CIA.

CEPAL. (2007). Demographic trends in Latin America. In *Observatorio demográfico No. 3: Proyección de población*. Retrieved January 25, 2013, from, www.google.com/url?sa=t&rct=j&q=&esrc=s&source=web&cd=1&cad=rja&uact=8&ved=0CB0QFjAA&url=http%3A%2F%2Fwww.eclac.org%2Fpublicaciones%2Fxml%2F0%2F32650%2FOD-3-Demographic.pdf&ei=qL-YU6bHOoaUyASimoKACw&usg=AFQjCNG7EA5hbeZLBi_SwBjs0Dw1dw3lng&sig2=qmvST1DKarhBlVWoS2zHGA. La Comisión Económica para América Latina (CEPAL).

Cotlear, D. (Ed.). (2011). *Population aging: Is Latin America ready?* Washington, DC: The World Bank.

Edwards, M., & Sen, G. (2000). NGOs, social change and the transformation of human relationships: A 21st-century civic agenda. *Third World Quarterly, 21*(4), 605–16.

Etzioni, A. (1993). *The spirit of community: Rights, responsibilities, and the communitarian agenda*. New York, NY: Crown Publishers.

Etzioni, A. (Ed.). (1995). *New communitarian thinking: Persons, virtues, institutions, and communities*. Charlottesville: University Press of Virginia.

Etzioni, A. (2000). *The third way to a good society*. London: Demos.

Ferro, G., & Castagnolo, F. (2010). On the closure of the Argentine fully funded system. *Pensions: An International Journal, 15*(1), 25–37.

Giddens, A. (1991). *Modernity & self-identity: Self and society in the late modern age*. Stanford, CA: Stanford University Press.

Giddens, A. (1994). *Beyond left and right: The future of radical politics*. Stanford, CA: Stanford University Press.

Giddens, A. (1998). *The third way: The renewal of social democracy*. Malden, MA: Blackwell Publishers, Inc.

Gross, D. L., Temkin-Greener, H., Kunitz, S., & Mukamel, D. (2004). The growing pains of integrated health care for the elderly: Lessons from the expansion of PACE. *Milbank Quarterly, 82*(2), 252–87.

Grzybowski, C. (2000). We NGOs: A controversial way of being and acting. *Development in Practice, 10*(3–4), 436–44.

Hayek, F. A. (1944). *The road to serfdom*. Chicago, IL: University of Chicago Press.

Hayek, F. A. (1959). *The constitution of liberty*. London: Routledge.

Hayek, F. A. (1976). *Law, legislation, and liberty, vol. 2: The mirage of social justice*. Chicago, IL: University of Chicago Press.

HelpAge International. (2009). *Working for life: Making decent work and pensions a reality for older people*. London, UK: HelpAge International.

Huber, E., & Stephens, J. D. (2006). Combatting old and new social risks. In K. Armingeon & G. Bonoli (Eds.), *The politics of postindustrial states: Adapting postwar social policies to new social risks* (pp. 143–67). London and New York: Routledge.

Hudson, R. B. (2005). *The new politics of old-age policy*. Baltimore, MD: Johns Hopkins University.

Idler, E. (2006). Religion and aging. In R. H. Binstock & L. K. George (Eds.), *Handbook of aging and the social sciences* (pp. 277–300). New York, NY: Academic Press.

International Federation of the little brothers of the Poor. (2013). *History*. The International Federation of the little brothers of the Poor. Retrieved from www.petits-freres.org/en/histoire.html.

Krause, N. (2006). Social relationships in later life. In R. H. Binstock & L. K. George (Eds.), *Handbook of aging and the social sciences* (pp. 181–200). New York, NY: Academic Press.

Lloyd-Sherlock, P. (2000). Population ageing in developed and developing regions: Implications for health policy. *Social Science & Medicine, 51*(6), 887–95.

Lynch M, Hernandez M, & Estes C. (2008). PACE: Has it Changed the Chronic Care Paradigm? Social Work in Public Health, 23(4), 3–24.

Martin, J. A., Hamilton, B. E., Ventura, S. J., Osterman, M. J. K., Wilson, E. C., & Mathews, T. J. (2012). *Births: Final data for 2010*. Hyattesvill, MD: National Center for Health Statistics.

Mead, L. M. (1986). *Beyond entitlement*. New York, NY: The Free Press.

Mead, L. M. (1997). Citizenship and social policy: T. H. Marshall and poverty. *Social Philosophy and Policy, 14*(2), 197–230.

Meals on Wheels and More. (2013). *Programs*. Austin, TX: Meals on Wheels and More.

Meals on Wheels Association of America. (2013). *History*. Alexandria, VA: Meals on Wheels Association of America.

Medina, J. (2013). Immigrant workers give new direction to Los Angeles unions. *New York Times*. Retrieved October 4, 2013, from www.nytimes.com/2013/05/18/us/los-angeles-labor-leader-puts-focus-on-immigrants.html?pagewanted=all.

Mesa-Lago, C. (2008). *Reassembling social security: A survey of pensions and health care reforms in Latin America*. Oxford and New York: Oxford University Press.

MIDES. (2012). *Plan Nacional de Envejecimiento y Vejez, 2013–2015*. Montevideo, Uruguay: Unidad de Información y Comunicación. MIDES – Consejo Consultivo del Instituto Nacional del Adulto Mayor – INMAYORES.

Mitchell, J. (2013). Who are the long-term unemployed? Washington, DC: The Urban Institute. Retrieved October 4, 2013, from http://media.oregonlive.com/opinion_impact/other/412885-who-are-the-long-term-unemployed.pdf.

Moren-Cross, J. L., & Lin, N. (2006). Social networks and health. In R. H. Binstock & L. K. George (Eds.), *Handbook of aging and the social sciences* (pp. 111–26). New York, NY: Academic Press.

Murray, C. (1994). *Losing ground: American social policy 1950–1980*. New York, NY: Basic Books.

Murray, C. (1996). Charles Murray and the underclass: The developing debate. In *Choice in welfare No. 33*. London: The IEA Health and Welfare Unit.

Murray, C. (1999). *The underclass revisited*. Washington, DC: AEI Press.

Murray, C. (2006). *In our hands: A plan to replace the welfare state*. Blue Ridge Summit, PA: AEI Press.

Myles, J. (2002). A new social contract for the elderly? In G. Esping-Andersen, D. Gaillie, A. Hemerijck, & J. Myles (Eds.), *Why we need a new welfare state* (pp. 130–72). New York, NY: Oxford University Press.

O'Connor, J. (1973). *The fiscal crisis of the state*. New York, NY: St Martin's Press.

Offe, C. (1982). Some contradictions of the modern welfare state. *Critical Social Policy, 2*(5), 7–16.

Orenstein, M. A. (2008). *Privatizing pensions: The transnational campaign for social security reform*. Princeton, NJ: Princeton University Press.

Orenstein, M. A. (2011). Pension privatization in crisis: Death or rebirth of a global policy trend? *International Social Security Review, 64*(3), 65–80.

Papadópulos, J., & Falkin, L. (2011). *Documento conceptual: personas adultas mayores y dependencia. Dimensionamiento de necesidades en materia de cuidados y alternativas de incorporación de servicios y población.* Montevideo, Uruguay: Sistema Nacional de Cuidados – Presidencia de la República.

Pereira, J., & Angel, R. (2009). From adversary to ally: The evolution of non-governmental organizations in the context of health reform in Santiago and Montevideo. In S. Babones (Ed.), *Social inequality and public health.* Bristol, UK: Polity Press.

Pereira, J., Angel, R. J., & Angel, J. L. (2007). A case study of the elder care functions of a Chilean non-governmental organization. *Social Science and Medicine, 64,* 2096–106.

Pierson, C. (2007). *Beyond the welfare state: The new political economy of welfare.* University Park, PA: The Pennsylvania State University Press.

Pierson, P. (2001). Coping with permanent austerity: Welfare state restructuring in affluent democracies. In P. Pierson (Ed.), *The new politics of the welfare state.* Oxford and New York: Oxford University Press.

Piñera, J. (1995/6). Empowering workers: The privatization of social security in Chile. *Cato Journal, 15*(2–3), 155–6.

Rosenfeld, J., & Kleykamp, M. (2009). Hispanics and organized labor in the United States, 1973 to 2007. *American Sociological Review, 74*(6), 916–37.

Salamon, L. M. (2003). *The resilient sector: The state of nonprofit America.* Washington, DC: Brookings Institution Press.

Sawhney, M. (2003). The role of non-governmental organizations for the welfare of the elderly: The case of HelpAge India. In P. S. Liebig & S. Irudaya Rajan (Eds.), *An aging India: Perspectives, prospects, and policies.* Binghamton, NY: The Hayworth Press.

United Nations. (2002). *Report of the Second World Assembly on Ageing, Madrid, 8–12 April 2002.* New York, NY: United Nations. Retrieved May 1, 2013, from www.c-fam.org/docLib/20080625_Madrid_Ageing_Conference.pdf.

United Nations Economic Conference for Europe. (2008). *A society for all ages: Challenges and opportunities. Report of the UNECE.* Proceedings of the UNECE Ministerial Conference on Ageing, 6–8 November 2007, León, Spain. Retrieved May 1, 2013, from www.unece.org/index.php?id=10834.

WHO and Milbank Memorial Fund. (2000). *Towards an international consensus on policy for long-term care of the ageing.* Geneva: WHO. Retrieved February 1, 2013, from www.milbank.org/uploads/documents/000712oms.pdf.

Willimore, L. (2006). Universal age pensions in developing countries: The example of Mauritius. *International Social Security Review, 59*(4), 67–89.

World Health Organization. (2000). *Home-based long-term care.* Geneva: WHO. Retrieved January 2, 2013, from http://whqlibdoc.who.int/trs/WHO_TRS_898.pdf.

World Health Organization. (2002). *Lessons for long-term care policy.* Geneva: WHO. Retrieved February 1, 2013, from http://whqlibdoc.who.int/hq/2002/WHO_NMH7CCL_02.1.pdf.

World Health Organization. (2003). *Key policy issues in long-term care.* Geneva: WHO. Retrieved February 1, 2013, from www.who.int/chp/knowledge/publications/policy_issues_ltc.pdf.

World Health Organization. (2013). *Health profile.* Geneva: WHO.

Xu, Q., & Chow, J. C. (2011). Exploring the community-based service delivery model: Elderly care in China. *International Social Work, 54*(3), 374–87.

Zaidi, A., Gasior, K., & Manchin, R. (2012). Population aging and intergenerational solidarity: International policy frameworks and European public opinion. *Journal of Intergenerational Relationships, 10*(3), 214–27.

INDEX

Page numbers in *italics* denote tables, those in **bold** denote figures.

Mexico: aging populations 108; Guanajuato 98–9, 107, 108; health care 111–12, 152; remittances 109–10; return of older migrants 111–12; *see also* U.S./Mexico border region
minimum wage 76, 77, 270
Mobile Medicare Unit (MMU) program, India 319
mortality 49, 50, 130, 132
MOWAM *see* Meals on Wheels and More (MOWAM)
Moynihan, Daniel Patrick 74
MS-13 (gang) 211
multiculturalism 10, 13–14, 21–35
Murdock, Stephen 51–2, **54**
Murray, Charles 71, 74
Muslim immigrants, Europe 14, 15

National Aging Network 253
National Association of Area Agencies on Aging 192
National Council on Aging 285
National Family Caregiver Support Program (NFCSP) 192, 253–5
National Hispanic Council on Aging (NHCOA) 323–4
National Survey of America's Families (NSAF) 272
Native American population 11–12, 21, 25, **50**, 292
negative assimilation 74
neighborhoods 202–26; age-friendly 222–4; defining communities 204–5; dispersion of Hispanic population 215–16, *216*; ethnic enclaves *47*, 48, 98–9, 209–14, 219–22; food deserts 218, **218**; and health 219–22; Hispanic barrios 46–8, *47*, 98–9, 209–14, 219–22; low quality 202–4, 210, 217–19; measuring quality 205–8
Netherlands 15, 16
New Jersey 182
New Mexico 173–4
New York 46–7, *47*, 213, 217
NFCSP *see* National Family Caregiver Support Program (NFCSP)
NGOs *see* non-governmental organizations (NGOs)
NHCOA *see* National Hispanic Council on Aging (NHCOA)
non-bank financial services 271
non-contributory pensions 302
non-governmental organizations

(NGOs) 22, 34–5, 304; eldercare 184–5, 188–90, 255–6, 314–24; financial advice 288–92
non-Hispanic black population **19**; age structures 51, **53**; asset accumulation *61*, 62, 82; divorce **55**; education 56–8, **56**, **57**, **58**; employment 58, *59*, 77–8, **77**; fertility rates **50**; incomes **60**, *61*, 79, **79**; inheritances **82**; life expectancy 130–1, **131**; marriage 53–4, **54**; neighborhoods 220, 221; occupation sectors **60**, 79–80, *80*; out-of-wedlock births **73**, 74; retirement incomes 83, 84–5, **84**; retirement plans **84**, 87, *87*, 277–80, **279**, **280**, 281; youth unemployment 80, **81**
non-Hispanic white population **19**; age structures 51, **52**, **54**; asset accumulation *61*, 62; divorce **55**; education 56, **56**, 57, **57**, **58**; employment 58, *59*, 77–8, **77**; fertility rates **50**; incomes **60**, *61*, 79, **79**; inheritances **82**; life expectancy 130–1, **131**, 132; marriage **54**; occupation sectors **60**, 79–80, *80*; out-of-wedlock births **73**; retirement incomes 83, 84–5, **84**; retirement plans **84**, 87, *87*, 277–80, **279**, **280**, 281; youth unemployment 80, **81**
Norway 16
nursing home industry 190–1
nursing homes 169–77, 239, 241–2, 244, 245
nutrition programs 183–4, 253, 289, 317–18

OAA *see* Older Americans Act (OAA)
Obama, Barack 117
Obamacare 113, 245, 272
obesity 135
Ocampo, Guanajuato, Mexico 108
occupation sectors 59, **60**, 79–80, *80*
Okin, Susan 27
Oklahoma Native Assets Coalition 292
Older Americans Act (OAA) 183, 192, 253, 254
older people: age-friendly communities 222–4; early retirement 88, 309; effects of low quality neighborhoods 202–4, 210, 217–19; financial exploitation 240,